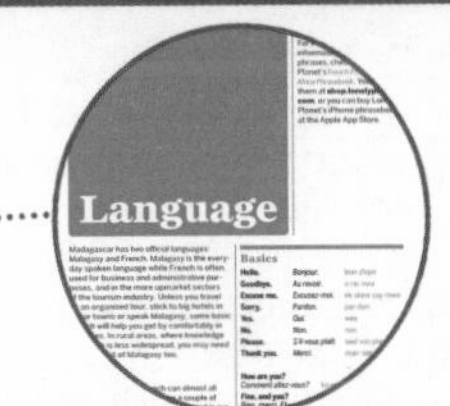

THIS EDITION WRITTEN AND RESEARCHED BY

Emilie Filou, Paul Stiles

welcome to Madagascar

What a Wonderful World

Madagascar is unique: 5% of all known ani-mal and plant species can be found here, and here alone. The remarkable fauna and flora is matched by epic landscapes of an incredible diversity: you can go from rainforest to desert in just 300km. Few places on earth offer such an intense kaleidoscope of nature. Making the best of it, however, can be challenging (and expensive): Madagascar is the world's fourth-largest island and its roads are dismal. But those who relish an adventure will come into their own: the off-road driving is one of a kind, and there are national parks that only see 100 visitors a year, regions that live in autarchy during the rainy season and resorts so remote you'll need a private plane or boat to get there.

Turn to the Sea

With 5000km of coastline, 450km of barrier reef and 250 islands, no stay in Madagascar would be complete without a few days on the island's shores. Divers will revel in the choice of sites, from underwater 'cathedrals' to shipwrecks, and will relish the chance to see rays, whale sharks, reef sharks and many other kinds of sharks. Snorkellers will be awed by the sheer grace of turtles and marvel at the rainbow of colours displayed by corals and fish. For those keen to keep their heads above water, the idyllic beaches will prove

Lemurs, baobabs, rainforest, beaches, desert, trekking and diving: Madagascar is a dream destination for nature and outdoor lovers – and half the fun is getting to all these incredible attractions.

(left) Sakalava woman carrying fish on her head, Morondava (p113)
(below) Crystal-clear waters of La Mer d'Emeraude (p145)

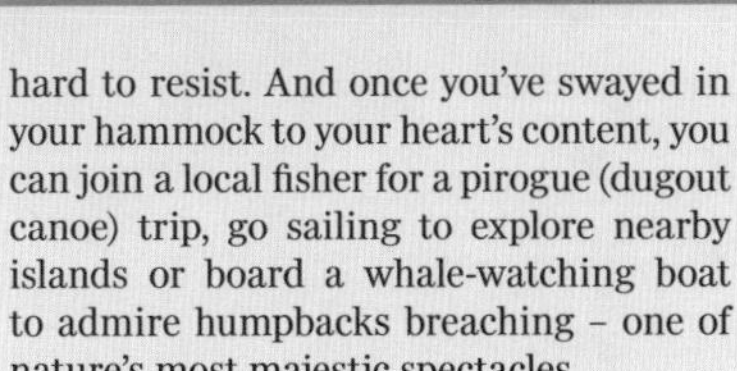

hard to resist. And once you've swayed in your hammock to your heart's content, you can join a local fisher for a pirogue (dugout canoe) trip, go sailing to explore nearby islands or board a whale-watching boat to admire humpbacks breaching – one of nature's most majestic spectacles.

Of Life & Death

Madagascar has been populated by successive waves of migrants from various corners of the Indian Ocean, each bringing their own customs and beliefs. This cultural melting pot has evolved into an intricate set of beliefs and rituals that revere ancestors' spirits. For travellers, getting accustomed to the central role that death plays in everyday life is often an opportunity to reassess their own beliefs, and attending a *famadihana* (traditional exhumation and reburial) or a traditional circumcision ceremony can be the highlight of a trip. There is much history to discover, too, from the 12 sacred hills of Antananarivo to the pirate cemetery of Ile Sainte Marie and the vestige of Madagascar's industrial revolution in Mantasoa.

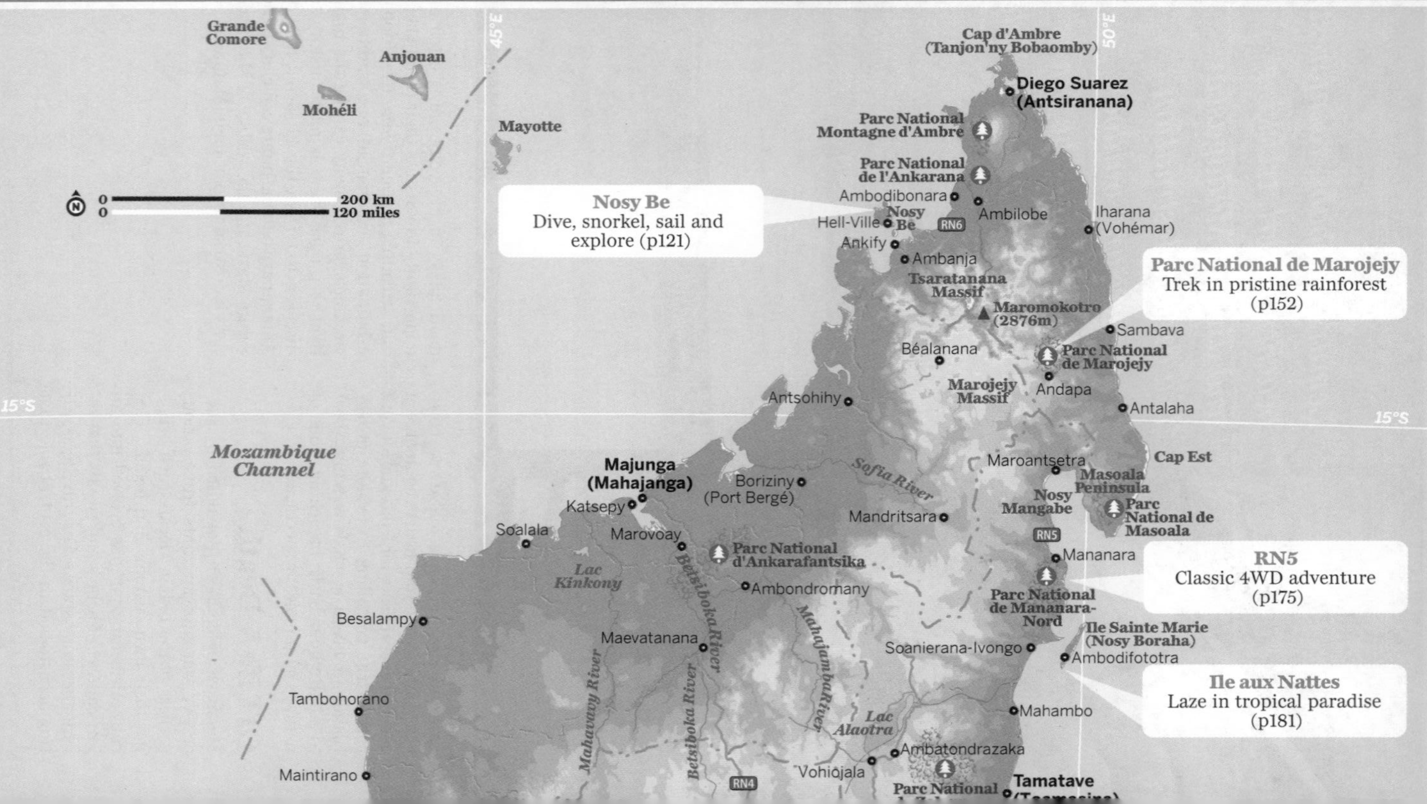
Nosy Be
Dive, snorkel, sail and explore (p121)
Parc National de Marojejy
Trek in pristine rainforest (p152)
RN5
Classic 4WD adventure (p175)
Ile aux Nattes
Laze in tropical paradise (p181)
Grande Comore
Anjouan
Mohéli
Mayotte
Mozambique Channel
0 200 km
0 120 miles
45°E
50°E
15°S
Cap d'Ambre (Tanjon'ny Bobaomby)
Diego Suarez (Antsiranana)
Parc National Montagne d'Ambre
Parc National de l'Ankarana
Ambodibonara
Ambilobe
Nosy Be
Hell-Ville
RN6
Ankify
Ambanja
Iharana (Vohémar)
Tsaratanana Massif
Maromokotro (2876m)
Sambava
Béalanana
Parc National de Marojejy
Marojejy Massif
Andapa
Antsohihy
Antalaha
Cap Est
Maroantsetra
Masoala Peninsula
Parc National de Masoala
Nosy Mangabe
RN5
Mananara
Parc National de Mananara-Nord
Ile Sainte Marie (Nosy Boraha)
Ambodifototra
Soanierana-Ivongo
Mahambo
Majunga (Mahajanga)
Katsepy
Boriziny (Port Bergé)
Sofia River
Mandritsara
Soalala
Marovoay
Parc National d'Ankarafantsika
Ambondromany
Lac Kinkony
Betsiboka River
Mahajamba River
Besalampy
Maevatanana
Mahavavy River
Tambohorano
Lac Alaotra
Ambatondrazaka
Maintirano
Vohiojala
RN4
Parc National
Tamatave

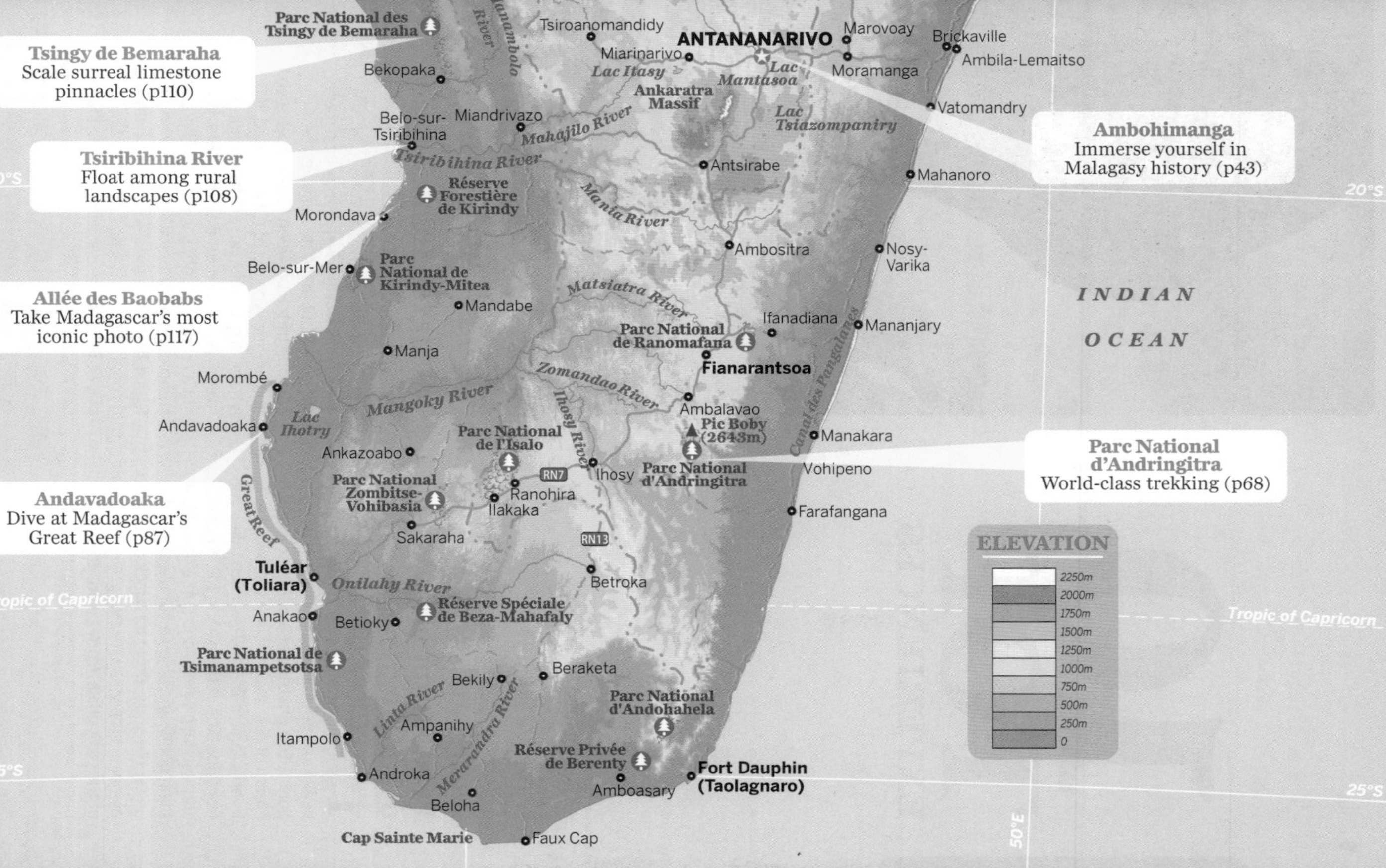

Tsingy de Bemaraha
Scale surreal limestone pinnacles (p110)
Tsiribihina River
Float among rural landscapes (p108)
Allée des Baobabs
Take Madagascar's most iconic photo (p117)
Andavadoaka
Dive at Madagascar's Great Reef (p87)
Ambohimanga
Immerse yourself in Malagasy history (p43)
Parc National d'Andringitra
World-class trekking (p68)
Parc National des Tsingy de Bemaraha
Manambolo River
Tsiroanomandidy
ANTANANARIVO
Marovoay
Brickaville
Ambila-Lemaitso
Miarinarivo
Lac Itasy
Lac Mantasoa
Moramanga
Ankaratra Massif
Bekopaka
Vatomandry
Lac Tsiazompaniry
Belo-sur-Tsiribihina
Miandrivazo
Mahajilo River
Tsiribihina River
Antsirabe
Mahanoro
20°S
Réserve Forestière de Kirindy
Morondava
Mania River
Ambositra
Nosy-Varika
Belo-sur-Mer
Parc National de Kirindy-Mitea
Mandabe
Matsiatra River
INDIAN OCEAN
Ifanadiana
Mananjary
Parc National de Ranomafana
Manja
Fianarantsoa
Zomandao River
Canal des Pangalanes
Morombé
Mangoky River
Ambalavao
Lac Ihotry
Ihosy River
Pic Boby (2643m)
Andavadoaka
Parc National de l'Isalo
Manakara
Ankazoabo
Ihosy
Parc National d'Andringitra
Vohipeno
Parc National Zombitse-Vohibasia
RN7
Ranohira
Ilakaka
Farafangana
Great Reef
Sakaraha
RN13
ELEVATION
2250m
2000m
1750m
1500m
1250m
1000m
750m
500m
250m
0
Tuléar (Toliara)
Onilahy River
Betroka
Tropic of Capricorn
Anakao
Réserve Spéciale de Beza-Mahafaly
Betioky
Parc National de Tsimanampetsotsa
Bekily
Beraketa
Parc National d'Andohahela
Linta River
Menarandra River
Ampanihy
Itampolo
Réserve Privée de Berenty
25°S
Androka
Fort Dauphin (Taolagnaro)
Amboasary
Beloha
50°E
Cap Sainte Marie
Faux Cap

10 TOP EXPERIENCES

Parc National d'Andringitra

1 With more than 100km of trails, a majestic mountain range, three challenging peaks and epic landscapes, this national park (p68) is a trekker's paradise. For the cream of the cream, follow the two-day Imarivolanitra Trail (p71), which takes you from one side of the park to the other via its summit, lush valleys and some natural swimming pools, and enjoy a couple of nights under the stars. Don't let a lack of forward planning stop you: hire everything you need at the park office, from guides to cooks, porters and even camping equipment.

Tackle the Infamous RN5

2 If you revel in the idea of a road challenge, this is it. It may be a *route nationale*, but make no mistake, the 240km stretch between Maroantsetra and Soanierana-Ivongo (p175) is no road. It is a track, a quagmire, an obstacle course, a river in places, a mountain in others, but not a road. Semantics aside, travellers who complete the journey will have anecdotes to last them a lifetime. Mananara, halfway through the trip, is also one of the few places in Madagascar where you're likely to see an aye-aye (p184).

1

ANDERS BLOMQVIST/LONELY PLANET IMAGES ©

2

PAUL STILES/LONELY PLANET IMAGES ©

Ile aux Nattes

3 If you've been dreaming of tropical island paradise, Ile aux Nattes (p181) is a dream come true. Standing at the tip of Ile Sainte Marie (pictured below), a short pirogue ride away or a leisurely walk at low tide, this is the place to come and do absolutely nothing. Nestle in a hammock at Chez Sika, laze on the beach and swim. And when you've had enough, cross over to Sainte Marie and zoom across the island on a motorbike (p177).

Sunset at Allée des Baobabs

4 Few things say Madagascar more than this small stretch of the RN8 between Morondava and Belo-sur-Tsiribihina (p117). Lined with majestic baobabs, it comes into its own at sunset and sunrise when the trees cast their long shadows on the red sand and the sky lights up with orange and purple hues. In addition to the Allée, you'll find plenty more baobabs across southern and western Madagascar. Some live for up to a thousand years and reach epic proportions: Majunga's sacred baobab (p99) measures 21m around its trunk!

3

ARIADNE VAN ZANDBERGEN/LONELY PLANET IMAGES ©

SHIU/IMAGEBROKER ©

FIONA MCINTOSH/GETTY IMAGES ©

Tsingy de Bemaraha

5 There is nothing else on earth quite like the jagged limestone pinnacles of Parc National des Tsingy de Bemaraha (p110). A Unesco World Heritage Site, the serrated, surreal-looking peaks and boulders are a geological work of art, the result of millennia of water and wind erosion. Just as remarkable is the infrastructure the national park has put in place to explore this natural wonder: *via ferrata* (fixed-cable routes), rope bridges and ladders, with circuits combining forests, caves, pirogue trips and even abseiling.

Diving & Snorkelling at Andavadoaka

6 Madagascar boasts the world's fifth largest coral reef, 450km of fringing, patch, and barrier reefs from Andavadoaka in the north to Itampolo in the south. The pearl of the barrier is Andavadoaka (p87), where work with local communities and a marine conservation area have kept the reef in top shape. Divers who make it all the way here will be rewarded with stunning corals and abundant fish. Other spots that will blow you away are the 'cathedrals' at Ifaty and Mangily (p84) and the serene village of Ambola (p91).

Tsiribihina River

7 Taking a trip down the Tsiribihina (p110) means disconnecting completely from everything: for two and a half days, there are no cars, no roads, and there's no mobile coverage. It is an experience of utter relaxation, with little more to do than admire the landscape, take in local life, chat to your guide, sing by the campfire and marvel at the night sky. For the real deal, hop on a wooden pirogue; for a little more comfort and conviviality, board a *chaland* (motorised barge).

Ambohimanga

8 This is Madagascar's only cultural site on Unesco's World Heritage list, and with good reason: Ambohimanga (p43) was the seat of King Andrianampoinimerina, the Merina sovereign who decided to unify the warring tribes of the island so that his kingdom would have no frontier but the sea. The cultural significance of the site goes beyond history: Ambohimanga is revered as a sacred site by the Malagasy, who come here to invoke royal spirits and request their protection and good fortune.

9

ANDERS BLOMQVIST/LONELY PLANET IMAGES ©

10

HEMIS/ALAMY ©

Parc National de Marojejy

9 With its pristine mountainous rainforest, thick root-filled jungle and waterfalls, Marojejy (p152) is a primordial place, where the 'angel of the forest', the endemic silky sifaka, inhabits misty mountains, and spectacular views of the Marojejy Massif open up through the canopy. A superb trail crescendos through the landscape, climaxing with a tough climb to the summit (2132m). Marojejy permits also provide entry to the remote and beautiful Réserve Spéciale d'Anjanaharibe-Sud (p154), where travellers will be rewarded with the wail of the indri.

Nosy Be

10 The 'big island' (p121) is a dream destination: you could spend two weeks here and in the surrounding islands (p133) and still feel like you haven't had enough. It's not just the world-class diving and snorkelling, the turquoise sea, the exquisitely soft light and arresting views: you can also visit spice plantations (p135), explore miles of inland trails, see fabulous wildlife in the marine and nature reserves, feast on an abundance of seafood and sail to dozens of small islands.

need to know

Currency

» The ariary (Ar)

Language

» Malagasy and French

When to Go

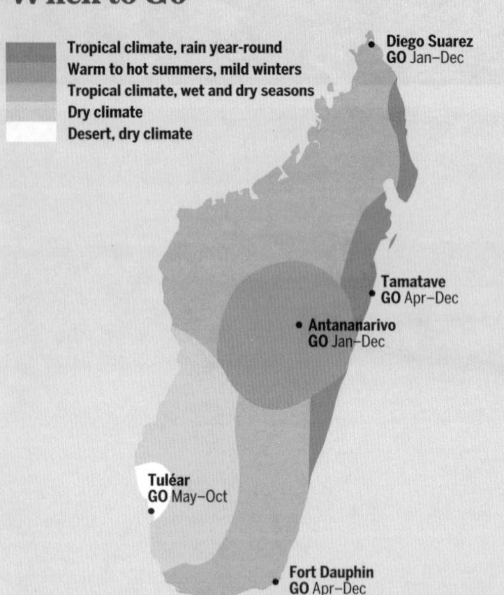

High Season
(Jul–Oct)

» July and August are especially busy because of European school holidays.

» It's winter – balmy temperatures by day and cool nights.

» There's also a spike of high-season activity at Christmas/New Year.

Shoulder
(Apr, May, Nov, Dec)

» Pleasant temperatures and fewer visitors.

» Some attractions have started closing or haven't quite reopened because of the rain.

Low Season
(Jan–Mar)

» Cyclone season, the east coast is particularly vulnerable but all coastal areas are susceptible.

» Rainy season everywhere – many areas inaccessible.

» Discounts available in most hotels.

Your Daily Budget

Budget Less than

€60

» Basic double (shared facilities) €5-12

» Food from *hotelys* (roadside stalls) for breakfast and lunch; dinner at a restaurant

» Travel between cities by taxi-brousse; chartered taxi for day trips

Midrange

€60-150

» Double room (mostly ensuite) €12-25

» A good meal costs around €10

» At the upper end, hire a car and driver

Top end over

€150

» Accommodation varies wildly, €25 in a guesthouse to €500 in a full-board resort

» Travel by private 4WD with driver; internal flights to save time

Money

» ATMs widely available in large towns and cities; in more rural areas, cash rules. Euros are the easiest foreign currency to exchange.

Visas

» Required for all visitors; free for up to 30 days, €45/70 for 60/90 days.

Mobile Phones

» Local SIM cards can be used in European and Australian phones; other phones will have to be set on roaming.

Transport

» Taxi-brousse (bush taxi) is the main public transport: slow, uncomfortable, cheap and omnipresent. Private vehicle and driver is a great but dearer alternative.

Websites

» **Lonely Planet** (www.lonelyplanet.com/Madagascar) Destination info, traveller forum.

» **Wild Madagascar** (www.wildmadagascar.org) Background information, conservation news.

» **David Attenborough's Madagascar** (www.bbc.co.uk/nature/collections/p00db3n8) BBC site with inspirational images.

» **Travel Madagascar** (www.travelmadagascar.org) Comprehensive travel info.

» **Madagascar Tourisme** (www.madagascar-tourisme.com) National tourist office site.

Exchange Rates

Australia	A$1	Ar2100
Canada	C$	Ar2100
Europe	€1	Ar2800
Japan	¥100	Ar2700
New Zealand	NZ$	Ar1600
South Africa	R10	Ar2600
UK	£1	Ar3300
US	US$1	Ar2100

For current exchange rates, see www.xe.com.

Important Numbers

Country code	☎261
Landline prefix	☎020
Mobile prefix	☎032, 033 or 034
Police	☎117
Fire	☎118

Arriving

» **Aéroport d'Ivato, Antananarivo**

Taxi – Ar30,000 during the day, Ar40,000 at night, 45-60 minutes to the city.

Navette Adema – Shuttle bus (Ar10,000, one hour) picks up and drops off passengers at selected hotels from 5am to 9pm (see p42).

Transport in Madagascar

Madagascar is a huge place, the roads are bad and travel times long: it takes 24 hours of solid driving from Antananarivo (Tana) to Diego Suarez (Antsiranana), 18 to Tuléar (Toliara), 16 to Morondava and so on. Be realistic about how much ground you want to cover or you'll spend every other day in the confines of a vehicle – heaven forbid it be in a taxi-brousse!

Internal flights can be huge time savers but they are expensive and do no good to your carbon footprint. If you decide to fly, you'll have to choose between booking your flight before setting off, which is more expensive but guarantees availability, or booking once in Madagascar, which is cheaper but less flexible in terms of timing.

if you like...

Beaches

With two oceans, 5000km of coastline and dozens of islands, Madagascar's beaches are one of the country's top attractions. Many rival the beauty of traditional beach destinations, with the added bonus of fewer visitors.

Anakao A perfect arc of white sand, turquoise water and laid back atmosphere, the pearl of the Great Reef (p89)

Anjajavy Only accessible by private plane or boat, the beaches on Anjajavy peninsula bring a whole new meaning to the word remote (p106)

Ile aux Nattes (Nosy Nato) A classic tropical island, with curving white-sand beaches, reclining palms and the most inviting sea (p181)

Salary Just one resort for 7km of beach, this is what exclusivity feels like (p87)

Nosy Iranja This postcard-perfect duo of islands becomes one at low tide, when a slim sandbank emerges; tour companies in Nosy Be arrange day trips (p135)

Wildlife

Famed for its wildlife, Madagascar is to nature lovers what France is to foodies. But you'll have to be patient, time your visit right and have lady luck on your side to see the best it has to offer.

Indri Madagascar's largest lemur is easily seen – and heard! – at Parc National d'Andasibe (p159)

Aye-aye Famed for its elongated 'magic digit', this highly endangered, curious-looking lemur is now a rare sight (p184)

Iconic baobabs Most commonly found in the southern half of the country, the giants' collection on Allée des Baobabs has become one of Madagascar's signature views (p117)

Humpback whales Every year from July to September, hundreds of whales make the long journey from Antarctica to mate and give birth in the warmer waters of the Indian Ocean and the Mozambique Channel (p180)

Turtles Beloved of divers and snorkellers, turtles thrive all along the Malagasy coast (p134)

Hiking

With such an alluring shoreline, it's easy to forget that about 70% of Madagascar's land surface sits at a lofty 1000m to 1500m. Cue superb mountains, extinct volcanoes and dramatic peaks, and ergo, fabulous hiking.

Parc National d'Andringitra & the Tsaranoro Valley Quite possibly Madagascar's most stunning national park, with world-class trekking and excellent facilities to make the best of what's on offer (p68)

Parc National Marojejy A trek through the primordial rainforest of the Massif de Marojejy progresses from scenic walk to full-on climbing expedition (turning back is possible!; p152)

Parc National des Tsingy de Bemaraha Scale the weird and wonderful Tsingy along the park's sensational *via ferrata* (mountain route; p110)

Les Trois Baies Battered by the winds and the might of the Indian Ocean's waves, this stretch of coast, with its pristine bays, is exhilaratingly wild and beautiful (p144)

ROBERT HARDING PICTURE LIBRARY LTD / ALAMY ©

» Zebu skewers with mango and rice

Food & Drink

Madagascar is a culinary delight: thanks to a mix of cuisines and prime fresh ingredients (plentiful seafood, succulent zebu meat, and fruit and vegetables bursting with flavour), you're certain to eat well wherever you go.

Camarons Try the Malagasy prawn (there are saltwater and freshwater varieties) for a fraction of what you'd pay back home (p102)

La Varangue Antananarivo's culinary gem. Make sure you treat yourself to outstanding Franco-Malagasy gastronomy (p36)

Société de Rhum Arrangé Flavoured rum is the red island's signature drink: there are dozens to try (and take back home) at this shop in Nosy Be, from vanilla to lychee, chocolate or ginger (p129)

Vanilla Madagascar's flagship plant grows in abundance on the northeast 'vanilla coast'; visit plantations in Antalaha (p154)

Millot Plantations Discover how spices, cocoa and aromatic plants are grown and processed at this beautiful plantation, and sample them as you go (p135)

Diving & Snorkelling

Madagascar is home to the world's fifth-largest coral reef, which partly explains why diving here is so good. The fauna is exceptional, with sharks, turtles, whales and rays.

Andavadoaka Part of the Great Reef of Madagascar, with all three types of reefs (fringing, patch and barrier), and an abundance of coral, fish and turtles (p87)

Nosy Be Dozens of dive sites within half an hour's boat ride, with a huge variety of seascapes, from shipwrecks to reefs and spectacular drops (p121)

Nosy Tanikely Now a protected marine reserve, Nosy Tanikely is one of the best and most accessible snorkelling spots in Madagascar. Turtles guaranteed (p134)

Ifaty & Mangily A great range of dives, including the famous 'Cathedral' – a network of stunning rocky arches (p84)

Ambola This serene spot on the southern reef gets as many points for the diving as it does for after-diving (p91)

History & Culture

Although many come to Madagascar for its incredible nature, the island has a rich and diverse culture, influenced by the waves of migrants who gradually populated the island and colonial powers who hoped to control it.

Ambohimanga The most sacred of Antananarivo's 12 sacred hills and long-standing home of Malagasy royalty (p43)

Tany Mena Tours Tour Madagascar with trained anthropologists, ethnologists and archaeologists and immerse yourself in Malagasy culture (p31)

Famadihana Visitors are often welcome at traditional exhumation ceremonies – an opportunity to re-assess our own beliefs about life and death (p51)

Ile Sainte Marie's pirate cemetery Overlooking the Baie de Forbans, where many pirates lived, this cemetery is a fascinating reminder of the island's lawless past (p180)

Tomb art Sakalava tombs are renowned for their erotic carvings, so much so that many have been pillaged; if you get to see one, know you are amongst a select few (p115)

» Woven-straw bags are a popular Malagasy souvenir

Shopping

Finding souvenirs is no hardship in Madagascar: there are woven baskets, gemstones, spices, clothes, rum, woodcarvings, leather goods and much more.

Sabotsy Market, Antsirabe A sprawling open-air market reminiscent of a North African souk, Sabotsy is as good for shopping as it is for people-watching (p50)

Marché Artisanal de la Digue, Antananarivo La Digue is like a shopping kaleidoscope of Madagascar: pretty much everything you have seen in the country is available here (p40)

Ring Road Ambositra is known far and wide for its *marqueterie* (objects inlaid with coloured woods) and this is the best place to buy fine examples of this art (p55)

La Teeshirterie, Antananarivo You'll see Madagascar's funky T-shirts everywhere, but this is the garment emporium of them all (p40)

Creature Comforts

If you've had enough of trekking, diving, wildlife-seeking and bumping around in a 4WD, put your bags down for a few days at one of these wonderful retreats.

Eden Lodge, near Nosy Be Remote, serene and ecofriendly, Eden Lodge is where to go to be at one with nature (p137)

Princesse Bora Lodge & Spa, Ile Ste Marie Pirogue tubs in the spa, suspended beds in the bungalows, a dizzying wine list: this is as close to perfection as you get (p180)

Chez Sika, Ile aux Nattes Swing in a hammock by the seaside, enjoy a spear-fishing trip with the owners and generally revel in this star budget establishment (p181)

Le Relais de la Reine, Isalo Elegance and refinement in the stark beauty of Parc National de l'Isalo, complete with spa and horse-riding club for a unique experience (p76)

Epic 4WD Journeys

If this were a TV program, it would open with 'don't try this at home'. Far from putting travellers off, though, many revel in the challenge that are Madagascar's roads, so here are our favourite bone-shaking, tyre-bursting, vehicle-bashing road trips.

RN5 from Maroantsetra to Soaniera Ivongo Depending on how you look at it, this is either the country's worst road, or its best 4WD adventure (p175)

Coastal road from Tuléar to Morondava The highlights of this journey are the northern end of the Great Reef of Madagascar, and an overnight stay at the serene village of Belo-sur-Mer, ensconced in the dunes (p118)

Coastal road from Tuléar to Fort Dauphin This road is practically a walk in the park between Tuléar and Itampolo – until it disintegrates and virtually disappears. The paved sections sport craters worthy of the moon (p88)

month by month

Top Events

1 **Reptiles & Amphibians**, February

2 **Famadihana**, July

3 **Whale-Watching**, August

4 **Mango Season**, October

5 **Baby Lemurs**, November

January

This is the beginning of cyclone season, which runs until March. Cyclones affect mostly the east coast, but they can strike the west coast too. Most areas have received some rains by now, turning arid landscapes into numerous shades of green.

February

The weather may be sweltering and humid, but for those who do make it at this time, the wildlife rewards are unique. Summer is also cruise-ship season, from Tamatave to Nosy Be.

Reptiles & Amphibians

After many months of hibernation or reduced activity, snakes and frogs come out in force in the hot and humid summer climate. This is the best time of year to admire their colourful displays and incredible variety.

April

Many areas that were inaccessible during the rainy season are starting to reopen. Be prepared for slower travelling times however, and copious amounts of mud.

May

In the north, the wind has picked up and will blow until the end of the year. Tourism starts picking up again.

Kitesurfing

A combination of fantastic wind and good surf has turned Baie de Sakalava and Mer d'Emeraude (northern Madagascar) into the Malagasy capital of this extreme sport. Tuition and equipment are available; a couple of hotels offer special kitesurfing packages.

Zegny'Zo Festival

For a shot of artistic zing, head to Zegny'Zo, an international street arts festival, bringing together musicians, painters, dancers, acrobats and many more for two weeks of exhibitions, parades, workshops, impromptu slam sessions and shows.

July

It's winter and temperatures regularly drop below zero in the Highlands at night; bring a very warm sleeping bag if you're camping and plenty of layers for heating-less hotels (surprisingly numerous!).

Famadihana

The 'turning of the dead', or exhumation, ceremonies to commemorate ancestors take place in the highlands from July to September. The practice is common from Antananarivo to Fianarantsoa and is an important celebration; foreigners are sometimes invited.

Game in Majunga (Mahajanga)

You're guaranteed to try zebu meat (a succulent cousin of beef) within a couple of days of arriving in Mada, but for something more original, why not try local game, such as fruit bat or comb duck? Hunting season runs from May to October.

Vanilla Season

The country's flagship plant is harvested between July and October. It is a labour-intensive process, as vanilla pods mature at different times. Flights are full in the vanilla-growing northeast region at this time of year, so book ahead.

August

With school summer holidays in full swing in Europe, August is peak tourism season in Madagascar. Book ahead for the most popular trips and in areas with limited accommodation, such as Parc National des Tsingy de Bemaraha.

Whale-Watching

Humpback whales migrate annually from their feeding grounds in Antarctica to the warm waters of the Indian Ocean and Mozambique Channel to mate and give birth. Famed for their spectacular breaching (jumping), they can be observed all along the coast from July to September.

September

With spring under way, this is the perfect time of year to come to Madagascar: temperatures are pleasant, there is little rain and the kids have gone back to school.

Birdwatching

Dry, deciduous forests are at their barest at this time of year – a godsend for birdwatchers. Deprived of their usual camouflage, Madagascar's 280 bird species, a third of them endemic, are easier to observe. Don't forget your binoculars.

Orchids

Madagascar has over 1000 species of this delicate plant, 90% of which are endemic. Many are endangered, however, so being able to see these floral works of art in the wild is an increasingly rare experience.

October

As with spring all over the world, there is stunning blossom, birth and mating – a great time of year to admire wildlife. Temperatures are also at their best, warm but not stifling.

Mango Season

The delectable mango bursts on to the scene, inundating market stalls and roadsides, and making its way into every dessert and fruit salad. The green fruit is picked earlier in August and September to make *achards* (a pickled condiment) and savoury salads.

Jacaranda Blossom

The exquisite purple blossom of the jacaranda tree is a sight to behold: its delicate colour contrasts beautifully with urban greys and country greens, while petals carpet the ground like a Technicolor version of snow.

Fossa Mating Season

The normally elusive fossa, Madagascar's biggest predator (and the baddie in *Madagascar* the cartoon), makes quite a show of its loud nuptials. It's best observed in the Réserve Forestière de Kirindy in western Madagascar.

November

Rains come early in parts of western Madagascar, making some roads inaccessible. Elsewhere, however, this is a lovely time of year, with visitor numbers petering out and the weather warming up.

Baby Lemurs

If you thought lemurs were cute, wait until you see the babies, clinging to their mother's fur or being carried by the scruff of the neck. The entire troop generally looks after the young.

Lychee Season

Madagascar provides around 70% of the lychees consumed in Europe, but fear not, there are plenty left in country to gorge yourself on. The season lasts until January, and lychees are a favourite Christmas food.

December

Christmas is a low-key event for Malagasies: families go to Mass and share a meal. Tourism peaks briefly around festive celebrations, with many Europeans enjoying the warm weather and tropical showers.

Whether you've got two weeks or two months, these itineraries provide a starting point for the trip of a lifetime. Want more inspiration? Head online to lonelyplanet.com/thorntree to chat with other travellers.

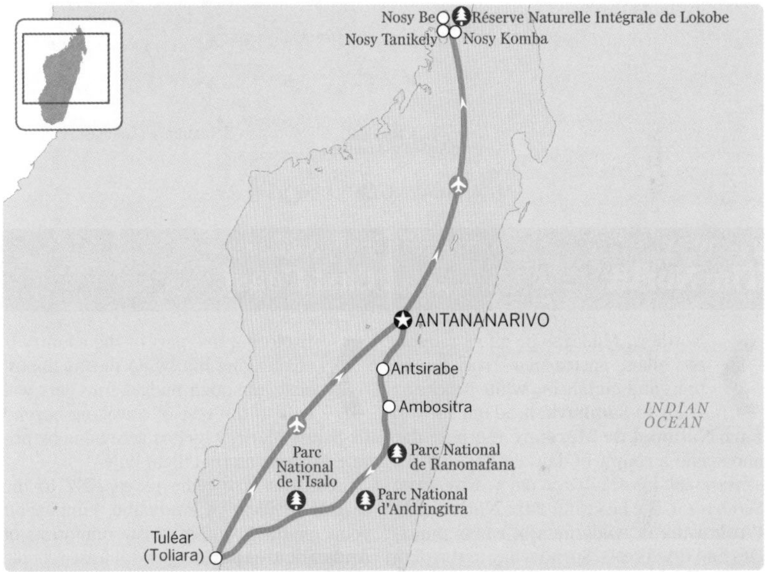

Two Weeks

Essential Madagascar

A combination of the classic RN7 with some island R&R. On day one, head down to the highland town of **Antsirabe**, with its wide colonial streets and colourful rickshaws.

On day two, wind your way down to **Parc National de Ranomafana** through the highland's scenic landscapes, stopping en route at the arts-and-crafts capital **Ambositra**. Spend day three hiking and searching for lemurs in Ranomafana's rainforest. On day four, drive to the superb **Parc National d'Andringitra**; spend the next two days on the **Imarivolanitra trail**, which takes in the summit of **Pic Boby**, Madagascar's second-highest peak.

On the seventh day, drive to **Parc National de l'Isalo**; spend day eight exploring the park's desert plains and canyons. On day nine, it's a long drive to **Tuléar (Toliara)**. On day 10, fly to Antananarivo (Tana), and then on to **Nosy Be**. Spend the morning at the beach and take a quad bike tour of the hinterland in the afternoon. On day 12, take a day trip to **Nosy Komba** and **Nosy Tanikely** for unrivalled snorkelling. On your last day, visit the **Réserve Naturelle Intégrale de Lokobe**. Fly back to Tana on day 14.

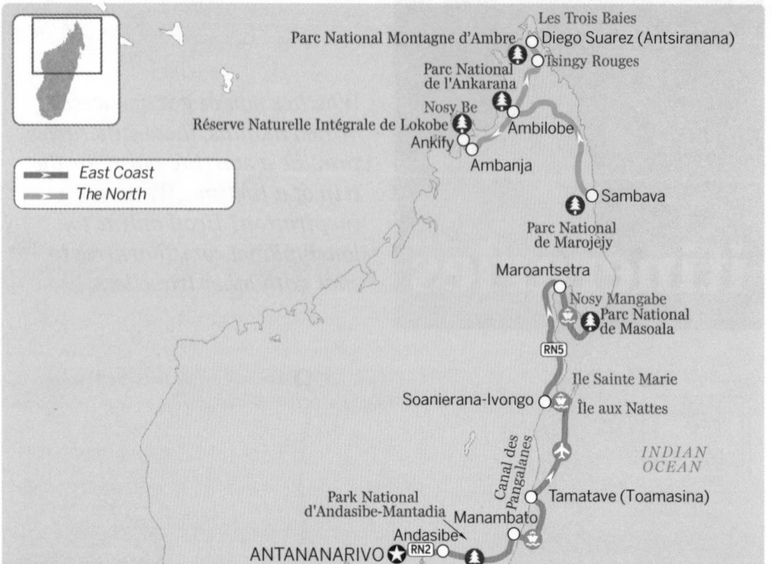

Two Weeks

The North

Northern Madagascar offers rainforest hikes, spectacular rock formations and tantalising white beaches.

Fly to **Sambava**; head out early to **Parc National de Marojejy** the next day and spend a couple of days trekking in this sensational massif. It's a day's drive from Sambava to the beautiful **Parc National de l'Ankarana**, a wilderness of caves, pinnacles and dry forests. Spend a day in the park and continue on to the northern belle of **Diego Suarez (Antsiranana)**, with a stop at the terracotta-coloured **Tsingy Rouges** on the way.

Take a day to discover Diego's heritage and explore the wild coastline of **Les Trois Baies** near Ramena. Take another day trip to the mountainous **Parc National Montagne d'Ambre**.

From Diego, it's half a day's drive to **Ambanja**, where you should visit the cocoa and spice plantations before boarding a boat at Ankify for **Nosy Be**. Spend three or four days enjoying the coral reefs and beaches and make sure you put a day aside for the fabulous **Réserve Naturelle Intégrale de Lokobe**. Fly back to Tana from Nosy Be.

2½ Weeks

East Coast

Exploring this part of the country is challenging but by no means impossible, although budget travellers will balk at the cost of travelling beyond Ile Sainte Marie, which is accessible by private 4WD or internal flight only.

Head east along the paved RN2 to the charming village of **Andasibe**, jumping-off point for the luxuriant, misty rainforests of **Andasibe area parks**. Spend at least a couple of days waking to the cries of the legendary indri (Madagascar's largest lemur), hiking and birdwatching before winding down the RN2 to the coast. In **Manambato**, organise a tour of **Canal des Pangalanes**, the picturesque gateway to the waterways and lakes. Travel to **Tamatave (Toamasina)** by cargo boat.

From Tamatave, fly to gorgeous **Ile Sainte Marie** and stay at the terminally laid-back **Ile aux Nattes**. Tour the island by quad or motorbike and take a whale-watching trip (July to September).

If you relish a challenge, take a boat to **Soanierana-Ivongo** and drive the infamous **RN5** (4WD only) to **Maroantsetra** (two days). Spend a night at **Nosy Mangabe** and a couple of nights in the pristine **Parc National de Masoala**. Fly back to Tana from Maroantsetra or on to Sambava in the northeast.

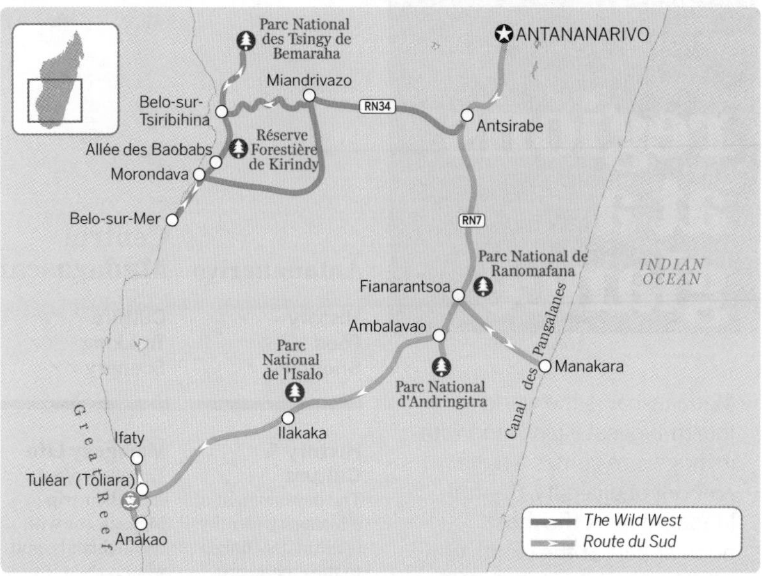

Three Weeks
Route du Sud

This classic route will whisk you from Antananarivo down to Tuléar along the famed RN7.

First stop is **Antsirabe**, where you should take a *pousse-pousse* (rickshaw) tour and explore Sabotsy market. Drive down to **Fianarantsoa** through spectacular mountain scenery. The next day, hop on the FCE train to **Manakara**; stay on the beach for a couple of nights and tour the **Canal des Pangalanes**.

Drive back to the RN7 to visit **Parc National de Ranomafana** and hike in the park's rainforest. Time your visit to the highland town of **Ambalavao** to coincide with Madagascar's largest zebu market, then spend a few days hiking among the granite peaks of **Parc National d'Andringitra**.

Further south is another wonderful protected area, **Parc National de l'Isalo**, with jagged sandstone massifs and cool canyons.

Stop at the sapphire boomtown of **Ilakaka** on your way to the coast. Eschew Tuléar and head straight for the perfect beaches of **Anakao** or **Ifaty**, and the **Great Reef**. From Tuléar, you can fly back to Antananarivo or travel on to Fort Dauphin or Morondava.

Two Weeks
The Wild West

This itinerary requires some planning ahead but once you've got your boat and your 4WD booked, you'll be off in a flash.

Book a descent of the **Tsiribihina River**. Trips start from **Miandrivazo**, a day's drive from Antananarivo. From there, it takes two and a half days to drift down to **Belo-sur-Tsiribihina**.

Arrange for a 4WD and driver to meet you at the boat landing in Belo and continue north to **Parc National des Tsingy de Bemaraha**. You'll need at least two days to explore the Grands and Petits Tsingy. It's then a day's drive through scorched landscape down to **Réserve Forestière de Kirindy**, home to the elusive fossa and the giant jumping rat. Make sure to go on a night walk. On your way to Morondava, stop at the iconic **Allée des Baobabs**.

After a day recuperating in the laid-back seaside town of **Morondava**, head down to the fishing village of **Belo-sur-Mer** for a couple of days. You can then drive on to Tuléar (during the dry season only), or go back to Morondava and fly or drive back to Antananarivo.

regions at a glance

Madagascar is the world's fourth-biggest island, and with its huge size comes a huge amount of diversity. Central Madagascar is the most popular part of the country, and the most accessible.

The coastal regions are the realm of the 4WD and can be challenging to travel in (the northwest being the exception). Southern Madagascar will appeal to divers and snorkellers. Beach bums will be better off in Ile Sainte Marie in the east or Nosy Be in the north.

Western Madagascar will delight those in search of something a little different, while activities enthusiasts will be at home in Northern Madagascar.

Eastern Madagascar is the most remote region, but those who make it there will be rewarded with pristine environments.

Antananarivo

History ✓✓✓
Food ✓✓✓
Shopping ✓✓

History & Culture

The development of a Malagasy identity is intimately linked to the emergence of Antananarivo (Tana) as a capital: this is the home of the kings who brought together the island's tribes. As one Malagasy put it, 'to understand our history is to understand us'.

Gastronomy

Foodies of the world, rejoice, Tana's got fusion cuisine down to a T. Imagine French gastronomy, prepared with the freshest Malagasy ingredients, add a soupçon of Creole, a smidgen of Indian, and voilà!

Retail Therapy

Tana is a mix of arts, crafts, clothes and delis. Bargain-hunters head for the markets, while more conventional shoppers love the well-stocked boutiques.

p26

Central Madagascar

Culture ✓✓✓
Trekking ✓✓✓
Scenery ✓✓

Malagasy Life

Travellers often start their trip in Madagascar with the highlands, and what a great introduction to Malagasy life: accessible homestays, colourful markets (including the biggest zebu market in the country), colonial architecture and plenty of artisans.

Amazing Treks

When it comes to trekking, Parc National d'Andringitra is in a league of its own. The trails are challenging, the views breathtaking and there is good infrastructure. The region's other national parks also offer great walks.

Scenic Highlands

Verdant peaks, majestic summits and stunning forests: one of the main draws of the highlands is their indisputable beauty.

p48

Southern Madagascar

Diving ✓✓✓
Beaches ✓✓✓
Desert ✓✓

Great Reef

It is the world's fifth-largest barrier reef, ergo one of the world's finest diving destination. There are multiple dive sites all along the reef and many professional outfits to choose from.

Beaches

Malagasy beaches rarely suffer from overcrowding, but many southern beaches are so off the radar that the likelihood of having the beach to yourself is actually quite high.

Desert

Much of southern Madagascar is a desert, but not just any kind of desert: with its frontier sapphire towns and rugged canyons, it could be a Western movie set, save perhaps for the giant baobabs.

p72

Western Madagascar

Baobabs ✓✓✓
Food ✓✓
Scenery ✓✓

Magnificent Giants

The Malagasies call them 'roots of the sky', after their crooked branches, and in western Madagascar, they come in all guises: in majestic avenues, intertwined, straight or bottle-shaped.

Seafood & Game

Food adventurers will rate the region for its variety: the seafood is abundant and cheap, including lobster and crayfish, and there are some truly off-the-beaten-track delicacies. Fruit bat, anyone?

Scenery

From meandering rivers to immense beaches, arid plains to deciduous forests, serrated peaks to undulating sand dunes, Western Madagascar is easy on the eye.

p98

Northern Madagascar

Activities ✓✓✓
Islands ✓✓✓
Plantations ✓✓

Diving & Trekking

Adrenalin junkies, look no further: here, you can trek in mist-shrouded rainforest, scale rock cliffs on deserted islands, kitesurf along unspoilt beaches and dive with whalesharks and rays. Oh, and beachcombing counts too.

Paradisiacal Islands

It's a cliché but the islands around Nosy Be more than live up to it; sadly, paradise doesn't come cheap.

Vanilla & Spice

If you've ever wondered where the delectable vanilla comes from, what a pepper plant looks like or how fruity cocoa beans become chocolate, visit one of the country's beautiful plantations to find out.

p120

Eastern Madagascar

Whales ✓✓✓
Rainforest ✓✓
Islands ✓✓✓

Humpback Migration

Ile Sainte Marie (Nosy Boraha) and Baie d'Antongil have been the nursing and mating grounds of humpback whales since time immemorial. Take to the water to admire these endangered giants in all their breaching glory.

Rainforest

Eastern Madagascar is one of the last areas in the country where huge tracts of rainforest remain. Explore it on foot or by boat in the Masoala Peninsula.

Tropical Islands

For sheer escapism, you can't do better than idyllic Ile Sainte Marie and Ile aux Nattes. Both cater admirably to those in need of R&R, but Sainte Marie also holds the promise of adventure in the north.

p156

Every listing is recommended by our authors, and their favourite places are listed first

Look out for these icons:

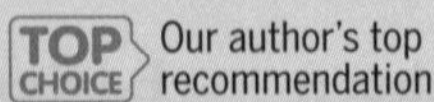

Our author's top recommendation

A green or sustainable option

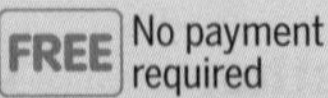

No payment required

See the Index for a full list of destinations covered in this book.

On the Road

Antananarivo

POP 1.2 MILLION

Includes »

Best Places to Eat

- » La Varangue (p36)
- » Le Café de la Gare (p36)
- » Le Saka (p36)
- » Le Petit Verdot (p36)
- » La Terrasse du Glacier (p36)

Best Places to Stay

- » Hôtel Sakamanga (p31)
- » Résidence Lapasoa (p32)
- » La Varangue (p32)
- » Hôtel Tana-Jacaranda (p34)
- » Le Manoir Rouge (p43)

Why Go?

Tana, as the capital is universally known, is all about eating, shopping, history and day trips. The town centre itself, with its pollution and dreadful traffic, puts off many travellers from staying, but bypassing the capital altogether would be a mistake: Tana has been the home of Malagasy power for three centuries and there is a huge amount of history and culture to discover by visiting its sacred hills.

In the city itself, the Haute-Ville, with its beautiful colonial buildings, steep streets and cool climate (average altitude in Tana is 1400m), is a great place to wander about. There are also some excellent markets and shops that stock products and crafts from across the country at very competitive prices. Finally, Tana is *the* place in Madagascar to treat yourself to a fine meal: some establishments rival Europe's Michelin-starred restaurants, but without the price tag.

When to Go

Antananarivo

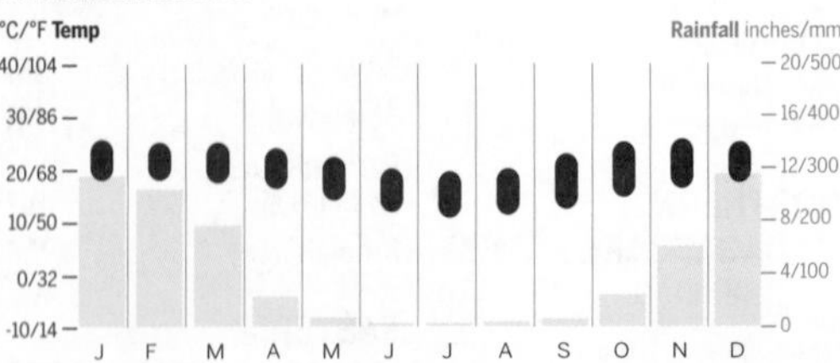

Jun–Aug Winter season in Tana, when night temperatures drop below 10°C.

Jul–Sep *Famadihana* season, when families exhume their ancestors' bones to communicate with them.

Oct The purple blossom of jacaranda trees lines the shores of Lac Anosy.

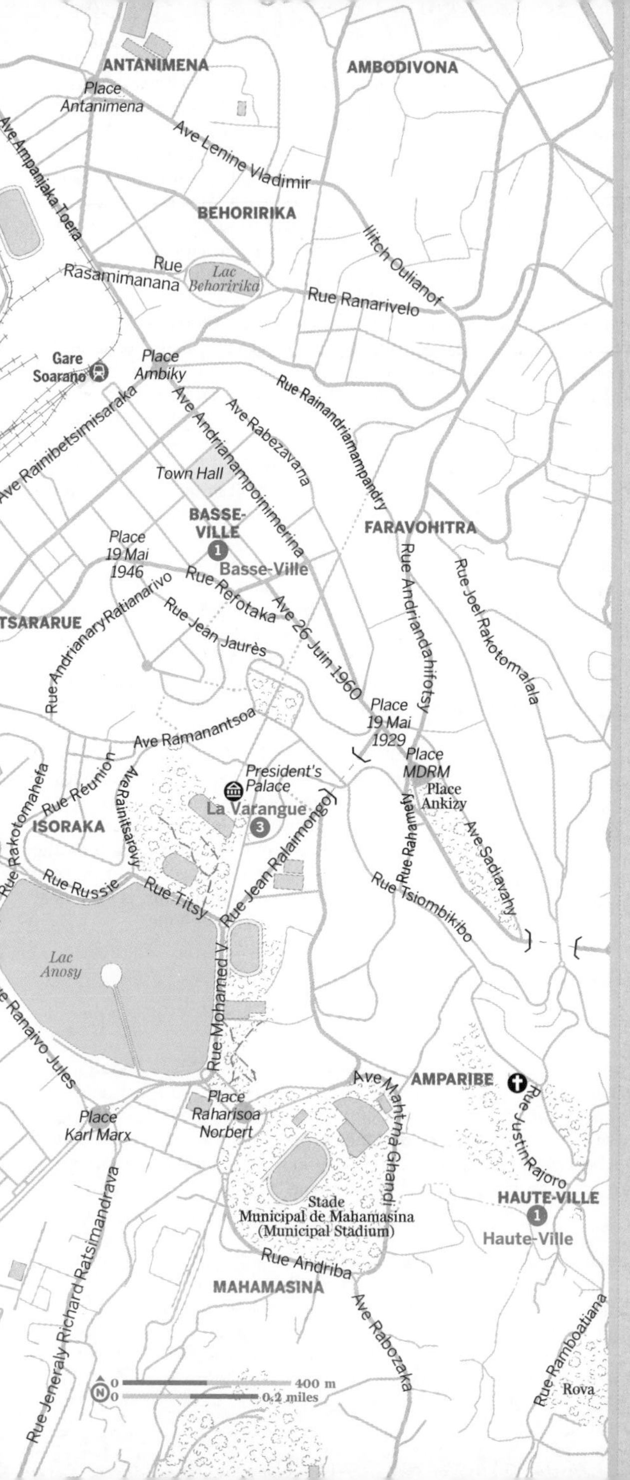

Antananarivo Highlights

1. Follow our walking tour through Antananarivo's lovely **Haute-Ville** and busy **Basse-Ville** (p33)
2. Spend an afternoon in the spiritual home of Malagasy identity, the royal hill of **Ambohimanga** (p43)
3. Splurge on dinner at **La Varangue** (p36)
4. Join a **guided tour** (p31) of Tana's sacred hills or the capital's surrounding villages
5. Shop till you drop (and haggle all you can) at **Marché Artisanal de La Digue** (p40)
6. Take a day trip to **Ambatolampy** (p46) in the highlands
7. Attend an afternoon of **hira gasy** (p39) – music, dancing and storytelling spectacles – in Tana or the surrounding villages

History

The area that is now Antananarivo was originally known as Analamanga (Blue Forest), and is believed to have been populated by the Vazimba, ancestors of today's Malagasy about whom little is known. In 1610 a Merina king named Andrianjaka conquered the region, stationed a garrison of 1000 troops to defend his new settlement, and renamed it Antananarivo, 'Place of 1000 Warriors'.

In the late 18th century, Andrianampoinimerina, the warrior king, moved his capital from Ambohimanga to Antananarivo, where it became the most powerful of all the Merina kingdoms. For the next century, Antananarivo was the capital of the Merina monarchs and the base from which they carried out their conquest of the rest of Madagascar.

Tana remained the seat of government during the colonial era, and it was the French who gave the city centre its present form, building two great staircases to scale the city's hills and draining swamps and paddy fields to create present-day Analakely. In May 1929, the city was the site of the first major demonstration against the colonialists.

Today the greater Antananarivo area is Madagascar's political and economic centre.

Sights

If your knees can withstand the long flights of stairs and steep, sloping streets, central Tana is a good place to explore on foot. Most of the attractive old buildings are in Haute-Ville, which is quieter and easier to stroll around than the hectic, exhaust-fume-ridden Basse-Ville.

Rova HISTORIC BUILDING

(Palais de la Reine; Rue Ramboatiana) Tana's *rova* (fortified palace) is the imposing structure that crowns the highest hill of Tana. Gutted in a fire in 1995, it is still under restoration and was not officially open to the public at the time of research. However, it was possible to enter the grounds by paying Ar5000 to the gatekeeper and coming in with one of the freelance guides hanging about (Ar5000).

The palace gate is protected by a carved eagle, the symbol of military force, and a phallus, the symbol of circumcision and thus nobility. The palace itself, known as Manjakamiadana (A Fine Place to Rule), was designed for Queen Ranavalona I by a Scottish missionary named James Cameron. The outer structure, built in 1867 for Ranavalona II, was made of stone, with a wooden roof and interior.

Succeeding rulers built (and destroyed) a number of other palaces on the premises; there are ruins scattered about. There is also a replica of King Andrianampoinimerina's palace at Ambohimanga.

The Rova is also the resting place of the country's greatest monarchs: the most imposing stone tombs are located to the left of the main gate. The plain grey ones are those of kings, while the queens' are painted red (red was the colour of nobility).

Remember that it is *fady* (taboo) to point your finger directly at the royal tombs or the palace itself. The Rova, which can be seen from almost anywhere in Tana, is located at the very top of the Haute-Ville.

ANTANANARIVO IN...

One Day

After breakfast at **InfiniThé** (p37), head up to the **Rova** (p28) and the **Musée Andafivaratra** (p29); arrange for a guide from **Ortana** (p41) to meet you there for a fascinating guided tour. Amble back down to the city centre following our walking tour through the Haute and Basse Villes. Stop at **La Terrasse du Glacier** (p36) for lunch. In the afternoon, head to **Marché Pochart** (p31) for a spot of shopping or book a relaxing massage at one of the town's **spas** (p35). Dine at the exquisite **La Varangue** (p36).

Two Days

Follow our day one itinerary. On the second day, charter a taxi and head for the hills. On the way, stop at one of Tana's **cafes** (p37) to buy a picnic. Start your trip at the royal palace of **Ambohimanga** (p43) for an introduction to Merina history. After exploring the site, settle for a picnic at one of the numerous viewpoints. After lunch, head to **Ilafy** (p43), one of Antananarivo's 12 sacred hills. Finish your day with some hard bargaining for souvenirs at **Marché Artisanal de la Digue** (p40). Have dinner at the atmospheric **Café de la Gare** (p36).

Musée Andafivaratra MUSEUM

(admission Ar5000; ⏲9am-5pm) Housed in a magnificent pink baroque palace, a few hundred metres downhill from the Rova, the Andafivaratra museum is the former home of Prime Minister Rainilaiarivony, the power behind the throne of the three queens he married in succession (Rasoherina, Ranavalona II and Ranavalona III) between 1864 and 1895.

The museum's collection is a dusty assortment of furniture, portraits and memorabilia from the age of the Merina kings and queens, but it illuminates some of the colourful characters that drove Madagascan history: mad Queen Ranavalona I, dumpy in a coral silk crinoline, scowls out from her oil painting like a psychotic Queen Victoria, while Jean Laborde, the French adventurer presumed to be her lover, glowers from beneath his beard in a black-and-white photograph.

There's also a huge gilt throne, originals of important trade treaties between Madagascar and the US, the UK and France, the Merina crown jewels, coats of chain mail and a random selection of presents from foreign crowns through the ages. Explanations of the exhibits are in English as well as French.

'Guides' generally loiter around the entrance and will try to win your custom; unfortunately, the majority don't know much about Malagasy history and will do little more than read the artefacts' captions. If you would like a guided tour, contact Ortana, the tourist office, to find an accredited (and knowledgeable) guide.

Presidential Palace HISTORIC BUILDING

This beautiful 19th-century manor was an official French residence for many years. It became the Malagasy presidential palace in 1975 and remained so until president Didier Ratsiraka decided to build a more modern complex about 15km south of the capital in 1991. The mansion remains an official residence but is generally quiet. In a bid to balance the colonial architectural influence, Andry Rajoelina, president of the high transitional authority (the administration in power since the 2009 coup), ordered that a replica of the King's Palace at Ambohimanga be built right next to it.

Lac Anosy LAKE

Antananarivo's heart-shape lake lies in the southern part of town, an easy downhill walk from Haute-Ville. The lake is particularly lovely in October, when the jacaranda trees are covered in purple blossoms. On an island connected to the shore by a causeway stands a large white angel on a plinth, the **Monument aux Morts** (Monument to the Dead; admission Ar5000), a WWI memorial erected by the French.

There's a daily **flower market** just across the road from the causeway entrance, where florists prepare kitschy but incredibly intricate bouquets and floral compositions. The market and entrance to the causeway are at the southern end of the lake.

The area around the lake has somewhat deteriorated over the last couple of years, so avoid wandering here on your own and definitely never after dark.

Gare Soarano HISTORIC BUILDING

Tana's old train station doesn't see much passenger traffic these days, so the lovely building has been converted into a small, but upmarket shopping centre. There are regular art shows of Malagasy artists downstairs, as well as chichi boutiques. Upstairs, you'll find clothes and jewellery designers offering their wares in an open-plan space.

FREE **Musée d'Art et d'Archéologie** MUSEUM

(Rue Dok Villette; ⏲9am-5pm Tue-Sat) This small museum in the Haute-Ville gives an overview of archaeological digs around the island, including displays of grave decorations from the south (known as *aloalo*), an extensive exhibition of musical instruments and a few talismans and objects used for in traditional ceremonies. A tip for the guide is customary.

HAVE YOUR SAY

Found a fantastic restaurant that you're longing to share with the world? Disagree with our recommendations? Or just want to talk about your most recent trip?

Whatever your reason, head to lonelyplanet.com, where you can post a review, ask or answer a question on the Thorntree forum, comment on a blog, or share your photos and tips on Groups. Or you can simply spend time chatting with like-minded travellers. So go on, have your say.

Central Antananarivo

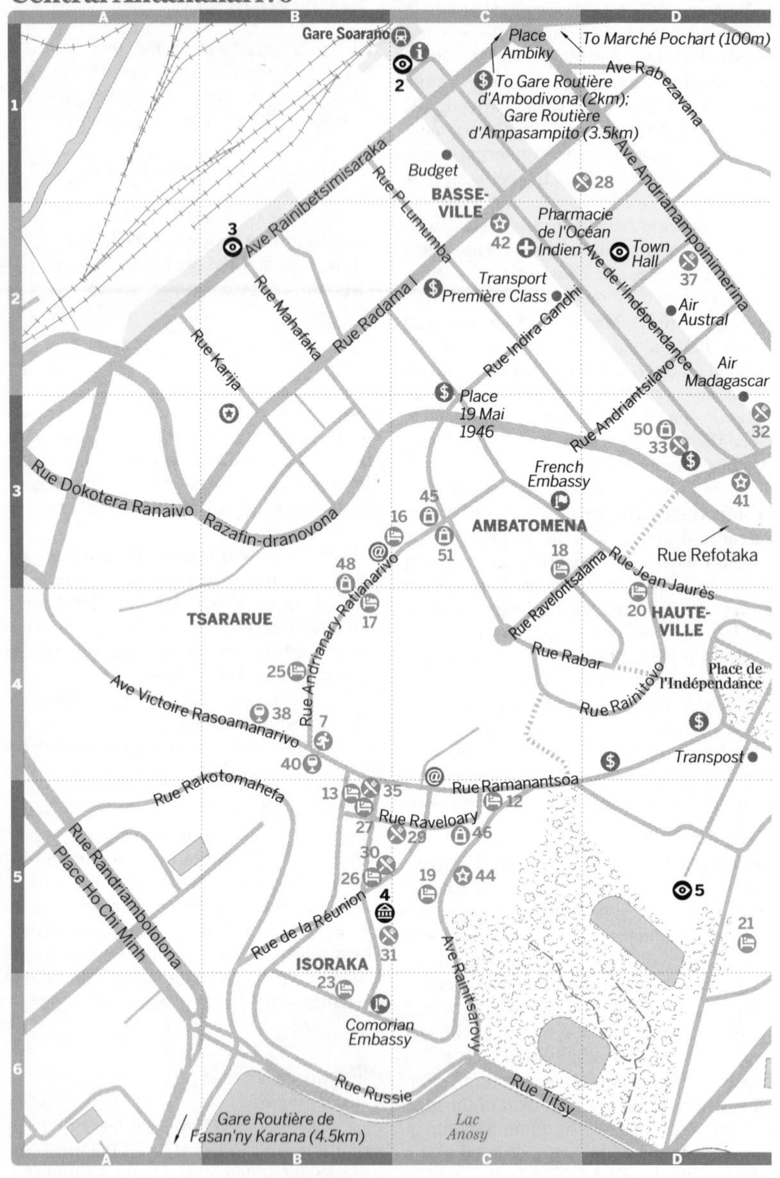

Markets MARKET

For Shakespeare, all the world was a stage; for Antananarivo it seems that all the world's a market, which must make at least half the population hawkers. Everywhere you look, vendors tout their wares from stalls, carts and inverted cardboard boxes, or simply wander the streets looking hopeful.

The main market is found in the 'pavilions' at **Analakely**; it's a shadow of the former *zoma* (market), for which Tana was legendary, but it's still a packed, teem-

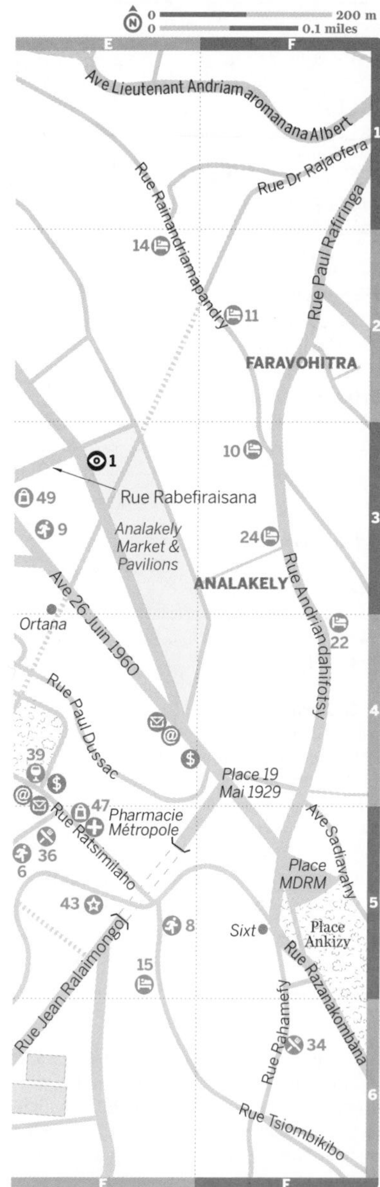

ing place, selling clothes, household items, dodgy DVDs and every food product you could imagine, plus a few you probably couldn't.

Another huge market is at **Andravoahangy**, about 1.5km northeast of the northern end of Ave de l'Indépendance. The smaller **Marché Communal de Petite Vitesse**, west of the train station, sells more or less the same goods, minus the food.

For souvenirs, the **Marché Pochart** is a nice alternative to Marché Artisanal de la Digue. Bargain hard.

Tours

TOP CHOICE Tany Mena Tours CULTURAL TOUR
(☎22 326 27; www.tanymenatours.com; Ave de l'Indépendance) This agency specialises in sustainable tourism and offers highly original tours around Antananarivo that combine historical highlights with cultural experiences: visits of local villages or traditional artisan workshops, attending Famadihana ceremonies etc (€37 per person for a group of three to five people). Most tours are led by trained historians or anthropologists (some English-speaking). Two-day trips in the surrounding highlands are also offered.

TOP CHOICE Ortana GUIDED TOUR
(www.tourisme-antananarivo.com; ☎22 270 51; Escalier Ravanalona I) This is the best place to go to if you would like a guide to visit historical sites around Tana such as the Rova and Musée Andafivaratra, Ambohimanga, Ilafy etc. Most guides are knowledgeable and many speak English and/or Italian as well as French. The office also organises one- to three-hour group walks around the Haute-Ville on Mondays, Wednesdays and Saturdays (Ar5000 to Ar20,000 per person depending on the circuit and the number of people).

Sleeping

Tana is one place in Madagascar where it is worth upping your budget if possible: the budget and midrange categories are remarkable by their mediocrity (with a couple of notable exceptions) whereas the top-end options are, on the whole, excellent value. A number of hotels offer 'day rates', which allow guests to keep their room until early evening as many flights to Europe leave late at night.

TOP CHOICE Hôtel Sakamanga BOUTIQUE HOTEL €€€
(☎22 358 09; www.sakamanga.com; Rue Andrianary Ratianarivo; d Ar50,000-135,000; ❄@📶) A perennial favourite, the Sakamanga offers fantastic accommodation for both midrange and top-end travellers setting store by a

Central Antananarivo

Sights

1 Analakely Market E3
Centre Culturel d'Art et d'Archéologie .... (see 49)
2 Gare Soarano C1
3 Marché Communal de Petite Vitesse B2
4 Musée d'Art et d'Archéologie B5
5 Presidential Palace D5

Activities, Courses & Tours

6 Balnéoforme Colbert E5
7 BioAroma B4
8 Homeopharma E5
Le Royal Palissandre Spa .... (see 24)
9 Tany Mena Tours E3

Sleeping

10 Chez Francis F3
11 Hôtel Brajas F2
12 Hôtel Isoraka C5
13 Hôtel Le Jean Laborde B5
14 Hôtel Moonlight E2
15 Hôtel Raphia E5
16 Hôtel Sakamanga C3
17 Hôtel St Antoine B4
18 Hôtel St Germain C3
19 Hôtel Tana-Jacaranda C5
20 Hôtel-Restaurant Shangaï D4
21 La Varangue D5
22 Le Karthala F4
23 Le Pavillon de l'Emyrne B6
24 Le Royal Palissandre F3
25 Merina Lodge B4
26 Résidence Lapasoa B5
27 Villa Isoraka B5

Eating

28 Blanche Neige D1
29 Chez Sucett C5
30 Kudéta B5
31 La Boussole B5
32 La Potinière D3
33 La Terrasse du Glacier D3
La Varangue .... (see 21)
Le Café de la Gare .... (see 2)
34 Le Petit Verdot F6
35 Le Rossini B5
Le Saka .... (see 16)
36 Pâtisserie Colbert E5
Saka Express .... (see 16)
37 Shoprite D2
Villa Isoraka .... (see 27)

Drinking

38 Bar Mojo B4
39 Buffet du Jardin E4
Kudéta .... (see 30)
40 Manson B4

Entertainment

41 Hôtel Le Glacier D3
42 Institut Français C2
La Café de la Gare .... (see 2)
43 Phoenix E5
44 Théâtre de Verdure C5

Shopping

45 Baobab Company C3
46 Epicerie Fine La Ferme de Morarano C5
47 Espace Loisirs E5
48 La Teeshirterie B3
49 Le Flamant Rose E3
50 Librairie de Madagascar D3
51 Roses & Baobab C3

Transport

Corsair .... (see 2)
Madarail .... (see 2)

friendly atmosphere, varied rooms, character decor and beyond-comprehensive services. The intriguingly mazy layout leads to a garden and cafe-bar-library, with enough artefacts in the corridors to open a museum. Reserve well in advance, as it is almost always full.

TOP CHOICE **Résidence Lapasoa** BOUTIQUE HOTEL €€€
(☎22 611 40; www.lapasoa.com; 15 Rue de la Réunion; d/ste Ar121,500/162,000;) The exquisite Lapasoa is a modern twist on colonial decor: there are polished wood floors, beautiful wooden furniture (including stunning four-poster beds), colourful fabrics, and light flooding in from skylights and big windows. The top-floor rooms, with their high, sloped ceilings, are the loveliest. The same owners run the superb Kudéta restaurant next door.

La Varangue BOUTIQUE HOTEL €€€
(☎22 273 97; www.tana-hotel.com; 17 Rue Prince Ratsimamanga; r/ste from €70/90;) Discreetly set down a steep lane next to the Presidential Palace, La Varangue's nine spacious rooms come in two categories: the cheaper ones have modern decor,

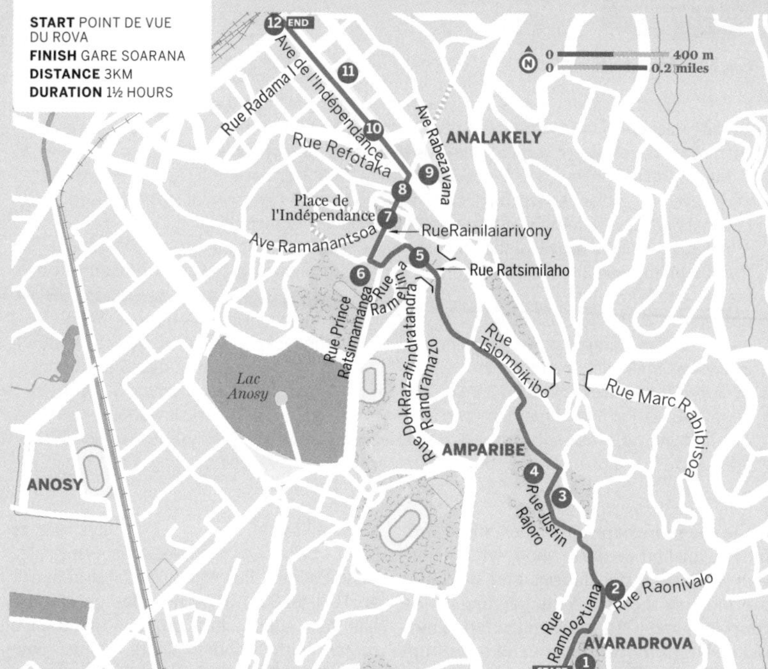

Walking Tour
Antananarivo

This walk starts at the viewpoint below the Rova, so you could combine it with a visit to the palace or come straight here by taxi (Ar10,000 from the centre).

The views from the lookout below the ❶ **Rova** make it clear why the city's rulers decided to build their palace here: the Malagasy landscape unfolds for miles in every direction.

A few hundred metres downhill is ❷ **Musée Andafivaratra**, housed in the magnificent pink baroque palace of Prime Minister Rainilaiarivony (r 1864–1895). From here, wend your way down to the reconstruction of ❸ **Jean Laborde's house**, a beautiful wooden building that served as Madagascar's first French consulate. At the end of the street is ❹ **Cathédrale de l'Immaculée Conception**, which was built on the spot where Queen Ranavalona I ordered Christian martyrs to be thrown from the cliffs.

From here, amble down through the Haute-Ville's quiet lanes to ❺ **Rue Ratsimilaho**, famous for its jewellers. Turn left on Rue Prince Ratsimamanga to have a look at the old ❻ **Presidential Palace**, with its white, green and red sentry boxes that match the Malagasy flag colours; at night, the fountains at the front are lit with multicoloured spotlights, adding a trendy touch to the classic facade.

Head up Rue Rainilaiarivony towards ❼ **Place de l'Indépendance**; cross the gardens and make your way down the lively ❽ **Escalier Ranavalona I**, with its souvenir stands, shoe polishers, rubber-stamp sellers and mobile-top-up hawkers. At the bottom of the steps, you'll see the pavilions of the ❾ **Analakely Market**.

Turn left towards ❿ **Ave de l'Indépendance**, Tana's main thoroughfare. Halfway up is the brand-new ⓫ **town hall**; the fountained piazza is open at the weekend. The avenue ends at ⓬ **Gare Soarano**, now a high-end exhibition and retail space, with a splendid restaurant where you should stop for a well-earned rest.

DON'T MISS

LA MICHELINE

In 1929, French engineer André Michelin, of tyre fame, patented the use of pneumatics on rail vehicles in a bid to improve passenger comfort. Trials were hugely successful and 'Micheline' wagons were soon zooming up and down the world's rail tracks.

Madagascar didn't escape the craze and got its first Micheline in 1932. By 1953, there were seven in regular service, but lack of maintenance and investment slowly caused the Malagasy railway system to fall into disrepair – Michelines included.

It wasn't until the revival of the rail system in the early 2000s that plans to restore the pneumatic wagons were hatched. Following restoration by the Michelin Museum in France, one **Micheline** (☎034 00 503 57; www.madarail.mg; Gare Soarano), which seats 19 passengers in old-world class, is now back in service and chugs its way between Tana and Andasibe (Périnet) or Antsirabe every weekend (one-way/return Ar90,000/130,000, including breakfast). The Micheline departs Tana at 8am on Saturday and arrives around 12.30pm; it then leaves around 2pm on Sunday afternoon and is back around 6.30pm (it goes to Andasibe three times a month and once to Antsirabe). The trip is obviously very popular with Tana residents, who enjoy the weekend break with family, but it is also a nice alternative to the taxi-brousse (bush taxi) for travellers. Advanced booking is essential.

while the more expensive ones are beautifully furnished in dark wood, with rustic-style furniture, rich fabrics and balconies overlooking the city. Vintage cars in the courtyard and a stunning collection of hurricane lamps in the lounges and restaurant complete the old-world feel.

Hôtel Tana-Jacaranda GUESTHOUSE €€
(☎22 562 39; www.tana-jacaranda.com; 24 Rue Rainitsarovy; d Ar50,000, without bathroom Ar39,000; @ wi-fi) Rooms at this super-friendly, family-run hotel are dark but quiet and clean. There is also a tip-top dining room with fabulous views of the Rova and the Haute-Ville, piping hot water in the showers, good wi-fi, a guest computer and multilingual, wonderfully helpful staff. It's in the popular neighbourhood of Isoraka, within walking distance of all the good restaurants.

Le Pavillon de l'Emyrne BOUTIQUE HOTEL €€€
(☎22 259 45; www.pavillondelemyrne.com; 12 Rue Rakotonirina Stanislas; s/d/ste €75/95/105; air-con wi-fi) In a beautiful 1920s house, the Emyrne has a handful of rooms with an exclusive feel. Each has been individually decorated with a refined mix of vintage and modern. The suites are an absolute steal (huge and with their own garden or verandah). The rooms on the lower ground floor are a little dark, however. Rates include breakfast, and staff will be happy to walk you to one of the neighbourhood's many good restaurants for dinner.

Merina Lodge GUESTHOUSE €€
(☎24 522 33; merinalodge@moov.mg; Impasse Ostie, off Rue Andrianary Ratianarivo; d/tr Ar54,000/81,000) This peaceful guesthouse has five simple but proudly maintained rooms with wooden floors, bright bedspreads and clean bathrooms. Its trump cards are the tranquil terrace – an unexpected find for such a central location – and friendly staff.

Hôtel Moonlight HOTEL €
(☎22 268 70; hasinaherizo@yahoo.fr; Rue Rainandriamapandry; s/d/tr without bathroom Ar23,000/29,000/34,000) This budget stalwart is an excellent option in a lively part of town with cool internet cafes and restaurants. Rooms have brightly coloured walls, parquet floors and clean bathrooms (some rooms have showers but all share toilets). There are two large communal terraces from where you can watch the world go by.

Hôtel St Germain HOTEL €€
(☎033 25 882 62; www.hotelstgermain.e-monsite.com; Rue Ravelontsalama; d Ar45,000; wi-fi) This attractive building near the French embassy is an excellent budget-friendly choice. Rooms are pocket-size but bright and immaculate. There is a convivial bar/breakfast room downstairs, and the friendly management will happily recommend restaurants nearby.

Hôtel-Restaurant Shangaï HOTEL €€
(☎22 314 72; www.shangai-hotel.com; 4 Rue Rainitovo; d/tr Ar50,000/65,000; wi-fi) Uninspiring but thoroughly acceptable for the price, this

family-run hotel in the embassy quarter is a little musty but has a lovely front courtyard with tumbling bougainvillea and swaying palms. Ask for a room on the 2nd or 3rd floor to make the best of the light and views of the city.

Villa Isoraka GUESTHOUSE €€€
(☎24 220 52; demay.christophe@yahoo.fr; Rue Raveloary; d Ar80,000-100,000, without bathroom Ar50,000-65,000; 📶) There are just five rooms in this beautiful French townhouse, a hotel-restaurant that was given a facelift in 2011. Two of the rooms don't have windows and feel a little claustrophobic, but all rooms share the same modern design, with beige and chocolate colour themes and comfortable furnishings. The garden and dining room are both exquisite for breakfast.

Hôtel Brajas BOUTIQUE HOTEL €€€
(☎22 263 35; www.hotelbrajas.com; 74 Rue Rainandriamapandry; d Ar85,000-100,000; ❄📶) A recent addition to Tana's hotel scene, the Brajas occupies a beautifully renovated, three-storey building with sensational views of the capital. The rooms are an odd mix of business and boutique, but for the comfort and the price, this is a trivial stylistic quibble. Rooms with panoramic views are more expensive; don't worry if you miss out however, since the bar and restaurant (specialising in Indian food) sport similar vistas.

Hôtel St Antoine HOTEL €€
(☎033 21 597 19; www.hotelstantoine.e-monsite.com; Rue Andrianary Ratianarivo; d Ar55,000, without bathroom Ar35,000; 📶) Recently renovated, the St Antoine has something of a Mediterranean feel, with its big patio and terracotta-colour walls. The 14 rooms vary in size, light and noisiness so ask to see a couple before you settle on one.

Le Karthala PENSION €€
(☎22 248 95; le_karthala@yahoo.fr; 48 Rue Andriandahifotsy; r Ar50,000) The Karthala's motto is 'a little bit like home', and Ariane and her family certainly have a way to make guests feel welcome: it's all about the long afternoons/evenings spent chatting in the pretty garden courtyard. The rooms do need updating, the bathrooms in particular, but on the whole, the place is spacious and clean. Rooms under the roof share a bathroom but are quieter. Rates include breakfast.

Chez Francis HOTEL €€
(☎22 613 65; hotelchezfrancis@yahoo.fr; Rue Rainandriamapandry; r Ar41,500) With its spotless tiled floors, pine furniture and bright interior, Chez Francis is reminiscent of a holiday camp or youth hostel. Ask for a room with a view.

CAPITAL PAMPERING

Balnéoforme Colbert SPA
(www.hotel-colbert-tananarive.com; ☎22 625 71; Hôtel Colbert, 29 Rue Prince Ratsimamanga; admission Ar50,000; ⏲6.30am-4.30pm Mon-Sat, from 10am Sun) For a truly indulgent experience, try this fantastic spa with a mosaic swimming pool, Finnish sauna and Turkish bath. The entrance fee also gives you access to the gym. For additional pampering, there is a treatment list an arm long including body wraps, bubble baths and every kind of massage imaginable – relaxing, slimming, water, ying-yang… It's not cheap (prices start at Ar100,000), but worth it if you've just arrived back in Tana after some hard trekking.

BioAroma MASSAGE
(☎22 326 30; 54 Rue Ramanantsoa; ⏲8am-6pm Mon-Sat, 8.30am-12.30pm Sun) As well as selling local oils and bath, spa and spice products, BioAroma offers a comprehensive range of massages (from Ar38,000 for one hour) as well as facials, scrubs, reiki, and manicures and pedicures.

Homeopharma MASSAGE
(☎22 686 47; www.madagascar-homeopharma.com; 47 Rue Ratsimilaho; ⏲8am-6pm Mon-Fri, 9am-5pm Sat) The state-approved natural-health chain Homeopharma has outlets all over Tana and throughout the country; many, such as this branch, offer massages and other treatments (Ar12,000).

Le Royal Palissandre Spa SPA
(☎22 605 60; www.hotel-palissandre.com; 13 Rue Andriandahifotsy; ⏲9am-9pm) Another gorgeous spa, with a beautiful heated outdoor pool and a *hammam* (Turkish bath); a number of treatments are available (from Ar90,000).

Le Royal Palissandre LUXURY HOTEL €€€
(☎22 605 60; www.hotel-palissandre.com; 13 Rue Andriandahifotsy; d from €87;) The rooms at the Royal Palissandre are unremarkable but the facilities definitely aren't: you won't get enough of the sweeping cityscapes, and the heated pool with its exotic garden is to die for. Rates include breakfast.

Hôtel Le Jean Laborde HOTEL €
(☎22 330 45; labordehotel@hotmail.com; 3 Rue de Russie; d Ar44,000-59,000, without bathroom Ar22,000-27,000) The welcome is pretty grumpy but this small hotel at the heart of Isoraka still does a brisk trade thanks to its excellent location and budget-friendly prices. The rooms have threadbare green carpet and pink walls, but the place is well kept and the more expensive rooms are very spacious.

Hôtel Raphia HOTEL €€
(☎22 253 13; hotelraphia@moov.mg; Rue Ranavalona III; d/tr Ar46,000/56,000, without bathroom Ar41,000/51,000) This family-run Haute-Ville option comprises an eccentric selection of wood-clad rooms with a traditional feel. All are spotless and those at the top have views. Guests get a 10% discount at the restaurant.

Hôtel Isoraka HOTEL €€
(☎22 355 81; saka@malagasy.com; 11 Rue Ramanantsoa; r Ar36,000-41,000) The Isoraka would be an excellent budget choice were it not for its lack of facilities and very noisy location. Rooms are clean, colourful and good value for the neighbourhood, but earplugs are a must.

Eating

Tana excels at eating: you'll find some of the country's best restaurants in the capital, and although they're slightly more expensive than in the rest of the country, they're often great value for the quality.

TOP CHOICE **La Varangue** INTERNATIONAL €€€
(☎22 273 97; www.tana-hotel.com; 17 Rue Prince Ratsimamanga; mains Ar21,000-35,000;) Currently the best address in the city for real gourmet cuisine, La Varangue has achieved a fantastic reputation thanks to kitchen maestro Lalaina Ravelomanana. The menu, an elaborate melange of French gastronomy and Malagasy flavours, is concise, but the dishes are truly divine. Lalaina is a chocolate specialist, so make sure you leave space for dessert: the ice cream explosion – a dark-chocolate sphere filled with the creamiest chocolate ice cream you've ever had – is sheer ambrosia. Meals are served either in the beautiful dining room, with its low lighting and antique furniture, or the terrace, which overlooks the hotel's charming garden.

TOP CHOICE **Le Café de la Gare** INTERNATIONAL €€€
(www.cafetana.com; Gare Soarano; mains Ar16,000-19,000;) The fabulous Café de la Gare is the flagship of the beautifully renovated Soarano train station. Inside, you'll feel as if you've just been transported to a brasserie at Paris' Gare du Nord, just even more beautiful. In the evenings, the open fire, candle-lit tables, magnificent chandeliers and low hubbub from Tana's cool crowd give it an exclusive feel. The food is stupendous too, with well-executed international staples such as prawn curry, zebu burger, pan-fried fish etc. On Sunday, brunch is served between 11am and 3pm.

Le Saka FUSION €€
(☎22 358 09; Hôtel Sakamanga, Rue Andrianary Ratianarivo; mains Ar1100-18,000) Striking the perfect balance between gastro French and straightforward local cooking, Le Saka is a Tana institution. The restaurant is housed in a gorgeous wooden house full of old black-and-white photos and local artwork. The chef whips up some mighty desserts using Malagasy chocolate. Make sure you finish your meal with a house rum or coconut punch.

Le Petit Verdot FRENCH €€
(27 Rue Rahamefy; mains Ar12,000-18,000; ⏰lunch & dinner Mon-Fri, dinner Sat) This tiny red-brick bistro, spread over three floors from cellar to mezzanine, scores high on homey atmosphere and hearty French food. The foie gras is terrific, there is a fantastic selection of meat and fish dishes, and the wine selection is the best in Madagascar (261 references from around the world, including some local vintages).

La Terrasse du Glacier MALAGASY €€
(www.hotel-glacier.com; Annexe Le Glacier, 2nd fl, Ave de l'Indépendance; mains Ar8500-16,000) Perched on a 2nd floor above Ave de l'Indépendance, La Terrasse is a fantastic vantage point to admire the hustle and bustle of Tana's main thoroughfare. The delicious food is Malagasy with a hint of French, with dishes such as tilapia in ginger and spring onion, zebu Bourguignon, and *romazava* (traditional Malagasy beef-and-vegetable stew). The three-course menu of the day is a steal at Ar9900.

Kudéta FUSION €€€
(☎22 281 54; 16 Rue de la Réunion; mains Ar14,000-18,000) Playing on the region's reputation for

political instability may not be very PC, but it really would take a coup d'état to unseat this stylish bar-restaurant from its position at the pinnacle of Tana's fashionable eating scene. The menu makes imaginative use of local ingredients, creating a sophisticated fusion cuisine that suits the chic ethnic decor perfectly. The sleek dining room is almost always packed with fashionable folk, so booking is advisable.

Saka Express FAST FOOD €
(☎032 41 412 57; www.sakamanga.com; Rue Andrianary Ratianarivo; mains Ar5000-10,000; ⌚breakfast, lunch & dinner Mon-Sat, lunch & dinner Sun) The Hôtel Sakamanga's snack cafeteria and takeaway outlet is the best place in town for lunch on the go. There are pizzas, kebabs and sandwiches, all bursting at the seams with fillings. There are a few tables inside, which fill quickly at lunchtime. Delivery to neighbouring hotels (including Isoraka) is possible.

Chez Sucett MALAGASY €€
(23 Rue Raveloary; mains Ar10,000-15,000) The dining room looks a little dim from the outside, but inside the atmosphere is jovial, with tables of budget-conscious travellers and locals in the know gingerly tucking into Sucett's Malagasy and Creole (a cuisine that is a blend of African, Asian and European influences) dishes. The selection of dips (peanut, aubergine, pickled cucumber etc) offered at the beginning of the meal are mouth-wateringly good, so skip starters!

Villa Vanille FRENCH €€€
(☎22 205 15; Place Antanimena; mains Ar18,000-30,000) In an old colonial villa, this classy establishment serves French gastronomy infused with vanilla (foie gras, crayfish, duck etc), with marvellous results. There is nightly music performed by bands from all across the region, and with the candle-lit atmosphere it all feels delightfully old-world and nostalgic. It's on Place Antanimena, about 400m north of Marché Pochart.

TANA'S CAFE CULTURE

Whether a remnant of French influence or a sign that Tananarivians have a sweet tooth, the Malagasy capital has a number of cafes, some in a league of their own when it comes to cakes and pastries, others a perfect halt for a quick and cheap lunch.

InfiniThé CAFE €
(Enceinte Motel de Tana Anosy; snacks Ar2500-5000; ⌚8am-7pm Mon-Sat) Tana's chic-est address, InfiniThé caters to the town's elite, who rush to buy its artisan breads and wondrous pastries or come to enjoy a cup of tea in refined surroundings. There are lovely sandwiches and quiches for lunch. It's 300m south of Lac Anosy, past the flower market.

Cookie Shop CAFE €
(Ave Rainizanabolone; snacks Ar2500-5000; ⌚8am-7pm Mon-Sat) This bright, sparky cafe used to be a favourite of American expats before the embassy moved out of town. It's still popular with foreigners but has also acquired a growing young and trendy Malagasy clientele, who love the bagels, cookies and muffins on offer. Brunch (Ar12,000) is served on Saturdays. Carry on Ave Toera past Marché Pochart and turn right on Ave Rainizanabolone.

Pâtisserie Colbert CAFE €
(Hôtel Colbert, Rue Prince Ratsimamanga; cakes & quiches Ar1300-5000; ⌚breakfast & lunch) This patisserie is a popular meeting place for local businesspeople and a great place for breakfast. The croissants are almost too buttery, but if you're not going to throw dietary caution to the wind here, where will you?

La Potinière CAFE €
(Ave de l'Indépendance; cakes from Ar800; ⌚7am-6pm) This Chinese-run bakery heaves at weekends, when locals come for a treat. As well as pastries, it has a range of quiches and sandwiches for a light lunch.

Blanche Neige CAFE €
(15 Ave de l'Indépendance; cakes from Ar800; ⌚7am-6pm Tue-Sun) With its Disney murals and good cakes, 'Snow White' is popular for its breakfasts (Ar3000 to Ar5000) and lovely ice creams and sorbets, including local flavours such as *corossol* (soursop).

LOCAL KNOWLEDGE

ANN HARIVOLA RAKOTONDRAZAKA, ARCHAEOLOGIST & GUIDE

Ann is an erudite guide specialising in cultural tours in and around Tana.

Culture vulture

I love the program at Institut Français, there are some wonderful shows. The **Centre Culturel d'Art et d'Archéologie** (Ave de l'Indépendance; ⌚9am-5pm Mon-Fri) is also good: it's a small place but one of the few where you'll find information and artefacts from the country's various archaeological digs.

Escape from the city

I like going out to Ambohirabiby in the north and Ambatolampy in the south. Both places are beautiful and rich in history. At the weekend, there are good *hira gasy* (music, dancing and storytelling spectacles) in the surrounding areas.

The Malagasy & Death

For many Malagasies, death is not the end per se. It's a passage between life on earth and life beyond. Many believe that life beyond is permanent, which is why you'll see families with small houses but massive stone tombs. *Famadihanas* (exhumations and reburials, literally 'the turning of the bones') allow those living on earth to communicate with those living beyond. *Famadihanas* are very happy occasions for Malagasy families, and a huge undertaking: a zebu (domesticated ox) costs €500 to €800 and a silk shroud for the bones costs about the same.

Le Rossini FRENCH €€€
(☎22 342 44; Rue Ramanantsoa; mains Ar15,000-22,000) You might not expect a visit to Madagascar to widen your knowledge of France, but this rarefied dining room should at least educate your palate: it specialises in cuisine from the southwest Périgord region using lots of duck and foie gras, all raised and prepared locally. If the weather is good, dining is possible on the 1st-floor terrace. Booking is recommended.

Villa Isoraka INTERNATIONAL €€
(Rue Raveloary; mains Ar9000-15,500) In a gorgeous private mansion reminiscent of wealthy Parisian suburbs, Villa Isoraka has opened an original restaurant. By day, it serves mostly the local business clientele in the garden or in the lovely dining rooms with tinted-glass windows, but at night it becomes a trendy restaurant-cum-wine bar. The food is good (an eclectic mix of French and Tex-Mex), although it's really for the atmosphere that people come to the villa.

La Boussole INTERNATIONAL €€€
(21 Rue Dr Villette; mains Ar15,000-22,000; ⌚lunch & dinner Mon-Fri, dinner Sat & Sun; 📶) The 'Compass', an attractive, lively bar-restaurant, has funky decor, and live bands on Thursdays. The restaurant serves mainly French brasserie-style dishes that are overpriced, while the bar whips out more prosaic snacks such as burgers and the like.

Chez Mariette MALAGASY €€€
(☎22 216 02; 11 Rue Joel Rakotomalala; set menu Ar44,000; ⌚dinner) Superchef Mariette Andrianjaka has cooked for notables as diverse as Paloma Picasso and Prince Albert of Monaco during her long career, and has even had a collection of her recipes published by Unesco. These days she entertains guests in her 19th-century villa, preparing elaborate 12-course set meals based on *haifi* cuisine – the traditional banquets once served to Merina royalty. The service and the atmosphere are stuffy, but the food is good and the portions gargantuan (skip lunch); drinks are extra. Advance reservation is required. Chez Mariette is up in the Haute-Ville – taxis know where to find it.

Shoprite SUPERMARKET €
(Ave Andrianampoinimerina; ⌚8.30am-7.30pm Mon-Sat, to 3pm Sun) Well-stocked supermarket.

Drinking

Nightlife in Tana has been relatively quiet since the coup. The busiest nights are Thursday to Sunday.

Manson BAR
(Rue Ramanantsoa) Manson wouldn't look out of place in Paris or London, so it should come as no surprise that this is the venue of choice for Tana's expat community. We like the graffiti decor outside, and the music inside is pretty good.

Bar Mojo BAR
(Rue Victoire Rasoamanarivo) A cool music space replete with crimson walls and oversize seats. DJs and bands often play at the weekend. It's suffered slightly from the popularity of Manson.

Buffet du Jardin BAR
(Place de l'Indépendance; ⏰24hr) This longstanding snack stop and bar is a favourite with taxi drivers; the terrace is a nice, low-key place for a beer.

Kudéta LOUNGE
(15 Rue de la Réunion) Tana's coolest restaurant doubles up as a bar/lounge in the evening, with fancy cocktails and expensive beer.

☆ Entertainment

To find out what's going on and where, buy any of the three national daily newspapers – *Midi Madagasikara*, *Madagascar Tribune* and *L'Express de Madagascar* – all of which have advertisements for upcoming events, particularly in the Friday issue. Posters around town also give plenty of notice of forthcoming concerts. Other good resources include the free fortnightly listings **Sortir à Tana** (www.sortiratana.com) and **No Comment** (www.nocomment.mg), which you will find in every hotel and restaurant in town.

Most nightclubs in Tana are packed with prostitutes, so unaccompanied guys can expect a bit of unsolicited attention.

Le Café de la Gare CINEMA
(☎22 611 12; www.cafetana.com; Gare Soarano; ⏰9am-11pm; 📶) The stylish Café de la Gare holds regular live music sessions as well as a cinema night every Sunday. Both the concerts and cinema are free (films are either in French or in English with French subtitles): just get yourself a drink at the bar and settle down for the night.

Hôtel Le Glacier LIVE MUSIC
(admission Ar3000; Ave 26 Juin 1960) This slightly disreputable bar has cabaret, bands and traditional music performances every night of the week; it's always full and the atmosphere is good.

Institut Français PERFORMING ARTS
(☎22 213 75; www.institutfrancais-madagascar.com; 14 Ave de l'Indépendance; ⏰Sep-Jul) Antananarivo's foremost cultural venue hosts excellent concerts, theatre events, dance performances, art exhibitions and film screenings almost daily. Pop in to pick up the bimonthly schedule or check it online. Booking is recommended for most of the shows.

Théâtre de Verdure CONCERT VENUE
(Ave Rainitsarovy) This amphitheatre has occasional shows featuring artists from the Malagasy charts, as well as regular gospel-music or church-choir concerts that set the crowd on fire. Tickets are generally very cheap.

Grill du Rova LIVE MUSIC
(Rue Ramboatiana, Avaradrova) This restaurant has regular music recitals, including a piano bar on Friday, traditional performances from noon to sunset every Sunday, and improvised musical soirées on the first and third Wednesday of each month. Find it about 100m downhill from the Rova.

Le Club NIGHTCLUB
(Ave Rainizanabolone; admission Ar5000; ⏰from 10.30pm Fri & Sat) Tana's biggest, flashiest club space, designed in a modern style, has the DJ spinning recent tunes from his lofty winged booth above the dance floor. It's about 200m past Marché Pochart.

HIRA GASY

Traditional Malagasy performances of acrobatics, music and speeches, *hira gasy* (p206) events are held most Sunday afternoons in the villages around Antananarivo. Check newspapers for details; entry is generally very cheap (Ar500 to Ar1000), and the experience is great fun.

Tana's regional tourist office **Ortana** (www.tourisme-antananarivo.com) also organises a *hira gasy* at **Jardin d'Andolaho** (⏰2.30-4.30pm Sun Aug-Sep) in the Haute-Ville to try and revive the tradition. It is free to attend, although spectators normally throw small notes (Ar100 or Ar200 for instance) to the team who performed best.

Phoenix NIGHTCLUB
(Rue Rabobalahy; admission Ar5000; ⌚Wed-Sun) Enter through the surreal giant mouth to access a strange mix of giant screens with faux-Moroccan decor. It's very quiet outside of Fridays and Saturdays.

Shopping

You will find plenty of arts, crafts, T-shirts, coffee and spices in the souvenir shops of central Tana.

TOP CHOICE Marché Artisanal de La Digue HANDICRAFTS
(La Digue; ⌚9am-5.30pm) The most popular place to pick up souvenirs is this market located about 12km out of town on a bend in the Ivato airport road. Artisans and middlemen from all over the country sell their products here; popular souvenirs include embroidered tablecloths, brightly coloured raffia baskets, woodcarvings, spices, vanilla, gemstones, recycled paper products and T-shirts. Bargaining is essential – halve the price you're quoted and work from there. A taxi (around Ar20,000 return) is the easiest way to get here and back with your purchases. Otherwise, if you're going to the airport with a taxi, leave an hour early and stop on your way there. Cash only.

TOP CHOICE Epicerie Fine La Ferme de Morarano FOOD & DRINK
(www.ladistilleriedumaido.com/madagascar.html; Rue Raveloary; ⌚9am-6pm Mon-Sat) This is the Tana shop of the wonderful organic Ferme de Morarano in Ambatolampy where you'll be able to buy everything from essential oils, to artisan jams, chutneys and spices. There are also natural lotions and potions (moisturiser, shampoo, soap etc) prepared with the farm's essential oils.

La Teeshirterie CLOTHING
(Rue Andrianary Ratianarivo) By far the best place to come for Madagascar's funky T-shirts. You'll find all the main brands here (Baobab, Carambole, Maki etc) and a large choice of models and sizes. Credit cards accepted.

Lisy Art Gallery HANDICRAFTS
(Rte du Mausolée; ⌚8.30am-6.30pm Mon-Fri, 8.30am-12.30pm & 2-6.30pm Sat) This huge shop stocks anything and everything you could possibly want to bring back from Madagascar, from beautiful bottles of *rhum arrangé* (homemade rum with fruit inside) to leather goods, raffia baskets, hats and spices. The only thing you won't find are gemstones. Prices are fixed but reasonable. It's a short taxi ride from the centre (Ar5000 one way). Card payments accepted.

Roses & Baobab ARTS & CRAFTS
(www.rosesetbaobab.com; Rue des 77 Parlementaires Français; ⌚9am-5pm Mon-Sat) A collective of local artists showcasing sculptures, wood carvings, paintings, metalwork and more.

Le Flamant Rose HANDICRAFTS
(45 Ave de l'Indépendance; ⌚9am-5pm Mon-Sat) Craft souvenirs, raffia items and embroidery.

CS Events OUTDOOR EQUIPMENT
(www.csevents-madagascar.com; Rte du Mausolée, Andrainarivo; ⌚8am-12.30pm & 1.30-6pm Mon-Fri, 8am-1pm Sat) For trekking, camping gear and the like; there is a wide but expensive selection of international branded products.

Baobab Company CLOTHING
(Rue Andrianary Ratianarivo) Universally popular T-shirts and clothes.

Espace Loisirs BOOKS
(Rue Ratsimilaho) The best selection of books in town, including French guidebooks, maps of Tana and the rest of the country, children's books and novels.

Librairie de Madagascar BOOKS
(38 Ave de l'Indépendance) A good selection of newspapers and magazines (mostly in French, plus books on Madagascar and the Indian Ocean region. Also sells maps.

Information

Dangers & Annoyances

Insecurity has increased in Tana since the political events of 2009. It is not safe to walk after dark and you should always travel by taxi at night.

Pickpocketing is rife around Ave de l'Indépendance, Analakely and Marché Pochart, so be very careful with your belongings.

Touts posing as official guides prey on travellers who haven't arranged to be met at the airport; stick to the official taxi rank or book one through your hotel.

Emergency

Ambulance (☎22 200 40, 033 11 613 05)
Fire (☎118)
Police (☎117)

Internet Access

Chillout Café (Rue Rainandriamapandry; per min Ar20-40; ⌚9.30am-10.30pm; wi-fi) Evening use is more expensive than daytime use; also a funky bar-restaurant.

Cyberpaositra (per min Ar30) Analakely (Ave 26 Juin 1960; ⌚8am-3pm Mon-Fri, 8-10.30am Sat); Haute-Ville (Rue Ratsimilaho; ⌚8am-5pm Mon-Fri, 8am-noon Sat) Both Tana's main post offices have cheap internet centres.

Outcool Web Bar (Rue Andrianary Ratianarivo; per min Ar50; ⌚9am-12.30am) Also functions as a sociable bar.

Teknet (Rue Ramanantsoa; per 45 min Ar2000; ⌚8am-6.30pm Mon-Sat, 2.30-6.30pm Sun) Look for signs for 'Cyber Sous-Sol'. Fax and phone services also available.

Medical Services

Clinique des Sœurs Franciscaines (☎22 235 54; Rue Dokotera Rajaonah, Ankadifotsy) Has X-ray equipment and is well run.

Dr Chapuis (☎22 208 88; 13 Ave de l'Indépendance) A reliable dentist.

Dr Rabedasy (☎22 358 70; 9 Rue de la Réunion) Another recommended dentist.

Espace Médical (☎22 625 66; 65 bis Rue Pasteur Rabary) A private clinic just east of the city, with laboratory and X-ray equipment.

Hôpital Militaire (☎22 397 51; Rue Moss, Soavinandriana; ⌚24hr) The best-equipped hospital in the country.

Pharmacie Métropole (☎22 200 25; Rue Ratsimilaho) One of Tana's best and most convenient pharmacies.

Pharmacie de l'Océan Indien (☎22 224 07; 118 Ave de l'Indépendance) Centrally located and well-stocked.

Money

All banks listed below change foreign currencies and travellers cheques and offer cash advances on credit cards (both Visa and MasterCard). Virtually all now have reliable ATMs (Visa only, except BNI-CA); not all are accessible after banking hours.

Bank of Africa (BOA) Basse-Ville (Ave de l'Indépendance); Haute-Ville (Place de l'Indépendance)

BFV-SG Basse-Ville (Ave de l'Indépendance); Haute-Ville (Rue Ramanantsoa)

BMOI (Place de l'Indépendance)

BNI-CA (74 Ave 26 Juin 1960)

Socimad (Rue Radama I) Bureau de change.

Post & Telephone

Post Office (Paositra; www.paositra.mg; ⌚8am-4pm Mon-Fri, 8-11am Sat) Basse-Ville (Ave 26 Juin 1960); Haute-Ville (Rue Ratsimilaho) Tana's two main post offices.

Tourist Information

Office National de Tourisme (www.madagascar-tourisme.com; Gare Soarano; ⌚9am-5pm Mon-Sat) Limited amounts of countrywide information.

IVATO AIRPORT

» The bureaux de change at Ivato airport offer similar rates to the banks in Tana; it also exchanges travellers cheques.

» BNI-CA has an ATM that accepts both Visa and MasterCard.

» All three phone networks have booths in the arrivals area where you can buy a SIM card and credit.

» Ariary are not accepted in the departure area, even at the cafe (euros or US dollars only).

Ortana (☎24 600 93; www.tourisme-antananarivo.com; Escalier Ranavalona I; ⌚8.30am-5pm Mon-Fri, to 4pm Sat) Very dynamic regional tourist office with keen staff, a full schedule of guided tours and lots of brochures on national attractions.

 Getting There & Away

Air

For details of flights from Ivato airport, see p255 for international routes and p256 for domestic services. The following airlines have offices in Tana:

Air Austral (☎22 303 31; www.airaustral.com; 23 Ave de l'Indépendance)

Air France (☎23 230 23; www.airfrance.com; Tour Zital, Rte des Hydrocarbures, Ankorondrano)

Air Madagascar (☎22 222 22; www.airmadagascar.com; 31 Ave de l'Indépendance)

Corsair (☎22 633 36; www.corsair.fr; Gare Soarano)

Bus

The following public-transport companies only offer the Tana–Majunga (Mahajanga) route for the time being, but at press time both had plans to expand their network so check what the latest schedule is.

Transport Première Class (☎032 40 134 76, 033 07 601 67; www.malagasycar.com; Hôtel Le Grand Mellis, 3 Rue Indira Gandhi) Runs comfortable, air-con vehicles between Tana and Majunga (Ar78,000, 10 hours, daily). It sits just two people to a row and includes a packed lunch. Departure is at 7am; drop-off is on the corniche in Majunga. Booking essential.

Transpost (☎22 302 27; Post Office, Rue Ratsimilaho) More punctual than normal taxis-brousses but similar in comfort and price, Transpost is run by Madagascar's postal service. It has minibuses between Majunga and

Tana (Ar25,000; 10 hours; Tuesday, Thursday and Saturday); pick-up and drop-off is at the central post office in both cities. Departure is at 7.30am sharp. Booking required.

Car

The best place to arrange a car and driver is from one of the reputable tour agencies (see p258) operating in the country. Big international car-rental agencies are also present in Tana, but they may not rent cars outside of Tana, or if they do, they may require a driver. Prices quoted are for short journeys.

Budget (☎032 05 811 13; www.budget.mg; 4 Ave de l'Indépendance) A compact/4WD with driver costs per day Ar180,000/324,000, plus fuel.

Sixt (☎22 621 50; sixtintermad@simicro.mg; 2 bis Rue Rahamefy) Self-drive only; a compact/4WD costs per day Ar75,000/256,000, bearing in mind that the deposit is Ar1,200,000/5,000,000.

Taxi-Brousse

For morning departures, turn up early (6am); for afternoon departures, come around 2pm. It may take up to four hours for some vehicles to fill.

There are three main taxi-brousse stations *(gares routières)*.

Gare Routière d'Ambodivona (Northern taxi-brousse station; Ambodivona) About 2km northeast of the city centre. A taxi to/from the centre costs Ar3000.

Gare Routière d'Ampasampito (Eastern taxi-brousse station; Ampasampito) About 3.5km northeast of the centre. A taxi to/from the centre will cost Ar6000.

Gare Routière de Fasan'ny Karana (Southern taxi-brousse station; Anosibe) About 4km southwest of Lac Anosy. A taxi to/from the centre costs Ar8000.

Train

There are no regular passenger trains from Tana, but **Madarail** (www.madarail.mg), Madagascar's main rail company, runs a weekend, tourist-oriented service to Antsirabe and Andasibe (see p34).

ℹ Getting Around

To/From the Airport

Ivato airport is 12km from the city centre. A taxi to/from the city centre costs Ar30,000 during the day, Ar40,000 at night. A much cheaper but slower alternative is **Navette Adema** (☎034 07 063 02; ⏰5am-9pm), a shuttle service running between the airport and selected hotels in the town centre, with a terminus at Gare Soarana (Ar10,000, one hour). To go to the airport, ask your hotel to book the shuttle (that way they can chase it if it's running late) and make sure you leave plenty of time as it's not possible to know how many pick-ups the shuttle will have to do before setting off.

Taxi

Tana's cream-colour taxis are plentiful and cheap, even at night; Fares are negotiable: a journey in town should cost Ar3000 to Ar5000 during the day, or Ar5000 to Ar7000 at night.

TAXIS-BROUSSES FROM ANTANANARIVO

DESTINATION	TAXI-BROUSSE STATION	PRICE (AR)	DURATION (HRS)	APPROXIMATE DEPARTURE TIME
Antsirabe	Fasan'ny Karana	17,000	3	All day
Ambanja	Ambodivona	50,000	16	Afternoon
Diego Suarez (Antsiranana)	Ambodivona	65,000	24	Afternoon
Fianarantsoa	Fasan'ny Karana	23,000	8	Morning
Fort Dauphin (Taolagnaro)	Fasan'ny Karana	85,000	36	Afternoon Tue & Thu, morning Sat
Majunga	Ambodivona	32,000	12	Morning & afternoon
Manakara	Fasan'ny Karana	37,000	13	Afternoon
Miandrivazo	Fasan'ny Karana	24,000	9	Afternoon
Moramanga	Ampasampito	5000	2	All day
Morondava	Fasan'ny Karana	45,000	16	Afternoon
Tamatave (Toamasina)	Ambodivona/ Ampasampito	20,000	10	Morning & afternoon
Tuléar (Toliara)	Fasan'ny Karana	45,000	18	Afternoon

Always agree on a price before leaving. You may pay a different rate for the same journey if it is downhill or uphill!

Taxi-Be

Large minibuses called taxi-be meander around Antananarivo and the outlying suburbs; the standard fare is Ar400. They are of limited use to travellers because of the difficulty to work out a) the route and b) where bus stops are. On straightforward journeys (to Ivato or Ambohimanga for instance), be very careful with your belongings as pickpockets are a real problem.

AROUND ANTANANARIVO

The highlands around Antananarivo are often ignored by travellers pushing on to other regions, but the whole area is perfect day-trip country. Keen cyclists will have a ball in the 12 sacred hills surrounding the city, and even a brief excursion offers plenty of spectacular views and an insight into the history and culture of the Merina people.

If you don't have your own transport, the best way to see the sites around Tana is to charter a taxi for the day; a lovely day trip would be to combine Ilafy, Ambohimanga and Ivato (expect to pay Ar100,000).

Ivato

About 13km from Antananarivo is the village-suburb of Ivato, where the international airport is located.

Croc Farm (Ivato; admission Ar10,000; ⌚9am-5pm) is an unusual place: a commercial crocodile farm that breeds crocs and sells their meat and skin, as well as a zoo where you can see the reptilian giants in all their basking glory, along with various species of lemur, chameleons and even the rare fossa (striped civet), Madagascar's biggest predator. The displays on the crocodiles are highly informative: many of the biggest specimens (well over 6m) have been brought to Croc Farm because they were becoming a danger to humans in their natural habitat.

You can also eat crocodile in the park's **restaurant** (mains Ar15,000). The park's about 3km from the airport. A taxi will cost around Ar10,000 return from Ivato, including an hour's wait.

Le Manoir Rouge (☎032 05 260 97; www.manoirrouge.com; r Ar56,000, without bathroom Ar33,000-42,000), an amiable backpacker-friendly guesthouse a scant 700m from the airport, has real charm, with its creaky floorboards, dining room, fireplace and lovely garden. The varied rooms (most with shared bathroom) sleep up to four people. Patrick, the jovial owner, is a passionate mountain biker and runs brilliant excursions around the capital every couple of days.

A taxi between the airport and Ivato village will cost Ar5000. A taxi from Ivato village to Antananarivo costs Ar25,000. Taxi-be route D (Ar400, one hour) links the taxi-brousse stand behind Gare Soarana in Tana to Ivato bus station near the market.

Ilafy

Originally called Ambohitrahanga, Ilafy was founded around the turn of the 17th century on a sacred hilltop and was used as a country residence by the Merina royal family. The wooden residence was redesigned in the 1830s by Ranavalona I and used as a hunting lodge by Radama II, whose body was initially buried in a modest tomb on the grounds and then transferred to the *rova*.

The hunting lodge was reconstructed in 1957, after the original had fallen into disrepair; it now houses the **Ethnographic Museum** (admission Ar3000; ⌚9am-noon & 2-5pm Tue-Sun), which illustrates tribal life around Madagascar with exhibits including model tombs, hunting and fishing tools, modern wooden carvings and information about magic and religious rituals. A knowledgeable guide will show you around; a tip of Ar2000 to Ar5000 is appropriate.

Ilafy lies 12km from Antananarivo just east of the road leading to Ambohimanga. You'll need your own transport to get here.

Ambohimanga

Ambohimanga ('blue hill' or 'beautiful hill') was the original capital of the Merina royal family. Even after the seat of government was shifted to Antananarivo for political reasons, Ambohimanga remained a sacred site, and was off-limits to foreigners for many years. The entire hill was listed as a Unesco World Heritage Site in 2001 for being 'the most significant symbol of the cultural identity of the people of Madagascar'.

The entrance to Ambohimanga village is marked by a large traditional gateway, one of the seven gateways to the eyrie-like hilltop. To one side is a large, flat, round stone.

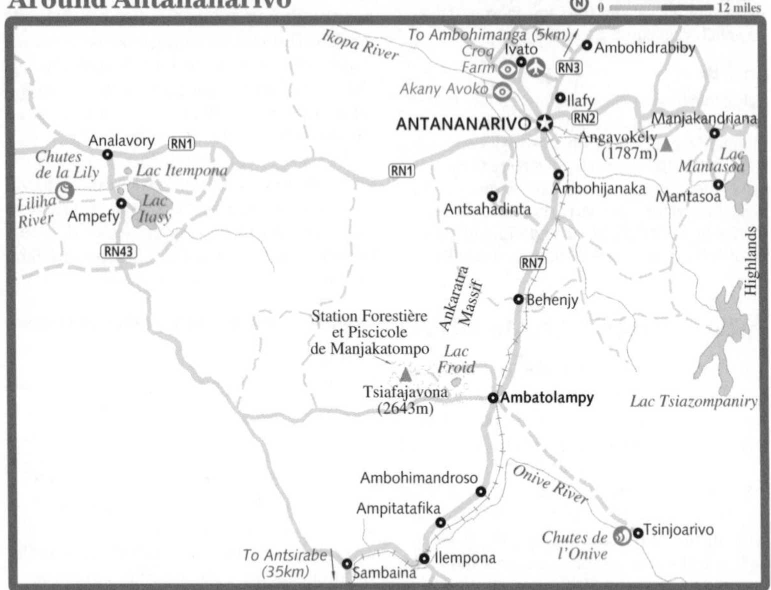

At the first sign of threat to the village, the stone would be rolled by up to 40 slaves, sealing off the gate.

Sights

TOP CHOICE Rova PALACE

(admission Ar7000; 9am-5pm) Poised atop the hill is Ambohimanga's Rova, the fortress-palace of the all-powerful Merina king Andrianampoinimerina.

Slaves were once sacrificed on the rock inside the palace's entrance, and the many pilgrims who come to ask the blessings of the royal ancestors sometimes still slaughter animals in the same spot. The fortress was constructed using cement made from sand, shells and egg whites – 16 million eggs were required to build the outer wall alone.

Inside the compound stands the blackened wood hut (1788) that was **King Andrianampoinimerina's palace** (the word 'palace' seems at odds with the simplicity of the structure, but palace it was). The original was thatched, but French engineer Jean Laborde replaced the grass roof with more durable wooden tiles in the 19th century.

The central pole of the hut is made from a single trunk of sacred *palissandre* (rosewood), which was reportedly carried from the east coast by 2000 slaves, 100 of whom died in the process. The top of the pole is carved to show a pair of women's breasts, a symbol of the king's polygamy. The king supposedly hid in the rafters when visitors arrived, signalling whether the guest was welcome by dropping pebbles onto his wife's head.

The royal bed is in the sacred northwest corner of the hut and is elevated to indicate the king's superior status. The simple furniture is aligned according to astrological rules.

Behind the hut are the open-air baths where the king performed his royal ablutions once a year, in the company of his 12 wives and diverse honoured guests. Afterwards his bathwater was considered sacred and was delivered to waiting supplicants.

Next door to King Andrianampoinimerina's hut, in a striking style contrast, is the elegant **summer palace** of Queen Ranavalona I (r 1828–1861), constructed by Jean Laborde in 1870 (who was thought to be Ranavalona's lover). It's been beautifully restored and has original European-style furniture inside. The dining room is lined with mirrors, which allowed the queen to check that no one was sneakily poisoning her food.

Ambohimanga is still revered amongst many Malagasies as a sacred site, and you will see offerings (zebu horns, blood, sweets, honey as well as small change) at various **shrines** around the compound where individuals or families have come to invoke royal spirits for luck and fertility. Don't disturb these sacred locations and never point at them with your finger outstretched.

There are sensational **views** of the surrounding countryside from around the compound.

Make sure you take a guide to go round the Rova to learn about the site's historical and cultural significance. Guides are available by the entrance where you pay your admission. Otherwise, contact the local tourism promotion office **OSCAR** (☎26 300 46), which organises guided circuits in the compound and surrounding area.

Getting There & Away

Ambohimanga is 21km north of Antananarivo and easily visited as a day trip in combination with Ilafy. Taxis-bes (route H) leave throughout the day from Ambodivona (Ar700, one hour). From the village, you'll need to walk 1km up the hill to the Rova.

Lac Mantasoa

This 2000-hectare artificial lake, built in 1931, is a good place for fishing, sailing and picnicking, and has become a popular weekend retreat for Antananarivo residents. The hotels on the lakeside all offer boating, waterskiing, pedalo, fishing and more. The lake also holds a special place in history as being the site where Madagascar's industrial revolution started.

In 1833, Frenchman Jean Laborde (see p196) built a country palace for Queen Ranavalona I, as well as carpentry and gunsmith shops, a munitions factory, an iron forge and a foundry. The primary aim was to supply the monarch with swords, arms and ammunition. Much of this was destroyed in 1851 when slaves rebelled, whilst other parts now lie underwater, but some notable buildings can still be seen and visited in the village of Mantasoa, offering a fascinating insight into Madagascar's heyday as an industrial powerhouse.

Laborde's home (⏰8am-4pm Mon-Sat, noon-4pm Sun) is a lovely traditional, wood-clad house complete with sculpted wooden tiles reminiscent of fish scales. Inside there are old photographs and sparse furniture but a fair amount of biographical information (in French).

You can also see Laborde's **grave** in the local cemetery at the top of the village: the industrialist rests in a grand stone mausoleum, surrounded by 12 soldiers' tombs. As for the old industrial complex, all that remains of the once massive enterprise are the old **munitions factory**, now a school, a couple of **staff houses** and an impressive **stone furnace**.

WORTH A TRIP

ANTSAHADINTA

Antsahadinta (Forest of Leeches), founded by King Andriamangarira in 1725, is one of the most remote and best-preserved hilltop villages around Antananarivo. The royal precincts, or **Rova** (admission Ar5000; ⏰9am-4pm), contain several terraced tombs and a well-maintained garden with evocative sacred trees and lovely views of the surrounding countryside.

As you enter the settlement, the large tomb on your right belongs to Queen Rabodozafimanjaka, one of King Andrianampoinimerina's 12 wives. Accused of disloyalty, she had to undergo an ordeal with *tanguin*, a strong poison, and no one today is certain whether or not she survived it.

There is a small **museum** with historical artefacts, photos and family trees. The whole compound has been well maintained, and the resident guide is a real character, a passionate of Malagasy history with enough anecdotes to keep you entertained for an afternoon (a tip will be expected).

As well as being of historical interest, Antsahadinta is a beautiful place; if you come, bring a picnic to feast on the views from the lofty Rova. The site is 14km southwest of Antananarivo, through paddy fields, sugar cane plantations and picturesque villages. As the road is in bad condition and there is no public transport, you will need your own vehicle to come here, preferably a 4WD.

With its country club feel, **Domaine de l'Ermitage** (☎42 660 54; www.ermitagehotel-mantasoa.com; d/f Ar80,000/150,000) attracts a wealthy Tana crowd who come here to enjoy some R&R by the lakeside on the weekends. It is rather quiet during the week (when good discounts can be negotiated).

The hotel itself is dated, but the facilities are excellent, with game rooms, a fireplace lounge, massive grounds and a host of water sports and activities (horse riding, trampoline, mountain biking etc) on offer. There is a very popular buffet lunch (Ar40,000) on Sunday.

Getting There & Away

Mantasoa village lies about 60km east of Antananarivo. If you're going by taxi-brousse (Ar3000), plan to spend the night there as it is impossible to know whether you'll find a taxi-brousse heading back to Tana in the afternoon.

Ambatolampy & Around

A charming and very typical plateau town, Ambatolampy lies on both the RN7 and the railway line, 68km south of Antananarivo. The surrounding area is a good place to do some walking, mountain biking and birdwatching among the picturesque forests and hills of the Ankaratra Massif.

Sights & Activities

La Ferme de Morarano FARM

(☎032 40 978 33; www.ladistilleriedumaido.com/madagascar.html; admission Ar5000; ⌚9am-6pm) This organic farm specialises in the production of essential oils. You can tour the plantation with a guide and see myriad aromatic and medicinal plants as well as fruit trees. If you liked what you saw, the farm shop sells pure essential oils as well as beauty products (from massage oils to shampoo) and a mouthwatering collection of jams, chutneys and spreads. The farm also has a phenomenal collection of butterflies (6000 in total) in its **Insect Museum** (admission Ar5000; ⌚9am-5pm).

Aluminium Pot Workshops VILLAGE

(admission Ar5000) Ambatolampy is famous for its aluminium pots, which you can see in every household and hotel up and down the country. A number of workshops are open to visitors for a small fee. The aluminium used to manufacture the pots is scavenged from car parts etc. It is melted in furnaces and then poured in handmade moulds of very fine laterite and coal powder. The workers are incredibly dexterous and fast: one team of two can produce up to 50 pots a day.

Station Forestière de Manjakatompo HIKING

(admission Ar5000) This forest reserve was badly burnt in 2011, but it is still a good area for walking. Make sure you get a guide to explore the area: they will generally be available at the forestry station gates. Or organise one via local hotels. Access is via a secondary road towards Ankaniheny.

Sleeping & Eating

La Pineta GUESTHOUSE €€

(☎43 493 02, 033 28 176 86; http://madagascar-alapineta.com; Route d'Antsirabe; r Ar40,000, without

THE MERINA

The region surrounding Antananarivo is known as Imerina (Land of the Merina Tribe). Historically, the Merina have been Madagascar's dominating tribe, reigning over the country for several centuries.

Merina hierarchy was based on a three-tier caste system, largely dependent on skin colour. The *andriana*, or nobles (generally fairer-skinned and with pronounced Asiatic rather than African features, reflecting their Indonesian ancestry), comprised the upper echelon, while the *hova*, or commoners, made up the middle class. The remainder – descendants of former slaves – were known as the *andevo* (workers).

The first Merina kingdoms were established around the 16th century, and by the late 19th century they were the dominant tribe in Madagascar. Ordinary Merina citizens customarily worked as administrators, shopkeepers, teachers and traders. Their position was enhanced by the choice of Antananarivo as the seat of the French colonial government, and by the establishment of an education system there.

Today, the Merina are still among the best-educated Malagasies and many remain at the forefront of public life: former president Marc Ravalomanana and the president of the transitional high authority Andry Rajoelina are both Merina.

DON'T MISS

MADAGASCAR'S HOME OF FOIE GRAS

The little village of **Behenjy**, about 40km south of Antananarivo on the RN7, is famous for its duck and its foie gras. In fact, much of the duck and foie gras you'll enjoy in Tana's restaurants come from around here. At the **Coin du Foie Gras** (☎033 11 033 26; aniriaandrianaivo@yahoo.fr; mains Ar5000-12,000), right at the heart of the village, you can stop for a gourmet lunch of foie gras or duck breast and buy home-made foie gras in 250g glass jars (Ar35,000) that will withstand the journey home (they keep for six months, even outside the fridge). Purists will love the plain blocks but those after something different can try the vanilla-flavoured variety, or those with peppercorns or raisins. Thanks to French influences, it is as good as the genuine article in France, but at much sweeter prices.

bathroom Ar26,000) With its vaguely Mexican-sounding name and vaguely Swiss-chalet feel, La Pineta is an unusual but tip-top option in Ambatolampy. The five pretty rooms have lovely wooden floors and bright colours. Meals are served either in the dining room or under the gazebo in the garden, and the friendly owners are an excellent source of information on treks and excursions in the area.

Le Rendez-Vous des Pêcheurs PENSION €€
(☎43 492 04; www.madagascar-parleshauts.com; r Ar40,000) Going strong since 1951, the Rendez-Vous is a local institution. Every tour travelling between Tana and Antsirabe or enjoying a day trip in the highlands seems to stop here for lunch (mains Ar9000 to Ar12,000). The dining room has the feel of an old-fashioned canteen and the food is hearty and great value. There are spacious rooms on the first floor; just like the dining room, the furniture hasn't changed since the 1950s, but it's immaculate and the manager is a mine of information on the area. He can also organise tours between here, Antsirabe and Ambositra.

Getting There & Away

All taxis heading south towards Antsirabe pass through Ambatolampy (one hour, Ar10,000).

Lac Itasy & Around

Lac Itasy (45 sq km) was formed when the valley surrounding it was blocked by lava flow about 8000 years ago. Although the area has been completely deforested and none of the original vegetation remains, the volcanic domes that rise above the landscape have a certain beauty of their own. The pretty town of **Ampefy** is now a firm weekend favourite amongst Tana residents.

There are good possibilities for hiking around the lakeshore: a new 17km trail has been created that takes in 13 small villages and panoramic views of the lake. The trail starts near Hôtel Kavitaha. Follow the red markings.

About 5km west of Ampefy, in the village of **Antafofo**, the Liliha River plunges more than 20m. In French, the falls are known as the **Chutes de la Lily** (admission Ar2000).

Sleeping & Eating

Hôtel Kavitaha HOTEL €
(☎033 09 325 99; kavitaha.ampefy@gmail.com; Ampefy; bungalows Ar20,000-35,000) On a lovely spot by the lakeside, the Kavitaha is a bargain: rooms are bright and clean, the garden is gorgeous and the pool fantastic. The restaurant serves good meals (mains Ar10,000) and has splendid lake views.

Chez Jacky BUNGALOWS €
(☎48 840 13; Ampefy; d Ar35,000, mains Ar6000-10,000) Jacky has gained a solid reputation for his excellent food, and Tana residents come here in droves at the weekend. The restaurant is a big thatched pavilion, full of bric-a-brac and with lovely views of the countryside. Small, thatched bungalows are available. It is very quiet on weekdays.

Getting There & Away

Lac Itasy lies near the village of Ampefy, 120km west of Antananarivo and south of Analavory (which lies along the RN1). It's doable as a day trip from Tana with your own vehicle, but you'll need to sleep in Ampefy if you go by taxi-brousse – take a vehicle for Tsiroanomandidy, get off in Analavory (1½ hours, Ar8000) and change to another vehicle going south to Ampefy (10 minutes, Ar2000).

You'll need your own vehicle to see the waterfalls.

Central Madagascar

Includes »

Best Places to Eat

» Surprise Betsileo (p62)
» Motel Violette (p56)
» Résidence du Betsileo (p68)
» Le Pousse-Pousse (p53)

Best Places to Stay

» Camp Catta (p70)
» Trianon (p51)
» Lac Hôtel (p65)
» Tsara Guest House (p61)
» Résidence du Betsileo (p68)
» Chez Billy (p51)

Why Go?

The classic tourist route from Antananarivo (Tana) takes you south along the RN7 through Central Madagascar, a high plateau stretching all the way to Fianarantsoa. You'll twist and turn through these highlands, a region of scenic hills and rice paddies that resists generalisation. Here you'll find a potpourri of traveller's delights: bustling market towns clogged with colourful *pousse-pousse* (rickshaws), a famous railway line, small villages of distinctive two-storey mudbrick homes with porches and thatched roofs, a mountain stronghold of lemurs, the legacy of French colonialism, national parks with landscapes ranging from thick jungle to wide-open grandeur, and some of the best trekking Madagascar has to offer. For many people this is their introduction to the country, and it's a good one, with a variety of attractions linked by a gentle road as well as friendly residents.

When to Go

Antsirabe

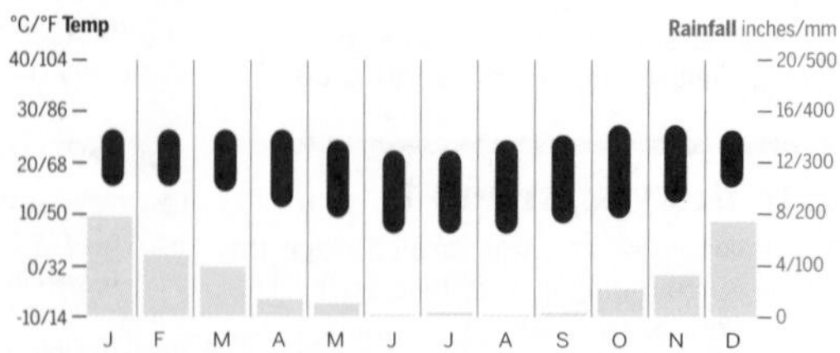

Jul–Sep *Famadihana* ceremonies take place in the Antsirabe area; visitors may be invited to attend.

Apr–May Countryside is greenest following the end of the rainy season.

Sep–Oct Best weather of the year, animals active, lemurs have babies.

Central Madagascar Highlights

1. Kick back on a *pousse-pousse* tour of **Antsirabe** (p51)
2. Search out chameleons on a night walk in **Parc National de Ranomafana** (p57)
3. Stroll through the eerie main street of **Ambalavao** (p67)
4. Commune with ring-tailed lemurs in **Réserve d'Anja** (p67)
5. Scale Madagascar's second-highest mountain, Pic Boby, in spectacular **Parc National d'Andringitra** (p68)
6. Sit by the village well in the paradisiacal **Tsaranoro Valley** (p68)
7. Ride the colourful **FCE railway** (p63) from Fianarantsoa to Manakara
8. Paddle a pirogue down the **Canal des Pangalanes** (p65)

Getting There & Around

Perhaps the most common itinerary in Madagascar is to head down the RN7 to Tuléar (Toliara) from Tana, sampling everything along the way, then fly back to Tana. Nearly all of Central Madagascar's towns and attractions lie near this two-lane highway, one of the few well-maintained roads in the country. Many people take a detour on the colourful FCE railway, continue on to the coast via Isalo, worship sun and reef a bit, then fly back to Tana.

Taxis-brousses (bush taxis) regularly ply the road between the capital and the coast. But unless you have lots of time and a streak of masochism, you will likely forgo that alternative in favour of renting a car and (mandatory) driver. Locally owned cars can be hired in Tana, Tuléar and Fianarantsoa, and sometimes in the smaller cities in between (ask at hotels or the bus station). But in our opinion, you can do no better than **Christophe** (032 64 822 45, 034 46 191 65; jtophy@gmail.com), the driver carefully selected for our own research trip throughout Central and South Madagascar. Along with a Land Rover, you will get an enthusiastic introduction to Malagasy music.

Antsirabe

POP 215,000

Madagascar's third-largest city, Antsirabe *(An-sra-bay)* assaults the senses with throngs of colourful *pousse-pousse* filling the dusty streets and a sprawling, vibrant market that can swallow you for hours. Behind the clamour lies a colonial past that emerges every so often, a reminder of a very different era.

Known for its thermal springs, the city has a long history as a spa town, first in the form of Norwegian missionaries, who built a health retreat here in the late 1800s, with cobblestone streets that can still be seen, and then French colonists, who turned it into a chic getaway from nearby Tana. Today, the great monument to its heyday, the Hôtel des Thermes, has been reopened, but has yet to dust itself off, while Le Trianon has come back in grand style. For the traveller, the omnipresent *pousse-pousse* makes getting around easy, and there are a surprising array of quality sleeping and restaurant options. Reserve ahead in the high season.

Sights & Activities

Sabotsy Market MARKET

A Malagasy version of a Moroccan souk, this sprawling open-air market, with distinct areas of jewellery, clothing, food, and more, will keep you occupied for hours either shopping or simply absorbing the spectacle. Located in a vast walled compound, it is a Pandora's box of unusual sights and sounds, not to mention things for sale, with all of local society seemingly on display. The shaded stalls are most welcome on a hot day, and the general lack of hard sales tactics makes visitors welcome. Just be careful of the open drains. Saturday is the main day, but there is action all week long.

FREE **Star Brewery** BREWERY

(usine.antsirabe@star.mg; Rue Danton; tours 9am & 2pm Tue, Wed & Thu) Wondering where all that Three Horses Beer comes from? Look no further. Madagascar's dominant and unmissable brand is made in this, the country's biggest brewery. Starting at the THB billboard on the corner of Ave Foch and Rue Danton, head west on Danton (toward Morondava) for 800m. Email ahead to book the thrice-weekly free tour. If you've seen breweries elsewhere, though, this will be familiar.

Antsenakely MARKET

If Sabotsy isn't enough for you, you can also visit the smaller Antsenakely (also known as Petit Marché), which is open every day.

Arotel SWIMMING

(Rue Jean Ralaimongo) If the summer heat is getting to you, do what the local expats do: head to this hotel for a swim in their attractive pool. Though they still exist, the historic **thermal baths** are too dirty for this purpose.

Tours

Antsirabe is a popular place to find a tour down the Tsiribihina River in western Madagascar (p110). These floating trips are often combined with a visit to Parc National des Tsingy de Bemaraha (p110) and last around seven days. You can also organise shorter excursions to places like Parc National de Ranomafana. Be sure to see the box (p64) on purchasing tours at national parks first.

Discover Madagascar TOUR

(032 40 322 50; discovermad@yahoo.com; Rue Jean Ralaimongo) In the Hotel Baobab, this company has a good reputation.

Madagascar Tropic Voyage TOUR

(032 44 434 46; www.madagascar-tropic-voyage.com; Ave Foch) This spin-off from Discover Madagascar has an energetic young leader who speaks English and sources all his talent locally.

DON'T MISS

THE POUSSE-POUSSE TOUR: A SHOPPER'S DELIGHT

Like most places in Madagascar, Antsirabe has a shortage of street signs, so navigation can be difficult. But have no fear: the *pousse-pousse* tour is here. For a most reasonable fee, you can float around for hours without a care, making seeing this town a breeze. There's even a hood if it rains.

This experience is particularly valuable if you are interested in local handicrafts – from elaborate woodwork to embroidery to miniatures. These are typically created by artisans who work out of small workshops or private houses, in places you would never find on your own. Your *pousse-pousse* driver will be able to take you right to the source, neatly sidestepping the middleman. These are not necessarily places set up for tourists, but they are authentic. Similarly, there are many producers of local foodstuffs, including wine, cheese, candy and honey, to discover. In fact, you can even visit the local *pousse-pousse* manufacturer, Garage Vony.

Your challenge is to arrange the tour. Virtually any *pousse-pousse* driver can do it, and there are an unlimited number of them prowling the streets, so try and find one that speaks some English and appears knowledgeable, as he is doubling as your guide. Prices range from Ar5000 per person per hour to Ar40,000 per person for a full day, with room to negotiate. Make absolutely clear what the cost will be, and whether that cost is per person or for the rickshaw. If haggling isn't your style, you can arrange your tour through virtually any hotel. This may make it easier to identify the right man for the job, but the cost will be higher. In any case, make clear to the driver what your interests are. They'll go out as far as Lake Andraikaba (p56).

Festivals & Events

Just when you thought you'd seen it all: June to September is the time for **famadihana** (literally, the 'turning of the bones'), the ritual exhumation and celebration of ancestors' bones by the Betsileo and Merina people. *Famadihana* are joyous and intense occasions, which occur in each family roughly every seven years (see p203).

Famadihana ceremonies take place in the *hauts plateaux* (highlands) region from Tana to Ambositra every year. Local tour operators or *pousse-pousse* drivers can help you find one and arrange an invitation. If you receive an invite, it's polite to bring a bottle of rum as a gift for the host family, and to ask before taking pictures. Foreigners are generally warmly welcomed, and most people find that the experience, far from being morbid, is moving and fascinating.

Sleeping

Antsirabe offers a fascinating array of sleeping options, better than anywhere else south of Tana. None of the hotels have heat, though, so come prepared in winter.

TOP CHOICE **Trianon** INN €€
(☎44 051 40, 034 05 051 40; hotel.letrianon@gmail.com; Ave Foch; s/d/tr Ar50,000/60,000/70,000; wi-fi) This charming throwback to the colonial era, a nicely renovated French chateau with grand embracing stairways, is just oozing with atmosphere, from its old airline posters to its uniformed staff. The classy restaurant and terrace strike just the right note, as do the chequered tablecloths in the breakfast room. Garçon!

TOP CHOICE **Chez Billy** INN €
(☎44 484 88; www.chez-billy.net84.net/accueil.html; Antsenakely; d/tr/q Ar16,000/24,000/31,000; @ wi-fi) This eclectic melange of guesthouse, music bar, internet cafe, and restaurant, awash in loud art, inspires a hostel-like conviviality among the Peace Corps staff, backpackers, Malagasy tourists, and in-the-know *vazaha* (foreigners) who form its crossroads clientele. Take your beer to the rooftop terrace and enjoy some rare free wi-fi in the best budget option in town. But act quickly: the eight rooms go fast.

Résidence Camélia INN €€€
(☎44 488 44; www.laresidencecamelia.com; Ave de l'Indépendance; d Ar70,000-126,000) A very genteel and well-done guesthouse with a tranquil shady garden and fresh, uplifting rooms in various shapes, sizes and prices. The charming restaurant (mains from Ar10,000), with its vaulted ceiling and winter fireplace, is a noteworthy bargain. But start with a drink in the piano bar.

Antsirabe

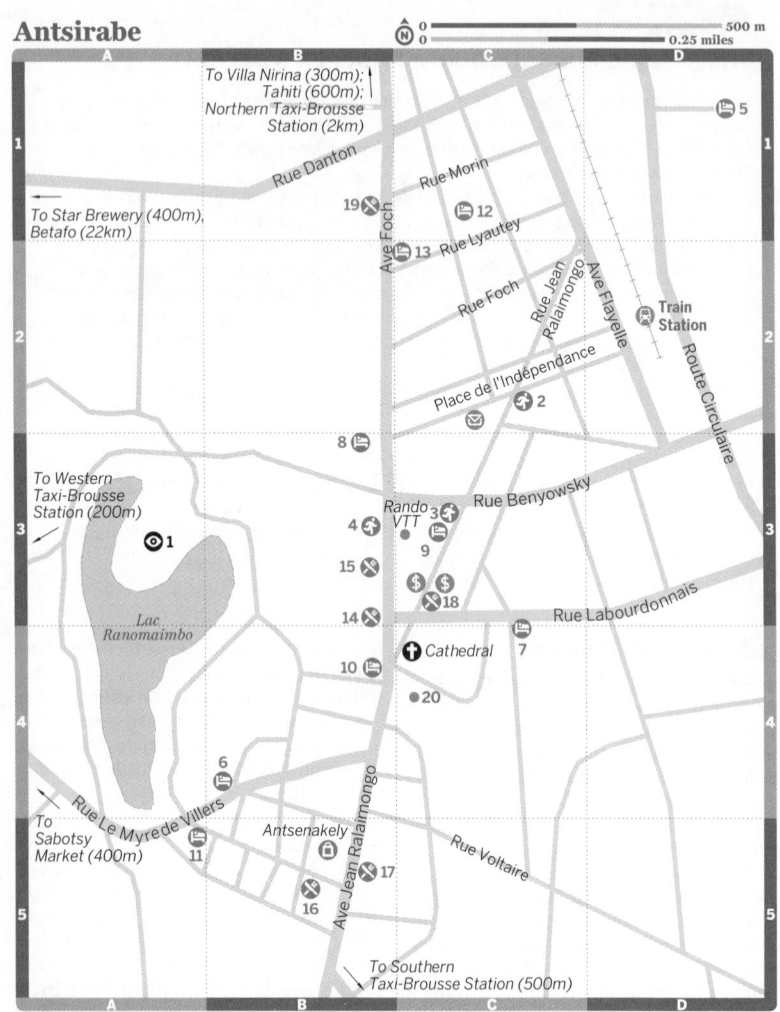

Chambres des Voyageurs PENSION €€€
(☎44 979 30, 032 40 866 22; www.chambres-voyageur.com; d/tr/q Ar70,000/90,000/130,000; 📶) This ecolodge is a rarity in Antsirabe, an island of nature on the edge of the city. There are extensive grounds where tortoises and chameleons roam about at a glacial pace, a central pond with an island, and brick bungalows that are simply furnished but spacious. If you are looking for the city, this is definitely not for you, but if you want to escape it, it's your first choice. Half-board supplements are Ar25,500.

Hôtel Hasina HOTEL €€
(☎44 485 56; hotelhasina@moov.mg; Ave Jean Ralaimongo; d Ar32,000) Right in the village centre, Hôtel Hasina is great value. There's lots of light, as well as comfy mattresses and cosy balconies. No wonder it fills up quick.

Green Park Hotel HOTEL €
(☎44 051 90, 034 08 725 13; Rue Labourdonnais, Tsarasaotra; camping per tent Ar6000, d/tr Ar30,000/40,000) This place has a beautiful garden and (somewhat iffy) pond. There are three excellent rooms in round towers, very nicely decorated, and a highly regarded res-

Antsirabe

Sights
1 Thermal Baths ... A3

Activities, Courses & Tours
2 Arotel ... C2
3 Discover Madagascar ... C3
4 Madagascar Tropic Voyage ... B3

Sleeping
5 Chambres des Voyageurs ... D1
6 Chez Billy ... B4
7 Green Park Hotel ... C4
8 Hôtel des Thermes ... B3
9 Hôtel Hasina ... C3
10 Nouveau Synchro Pub ... B4
11 Pension de Famille Sulby ... A5
12 Résidence Camélia ... C1
13 Trianon ... C2

Eating
14 Au Bon Coin ... B3
Chez Jenny ... (see 7)
15 L'Arche ... B3
16 Le Pousse-Pousse ... B5
Relais des Saveurs ... (see 9)
Résidence Camélia ... (see 12)
17 Restaurant Razafiramamonjy ... B5
18 Shoprite ... C3
Trianon ... (see 13)
19 Zandina ... B1

Information
Cyber Kool ... (see 17)
20 Voyages Bourdon ... C4
Zandina ... (see 19)

taurant, **Chez Jenny**, known for having the best pizza in town. Reserve in high season.

Villa Nirina B&B €€
(☎44 486 69; bbvillanarina@hotmail.fr; Ave Foch; d/tr Ar50,000/70,000) The five rooms at this family-run B&B are rather small and come with shared bathroom. The exterior yard is well kept, and in a walled compound that provides welcome privacy from the hectic streets. The owner (but not the staff) speaks English.

Pension de Famille Sulby HOTEL €
(☎032 80 467 22; pfsulby@yahoo.fr; Antsenakely; d Ar20,000) If you are out of luck with budget accommodation, this one will do fine. It's centrally located, has clean rooms, the owners are friendly and the prices are rock bottom. The street can get a bit noisy.

Nouveau Synchro Pub HOTEL €
(☎44 962 24, 033 14 212 09; www.synchropub.com; Antsenakely; d Ar25,000) Don't be thrown by the name. This is a hotel with a pub (set menu Ar10,000), and a strong budget option at that: quiet, on a hill overlooking the city, with a nice rooftop cafe, and close to town without feeling so. Room No 1, a corner room with views, manages to be romantic.

Hôtel des Thermes INN €€€
(☎44 487 61, 44 487 62; d Ar125,000-256,000; 🏊) Once the Grand Dame of Antsirabe, the Old Lady just ain't what she used to be. Everything is falling apart, something even the creepy lighting can't hide, making the prices laughable. It's too bad: once you get past the surreal lobby, you can sense the grandeur that once was.

Eating

Food is very inexpensive in Antsirabe, even at major hotels. Among the latter, **Trianon**, **Résidence Camélia** and **Chez Jenny**, at Green Park, have good reputations.

There are numerous places serving inexpensive Malagasy food and more in the southern end of town, south of the cathedral. The best-stocked supermarket is the huge **Shoprite**, near Antsenakely.

TOP CHOICE **Le Pousse-Pousse** FRENCH, MALAGASY €€
(Antsenakely; mains Ar8500-12,000; ⏲11.30am-1.30am Thu-Tue) This charming place, where you eat inside a *pousse-pousse*, is known for its cheeseburgers – rare hereabouts – and occasional live music. Menu in English, too.

Restaurant Razafiramamonjy CHINESE, MALAGASY €
(Rue Jean Ralaimongo; mains Ar3000-5000) This locally recommended place, frequented by Malagasy families, offers meat, chicken and seafood cooked many different ways, although it's a bit dark. There is music at night, and the attached internet cafe stays open late. Look for Cyberkool sign.

L'Arche FRENCH, PIZZERIA €
(Ave Foch; mains Ar6000-9000; ⏲Mon-Sat) This eatery serves homey French favourites and pizzas to expats, river guides and tourists – a tour company is based out of the bar.

Zandina EUROPEAN, MALAGASY €€
(5 Ave Foch; mains Ar13,000; ⏲11.30am-1.30am; 📶) If you can deal with the lame art on the walls, this is a good place for pizza and grills, the latter served on an enclosed patio with a brick oven.

Relais des Saveurs DESSERTS €
(Rue Ralaimongo; smoothies Ar2000) The best smoothies in town, here known as 'smoozies'. Good omelettes, too. Next to Hôtel Hasina.

Au Bon Coin MALAGASY, CHINESE €
(Ave Foch; mains Ar4000-5000) A charming budget choice, with rare rooftop seating, a casual ambience and great breakfasts.

Drinking & Entertainment

Nightlife in Antsirabe doesn't match the array of hotels and restaurants. The **Tahiti nightclub** (Rte de Tananarive) at the Hotel Diamant is the longstanding choice for dancing. Otherwise, people tend to congregate in hotel and restaurant bars, such as Chez Billy, or Restaurant Razafimamonjy.

Information

For more reviews, insider tips and planning advice on Antsirabe, head to www.lonelyplanet.com/madagascar/central-madagascar/antsirabe.

There are numerous ATMs at the banks. The **BNI** (Rue Ralaimongo) ATM is open 24 hours and takes both MasterCard and Visa.

Cyber Kool (Rue Jean Ralaimongo; internet per min Ar30; ⏲8am-midnight) Attached to Restaurant Razafiramamonjy.

Voyages Bourdon (Ave de l'Indépendance) Arranges car rental and airline tickets.

Zandina (Ave Foch; internet per min Ar30) The restaurant also offers free wi-fi to clients. Good enough for Skype video.

Getting There & Away

Antsirabe is 170km south of Antananarivo. There are three taxi-brousse stations: one for Antananarivo (Ar8000, four hours) and all other points, about 2.5km north of town, behind the Jovenna petrol station; one in the southern end of town for transport to Ambositra (Ar5000, three hours) and Fianarantsoa (Ar15,000, six hours); and another one on the western edge of town for transport to nearby villages. A lot of the taxis-brousses for Tana try to catch you at the two gas stations (Total, Galana) on the way to the taxi-brousse station.

The vintage Micheline train (p34) also has limited service to Antananarivo.

Getting Around

Antsirabe can be easily negotiated on foot, but there are also a few taxis that can be chartered for getting around town and to destinations in the surrounding area, or you can take the bus. Car rental can be arranged through **Voyages Bourdon** (☎44 484 60; Ave de l'Indépendance) or directly with a driver named **Andry** (☎032 40 676 70), who speaks excellent English.

THE RICKSHAWS OF MADAGASCAR

Antsirabe is the *pousse-pousse* capital of Madagascar. Brightly painted and sporting racy names, such as 'Air France' and 'Zidane', *pousse-pousse* (literally, 'push-push') are the Malagasy version of the Asian rickshaw. Hundreds of them fill the wide avenues of Antsirabe, clustering like oversize prams and pooling in front of the post office and the market. Most drivers rent their vehicles, and have to make a certain number of rides a day just to break even. In pursuit of their goal, they hound pedestrians relentlessly with whistles, hisses and cries of *'pousse!'*. Passengers and freight vary – from teenage girls, reclining like queens, to bleating goats.

Within the *pousse-pousse* universe, there are three major species. The basic model is just a cart pulled by a man. It may feel uncomfortable to be towed around by someone in this fashion, but remember this is the driver's living, and your patronage will be most welcome to him. It is also a great way to see a city. One cruises in shade at just the right pace, and if you land an English-speaking driver, you get a tour guide, too – one who knows Antsirabe like the back of his hand. The *cyclo-pousse*, in which the cab is attached to a bicycle, is a step up, at least as far as the driver is concerned. And then there is the top of the food chain, the *kinga*, or motorised *pousse-pousse*.

Prices are always negotiable with drivers, but there are general guidelines. In Antsirabe a single trip from the taxi-brousse station to Antsenakely, for either *pousse-pousse* or *cyclo-pousse*, usually goes for nearly Ar2000, although the asking price may be Ar5000; most trips in the city are Ar1000 to Ar2000. When it rains, the price doubles – for *pousse-pousse*, *cyclo-pousse* or *kinga*.

Ambositra

POP 38,000

Ambositra is located in the centre of a very broad valley ringed by verdant peaks. It's a lot quieter, cleaner and prettier than Antsirabe, so it makes for a pleasant contrast. It's also a lot smaller, so the sleeping and eating options are reduced, particularly the latter. You're definitely getting away from the world here: there is no internet available save for one slow cafe. On the other hand, this rustic town is an overachiever in arts and crafts, offering woodcarvings, raffia baskets, polished stones, *marqueterie* (objects inlaid with coloured woods) and paintings. This is a place to wander crooked streets in search of a gift, or sip some tea by the side of a rice paddy, enlivened by fresh mountain air.

Sights & Activities

Ring Road NEIGHBOURHOOD

Many of the arts and crafts in town are located on the ring road at the heart of town, particularly the western loop. So the thing to do is simply to stroll around and have a look. The number of enterprises is a lot smaller than you'll find in the markets of Antsirabe or Fianarantsoa, but you can step into a shop, learn how things are made and take your time examining them here in ways you can't elsewhere.

Benedictine Monastery MONASTERY

At the western edge of town is a Benedictine monastery, where the monks and nuns sell postcards, cheese and jam in a small **shop** (⏲to 6pm). The church warrants a look if open.

Village Walks WALKING TOUR

There are many good walks from Ambositra through nearby villages, where you can see the artisans at work in their homes, carving wood with homemade tools or spreading brightly dyed raffia out in the sun to dry. If this interests you, the best thing to do is to stop by the Maison des Guides.

Tours

Maison des Guides WALKING TOUR

(☎47 714 48; lamaisondesguides.ambositra@yahoo.fr; guides per half day Ar35,000) This local co-operative, a kind of clearinghouse for guides, can usually arrange a guide who speaks some English, and customise an itinerary for you, for less than other tour operators. In fact, it operates much like the MNP offices at a national park. Short trips to a nearby waterfall and some palace ruins, as well as multiday forays into the Zafimaniry villages, are on offer. Hotels can also arrange tours, but this is the source of many.

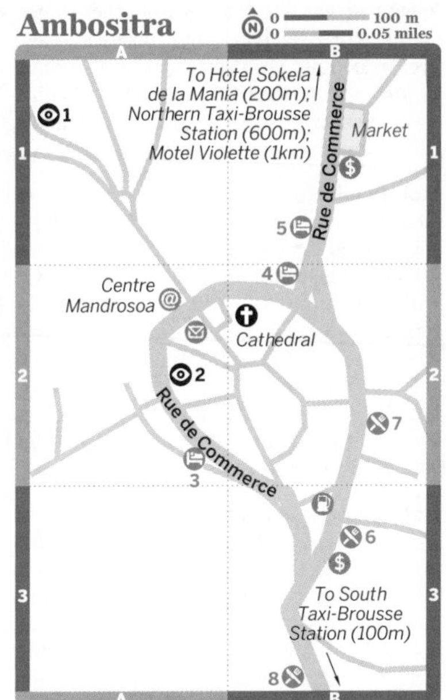

Ambositra

Sights

1	Benedictine Monastery	A1
2	Maison des Guides	A2

Sleeping

3	Hotel Angelino Tsaralaza	A2
4	Hotel du Centre	B2
5	Hôtel Mania	B1

Eating

6	Hotel-Restaurant Jonathan	B3
7	Hotely Tanamasoandro	B2
8	Oasis	B3

Sleeping

Winter nights are beyond chilly here; make sure your hotel provides blankets.

Hotel Angelino Tsaralaza HOTEL €€

(☎032 07 868 81; angelino-hotel@moov.mg; d Ar44,000) Don't let the humble facade fool you: there's a real gem here. With its white plaster walls, varnished wood, and irregular geometry, it feels like a homemade mountain lodge, with views to match. Go out back (watch your head!) to the porch, and you are knocked over by a grand vista across green hills. Suite 12 (Ar55,000) is the best room in town, with a surprisingly contemporary glass shower and a sitting area that could be in Bhutan.

Motel Violette HOTEL €€
(☎47 610 84, 032 56 117 23; motel-violette@wanadoo.mg; Rue du Commerce; r Ar28,000, bungalows Ar41,000) This is the best-run hotel in town, with a lively manager who understands customer service. The cottage-style bungalows, across the street from the main building, are spacious and clean, with plenty of blankets, but the real winner is the outdoor restaurant, with its dreamy views across a verdant rice paddy. A great place to breakfast.

Hotel Sokela de la Mania HOTEL €€
(☎47 711 95; Rue du Commerce; d/tr Ar35,000/45,000) On the outskirts of town, this quiet place has fabulous views, especially at sunset. Rooms are in a big white colonial building and offer lots of space and light with huge windows – get one facing the rice paddies. There is an on-site restaurant serving simple meals.

Hôtel Mania HOTEL €€
(☎47 710 21, 033 15 005 13, 032 04 620 91; toursmania@moov.mg; Rue du Commerce; r from Ar42,000) Tucked away in a leafy, gated courtyard in the centre of town, Mania has big, clean rooms with a peach colour scheme and spotless marble bathrooms.

Hotel du Centre HOTEL €
(☎032 86 658 39, 034 47 710 36; hotelducentre.mada@yahoo.fr; Rue du Commerce; d Ar30,000) This brand-new concrete hotel right on the ring road can be loud, so take the interior rooms facing the park.

Eating

Motel Violette FRENCH, MALAGASY €€
(Rue du Commerce; set menu Ar16,000, Malagasy breakfasts Ar7000; ⊙breakfast, lunch & dinner) Don't miss a chance to come here for a meal overlooking the rice paddies – and not just for the view, either: locals give the grills and pizza here consistently high marks, and there is a variety of French, Chinese, and Malagasy options, as well. It's a popular breakfast stop, too. English-language menu.

Hotel-Restaurant Jonathan MALAGASY, PIZZERIA €
(Rue du Commerce; mains Ar3000-7000, pizzas Ar8000-12,000) A reliable favourite for local expats, this busy hotel-restaurant offers a mix of pizza and Malagasy favourites that outshines the quality of its accommodation.

Oasis CHINESE, VEGETARIAN €
(☎47 713 01; RN7; mains from Ar3000) Another *vazaha* hangout, this place near the southern taxi-brousse station has an inexpensive and tasty menu with lots of veggie and Chinese options and a popular outside terrace.

Hotely Tanamasoandro MALAGASY €
(Rue du Commerce; mains from Ar2400) This unpretentious local favourite is popular for both its ambiance and huge portions of cheap Malagasy food.

Information

Centre Mandrosoa (Rue du Commerce) is the only internet cafe in town. Connection speed has been a problem. ATMs are available at BNI-CA and Bank of Africa.

WORTH A TRIP

A TRIP TO THE LAKES

There are two attractive lakes outside of Antsirabe that are popular day trips from the city. **Lake Andraikaba**, the closest and largest of the two, is 7km west off the road to Betafo. Frequented by Malagasy tourists, it has craft booths with some annoying hawkers, but it's also easy to get away for a nice quiet walk or picnic. The turquoise **Lake Tritiva**, a further 12km away, also has a hawker problem, and there is a Ar3000 entry fee, but otherwise this crater lake is even prettier, and the path around it makes for an easy circumnavigation.

Andraikiba can be reached by taxi-be 4, 5, and 11. Tritiva is more difficult to get to, as the 4 only goes about 5km of the way there. However, another option that gets a thumbs up from local expats is to bike to the lakes. At **Rando VTT** (Ave Foch, Antsirabe) you can get a good mountain bike with a lock and pump for Ar20,000 per day or Ar10,000 per half day. The Green Park hotel also rents bikes. Either one should be able to give you directions in English.

WORTH A TRIP

SANDRANDAHY

If you have come to Ambositra for crafts, there are some outlying areas you may be interested in too. The Zafimaniry villages are well known for their woodcarving, one reason for their designation as a Unesco World Heritage Site (for access, see p68). Likewise, Sandrandahy is known for its silk. In 2006 a federation of silk-weavers called Sahalandy was founded here to empower women in the community by establishing foreign markets, which it has done successfully. Silk has traditionally been a sign of nobility in Madagascar, and the process has been passed down through the generations for centuries. You can see the entire process here, beginning with cocoons, and ending with scarves, blankets, hammocks, pocketbooks, tablecloths, and much else. Sandrandahy is 20km north of Ambositra, and a beautiful drive; there is also a large market on Wednesdays. For more information visit the Sahalandy cooperative website, http://sahalandy.org.

Getting There & Away

Transport to points north, including Antsirabe (Ar7000, two hours) and Antananarivo (Ar10,000, five hours), departs from the far northern end of town, about 600m north of the fork and down a small staircase from Rue du Commerce.

Departures for Fianarantsoa (Ar6000, four hours) and other points south are from the southern taxi-brousse station.

Around Ambositra

IALATSARA LEMUR FOREST CAMP

Created in 2002, this small (10 sq km) **private reserve** (75 614 42; www.madagascar-lemuriens.com; admission Ar17,000) lies 83km south of Ambositra on the RN7, making it a very convenient stop, and a logical one if you are not going to visit Ranomafana. It's also a nice way to break up the long drive to the coast. There are a number of simple yet charming bungalows (Ar27,500) with balconies and bucket showers in a camp setting, and good family-style meals (Ar14,500).

Unlike in the national parks, you are free to walk around without a guide, although forest tours are available for four to 12 people (Ar25,000). The reserve is home to six species of lemurs and seven species of chameleon. Overall it's mildly pricey, but if this is your only chance to wander the jungle in search of wildlife, you should take it, at least for one night. The experience is quite similar to that at national parks without the time and expense of a long trek. The owner speaks English.

Parc National de Ranomafana

Like Antsirabe, the village of Ranomafana ('hot water') first evolved as a thermal bath centre popular with French colonials. In 1991 a large area of nearby forest was turned into a national park, largely to protect two rare species of lemur – the golden bamboo lemur and the greater bamboo lemur. Today the Parc National de Ranomafana is one of Madagascar's more popular parks, with 400 sq km of oddly shaped rolling hills carpeted in jungle and fed by rushing streams.

Meanwhile the town of 5000 has expanded with the influx of visitors, so that it and the park have closed the distance between them. While most accommodation will require a taxi to the park entrance, some are walking distance. Unfortunately, while there is a variety of excellent hotels to choose from, there are no banks or ATMs.

Ranomafana appears after a fantastic entrance through a dry rocky valley spotted with two-storey highlands houses. After a long day's travel, it feels like you have reached a mysterious island. The air is fresh and cool, and the nearby presence of the forest, with all of its strange sounds, alluring. Here you'll walk through jungle trails looking for elusive lemurs, or search out chameleons by the road at night. But be prepared for rain and temperature swings, particularly in winter, when a 25°C day becomes a 10°C night.

Park Entry & Fees

The **MNP Office** (8am-6pm Mon-Fri) is located on a dirt road a half-mile northeast of the Ranomafana town centre. Park visitors

PARC NATIONAL DE RANOMAFANA

Best time to visit Between September to December, when the weather is warm and dry.

Key highlight Spotting a bamboo lemur.

Wildlife Lemurs, birds, frogs, chameleons.

Habitats Primary and secondary rainforest.

Gateway town Ranomafana.

Transport options Taxi-brousse from Fianarantsoa (Ar5000).

Things you should know Park management leaves much to be desired: hunting of lemurs in the park persists.

pay an entry fee (one/two/three/four days Ar25,000/37,000/40,000/50,000), part of which goes to the community, and a guide fee (two/three/four hours Ar15,000/22,00/35,000, full day Ar60,000). Guides are mandatory and will assist you in working out an itinerary. There are many guides available; several speak English. A knowledgeable one is **Theo** (☎034 45 511 89, 033 09 793 30), who calls to the birds with his own jukebox of songs. It is customary to tip the guide; 10% is the norm.

Sights

Centre ValBio RESEARCH CENTRE
(☎033 02 753 98, 034 13 581 71; www.icte.bio.sunysb.edu; centrevallbio@gmail.com) This international training centre for the study of biodiversity, funded by several international universities, is housed in attractive buildings on the edge of the park, including a new and striking outreach centre. If you have any interest in the scientific research going on in the park, stop by here and someone will be happy to speak with you.

Thermal Baths BATHHOUSE
(baths/pool Ar1000/5000) The hot springs for which Ranomafana is named are across a bridge near the now-defunct Hôtel Station Thermale. The setting is pretty, but the individual baths, housed in little huts, are a bit dingy. Another option is the adjacent swimming pool, also fed by the springs, which is popular with locals. Best to swim here on Wednesday, as they clean the pool by emptying and refilling it on Tuesday. It's worth seeing even if you choose not to swim.

Ranomafana Arboretum BOTANICAL GARDEN
(RN7; admission Ar5000; ⊙8am-noon & 2-4pm) If you have any interest in local botany this is your first stop. It features over 150 species of native trees, 50 of which are fruit trees. There's a self-guided walking trail in English.

Sights & Activities

Wildlife

The park is divided into three parcels of land containing both primary and secondary forest. The former is more impressive, with enormous trees, but takes more hiking to reach. The park is known for its diverse wildlife, although some of it is quite elusive. There are 29 mammal species, including 12 species of lemur. On a typical day's walk, you are likely to see red-bellied lemurs, diademed sifakas and red-fronted lemurs. With luck (and a good guide), you may also see a golden bamboo lemur. This species was first discovered in 1986; Ranomafana is one of its two known habitats. The forest abounds with reptiles and amphibians; on a single night walk you may see 10 different species. The park's birdlife is also rich, with more than 100 species, of which 68 are endemic to Madagascar. Although most visitors come for the animals, the plant life is just as impressive, with orchids, tree ferns, palms, mosses and stands of giant bamboo.

Hiking

In Parcel III, the short **Talatakely Trail** (Petit Circuit) takes a leisurely two hours up and back and heads as far as the lookout at Bellevue, with lemur-spotting along the way. A branch heads to the Petite Cascade, which flows into a forest pool. In Parcel I, the three- to four-hour **Vohipara Circuit** goes a bit further in its search for lemurs, and is one of the best birding spots in Madagascar.

If you want the full-on experience, multiday treks take you even deeper into the park's primary forest, where the other tourists disappear. They also allow you to spend the night. This usually involves taking the **Soarano Circuit** into Parcel III, where there is another waterfall. Parcel II is rarely visited.

There are no longer any night walks into the forest; these now take place along the main road, where one moves down a wall of green looking for mouse lemurs and chameleons. This is a great experience – and what else are you going to do here at night?

Sleeping & Eating

Ranomafana has an extraordinary range of interesting lodging options for its size. Almost all the hotels are spread along a 10km stretch of the RN7 to the east of the park entrance. This means that you will likely need a ride to the park, although it is possible to walk along the road as well.

TOP CHOICE Cristo LODGE €€€

(☎034 12 353 97; http://cristohotel.cabanova.fr; d Ar90,000, bungalows Ar70,000) This relatively new lodge on the outskirts of town, perched on a gorgeous bend in the Namorona river, has the best view of any property in the area. From the fabulous wraparound verandah, one can see a breathtaking tropical sunset break over green hills, with a *ravinala* (travellers' palm) tree in the foreground spreading its leaves like a huge peacock. The upper-floor rooms share this panorama, and riverside bungalows are also available. An attractive restaurant with open fire is another draw, particularly on a rainy day, as are the amiable owners.

Hôtel Domaine Nature LODGE €€€

(☎75 750 25; desmada@malagasy.com; d/ste Ar62,000/136,000;) Located on both sides of the road, this aptly named hotel thrusts you right into the forest. Airy hillside bungalows with platform beds and space heaters are surrounded by jungle and the sound of rushing water; you look out into the canopy. A brand-new glass restaurant (mains Ar12,000) and super pool add creature comforts. It shows some wear, but the ambiance is what you came for. (Be warned: there are a lot of steps to the upper bungalows.)

Rianala Gite HOSTEL €

(☎033 14 905 69, 034 06 298 45; edm@moov.mg; dm Ar10,000, camping Ar3000) This is a great budget option. Right near the park entrance, you feel immersed in the forest. The rooms are clean and come with blankets and hot water, and there is a nice porch to sit on. There is also a restaurant, which you'll need unless you bring your own food. There are some great campsites a short walk away, too, with pitched thatched roofs overlooking the forest and the sound of a rushing stream below. Don't confuse them with the nearby MNP campsites, which aren't as atmospheric and cost Ar2000 more. Camping in the park itself is only allowed on guided treks.

Chez Gaspard B&B €€

(☎032 87 115 15, 033 01 155 05, 034 02 115 15; chezgaspard.ranomafana@gmail.com; bungalows Ar42,000-85,000) This line of bungalows, in a scenic tropical setting stretching along the river, are great value. Those furthest upstream are best, with No 14 a great family room that holds five. Avoid the rooms attached to the church, however, which are also rented from here.

Hôtel Manja HOTEL €€

(☎033 09 010 22; hotelmanja@gmail.com; bungalows Ar45,000, without bathroom Ar20,000) There are two classes of bungalow here, some older weathered ones without bath and some new ensuite cement ones that sit up high on a hill offering majestic views – if you don't mind the stairs. The hotel's best asset is the gigantic wooden restaurant, with a porch overlooking the river, which serves tasty, inexpensive Malagasy meals (mains Ar5000).

Setam Lodge LODGE €€€

(☎22 234 31; www.setam-madagascar.com; d Ar160,000) This upmarket ecolodge has outstanding attention to detail. The impressive reception and restaurant area features walls of glass framing a gorgeous view of the forest below. However, for this price, the rooms are on the Spartan side, and there is a golf-course feeling to the grounds that clashes with the forest setting. Breakfast is Ar8000 to Ar10,000, and set menus are Ar35,000.

Ihary Hotel HOTEL €€

(☎034 13 434 57, 033 12 857 22, 032 02 526 98; iharyhotel@gmail.com; bungalows from Ar42,000) We loved Ihary's tranquil thatched-roof bungalows right on the river, with their great views beyond. Bungalows are small, but very tidy and breezy with lots of windows. The restaurant serves good food (mains from Ar6000), although it may take awhile.

Centrest Sejour HOTEL €€€

(☎75 523 02; centrestsejour@gmail.com; d/f Ar110,000/160,000) This is a very calm, peaceful, and tidy hotel, with a lush tropical garden filled with local flowers and trees. The best rooms are down a sky-lit hallway that is kept spotless. The restaurant gets high marks, and has a mostly French menu (mains from Ar6000). Guests can visit the hotel's private reserve at Mahakajy, 9km away, which has chameleons and 80 species of orchid. English is spoken.

Information

Be forewarned: there are currently no banks or ATMs in Ranomafana. The nearest banks are 1½ hours away in either Fianarantsoa or Mananjary. Credit cards are not accepted anywhere.

Getting There & Away

Taxis-brousses go daily from Ranomafana to Fianarantsoa (Ar5000, 1½ hours) and Manakara or Mananjary (Ar15,000, five hours). Taxi-brousses to Fianarantsoa stop at the park entrance between 7.30am and noon. Taxis-brousses from Manakara usually arrive in Ranomafana around 9pm or 10pm. When arriving, let the driver know if you want to get off at the park entrance or in the nearby village.

To get to the park from your hotel: if you don't have a private car, some hotels will drive you, or arrange a ride for about Ar5000. There's lots of traffic on the road so hitching is also a realistic option.

Fianarantsoa

POP 193,000

Madagascar's second-largest city, Fianarantsoa *(Fi-a-nar-ant-soo)*, or Fianar for short, is like a mild version of Tana. Surrounded by hills, it is both a regional commercial, administrative, and religious centre, and a major transit point. Tourists typically come here to spend the night on their way to Ranomafana or Isalo, or to take the famous train to Manakara. Oddly enough, the airport has no regular flights anymore. You won't find many *vazaha* living here, either. But visitors can enjoy a historic old town, a great local market, some interesting places to stay, and a more laid-back ambience than the capital.

The city is divided into three parts. Basse-Ville (Lower Town), to the north, is a busy, chaotic area with the main post office and the train and taxi-brousse stations. Up from Basse-Ville is Nouvelle Ville (New Town), the

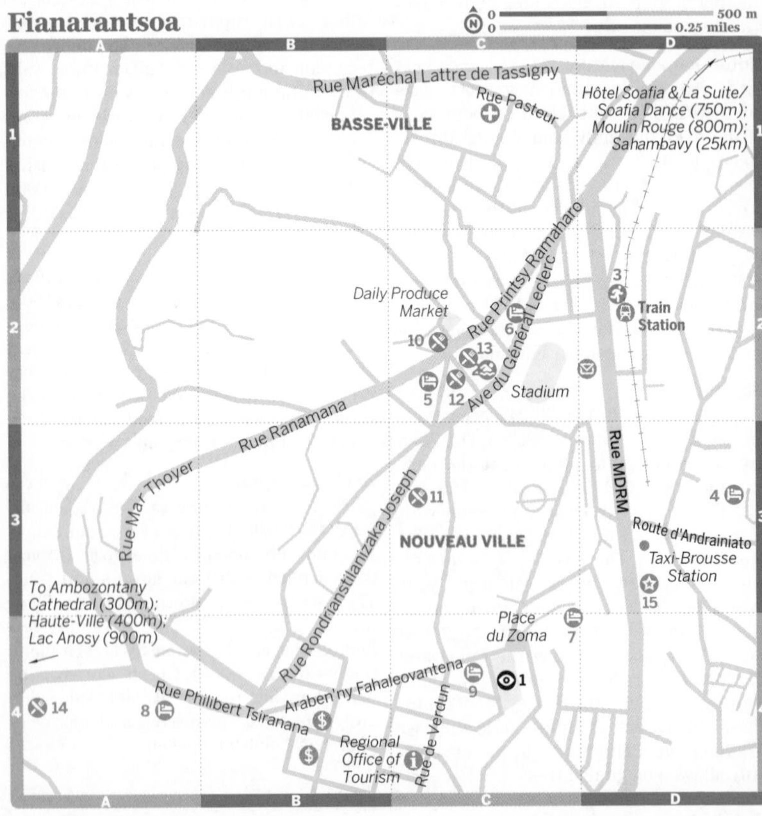

business area, with banks and several hotels. Further southwest and uphill is Haute-Ville (Upper Town), which has cobbled streets, a more peaceful atmosphere, numerous church spires and wide views across Lac Anosy and the surrounding rice paddies.

Sights & Activities

Haute-Ville NEIGHBOURHOOD
The oldest and most attractive part of town is the Haute-Ville (known as Tanana Ambony in Malagasy). A stroll (or climb) around the cobbled streets here offers great views of the surrounding countryside. In the centre of Haute-Ville, and dominating the skyline, is the imposing **Ambozontany Cathedral**, which dates back to 1890.

Lac Anosy LAKE
Located below, and visible from, the Haute-Ville, this lake is surrounded by flowering trees and is a popular place for a stroll.

Zoma MARKET
Fianar is a market town, with at least one small market open every day. The largest is the Zoma, where you'll find everything under the sun. It's held every day along Araben'ny Fahaleovantena, although Tuesday and Friday are best.

Fianarantsoa

Sights
1 Zoma C4

Activities, Courses & Tours
2 Hôtel Tombontsoa C2
3 Maison des Guides D2

Sleeping
4 Hôtel Arinofy D3
5 Hôtel Cotsoyannis C2
6 Hotel Soratel C2
7 Raza-ôtel C4
8 Tsara Guest House A4
9 Zomatel 1 & 2 .... C4

Eating
10 Chez Dom C2
11 Chez Ninie C3
12 Panda C2
13 Supermarché 3000 .... C2
14 Surprise Betsileo A4

Entertainment
15 Chez Tantine D3

Hôtel Tombontsoa SWIMMING
(75 514 05; Blvd Hubert Garbit; admission Ar5000) In hot weather, head for the large pool at the Hôtel Tombontsoa. There's also a sauna.

Tours

Most hotels and tour operators in Fianar also organise excursions to Parc National de Ranomafana and the Sahambavy Tea Estate. Apart from the need for transportation, there is no reason you couldn't do this yourself.

Maison des Guides WALKING TOUR
(034 03 123 01, 032 02 728 97; coeurmalgache@hotmail.com; 8am-5pm) Smartly located in an old railway car in front of the train station, this cooperative of local guides is your best choice for arranging a local tour. They know everything about the region, and specialise in treks to the picturesque Betsileo villages nearby. The guide **Eugène** (033 28 834 10; ranco_5213@yahoo.fr) speaks English.

Sleeping

TOP CHOICE **Tsara Guest House** GUESTHOUSE €€
(75 502 06, 032 05 516 12; www.tsaraguest.com; Rue Philibert Tsiranana; d Ar48,000-175,000) This classy and very popular plantation-style guesthouse brings a welcome sophistication to the town. The public spaces are excellent: the reception area, with a roaring fire and bright-red walls, a glass-walled restaurant serving delicious food (mains Ar5000 to Ar15,000) and a charming outdoor terrace with great views. The rooms come in four grades, all of them overpriced, but you're here for the amenities. Advance bookings recommended. An 8% fee is charged for credit cards.

Hôtel Arinofy GUESTHOUSE €
(75 506 38; hotel_arinofy@yahoo.fr; camping Ar12,000, d/tr Ar23,000/40,000) Your best budget option, this friendly guesthouse in a peaceful enclave has well-kept grounds, a professional uniformed staff, and a pleasant ambiance. There are a variety of rooms available, some en suite, and overflow camping (tents provided in the price) when rooms are full. The small restaurant serves a variety of dishes (mains from Ar5000), and there's a very clean kitchen for self-caterers. With a little paint it would be our top choice.

Zomatel 1 & 2 HOTEL €€€
(75 507 97; www.zomatel-madagascar.com; Araben'ny Fahaleovantena; d Ar83,000-100,000;) These twin business hotels, the result

WILD EXPECTATIONS

Many first-time visitors naturally associate Madagascar with two things – Africa and wildlife – leading to visions either of East African game parks, or of zoo-like rainforests. The reality is quite different. First, there are no plains full of roaming beasts here. In fact, there are no wild animals larger than a small dog. Outside the parks the most common impression is of the *absence* of wildlife. One can drive for days through the spiny forest in the south, for example, and see virtually nothing but a few domesticated zebu. Likewise, along the lush wetlands of the Canal des Pangalanes there are hardly any birds. There are many reasons for this, beginning with the impact of hunting and deforestation, which has decimated animal populations. But even the great biological diversity in the forests is not always obvious. Some animals are nocturnal, or shy of humans, or simply rare. The broad-nosed gentle lemur, for example, was thought to be extinct until it was rediscovered in Ranomafana in 1972. It was observed again in the late 1980s and is only occasionally seen today. Many fascinating animals, such as the world's smallest chameleon, are simply tiny. And rainforest is, by its very nature, a fairly effective shield for its inhabitants. So when seeking out this country's wildlife, it is best to adjust your focus to a smaller scale, look carefully around you, be patient, and hire a good guide. It can be challenging to spot that bamboo lemur in the canopy, but that's what makes it so rewarding when you do.

of a recent expansion, form a complex that includes an iffy restaurant (mains Ar5000 to Ar13,000), internet centre, low-key pizzeria and cheery staff. The newer Zomatel 2 is pricier but has surprisingly sophisticated modern rooms, with lots of light, great design and super beds. There's a nice indoor pool, too. English spoken.

Hôtel Soafia HOTEL €€
(☎75 503 53; www.soafia-hotel.com; Nouvelle Route d'Antananarivo; s/d/tr/q Ar42,000/62,000/72,000/87,000; ❄🏊) Here's a strange one: an enormous Chinese cruise ship sailing through Fianar. At least that's what it feels like. There's a large swimming pool, a vast restaurant (mains from Ar7000), a travel agency, a disco and an arcade of shops, linked by pagoda walkways. Labyrinthine corridors lead to strange rooms with gilt trim and enormous baths; Room No 112 could hold a Great Wall bus tour. Standard doubles are cheap as take-away, however, so how can you not love it?

Hôtel Cotsoyannis HOTEL €€
(☎75 514 72, 032 40 209 86; cotso@malagasy.com; 4 Rue Printsy Ramaharo; d from Ar51,000; 📶) 'Le Cotso' has a garden courtyard and rustic, attractive rooms that are good value for money. The cosy restaurant is a great place for afternoon dining (mains from Ar7500), with a log fire and good pizzas and crêpes.

Hotel Soratel HOTEL €
(☎75 516 66, 033 08 988 88; www.soratel.com; Rue Printsy Ramaharo; d/tr incl breakfast Ar36,000/46,000; 📶) This hotel does the basics well, with high-pressure hot-water showers, free wi-fi and a central location, all at a very reasonable price.

Raza-ôtel GUESTHOUSE €
(☎75 519 15; d Ar24,000) At the end of a rough side road, this is a welcoming family-run guesthouse with a dose of familial chaos. There are just four rustic rooms, unfortunately with saggy mattresses, and a cosy restaurant (mains from Ar6000) and bar.

Eating

TOP CHOICE **Surprise Betsileo** ITALIAN, MALAGASY €€
(☎034 01 998 04, 033 03 388 19; www.lasurprisebetsileo.com; Rue Pasteur; mains from Ar12,000) On the main road up to Old Town, this new addition is the stylish dining experience Fianar has been waiting for. The Italian owner has elegantly restored a 19th-century colonial villa and converted it into a sophisticated restaurant offering an interesting melange of Italian and Malagasy cooking. There are only eight tables, so book ahead.

Chez Ninie MALAGASY €
(Rue Rondriantsilanizaka Joseph; mains Ar3000-5000) Don't be fooled by the facade: lurking out back is open-porch dining with an extensive, inexpensive and very tasty Malagasy menu that keeps this place very popular. Dirt cheep beer (Ar1900), too.

Chez Dom FAST FOOD €
(Rue Ranamana; mains from Ar6500; @) A small, smoky cafe offering local rum and a quick menu. Frequented by backpackers, French

expats and tourists. Local guides may try to find you here.

Panda Restaurant CHINESE €€
(☎75 505 69; Rue Ranamana; mains from Ar12,000; ⊙Mon-Sat) If your ultimate fantasy involves dining on sautéed bat while staring at murals of copulating pandas painted on a restaurant wall, fulfil it here. Definitely a top contender for Madagascar's most eclectic eating establishment, Panda offers bat, pigeon, frog and wild duck. It also does excellent Chinese. Ring ahead if you're absolutely craving crocodile, as they are not always available.

Supermarché 3000 SUPERMARKET
(Rue Printsy Ramaharo) Supermarché 3000, in Basse-Ville, is the best-stocked place for self-caterers.

Entertainment

Besides La Suite/Soafia Dance, other weekend options include **Le Moulin Rouge**, at the northeastern end of town, which plays everything from Malagasy hits to Europop, and **Chez Tantine**, by the taxi-brousse station, which attracts a lively local crowd.

La Suite/Soafia Dance DJ
(admission Ar4000; ⊙9pm-late Tue & Thu-Sat) This is the best dance club in town. Located at the Hôtel Soafia, it has a bare-bones interior but plays great Euro/American music, including requests. Gets going after 11.30pm. The cover is for men only and includes one drink.

Information

Internet Access

There is free wi-fi available to nonguests at the Hotel Soratel. There are internet terminals at the main post office.

Money

Fianar has many banks with ATMs that also change currency and do Visa card cash advances.

Tourist Information

MNP (☎75 512 74; Antsororokavo) Located near the Hôtel Soafia and provides information and permits for the parks near Fianarantsoa. Permits can also be purchased at the parks themselves.

Regional Office of Tourism (Rue de Verdun; ⊙8.30am-12.30pm Mon-Fri) Good for its free public toilets, but that's about it.

THE FCE RAILWAY

One of the more popular things to do in Madagascar is to take the FCE (Fianarantsoa–Côte Est) railway from Fianar to the east coast. The train leaves its charming station around 7am in the morning and chugs along at 20km to 35km per hr on lines built in the 1930s, reaching Manakara seven to 12 hours later (yes, it's that variable). Along the way you pass plantations, waterfalls and green hills, cross 67 bridges and go through 48 tunnels, all the while dropping steeply in elevation. Despite its antiquity and unreliability, the train is still an economic lifeline for the people of the inland villages, who use it to transport their cargoes of bananas and coffee to be sold and exported. Stopping at each tiny station is a colourful experience, with Malagasy passengers leaning out of the windows to haggle with hordes of vendors balancing baskets of bananas, crayfish or fresh bread on their heads. For more details, see p64.

For the best views of the cliffs, misty valleys and waterfalls en route, sit on the north side of the train (ie the left side when going from Fianarantsoa to Manakara). However, the most impressive waterfall is on the right as you go towards Manakara – just after Madporano, about two hours from Fianarantsoa. Bring water, and, if you're making the journey in winter, plenty of warm clothes – it's often freezing early in the morning, when some of the best views can be hidden by fog. Food is available at stops along the way. Certain stops have no road access, so if you get off you are waiting for the next train.

This fascinating journey takes an entire day, leaving you with two options at the end. Many people stay over in Manakara and take a car back to Fianar in the morning, resuming their journey down the RN7. A better option is to spend another day in Manakara, as it has much to offer, including some excellent accommodation, the beach, and the Canal des Pangalanes (see p65).

For a more detailed history of the railway and the regions through which it passes, pick up a booklet called *The FCE: A Traveler's Guide*, by Karen Schoonmaker Freudenberger. It's available in English and French for Ar6000 at the station.

TOURS, GUIDES & NATIONAL PARKS

If you are planning your own itinerary in Madagascar and would like a tour of a national park, your first stop should not generally be a tour company, but the local office of Madagascar National Parks (MNP). The park office is a reservoir of knowledgeable local guides. They can arrange everything you need, from an hour's walk to a multiday trek, on the spot (although for multiday treks it may take an hour or two to procure food). They are also much less expensive than many tour companies, which can charge 200% to 300% more.

If you're travelling independently, organising your own expedition can be part of the fun of a national park outing and, with the MNP, easy and relatively inexpensive to accomplish.

Getting There & Away

Air

There is an airport in Fianar, but no regularly scheduled flights.

Taxi-Brousse & Minibus

Frequent taxis-brousses connect Fianarantsoa with Ambositra (Ar7000, three hours), Antsirabe (Ar14,000, six hours) and Antananarivo (Ar18,000, eight to nine hours).

Minibuses also go daily to Ambalavao (Ar2000, two hours), Ranohira (Ar9000, seven hours) and on to Tuléar (Ar25,000, 11 hours). Departures from Fianarantsoa to Tuléar are at around 5pm, arriving at about 4am the next day. Heading east there are multiple vehicles daily between Fianarantsoa and Ranomafana (Ar4000, two hours) and Manakara (Ar13,000, eight hours).

Train

Fianarantsoa is connected to Manakara on the eastern coast by the famous FCE (Fianarantsoa–Côte Est) railway. Departures from Fianarantsoa are scheduled for Tuesday, Thursday and Saturday at 7am, and from Manakara on Sunday, Wednesday and Friday at 7am. There are frequent delays and cancellations, making it wise to visit the station the day before to confirm. The trip can take anywhere from seven to 12 hours. Tickets cost Ar20,000/14,000 in 1st/2nd class; the only actual difference is that 1st-class seats and windows are bigger and it's less crowded. First class is generally only used by tourists. Advance reservations are Ar10,000 more.

Getting Around

Taxis operate day and night. The daytime price anywhere in the city is usually Ar2000, and Ar2500 to Ar3000 at night.

Villages and destinations in the surrounding area are served by *taxi-be* (minivans), which have route numbers marked in their front window. The fare to all destinations is Ar300; departures are from the taxi-brousse station.

Around Fianarantsoa

There are a few sites to the north of Fianar that can all be visited in the same half-day trip.

Maromby Trappist Monastery MONASTERY
(www.maromby.org; Maromby; admission Ar1000; 9.30-11.30am & 3-4.30pm) This is an interesting stop, as the monk on duty will give you a personal tour (pray he speaks your language). The monastery is the contemplative side of a larger religious community with a neighbouring active order. The Trappists here do what they have for centuries, making wine (red and white, and flavoured aperitifs) and honey, as well as growing a lot of their own food. The church, with its striking stone altar and parquet ceiling and floors, is particularly interesting as it reflects the integration of Christianity and Malagasy culture. Its doors were carved by the brothers. The monastery is located 7km northeast of Fianarantsoa. A taxi is about Ar10,000 return.

Sahambavy Tea Estate PLANTATION
(admission Ar7000; 7am-4pm Mon-Fri, to 9.30am Sat) Ever wonder where tea comes from? This local plantation will take you through the entire life cycle, from the fields to the processing plant to the free tasting at the end. It's a worthwhile trip, and unique in Madagascar. The tour is in French, but if you don't understand French, you can easily grasp the process (and if you have a driver, they may be able to translate).

The Tea Estate is the first exit on the RN7 about 15km north of Fianarantsoa (turn at the petrol station). You can also take a taxi-brousse, or take the train to Sahambavy station (the second stop after Fianar on the FCE railway) and walk about 500m.

Lazani Betsileo Winery WINERY

(☎75 901 27, 032 02 313 75; www.lazanibetsileo-vin.com; admission Ar3000) There are several vineyards in the Fianarantsoa area, but this is the most popular to tour. We don't vouch for the finished product, but wine aficionados will undoubtedly find this intelligently laid-out tour interesting. The vineyard is about 15km north of Fianarantsoa. Ring in advance, or else hunt down the man in the white coat.

Sleeping

TOP CHOICE **Lac Hôtel** HOTEL €€€

(☎75 959 06; www.lachotel.com; bungalows Ar70,000-130,000) One of Madagascar's many surprises, this well-executed boutique hotel just steps from the Sahambavy train station is a common stop for passengers coming back from the coast. It has extensive gardens, a winning French menu (set meals Ar25,000) and a variety of accommodation, including some real show-stoppers. The mini safari lodges perch on stilts over a lake, affording great views. Most interestingly, they are furnished with fantastic local carvings and fabrics to form a refined Malagasy style. In a country full of bungalows, these are some of the very best.

Manakara

POP 44,000

While Manakara is geographically on the east coast, virtually all travellers visit on a round-trip from Fianarantsoa, often by the famous FCE railway, making Manakara an important part of many a highlands itinerary. It is also a highly underrated destination that should not be overlooked. For those not planning on visiting the Canal des Pangalanes elsewhere, this is your chance. It can also be a welcome beach break from the highlands, particularly after trekking in the parks.

The town is innately interesting, as it is divided into two parts by the canal. The warm inland side, known as Tanambao, has a dynamic Caribbean vibe, with sandy streets, tin-roofed shacks and a buoyant daily market, while on the other side of the bridge lies the breezy seaside district of Manakara-Be, with its attractive waterfront accommodation. Furthermore, as a barrier beach, Manakara-Be stands astride ocean and canal, allowing you to experience two worlds at once. The entire region is easily traversed by *poussse-pousse*, but before setting off, note that many places go on siesta between noon and 3pm.

Tours

The primary tour guide in Manakara is **Ignace** (☎032 40 481 02, 033 08 947 74, 034 12 308 22; magnarobo@moov.mg), who can handle any request you throw at him. One standard offering is a full-day (8am to 5.30pm) **pirogue tour** of the canal for Ar40,000 per person. This includes visiting a vanilla plantation, and lunch (including lobster) at a natural ocean pool where you can swim. His English is limited, but an English-speaking guide can also be provided.

If you really want to strike out on your own you can rent **kayaks** (per hr Ar3000) at La Guinguette.

THE BETSILEO

The Betsileo, Madagascar's third-largest tribe, inhabit the *hauts plateaux* area around Fianarantsoa and Ambalavao. They only began viewing themselves as a nation after being invaded and conquered by the Merina in the early 19th century.

The Betsileo are renowned throughout Madagascar for their rice-cultivation techniques – they manage three harvests a year instead of the usual two, and their lands are marked by beautiful terracing and vivid shades of green in the rice paddy fields. Betsileo herdsmen are famous for their trilby hats and the blankets they wear slung in a debonair fashion around their shoulders. Betsileo houses are distinctively tall and square, constructed from bricks as red as the earth of the roads.

As well as the *famadihana*, which was adopted from the Merina after the unification of Madagascar, an important Betsileo belief centres on *hasina*, a force that is believed to flow from the land through the ancestors into the society of the living. Skilled traditional practitioners are thought to be able to manipulate *hasina* to achieve cures and other positive effects. The reverse of *hasina* is *hera*, which can result in illness and misfortune.

Manakara

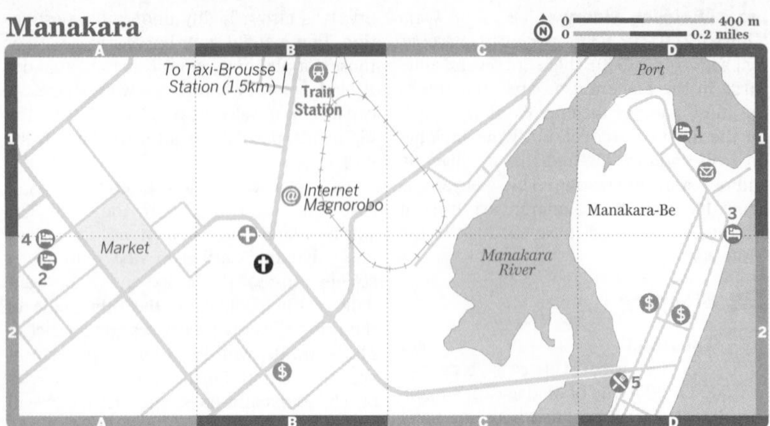

Sleeping & Eating

Tanambao has a number of serviceable concrete hotels with little to differentiate them except air-conditioning. In general it is much better to pay up a bit and stay on the beach, particularly in summer, when inland can be sweltering.

TOP CHOICE **Club Vanille** BUNGALOW €€
(☎72 210 23, 034 17 209 68; hotellavanillemanakara@yahoo.fr; Manakara-Be; bungalows Ar50,000) Madagascar breeds end-of-the-earth locations (see p167), and this is one of the better ones. Just don't mistake this satellite operation for the main Hotel Vanille in downtown Tanambao. You get here by crossing the bridge to the beach, turning right, and driving 8km down the peninsula. There you'll find some canal-side bungalows and a restaurant offering catches of the day and cold beer. Best of all, you are caught between the absolute roar of the surf on one side, and the placid canal on the other. It's a long way from town but perfect downtime. Shuttle service (Ar5000) available.

Délice de l'Orient Annex BUNGALOW €€
(☎72 217 34, 032 41 747 95; delicehotel@orange.mg; Manakara-Be; bungalows Ar65,000) Like the Vanille, make sure you don't confuse the Delice Hotel located in Tanambao with this superb annex on the beach, even though you must reserve through the former. It has a fantastic canal-side location with four waterfront bungalows that are the best in Manakara.

Manakara

Sleeping
1 Délice de l'Orient Annex D1
2 Les Flamboyants A2
3 Parthenay Club D1
4 Sidi Hotel A2

Eating
5 La Guinguette D2

Entertainment
Eden Sidi .... (see 4)

Parthenay Club BUNGALOW €€
(☎72 216 63, 034 29 803 14; Manakara-Be; bungalows Ar70,000) If you can overlook the perpetually empty pool front and centre, these tiki-hut bungalows set in a well-landscaped compound on the beach are a great way to enjoy the unique feeling of straddling both canal and sea. Bungalow 'CH' is right at the tip of a peninsula and the honeymooners' choice.

Les Flamboyants HOTEL €€
(☎72 216 77; lionelmanakara@dts.mg; Tanambao; d Ar20,000-25,000, bungalows Ar40,000, breakfasts Ar4000; @) This is a good-value hotel in the centre of Tanambao, with a shady 1st-floor terrace, fans and lots of new renovations. The attentive owner doubles as French consul.

Sidi Hotel HOTEL €€
(☎033 02 803 90; sidihotel@moov.mg; Tanambao; d Ar50,000-100,000; ❄) Big, pink, Floridian and concrete pretty much sums up the appearance of this U-shape monster with

drive-in courtyard in Tanambao. Rooms are noted for their iridescent bedspreads and occasional tub. The local disco, **Eden Sidi**, is here too.

La Guinguette FRENCH, MALAGASY €
(☎72 213 92; Manakara-Be; mains Ar8000-10,000; ⏰Wed-Mon) You can't miss this place, located at the base of the bridge in Manakara-Be. It's a great spot to sit and have a drink overlooking the canal, while the local fishers cast their nets. Or stay and enjoy the fresh seafood.

Information

Magnarobo (Tanambao; per min Ar50; ⏰8am-noon & 2-6pm Mon-Fri, 8am-noon Sat) is slow but the best option for internet. Manakara has several banks and ATMs to choose from.

Getting There & Away

TAXI-BROUSSE There are usually two taxis-brousses per day between Manakara and Ranomafana (Ar11,000, five hours), continuing to Fianarantsoa (Ar13,000, six hours). These leave at 7am and 3pm or 4pm. The taxi-brousse station is 2km north of town.

TRAIN Most travellers prefer to travel at least one way by train from Fianarantsoa; see p64 for details.

Getting Around

Take a *pousse-pousse* everywhere. Fares to Tanambao/Manakara-Be from the railway station are Ar1500/2000. These double at night.

Ambalavao

POP 35,000

Set amidst beautiful mountainous countryside with numerous boulder-like peaks, Ambalavao is like a charming French village reduced through years of neglect to a Wild West outpost. Some people find it beautiful. Others find it haunting. Everyone finds it interesting. And that's why you must go: because it is going to make you think.

The first thing you see when you approach is a massive Gothic cathedral towering over all else, as if parachuted in from the Loire Valley. This turns out to be in a state of long-term disrepair. Then, as you walk down the main street, you find it covered in blowing sand and lined by once-charming shops covered in grime and slowly succumbing to the elements, bearing testimony to some event that seems beyond explanation. Meanwhile people throng the street as if arriving for a party. All manner of highlands culture passes by, a fascinating distillation. It is as if you have entered a lively ghost town, one of many poignant results of postcolonial rule.

This is an easy place to see: all you have to do is get off the RN7, find the adjacent main street of the town, and walk from one end to the other. At some point amazement is guaranteed, for one reason or another.

Sights

Réserve d'Anja WILDLIFE RESERVE
(Iarintsena; admission Ar7000, guide fee per 2hr Ar8000) This nifty little 37 hectare reserve, about 7km from town, encompasses three mountain-size boulders ('the three sisters') ringed at the base by a narrow forest full of ring-tailed lemurs. You reach the lemurs by passing through a narrow cave into a secluded area that feels like a private world. There are excellent views as you navigate the surrounding rocks.

The reserve is a completely community-run initiative, one that promotes regional tourism, creates jobs and teaches the value of conservation. It has also been highly successful, hosting 10,000 tourists a year, so you are unlikely to be alone, particularly from April to November. Certain climbing options are not for the faint-hearted. A good English-speaking guide is Daniel.

You can also stay here in some new **bungalows** (d Ar50,000). The incredible stars and the sound of calling lemurs might well be worth it. The park is located about 12km south of Ambalavao on the RN7. To get here take a taxi-brousse south and ask the driver to stop at the **park office**.

FREE **Fabrique de Papier Antaimoro** ARTS CENTRE
(Antaimoro Paper Factory; ☎75 340 01; ⏰7.30-11.30am & 1-5pm) Located behind the Hôtel Aux Bougainvillées, this factory showcases the production of a unique kind of paper, made from the bark of a local bush, which has flowers pressed into it. Antaimoro cards, envelopes, and picture frames are all for sale.

Zebu Market MARKET
Ambalavao hosts the largest zebu market in the country every Wednesday and Thursday morning, with tough, wizened herdsmen walking from as far away as Tuléar to sell their cattle. Located about a mile south of town on the RN7, it starts well before dawn.

Soalandy ARTS CENTRE
(☎033 14 987 45; RN7; ⏰7.30am-5pm) The fascinating process of silk production is laid out here, with a gift shop to boot. Soalandy is in the purple building on the right just as you enter town from the north, across from Le Tropik Hotel.

Tours

Adrien (☎032 64 822 45; adrientrek@yahoo.fr) is a well-known guide based at the Hôtel Aux Bougainvillées. He runs a variety of all-inclusive tours in Parc National d'Andringitra, as well as a new five-day hike from Ambalavao to Manakara for Ar130,000 per person per day.

There is an **MNP office** about a mile north on the RN7, but if planning a trip to Andringitra, it is best to use the one there.

Sleeping & Eating

TOP CHOICE **Résidence du Betsileo** HOTEL €€
(☎033 02 863 89, 032 44 285 60; residencedubetsileo@gmail.com; d/tr Ar34,000/44,000) This charming bargain is the best place to stay – and eat – in town. Located in a renovated store right on Main St, it has great views out back, and a nice patio restaurant, too (mains Ar7000 to Ar10,000). Choose the off-street rooms.

Hôtel Aux Bougainvillées HOTEL €€
(☎75 340 01; ragon@wanadoo.mg; d/tr/q Ar45,000/60,000/85,000, camping per tent Ar20,000) Draped in its colourful namesake plant, this hotel has a bit of character. The rooms are comfortable and clean, but only the more expensive ones have hot water and private bathrooms. There's a decent restaurant (mains Ar10,000), which is popular with tour groups at lunch.

Tropik Hotel HOTEL €
(☎033 14 183 83; d/tr Ar27,000/36,000) This basic concrete hotel has clean rooms enlivened by blinding pastels.

Getting There & Away

Ambalavao lies 56km south of Fianarantsoa. The town has direct taxi-brousse connections with Fianarantsoa (Ar3000, 1½ hours), Ihosy (Ar5000, two hours) and Ilakaka (Ar6000, five hours). For destinations further north, you'll have to go to Fianarantsoa first.

Parc National d'Andringitra & the Tsaranoro Valley

Andringitra *(An-dring-i-tra)* is the greatest national park south of Tana, and perhaps in Madagascar. It encompasses a majestic central mountain range with two gorgeous

WORTH A TRIP

THE HIGHLANDS HOMESTAY

A common ecotourism option in Madagascar is a homestay, in which you are offered the chance to stay with a family in a local village. Accommodation generally includes a bucket shower and composting toilet, a straw mattress, and traditional rice-based meals. There may be little or no English spoken. You may also get the chance to participate in traditional crafts, and to participate in multiday treks. There are two popular destinations, and the best time to visit is May to September.

Zafimaniry villages A cluster of villages southeast of Ambositra that are known for their woodcarving, and a Unesco World Heritage Site. The best villages to visit are Sakaivo, Falairivo and Antetezandotra. You will need to go to the largest and otherwise missable village, Antoetra, to hire a guide. Alternatively, speak with Maison des Guides in Ambositra (p55).

Ambohimahamasina This scenic area about 50km east of Ambalavao, in the rainforest corridor linking Ranomafana and Andringitra national parks, contains many Betsileo villages connected by walking trails. A local ecotourism initiative named FIZAM combines homestays with walking itineraries, including an ascent to the summit of the sacred mountain Ambondrombe with French- and English-speaking guides. For more information contact the FIZAM office in Ambohimahamasina (must be done in person) or their sponsor, the NGO **Ny Tanintsika** (☎75 512 43, 032 40 527 38; nytanintsika@yahoo.fr; Fianarantsoa), which has been set up by a Scottish charity, **Feedback Madagascar** (www.feedbackmadagascar.org). The Maison des Guides in Fianar and Ambositra also handle this destination.

Parc National d'Andringitra & the Tsaranoro Valley

valleys on either side, the Namoly and the Tsaranoro (sometimes called the Sahanambo, for the river that runs through it) forming a paradise for walkers and climbers. One can easily spend a week hiking in this area. There are spectacular views in all directions, 100km of well-developed hiking trails, excellent accommodation, interesting villages, plus three extraordinary peaks: Pic Boby (Imarivolanitra), at 2658m the second-highest peak in the country; the Tsaranoro Massif, which reaches 1910m, including an 800m vertical column considered to be one of the most challenging climbs in the world; and the great stump of Pic Dondy (2195m). The latter two form the Gates to Southern Madagascar, separating the Betsileo and Bara regions.

Now here's the most amazing part of all: there is hardly anyone here! For various reasons relating to its distance from the RN7, the state of the roads, and the relatively young age of the park, which has emerged during a difficult period of political instability, Andringitra currently sees only 1200 visitors a year. Imagine having Yosemite to yourself, and you're not far off the mark. This rare combination of natural wonder and unspoiled seclusion makes Andringitra a world-class off-the-beaten-track destination. But perhaps we shouldn't have said that.

Technically most of the Tsaranoro Valley lies outside the park boundaries, but when people speak of Andringitra they tend to imply this entire region. There are two ways into the region, the western entrance in the Tsaranoro Valley, and the eastern entrance in the Namoly Valley. The main MNP office is in the Namoly Valley, making this the most common starting point for treks.

Park Fees & Guides

The **MNP office** (☎75 340 81, 033 12 340 81, 034 49 400 96; www.parcs-madagascar.com) in the Namoly Valley has all you need to trek

PARC NATIONAL D'ANDRINGITRA

Best time to visit October to November during orchid bloom; park closed January to March.

Key highlight Sunrise from the summit of Pic Boby.

Wildlife Ring-tailed lemurs, multicoloured grasshoppers.

Habitats High plateau, meadows, rocky peaks, some primary rainforest (Imaitso).

Gateway town Ambalavao; head from there to either park entrance.

Transport options Private car, transfer to Camp Catta, intermittent taxis-brousses.

Things you should know Water freezes at night during winter.

into the park, including **entry permits** (per 1/2/3/4 days Ar10,000/15,000/20,000/25,000). Here you can hire guides, porters, cooks, and equipment. Food can be arranged too, if you call one day ahead. Otherwise arrive with your own provisions, which will further give you your own choice of meals. Don't bring any pork as it is *fady* (taboo) in the park. Guide fees start at Ar15,000 and cooks and porters about half that, with prices dependent on how long you want to hike.

In the winter, temperatures fall into the cold-as-hell zone, reaching as low as -7°C at night. You will definitely need extra-warm clothing and a good sleeping bag if camping during the winter. If renting a sleeping bag, confirm it is sufficient. The park is officially closed from January to March, when heavy rains make access difficult. Afternoon mists are common, and you should be prepared for bad weather at any time of year. If you are climbing Pic Boby, you will need a flashlight with several hours of battery life.

The Tsaranoro Valley has a tiny **MNP office** in Morarano, near Camp Catta, where you can buy a permit and find a guide – if staff are present. Guides tend to look for business at Camp Catta too.

Sights & Activities

Wildlife

Andringitra is mainly about hiking in spectacular scenery; it is not primarily a wildlife destination. Ironically, 14 lemur species have been identified here, more than in any other park in Madagascar, but sightings by visitors are rare since most of their habitat is outside the tourism zone. Ring-tails are the most commonly seen. The park's rich flora includes more than 30 species of orchid, which bloom mainly in October and November.

Hiking

The national park proper offers 100km of trails that traverse a variety of habitats and offer fantastic trekking. There are five main circuits catering to various abilities, but if you are going to come here, and are in good shape, take the **Imarivolanitra Trail** to the summit of Pic Boby to get the full Andringitra experience. You will need at least two days for this, but better to take three so you can explore the Tsaranoro Valley and exit the other side of the park rather than retrace your steps.

Other circuits include the easy **Asaramanitra** (6km, about four hours), which includes waterfalls and a cave, and the scenic **Diavolana** (13km, six to seven hours) which is the next best choice after Imarivolanitra, as it takes in much of the plateau beneath the mountains. The best route for lemur-spotting is **Imaitso** (14km, about eight hours) which goes through the eastern forests. **Isahavato** is a long (12km, 15 hours) trek into a zone of rare palm trees with a natural pool. Details of the various routes are available from the park office and website.

Reaching the Tsaranoro Valley requires a further trek across a pass through the central range and down, crossing the park boundary. Here there are three major trails to villages along the valley floor and around the Gates of the South. The presence of Pic Dondy and the Tsaranoro Massif are impressive from all angles. See the trail maps at Camp Catta reception for further information.

Sleeping

Camp Catta LODGE €€

(☎75 923 58, 033 15 347 19; camping tent rental Ar24,000, bungalows Ar60,000, without bathroom Ar48,000, 5-person chalets Ar144,000) This the place to stay in the Tsaranoro Valley, with a breathtaking location at the foot of the Massif, direct access to a pristine forest at its base, and quality accommodation and food. It's not cheap, but you are a long way from anywhere. Transfers available from Fianarantsoa (Ar175,000) and Ambalavao (Ar125,000). You will find the manager strumming his guitar at the entrance, and well he should.

THE BEST OF ANDRINGITRA

The best way to do Andringitra is on the **Imarivolanitra Trail**. Enter through the Namoly Valley, summit Pic Boby, descend into the Tsaranoro, and exit through Morarano, with an overnight at Camp Catta. First, you begin at the Namoly park office, and arrange your trek. Then you ascend to the final camp. This entails hiking up 1000m or so until you reach a high plateau that hugs the rocky skyline for miles. It's a generally gentle climb, with a few steep 50m ascents, that takes four hours. The camp is by a stream, so you can fall asleep while listening to a waterfall beneath the stars. Awake early, and depart by flashlight at 4am for a two-hour trek to the summit, which is not where you think. When you reach the top of the skyline, with the sky beginning to lighten, you finally see what looks like Gibraltar sitting on top. This strenuous last leg takes you to the roof of Madagascar, just in time for sunrise. Here you stand astride the entire island, a sea of clouds on one side, and an unbroken vista on the other. Beneath a cairn lies a metal box, where you can leave a handwritten note behind.

Now it's back to the camp for breakfast, and onwards to new territory. You walk along the flat plateau for hours, breathing in the finest scenery. The sky is huge, the ridgeline dramatic. After crossing over the mountains through a deep pass, the Tsaranoro Valley comes into view, a grand vista. You pass through an alluring desert landscape, with the unforgettable sight of the great Massif's vertical drop ahead. Then it is down, down until you reach the valley floor, and the first few villages, where the local children have never even seen a pair of binoculars. Finally it's on to Camp Catta for dinner, with the Gates of the South towering above. The next day you can hike more of the valley, as you wish, before heading back to the RN7. Unforgettable.

Gîte HOSTEL **€**
(☎75 340 81; dm Ar5000, s/d Ar13,000/30,000) This rustic and incredibly scenic farmhouse with a fireplace and great wraparound porches in the middle of the Namoly Valley, about 5km or so from the trailheads, is just what you imagined a mountain hostel should be. One walks out into the arms of an encircling skyline of rock. Self-catering kitchen with cook on site. Advance reservations recommended.

Park Campgrounds CAMPGROUND **€**
(camping per tent Ar5000) The park circuits contain five wilderness camping grounds with roof-only sites, a cooking hut, running water and toilets. Tents can be rented at the park office.

Tranogasy LODGE **€€**
(☎033 14 306 78; www.tranogasy.com; d Ar60,000) These chalets near the Namoly park entrance are a great place to stay if you want to arrive in the afternoon, arrange your trek, and start off the next morning. The mountain valley setting is incredible.

Tsara Camp LODGE **€€€**
(☎22 530 70, 033 14 251 77; www.tsaracamp-madagascar.com; per person incl meals Ar155,000) If Camp Catta is full, you can default here. It, too, has an awesome location in the centre of the Tsaranoro Valley, but the ambience isn't as nice, it's pricey, and full board is mandatory (what if you wish to eat at Camp Catta?).

ℹ Getting There & Away

NAMOLY VALLEY The Namoly Valley is a nearly three-hour drive from Ambalavao, with some iffy bridges, but it is also a scenic trip through rocky hill country full of small villages, rice paddies, and smiling children, and part of the whole experience. We met only one other car on the way.

There is a toll of Ar3000 to Ar4000. The road has deteriorated and requires a 4WD. Sturdy taxis-brousses leave Ambalavao for Namoly on Tuesday and Thursday from the western side of the market.

TSARANORO VALLEY The Tsaranoro Valley entrance is further from Ambalavao (60km) but takes the same amount of time (three hours) as part of the way is paved. There is at least one toll of Ar3000 to Ar4000.

Southern Madagascar

Includes »

Best Places to Eat

» Isalo Rock Lodge (p76)

» Corto Maltese (p82)

» Chez Cecile (p86)

» Anakao Ocean Lodge (p90)

» Auberge Peter Pan (p90)

Best Places to Stay

» Bakuba (p82)

» Anakao Ocean Lodge (p90)

» Le Relais de la Reine (p76)

» Le Relais d'Ambola (p91)

» Satrana Lodge (p76)

Why Go?

Southern Madagascar is a wide-open adventure among some of nature's most dramatic forms. The stark desert canyons of Isalo rival those of Arizona. The western coast offers a massive coral reef, the fifth largest in the world. The cape is the last stop before Antarctica. And miles and miles of spiny forest contain the strangest and most formidable plants on Earth. There are also two scruffy cities, Tuléar (Toliara) and Fort Dauphin (Taolagnaro), but that is not why you came. The question is how to tackle a region of this size. For many, a lodge in Isalo and a slice of beach are enough. But for others, the south is the perfect recipe for off-road exploration, an episode of *Top Gear* you can write yourself. There are thousands of kilometres of dirt tracks, many of them reasonably good, with no one on them. Renting a 4WD isn't cheap, but everything else is, so get your expedition underway.

When to Go

Tuléar

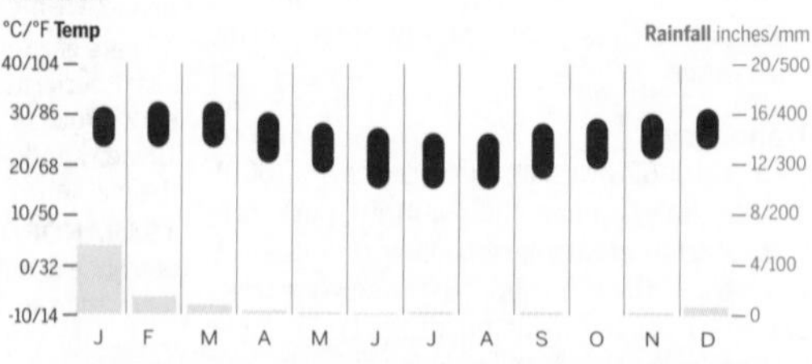

Jul–Sep Whale-watching season on the Great Reef.

Sep–Nov Ideal four-wheeling season.

Dec–Mar Rainy season makes travel difficult; many dirt roads impassable.

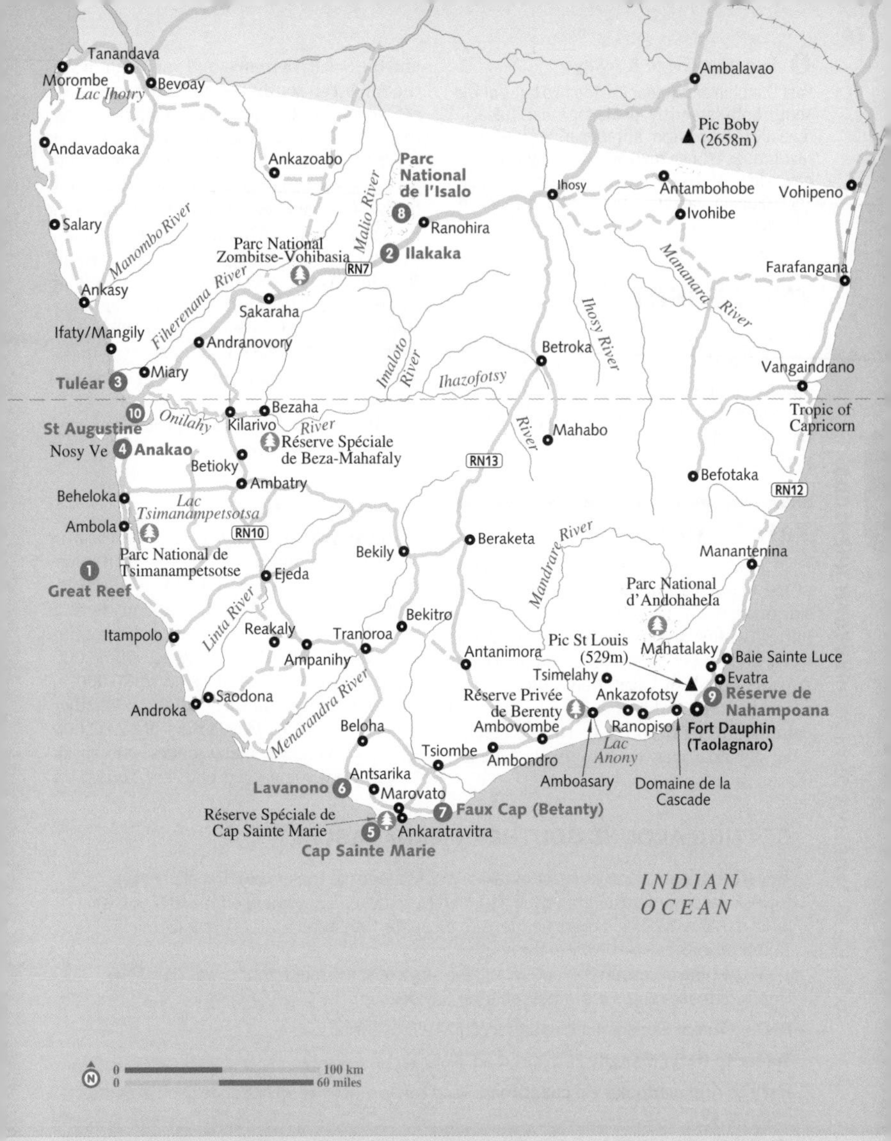

Southern Madagascar Highlights

1. Snorkel, dive, fish, or paddle the **Great Reef** (p78)
2. Visit the sapphire mines of **Ilakaka** (p77): that ring will never look the same
3. Drive the coastal sand track through the spiny forest north of **Tuléar** (p84)
4. Arrive in style: take the speedboat from Tuléar to **Anakao** (p89)
5. Stand at the very tip of the 'eighth continent' at **Cap Sainte Marie** (p92)
6. Hang out with the surfers at **Lavanono** (p91)
7. See elephant bird eggshell fragments in **Faux Cap** (p92)
8. Take a dip in the Piscine Naturelle at **Parc National de l'Isalo** (p74)
9. Say hi to the lemurs at **Réserve de Nahampoana** (p96)
10. Lunch by the mouth of the Onilahy River in the remote town of **St Augustine** (p89)

Getting There & Away

Fort Dauphin and Tuléar are the two hubs of the south, both served by Air Madagascar. Tuléar is easily reached from Antananarivo (Tana) by taxi-brousse (bush taxi) or private car via the paved RN7, and is the gateway to the Great Reef. Fort Dauphin and the cape can only be reached by 4WD.

THE DESERT

Heading south from Ambalavao, you know you've left the highlands when a vast plain swallows the RN7. This mostly empty desert harbours one great national park, and a nearby sapphire boomtown. They make a perfect stop on the way to Tuléar.

Parc National de l'Isalo

Isalo is like a museum dedicated to the art of the desert canyon. Canyons full of yellow savannah grass, bone-dry canyons, sculpted buttes, white-washed canyons, vertical rock walls, and best of all, deep canyon floors with streams and lush vegetation, and pools for swimming. All of this changes with the light, culminating in extraordinary sunsets beneath a big sky. Take away the lemurs, the baobabs, and the Sakalava tombs, and you might be in the American southwest. Add all this to easy access off the RN7, and you understand why this is Madagascar's most visited park, even if it is not our top choice. At more than 80,000 hectares, it's also a large park, so if you want to go off on your own there is plenty of room for exploration, including week-long hikes. The park is served by the small town of Ranohira, which contains the park office and a handful of hotels and restaurants, but don't stop there: resorts extend all along the park's southern border, including some of the finest in the country, making this a great chance to indulge yourself.

Isalo can get very hot during the day. Bring sunscreen, a hat, and enough food and water for your visit.

Park Fees & Guides

The **MNP Office** (☎033 13 172 58; ⏲7am-5pm) is an innocuous building facing the main intersection in the centre of Ranohira. You can arrange a mandatory guide and itinerary here; a map of all the current routes is on display. Entry fees are Ar25,000/37,000/40,000/50,000 for 1/2/3/4 days. Guide fees are Ar20,000 to Ar30,000 per circuit, depending on whether you go by foot or car. Porters are Ar13,000 per day. There are many guides who speak English, but some good ones are **Toussaint**

GETTING AROUND SOUTHERN MADAGASCAR

Travel in cities is an easy matter of taxi or *pousse-pousse* (rickshaw). Travel between towns is another matter entirely. If you wish to go by road anywhere off the RN7 you will need either a 4WD or, if there happens to be public transport, a very strong stomach. Taxi-brousses can be brutal in the south.

At the time of research (September) the state of some major routes was as follows (many of these routes are impassable in rainy season):

RN7 to Tuléar Excellent paved surface, no 4WD necessary.

Tuléar to Ifaty/Mangily Firm dirt road, 4WD in rain.

Ifaty to Andavadoaka via coast road Sand track, mostly good but deep sand in spots, requires 4WD.

Ifaty to Andavadoaka via RN9 Reportedly worse than coast road.

Tuléar to Itampolo via coast road Excellent sand track, but requires 4WD.

Itampolo to Ampanihy via Androka Very bad, often rocky road, confusing tracks, maps not accurate. Use local guide.

Androka to Lavanono via coast road Impassable at Menarandra River; use RN10.

Ampanihy to Ambovombe Improved dirt road, particularly good on first half.

Ambovombe to Ihosy Variable dirt road rutted by *camions-brousses* (large trucks). Ambovombe to Antinimore has deteriorated badly, as has Betroka to Ihosy.

Ambovombe to Fort Dauphin Terrible road, a deteriorated paved surface with craters worthy of the moon.

(☎032 43 831 88), **Albert** (☎034 63 971 11), **Rolland** (☎033 08 437 94) and **Parson** (☎034 12 241 84). It is customary to tip the guide when you are through; 10% is the norm. If you wish to take a car to certain trailheads, your guide can arrange this.

Sights

FREE **Maison de l'Isalo** MUSEUM
(⏲7am-6pm) This kid-friendly museum about the history, culture, and geology of the park is a bit underwhelming, as it occupies one room in a much larger building. It's free, though, and the only museum around, so if you are driving by it's worth a stop.

Rock Formations ROCK FORMATION
If you like finding figures in stone, **La Reine de l'Isalo** (the Queen of Isalo) sits about 3km south of the museum, on the left hand side of the road. Keep on going and you'll come to another rock formation, **La Fenêtre de l'Isalo**, a natural window that affords an interesting view over the plain. It's a popular place to watch the sunset.

Activities

Wildlife

Although animal life isn't the park's most prominent feature, there are some interesting lemur species to watch out for, including grey mouse, ring-tailed and brown lemurs, and Verreaux's sifaka. There are more than 50 bird species as well. The park is covered with dry grassland or sparse, low deciduous woodland. Near streams and in the lush pockets of forest in the deeper canyons, there are ferns, pandanus and feathery palm trees. At ground level in drier areas, look for the yellow flowering *Pachypodium rosulatum* (especially beautiful in September and October), which resembles a miniature baobab tree, and is often called 'elephant's foot'.

Circuits

There are numerous circuits in the park, which can be combined in various ways. The length of time they require depends on whether you take a car to the trailhead, as listed here; otherwise you must walk from Ranohira, which is a long way away in some cases.

Malaso Mostly rocky landscapes; 7km by car, 4½ to six hour hike, somewhat difficult.

Piscine Naturelle The most popular trail. Short and easy trek to a beautiful natural pool. Occasionally crowded; 3km by car, 3km on foot.

Parc National de l'Isalo

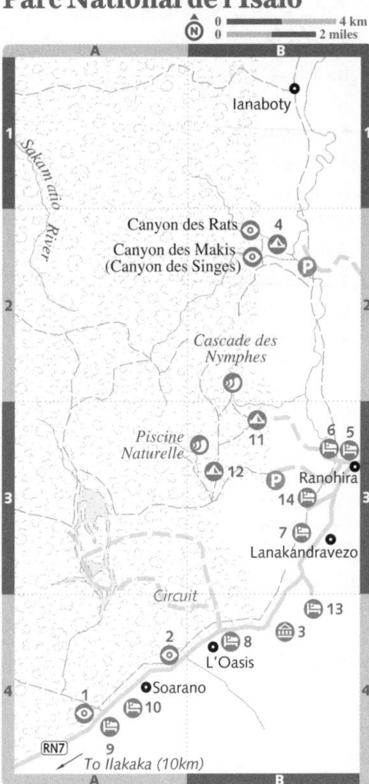

Parc National de l'Isalo

Sights

1 La Fenêtre de l'Isalo A4
2 La Reine de l'Isalo A4
3 Maison d'Isalo B4

Sleeping

4 Canyon des Makis Camping Ground B2
5 Chez Alice B3
6 Hotel Berny B3
7 Isalo Ranch B3
8 Isalo Rock Lodge B4
9 Jardin du Roy A4
10 Le Relais de la Reine A4
11 Namaza Camping Ground B3
12 Piscine Naturelle Camping Ground B3
13 Satrana Lodge B4
14 Toiles de l'Isalo B3

PARC NATIONAL DE L'ISALO

Best time to visit May–June or September–October

Key highlight Piscine Naturelle

Wildlife Sifaka, *Pachypodium*

Habitats Dry desert rock, spring-fed oases

Gateway town Ranohira

Transport options Taxi-brousse or car (4WD in park)

Things you should know While the luxury resorts are expensive for Madagascar, they are a bargain compared to other parts of the world.

Namaza Follows a stream through some deep gorges to a high waterfall, the Cascade de Nymphes; 3km by car, somewhat difficult 2km hike.

Falls of Anjofo A new trail. Hike by river's edge to two waterfalls; 27km by car, somewhat difficult 3km hike.

Canyons Takes in the Canyon des Makis (aka Canyon des Singes), the premier lemur-spotting area, and the Canyon de Rats burial area; 15km drive, easy 2km hike.

Grand Tour An 80km, six- to seven-day hike that takes in as much as the park can offer, including the Portuguese Grotto, a picturesque cave some 30m long. The way to get away from it all.

4WD Circuit Takes you out into the savannah and to the edge of some canyons, with stops at some amateurish trails. Not the best way to see the park.

Sleeping & Eating

Accommodation extends westward from Ranohira, along the southern border of the park. You can't go wrong with any of the premier properties here. Dining is done exclusively in hotels, but the quality is very high everywhere.

TOP CHOICE Le Relais de la Reine BOUTIQUE HOTEL €€€
(☎22 336 23; www.lerelaisdelareine.com; d €80, bungalows €70; @ 🏊) This hotel has the perfect name, because it is indeed the queen of properties in this area. Beautifully designed, it sits among canyons with a stately elegance, wedded perfectly to its site, with a castle-like feel that's not heavy or formidable. On the contrary, there is an energy here that elevates you. The gracious family that owns it understands the nature of hospitality from entry to exit. There are all the usual accoutrements one would expect from a property at this level, including pools, tennis, a fine restaurant (mains from €10) and stylish bar, but of note is the private airfield, the spa with its long menu of relaxation treatments, and the equestrian centre for sunset gallops across the savannah. What is truly surprising is the more-than-reasonable price.

Satrana Lodge LODGE €€€
(☎034 14 260 87; satranalodge@yahoo.fr; d €75; 🏊) This wonderful new lodge beautifully situated beneath a range of sandstone cliffs has a majestic pool with endless desert views, a classy restaurant (dinner set menus €14) with live music, atmospheric safari-tent rooms (albeit without sound-proofing) with beautiful writing desks, and fine woodwork throughout. The owners get an A+ for creativity everywhere, including an outdoor astronomy bar that makes for an unforgettable desert night. With evening drink in hand, you use a computer screen to zoom in on a chart of the galaxy, the adjacent telescope whirrs...and there you are.

Isalo Rock Lodge LODGE €€€
(☎22 328 60; www.isalorocklodge.com; s/d/f incl breakfast €104/114/150; ❄ 🏊) If you prefer contemporary design, another magnificent option is this stylish hotel, with a beautiful terrace overlooking sandstone formations, a spa and fitness room, a rare conference room, and a fluorescent pool with ever-changing colours. The restaurant serves works of art (breakfast/lunch/dinner €6/14/16). There's a walking trail with a natural pool, and a steep ascent to a viewpoint at the summit of a nearby formation. A sharp manager ensures perfection in-house, but the website needs an overhaul.

Chez Alice BUNGALOW €
(☎032 04 042 22, 032 02 055 68; camping with tent Ar6000, paillotte Ar25,000, d/tr/q bungalow Ar35,000/45,000/55,000) A rough drive in hides this convivial backpacker's hangout and budget gem conveniently located near the centre of Ranohira. Run by the irrepressible Alice, who would otherwise be running an Old West saloon, there are bun-

galows of various types and prices, with the *paillottes* being the best deal, even if they look like termite mounds. The restaurant is a super place to hang out, and the food (mains Ar6500, breakfast Ar5000) ain't bad either, partner. If you're ridin' the range, they'll pack a picnic (Ar8000), too.

Jardin du Roy BOUTIQUE HOTEL €€€
(☎22 351 65; www.lejardinduroy.com; bungalow €100; ❄) This new property shares amenities with the adjacent Relais de la Reine, and is owned by the same family of hoteliers. They have put extraordinary work into creating unique stone bungalows, including custom hand-crafted furniture, and all rooms are air-conditioned. Like its sister property, it is situated within sandstone formations, but it's not as well placed; the lawn is vast, and the buildings a touch heavy.

Isalo Ranch BUNGALOW €€
(☎26 011 11; www.isalo-ranch.com; d Ar87,000) While not presenting well from the road, the sand pathways of this lodge tie its bungalows together into a welcoming little village, aided by a shady and cosy restaurant with an international menu (set menus Ar25,000).

Toiles de L'Isalo BUNGALOW €€
(☎22 245 34, 33 11 025 25; www.hotel-toiles-isalo.com; d incl breakfast Ar65,000, tr Ar75,000; ≋) Another series of bungalows with a pool and central restaurant overlooking the sandstone cliffs. Cheaper than Isalo Ranch, but showing more wear.

Park Camp Sites CAMPGROUND €
(camping Ar5000) There are several camp sites in and near the park, including **Canyon des Makis**, **Piscine Naturelle** and the entrance to the **Namaza** circuit. Piscine Naturelle is best equipped with showers, toilets, sheltered dining and a large cooking area. Camping elsewhere in the park is possible if you are going on a longer trek, but you'll need to obtain permission from the MNP office (p74).

Hotel Berny HOTEL €
(☎75 801 76; http://hotel-ranohira-ihosy-isalo.lagrandeile.com; d & tr Ar62,000) We only stood back in amazement when the owner of this more-than-eclectic establishment, the aging mayor of Ranohira and a national institution, began his tour by taking us to his homemade sewage treatment plant. And yet, if one overlooks the front yard, with its forlorn vehicles, piles of firewood, totem poles, ancient gas pumps and car radiator sculpture, one finds a large stone hotel whose interior is immaculate, with Tintin toilet seats and zebu horn paper holders to help keep you amused. Meanwhile, Berny's adjoining restaurant (open breakfast, lunch and dinner) is the best in Ranohira, with hearty home-cooked meals at a reasonable price. Go figure.

ℹ Information

There are no internet cafes. The Relais de la Reine is the only hotel with high-speed internet access.

There are no banks or ATMs in Ranohira. The nearest bank is in Ihosy, 91km away. Be sure to ask if your hotel takes credit cards.

For more planning advice, author recommendations and insider tips on Parc National de l'Isalo, head to www.lonelyplanet.com/madagascar/southern-madagascar/parc-national-de-lisalo.

ℹ Getting There & Away

For points north, you may be lucky enough to find a taxi-brousse travelling between Tuléar and Antananarivo with an empty seat. You can always ask around in the hotels to see if any empty tourist vehicles are going back to Antananarivo, too. Each morning one or two taxis-brousses connect Ranohira directly with Ihosy, 91km to the east (Ar20,000, two hours), from where there are more options.

Public transport from Tuléar generally arrives in Ranohira between 10am and 1pm, while vehicles from the north usually arrive before 10am.

Ilakaka

POP 25,000

Ilakaka is the perfect setting for a James Bond movie. Driving through the middle of nowhere about half an hour west of Ranohira, you come upon a sapphire boomtown that has spontaneously erupted astride the RN7. The main street is lined with ramshackle structures selling provisions for the miners, from shovels to cell phones. Side streets are lined with gem buyers in shaded huts and women with painted faces squatting on the pavement organising piles of stones by quality. The highlight is the nearby mining area, where hand-dug mines pock-mark the earth (see boxed text, p78). One can imagine 007 running across this landscape pursued by the henchman of some evil gem lord.

In any case, you have to see this. By accident it has become one of the more fascinating sights in Madagascar, all the more so because it appears completely unconscious of the fact. The gem dealer **Color Line** (☎033 73 252 13, 033 14 737 57; colorlineilakaka@gmail.com; main street; ⏰7am-7pm) has caught on, however, and now offers **tours** (per person Ar16,000; ⏰7-10am & 1.30-3.30pm). Far from destroying the authenticity, it is fully part of it. It owns a secretive gem and fossil shop on the main street, where you will be thoroughly looked over upon entering and exiting. The manager, Philippe Ressigeac, is straight from central casting, with his Indiana Jones hat, trailing cigarette, and low-toned references to 'the stone'.

To really enter this scene yourself, attend the gem dealers' party starting at 1am every Friday night at Color Line's adjacent bar, known as **Al2O3** (the formula for sapphire, naturally). Coming into town from Ranohira, it's about a kilometre along on the left, near the mosque. We suggest parking nearby.

Ilakaka has long had a reputation for being dangerous, a reputation that seems to have been warranted in the past when the boom was hot, but has waned as it has tapered off into some kind of thin normality. You don't have anything to worry about here during the day, particularly during a tour, but we can't vouch for 3am, when the party ends. Travellers have reported encountering corruption here and some have had run-ins with police. But would Hollywood have it any other way? Round up the usual suspects!

Getting There & Away

If you are in Isalo and want to take the tour, call Color Line and it will arrange transport. Otherwise any taxi-brousse heading west on the RN7 will get you here. If you are driving west on the RN7, you will pass through town as well.

From Ilakaka, taxis-brousses leave every morning and afternoon for Tuléar and Ambalavao (Ar20,000, six hours), and sometimes continue to Fianarantsoa.

THE GREAT REEF

A great reef stretches over 450km along the southwestern coast of Madagascar, making it the fifth-largest coral reef in the world. It is the main attraction in the region, from Andavadoaka in the north to Itampolo in the south, with its own changing personality. Interestingly, no one knows what to call it. Some use 'the Great Reef of Tuléar', but that actually refers to a particular barrier reef off that city. So The Great Reef of Madagascar it is.

The Great Reef comes in three potential forms, a fringing reef close-in, a patch reef of coral heads, and an outer barrier reef. The latter creates very broad and shallow in-shore lagoons, and makes for dramatic scenery, with large waves crashing in the distance, forming a vibrant line of white. The beaches range from broken coral to spectacular white powder. There are many popular activities to pursue here: sunbathing, snorkelling, diving, fishing, whale-watching (July to September), surfing, and sailing among them. There are also several offshore islands that make for interesting outings.

The diving, however, can't compare with other spots in the West Indian Ocean, like Pemba, Mayotte, or northern Mozambique. In recent decades over-fishing, river runoff, and other human disturbances have degraded reef health, particularly in shallow, nearshore, and lagoonal reefs. The most remote

DON'T MISS

MINING THE OLD FASHIONED WAY

The sapphire mining process begins with a bore-hole large enough to lower a man 30m into the earth. If round stones are found, the signs of an ancient river bed, sapphires might be found as well. This leads to the digging of a second hole by the mining equivalent of a bucket brigade, one man shovelling to the next, and so on, for a very, very long time. If it rains, walls collapse and the digging begins anew. Some mines are dug by individual owners, while others are financed by groups of investors. Some yield valuable sapphires, others yield nothing. There have been enough of the former to create a sapphire rush in Ilakaka involving tens of thousands of people. In fact, Ilakaka sits on top of the biggest sapphire deposit in the world, all 4000 hectares of it, even though you will not see a single piece of mining machinery beyond a spade. Once you visit, you will never be able to look at a jewellery store the same way again. Just be careful what you are offered in the street. As the saying goes, 'the closer you get to the mine, the more synthetic you find'.

sites, particularly those further offshore, are in the best shape. In any case, divers are advised to thoroughly check over any rental dive equipment.

Each entry point to the reef has its own pros and cons to assess. There are several properties with spectacular natural locations – Salary Bay, Anakao Lodge, Manga Lodge, and Valahantsaka, to name a few – and some wonderful end-of-the-world spots, too, like Andavadoaka, St Augustine, and Ambola. There's an outstanding art hotel, Bakuba, and the best budget hotel south of Tana, Peter Pan (p90). On the downside, fresh water and electricity can be an issue, necessitating generators during limited hours and water conservation measures, and local villages tend to use the sea as a latrine. But the major problem, as ever, is transport. On the other hand, if it were easy to get to any of these places, you wouldn't be off the beaten path, would you?

Getting There and Away

Tuléar is the hub of the Great Reef. North of Tuléar, there is no public transportation after Mangily. With the exception of private planes, the northern hotels are all reached by private 4WD. Transfers can be arranged, but are expensive. Sometimes the more northern hotels are better reached by driving south from Morombé, but there is only irregular service there from Air Madagascar.

South of Tuléar, there are boat transfers to Anakao, which is a quick and wonderful way to arrive, but south of Anakao you need a private 4WD again, or *lots* of time. At the time of research a ferry service was due to begin soon across the Onilahy River south of Tuléar. It will shave a day's drive off a road trip to Anakao, making the rest of the southern reef much easier to reach.

Tuléar (Toliara)

POP 136,000

Tuléar is mostly known as a transit point. It has a bit of Antsirabe about it, with a sea of *pousse-pousse* bouncing down dusty lanes, and the same crumbling relics of the colonial past. But while few people see this as a vacation destination, it actually offers some interesting ways to spend your time, if you know where to look, most of it on the seafront. The concentration of travellers has bred some fascinating accommodation, and some actual nightlife, too. Add this to a somewhat raffish tropical ambiance fuelled by the local French expats, and you have the setting for your first novel. Do take taxis after 9pm.

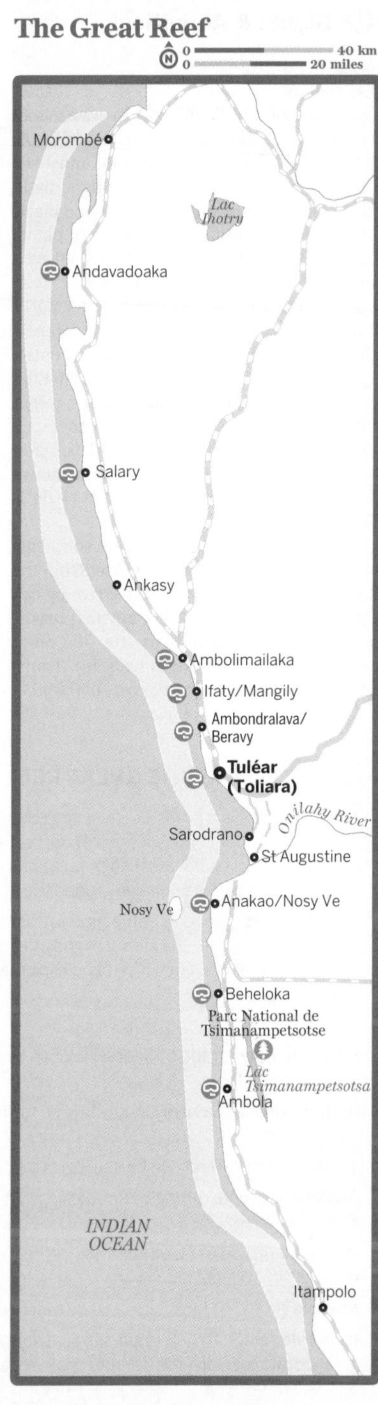

Sights & Activities

TOP CHOICE Arboretum d'Antsokay GARDENS

(☎032 02 600 15, 034 07 600 15; www.antsokayarboretum.org; admission incl guide Ar10,000; ⏲7.30am-5.30pm) This is the one must-see attraction in Tuléar. It is essentially a distillation of the entire spiny forest in one place, a fantastic collection of 900 species of plants that will fascinate anyone. Established by a Swiss botanist and conservationist in 1980, it is also a model for how much larger parks should be run, even though it is only 40 hectares. There is a classy interpretation centre, a small museum, self-guided tours in English, a very stylish **restaurant** (set menus Ar22,000, breakfast Ar6500), and some excellent, inexpensive **bungalows** (d bungalow Ar30,000, camping Ar10,000) with an attractive pool. MNP take note: all you have to do is clone this place.

The arboretum lies about 12km southeast of town, just a few hundred metres from the RN7, so it's a good stop as you arrive by car. Otherwise take a taxi, or ask any taxi-brousse heading toward Befety to drop you off at the junction (you'll have to walk in). Transfers to Tuléar or the airport cost Ar10,000.

La Table MOUNTAIN

This table mountain is unmissable as you approach Tuléar down the RN7, about 10km from town. There's a relatively easy trail to the top, which takes about 15 minutes to climb, and is a great place to watch the sunset. Go early or late in summer. For Ar25,000 you can hire a taxi in town to take you here and the nearby Arboretum.

Musée Cedratom MUSEUM

(admission Ar2300; ⏲8-11.30am & 2.30-5.30pm Mon-Fri) Features exhibits on local culture, an elephant bird egg, and other oddities including an ancient mask with real human teeth. Cedratom is the name for the local university.

Sleeping

If you're waiting for a flight, there's no need to be near the airport for traffic reasons, as there isn't any. Any of the listings are close enough, including Bakuba and Famata Lodge.

Along with the hotels listed, there are also two adjacent hotels on the ocean that manage some downtrodden charm: **Hotel Le Recif** (☎94 446 88, 032 40 755 39; Blvd Lyautey; d Ar25,000-40,000) and **Hotel Manatane** (☎94 412 17, 032 05 309 09; hotel.manatane@yahoo.fr; Blvd Lyautey; d Ar20,000-30,000). The latter

SNORKELLING THE GREAT REEF

The Great Reef is a prime snorkelling ground. However, human proximity has taken its toll, meaning that some sections of the reef are in better shape than others. Using information on coral health and fish populations supplied by local marine conservation NGO Blue Ventures (see p87) we've graded the quality of the reef from 1 (low) to 10 (high).

Andavadoaka (grade 7) Some nice small bommies (shallow, isolated patches of reef) can be reached from the shore. Slightly deeper reefs are a short pirogue (dugout canoe) trip from the village. Longer pirogue trips reach shallow sites off the island of Nosy Hao.

Salary (grade 6) Good sites are really too deep to snorkel but there are some small bommies inshore.

Ifaty/Mangily (grade 6) Snorkelling can be done by pirogue in the Rose Garden Marine Reserve (for a fee).

Ambondralava/Beravy Good sites are really too deep to snorkel but there are some small bommies inshore.

Tuléar (grade 4) Reef can be shallow but requires a short pirogue/boat trip.

Anakao/Nosy Ve (grade 5) Snorkelling in the marine reserve off the northern tip of the island (for a fee).

Beheloka (grade 6) Good sites are further offshore and need to be reached by a pirogue trip from the village.

Ambola (grade 6) Most sites can be reached by a pirogue trip from the village.

Itampolo (grade 8) One great site for snorkelling straight off the beach in the north, great coral cover, diverse fish and shallow depth.

has an interesting cabin restaurant, but otherwise you're flipping a coin.

Famata Lodge LODGE €€€
(☎94 937 83, 032 02 108 48; www.famatalodge-tulear.com; d €30, f €55;) Further down the coast from Bakuba, 16km from town and 11km from the airport, lies this interesting ecolodge. Located in the mangroves, it has five bungalows and three safari tents, all with private bathroom, hot water and a large terrace, a restaurant, and a great pool. The family bungalow is a steal, with an open

Tuléar (Toliara)

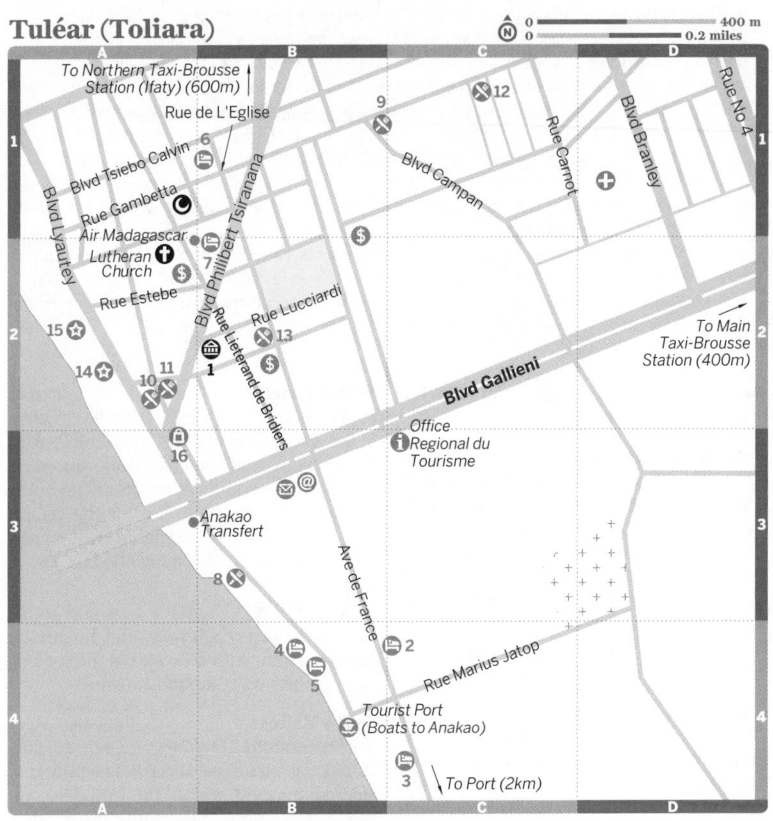

Tuléar (Toliara)

Sights
1 Musée Cedratom B2

Sleeping
2 Chez Lala C4
3 Hotel Hyppocampo C4
4 Hotel Le Recif B4
5 Hotel Manatane B4
6 Saïfee Hotel B1
7 Serena B2

Eating
8 Bo Beach B3
9 Corto Maltese B1
10 Etoile de Mer A2
11 Food Stalls A2
12 Gelateria C1
13 Nandih B2

Entertainment
14 Tam Tam A2
15 Zaza Paradise Club A2

Shopping
16 Craft Market A3

DON'T MISS

BAKUBA

Tuléar's great anomaly is **Bakuba** (☎034 64 927 82; www.bakubaconcept.com; r €80, ste €120) a new guest house on the sea 14km southeast of the city centre and only 7km from the airport. The creation of Bruno Decorte, who has lived much of his life throughout Africa, it would be more accurate to describe it as a work of art that you stay in, with creative genius on display throughout. The house is anchored by large towers reminiscent of baobab trees. One serves as a hidden water tower, another as a hammam and conversation room. The interior contains a vast hall inspired by Mauritanian temples. Doorways are lined by real palm trunks; lamps are constructed from gourds. There are three unique guest rooms, one with a wall of water that also feeds an underground cooling system. The decor includes a fetching statue of a West African chief – Bakuba himself. The highlight is the external suite, a massive 200 sq metre bungalow, which contains a dugout canoe as a bathtub, and a shower room open to the sky. If any of this sounds like kitsch, guess again. Decorte has managed to integrate everything with a strong sense of naturalism, in the manner of Gaudí.

The hotel also has some more run-of-the-mill benefits, like 100m of beachfront, catamarans and canoes, and quads for hire. So if you want to spend a few days, you can. But if you only have one night in Tuléar before taking your flight, we recommend spending it here. The hotel was nearing completion during research. See the website for more.

wall facing the sea. A bit garish in spots but otherwise well done.

Hotel Hyppocampo HOTEL €€€
(☎94 410 21; www.hyppocampo.com; Ave de France; d Ar135,000, ste Ar189,000; ❄@≋) With its great oceanfront setting, asymmetric pool, design focus and well-appointed rooms, the Hyppocampo is the high end of in-town accommodation. The suites have huge tubs and queen beds tucked away from a sitting room. Clientele is an even mix of European tourists and business people.

Chez Lala HOTEL €
(☎94 434 17; Ave de France; d Ar21,000, without bathroom Ar15,000; ❄📶) This laid-back and genial guesthouse is your best budget option. The cosy rooms in the tropical courtyard are smaller than those in the parquet-tiled main block, but they are all great value. A TV lounge, great espresso, loads of info, and free wi-fi help clinch the deal.

Serena HOTEL €€
(☎94 411 73, 032 45 377 55; www.serenatulear.com; Blvd Tsiranana; d Ar47,500, tr Ar72,500; ❄📶) The rooms here have been beautifully designed by Bruno Decorte, owner of Bakuba, in 'African tribal chic' style, elevating this hotel above the pack. Take your morning espresso in the glassed-in restaurant, the perfect place to watch the *pousse-pousse* carts gliding past below.

Saïfee Hotel HOTEL €€
(☎94 410 82, 032 05 410 82; saifee_hotel@yahoo.fr; Rue de l'Eglise; d Ar60,000, tr Ar100,000; ❄📶) This is a business hotel that works for everyone, with a sparkling open-air atrium in the centre, enjoyable balconies off the rooms, and a public TV room if you must, all in perfect condition. Breakfast included.

Eating

French, Malagasy, Chinese, and Italian are the norm here, with zebu steaks and seafood finding their way onto most menus.

Corto Maltese INTERNATIONAL €€
(cnr Rue Gambetta & Blvd Campan; mains Ar10,000-18,000; ⏰lunch & dinner Mon-Fri) Generally considered the best restaurant in Tuléar, yet moderately priced, this creative bistro offers an eclectic menu including steaks that actually look the part. Nice outdoor seating, too.

Bo Beach BURGERS €
(mains Ar6000-15,000; ⏰from 7.30am; 📶) This lively sports bar and expat hangout with its own private beach is *the* place to come for breezy waterfront dining, with enough beer, burgers, pizza, and kebabs to displace the memory of all that rice you've been eating.

Gelateria ICE CREAM €
(Rue Gambetta; sundaes Ar7000; ⏰Tue-Sun) Have confidence in this place: it is owned by an Italian, and he has not forgotten the motherland. Great ice cream, pizza, and sandwiches

follow, along with a pâtisserie for the early hours. Throw in free wi-fi and you have the perfect snack stop.

Chez Alain FRENCH €€
(Sans Fil; mains Ar7000-15000; ⌚lunch & dinner) The restaurant here is a local institution known best for its robust French menu, with serious zebu steaks topped with various sauces. Basic bungalows available too. Chez Alain is half a kilometre from the city centre – follow Blvd Gallieni out of town, turn right, then after 200m, right again.

Etoile de Mer FRENCH/INDIAN €
(☎94 428 07, 034 07 605 65; Blvd Lyautey; mains from Ar1000; ⌚lunch & dinner) Dishing up good Indian food as well as some of the best pizzas in Tuléar, this place has been around forever. Try the fresh seafood, too.

Nandih MALAGASY €
(mains Ar2000-4000; ⌚lunch & dinner) Put a *hotely* (small roadside place serving basic meals) in a cabin and elevate the menu a bit and you get this tasty and incredibly cheap eatery offering a range of Malagasy cuisine.

Food Stalls BARBECUE €
(Blvd Tsiranana; brochette Ar500; ⌚from 9pm) Grab a stool, this is where you down your brochette and beer for the cheapest dinner in town. Popular into the wee hours.

☆ Entertainment

Nightlife in Tuléar revolves around two hot clubs on the ocean, **Tam Tam** (Blvd Lyautey; beer Ar3500) and the large **Zaza Paradise Club**(Blvd Lyautey; beer Ar3500), which are right near each other. Evenings generally get going at the former after 11pm, and rotate to the latter around 1am. Tam Tam is more of a *vazaha* (foreigner) hangout; Zaza tends toward Malagasy music. In either case, make sure you separate the tourists from the professionals, and take a taxi back to your hotel, even if it is close by.

Shopping

There is a decent **craft market** near the seafront full of strange curios. Be prepared to haggle. If you're short on transport, there's also a zebu market east of town. You can get one for around Ar780,000.

Information

There is free wi-fi available at Bo Beach and Etoile de Mer. There are plenty of banks and ATMs in Tuléar. BNI-CA is the only ATM that accepts MasterCard; the rest take Visa.

Cyber Paositra (per min Ar30; ⌚8am-8pm Mon-Sat) Behind the post office.

Office Regional du Tourisme (☎94 446 05; www.tuléar-tourism.com; 2nd fl, Chamber de Commerce, Blvd Gallieni) There's a person here to answer questions, but that's about it.

ℹ Getting There & Away

Air

Air Madagascar (☎94 415 85, 94 422 33) has an office in town, but not at the airport. It flies from Tuléar to Antananarivo (€192), Fort Dauphin (€50-150) and Morondava (€192). The schedule is a moving target so check the website, or better yet, visit in person. Planes fill up in tourist season.

Boat

Anakao Transfert (☎94 92416, 034 60 072 61; anakaotransfert@moov.mg; one-way Ar50,000), an enjoyable speedboat, departs from the tourist port for Anakao every day at 9am. The best and safest option.

Travel south of Tuléar has long been delayed by the lack of a ferry across the Onilahy River. During research a new vehicle ferry, the **Bac Fiavota** (☎032 02 127 74, 033 11 545 73, 034 13 800 50), had arrived at the port and was reportedly awaiting the construction of landing points. How long this will take is unclear.

Camion-Brousse

The mother of all taxis-brousses, the *camion-brousse* is a troop transport that plies the god-awful roads between Tuléar and Fort Dauphin (Ar36,000), with stops in Betioky (Ar13,000), Ampanihy (Ar20,000) and Ambovombe (Ar28,000). This takes a whopping 30 to 60 hours depending on breakdowns and road conditions. But beware: these amusement park rides are packed beyond capacity. Passengers bounce around, and are frequently ill. There are a limited number of breaks. You'll need a scarf and pullover for the dust and wind. To make matters worse, if you do the trip in stages, you could spend a lot of time waiting for a seat, as the vehicles that pass the towns en route are often full. Finally, provisions are sparse along the way, so you need to stock up ahead of time. All things considered, we have never seen a rougher form of public transport.

Hitching

It's relatively easy to hitch a lift from Tuléar to Antananarivo as many tourist vehicles and supply trucks from Antananarivo return to the capital empty. Expect to pay a bit more than the taxi-brousse fare. The best places to ask are the major hotels, particularly the **Hotel Escapade** (☎94 411 82, 034 94 411 82; Blvd Gallieni).

Taxi-Brousse

Taxis-brousses leave the main station very early every day for Antananarivo, arriving a day later. Vehicles to Antananarivo may fill up quickly, so get to the station early or book a seat the afternoon before. Destinations and fares along the way include the following.

DESTINATION	FARE (AR)
Ambalavao	26,000
Ambositra	36,000
Antananarivo	45,000
Antsirabe	40,000
Fianarantsoa	30,000
Isalo/Ranohira	20,000

Transport along the sand road north to Ifaty/Mangily (Ar6000, three hours) and Manombo departs from the northern taxi-brousse station on Route de Manombo. There are a few trucks daily to both destinations, generally departing between 6am and early afternoon.

A taxi-brousse leaves for Morondava a few times weekly (Ar45,000, two days). The road is very rough, and you will need to overnight in Manja (Ar30,000) on the way.

Taxis-brousses also connect Tuléar with St Augustine (Ar2000, two hours) via a good sealed road once a day Tuesday to Saturday. Departures are at noon from Tuléar and 2am from St Augustine.

There's a taxi-brousse every Thursday to Beheloka and Itampolo (12 hours).

Getting Around

To/From the Airport

A taxi between the airport and the centre of town costs a standard Ar15,000 and many hotels in Tuléar and Ifaty do airport transfers.

Car

These companies hire 4WD vehicles. Remember, it's open-season on negotiation.

Kintana (☎032 07 760 84)
Michel Balbine (☎032 41 153 07)
Touramada (☎032 52 262 18)
Transmalala (☎032 07 573 49)

Pousse-Pousse

Standard rates for *pousse-pousse* rides start at about Ar500.

Taxi

For rides within town, taxis charge a standard rate of Ar2000 per person, but can climb as high as Ar15,000 at night. Don't be afraid to bargain.

Northern Reef

The reef north of Tuléar is a gentle curve punctuated by a number of villages and resorts all the way to Andavadoaka some 207km distant. There is a dirt road to Mangily, then a coastal sand track the rest of the way which requires a local guide. Locations along the road are commonly indicated in kilometres north of Tuléar. Villages typically have no signs; look for the hotel signs. Transfer costs increase the further north you go, naturally, but remember: once you get past Mangily you are slithering down a sandy track through a spiny forest full of huge baobab trees and wandering tribesmen. Not your average trip from the airport.

AMBONDROLAVA & BERAVY

On the left 15km north of Tuléar you'll come upon a humble sign for the **Mangrove Information Center** (www.honko.org), a 200-hectare wetland complex created by HONKO, a Belgian NGO, in Ambondrolava. The main attraction is a 1.5km wooden boardwalk. It's a nice place to stretch your legs on the way north, with a trail through the mangroves, educational placards, and a lovely tower overlooking a river at the end.

Two kilometres further takes you to **Le Jardin de Beravy** (☎032 40 397 19; www.hotel-jardindeberavy-tulear.com, d €34-36, set menus from €10), a hotel and restaurant on the sea. There's a nice beach here with a view of the waves crashing on the outer reef. The rooms are a bit claustrophobic except those with a verandah, which includes the excellent corner room. It also does transfers to the airport (€20) so if coming south you could stay here before heading out. There's a local dive centre.

IFATY & MANGILY

Ifaty and Mangily, 27km north of Tuléar, are two separate villages 3km apart that share the same beach, confusingly known as Ifaty Beach (the Dunes d'Ifaty, for example, is in Mangily). Ifaty is by far the smaller tourist destination, even while its name continues to usurp the latter. The popularity of this area is largely due to its location close to Tuléar and the decent dirt road that connects them. The beaches are really quite poor relative to other options: rocky at times, very shallow for much of the day, and with seagrass beds rather than sandy bottoms. The unkempt villages, saturated by go-go tourism, are not very attractive, either. Nevertheless, the snorkelling is good, the whales come here, and there are a lot of resorts to choose from, including some good ones.

Sights

If you visit Ifaty village around 1pm to 2pm you can enjoy watching the local fishermen beach around 50 pirogues (dugout canoes) full of catch.

Reniala Nature Reserve WILDLIFE RESERVE
(☎94 417 56; http://reniala.jimdo.com) This is a 60-hectare spiny forest full of baobab trees and some birds. There are two circuits, one of 45 minutes to an hour and the other of 1½ to two hours. If you have been to the Arboretum in Tuléar, which is better done, you don't need to repeat that experience here, unless you have a strong interest. You can also stay in the **accommodation** (d bungalow with shared bathroom Ar20,000, r Ar30,000-40,000, breakfast Ar5000) here.

FREE **Village des Tortues** WILDLIFE RESERVE
(☎032 02 072 75; Ar6000; ⏲9am-7pm) Near Reniala, this 7-hectare park protects over a thousand radiated and spider tortoises. A guided tour of the grounds in English tells you the full story of these endangered animals and how they are being conserved. It's less than an hour, so a worthy break from the beach.

Activities

Most hotels in this area provide activities for guests, directly or indirectly. In the latter case, it may be in your financial best interest to go direct where possible. For fishing and kite-surfing see Yannick at the **Hotel de la Plage** (☎032 04 346 63, 032 04 362 76). For snorkelling, pirogue trips and forest/village tours see **Aubin and Florent** (☎032 41 439 52, 034 40 925 78; per person Ar15,000-30,000). For diving there are several centres to choose from, but the highest marks consistently go to two.

Le Grand Bleu DIVING
(☎034 64 781 76, 032 54 242 94; http://mangilyplongee.wordpress.com; 1 dive Ar100,000, 2 tanks Ar160,000) This outfit provides many options, from snorkelling with a local guide (Ar20,000 per person), to shallow inshore 5m to 10m dives, to 26m dives on the edge of the barrier reef. The latter focuses on two passes, north and south, with the former containing a famous network of rocky arches called the Cathedral. While most sections of the reef are damaged, there is a variety of fish. Le Grand Bleu also organises whale watching in season (Ar80,000, minimum two people) and surfing (Ar50,000, minimum two people).

Atimoo DIVING
(☎034 02 529 17; www.atimoo.com) In addition to local trips like those organised by Le Grand Bleu, this outfit takes a more adventurous approach, ranging from one end of the reef to the other in small dive parties that sometimes rough it ashore. Prices vary from €100 to €900, depending on the destination.

Sleeping & Eating

There are only three hotels in Ifaty, and some 20 in Mangily. A sound strategy here is to shop around by walking the Mangily beachfront before making a decision, at least in the low season.

Auberge "In" BUNGALOW €
(☎034 18 218 01; www.laubergine.free.fr; s Ar25,000, d Ar50,000) This one is located 100m from the beach, but manages to be the best budget option in Mangily anyway. The dirt-cheap country bungalows with thatched roofs and small porches in a carefully groomed yard are quaint and attractive, and management is cheery too.

Dunes d'Ifaty LODGE €€€
(☎22 376 69, 034 07 109 16, 032 07 109 16; www.lesdunesdifaty.com; d bungalow incl breakfast €136; 📶) This high-end property has a magnificent thatched roof lodge for eating and conversation. Super bungalows made of locally quarried stone offer large porches to take advantage of prime views and breezes, and elegant interiors with brightly painted walls, Italian baths and thoughtful amenities. Airport transfers cost €45. Beach security keeps away hawkers and ensures privacy, which is a problem further north. You pay for it, though: this is a *lot* of money for Madagascar.

Hôtel Le Paradisier LODGE €€€
(☎032 07 660 09; www.paradisier.net; d €80, ste €100; 📶) Another luxury option, and more attractively priced, this Ifaty property has a tropical jungle lobby that opens onto a sea-facing courtyard dining room, and a shimmering infinity pool. The waterfront bungalows are nicely integrated into the beach rather than manicured. The sole suite is one of the best accommodation options in this area, a private house with a broad verandah and magnificent views to sea. Rooms have no electrical outlets,

however, and the food is average. Be careful of pricey extensions.

Nautilus BUNGALOW €€€
(☎94 418 74, 032 07 418 74); www.nautilusmada.mg; tr €50; ❄📶🏊) This is a family hotel with modern bungalows, including some cleverly shaped like a nautilus shell, in Ifaty. The problem is that as you wind toward the centre of the shell, you end up facing...the toilet. But no matter: the beachy grounds, beautiful infinity pool, and excellent seafood restaurant will hopefully take up more of your time.

Chez Alex BUNGALOW €
(☎034 08 266 64; d Ar30,000, tr without bathroom Ar20,000) These clean beachfront bungalows, some with shared bathrooms, are the cheapest on the beach – and there's a seafood restaurant to match. Free beach chairs, too.

Mora Mora BUNGALOW €€
(☎034 46 431 72, 034 29 102 99; http://hotelmoramora@free.fr; d incl breakfast Ar45,000) Another budget option, these beach shacks are clean although set back from the water in an open field. The welcome shade of the bar, however, is front and centre. Cold water. English spoken.

Bamboo Club BUNGALOW €€
(☎94 902 13, 032 66 552 31; www.bamboo-club.com; thatched d bungalows Ar58,000-72,000, solid d bungalows Ar87,000; 🏊) This place caters mostly to divers, but offers neat grounds, comfortable bungalows on the beach, a small swimming pool, and an excellent terrace **restaurant** (mains Ar20,000) serving Indian Ocean specialties. If you can, opt for one of the new solid bungalows over the older thatched versions.

Chez Cecile SEAFOOD €
(☎034 94 907 00; www.surlaplagechezcecile.com; mains from Ar6000) There are some decent rooms in this **bungalow village** (d Ar35,000-45,000, without bathroom Ar20,000, f Ar55,000-75,000), which do all the simple things right, but they are still outshone by its sand-floor restaurant. This is Mangily's best informal dining option, with huge plates of pasta and seafood grills just steps from the sea.

Getting There & Away

Ifaty village lies 22km north of Tuléar along a sandy, pot-holed road. Several taxis-brousses leave daily from the northern taxi-brousse station in Tuléar, usually between 6am and early afternoon; the trip costs Ar6000 and takes three hours. You can get out anywhere in between, just tell the driver. Transfers provided by the hotels for their clients cost around Ar27,000 per person, while taxis in Tuléar charge around Ar60,000. Travel to Andavadoaka and points north can also be done by boat (see p88).

AMBOLIMAILAKA

You might consider this a smart alternative to Mangily, if you really want to get away from it all. There are three upmarket hotels to consider, all of them following the lodge-and-bungalow model, and offering a similar, and very broad, range of a la carte activities: zebu trips, forest excursions, kite surfing, diving, whale watching, fishing, quad biking, and horse riding among them. Transfers can be arranged from Tuléar (38km away) for approximately Ar85,000 per vehicle. Stay or no, it is definitely worth stopping by here around noon to watch the return of the fishing fleet, over 200 pirogues strong, just below Hôtel Belle Vue. The hotel signs will announce your arrival.

Sleeping & Eating

Hôtel Belle Vue BUNGALOW €€€
(☎032 04 747 22; www.bellevue.hoteltulear.com; d Ar100,000) This hotel and **restaurant** (set menus Ar25,000) is aptly named, as it sits up high on a bluff overlooking the sea, with a panoramic view of the fishermen's village shared by rooms and bungalows alike.

Hotel de la Plage BUNGALOW €€€
(☎032 04 362 76, 032 04 346 63; www.hotelplage-tulear.com; bungalows Ar115,000-200,000) Located between two fishing villages, this resort offers some neat circular bungalows strung along an elegant arc of beach. The local dive centre is located here.

Au Soleil Couchant BUNGALOW €€
(☎032 47 360 15; www.hotel-ifaty.com; d/tr/q bungalows Ar60,000/75,000/90,000) Located next to Hotel de la Plage, this resort has virtually identical bungalows, yet is considerably less expensive.

ANKASY

If you want to get away *even further,* you can come to this one-hotel outpost, 100km north of Tuléar. With four massive (100 sq metre) high-end bungalows, on a broad and beautiful 1.3km of private beach, the family-friendly **Ankasy Lodge** (☎032 05 400 42; www.ankasy-lodge-spa.com; per adult per day all-inclusive €90) lodge operates on an all-inclusive model, in which all accommodation,

LOCAL KNOWLEDGE

BIC MANAHIRA: DIVE INSTRUCTOR

Bic Manahira is the first Malagasy native to be certified as a dive instructor; he works for Blue Ventures.

Where is the best town to dive on the Great Reef? Andavadoaka. Perhaps I am biased, since that's where I live and work, but I have dived all along this coast and I think it's the best. Certainly better than Ifaty.

What makes Andavadoaka special? We have all three types of reef: fringing, patch, and barrier. We have a marine conservation area, too, known as Velondriake, so the quality of the reef is much higher here than elsewhere, both in terms of coral and fish populations. And there's not a lot of visitors. The people who come here really like to dive. Many have been all over the world.

Where's your favourite spot, and why? The barrier reef. It's the best place to see the big fish, turtles, and sometimes sharks.

food and local activities – and there are a lot of options, including a small spa – are €90 per day per adult, €30 per child under 12. Food is straight off the pirogue. Transfers from Tuléar are Ar300,000 per car. Look for the hotel sign.

SALARY

The **Salary Bay** (☎75 514 86, 032 49 120 16; www.salarybay.com; d bungalow €80) resort sits up high on a sandy peninsula, affording a spectacular 270-degree view from the restaurant, including the sight of a broad lagoon, and the resort's own enormous 7km of beach!

It's a long trip here, 129km from Tuléar, unless you come in by private plane (it has its own airfield) but once you have arrived it is heavenly. A popular choice for honeymooners and divers (the local dive centre is here). Transfers available from north or south.

ANDAVADOAKA

Yes, it's a long 78km from Salary, but this remote and laid-back outpost of some 1500 people is the most interesting spot north of Tuléar. After passing through the local village, which is the tidiest of them all, one ends at the tip of a sandy peninsula spotted with beach bungalows and a most welcome sight, a pizza restaurant that serves cold beer. At night this is surprisingly populated by people from all over the world, who are not tourists. They are the staff and volunteers of Blue Ventures, an NGO whose marine-conservation programs are spreading throughout the length of the reef, helping staunch its decline.

Not surprisingly, what this means for tourists is some of the best diving in the south, with an abundance of turtles, sharks, rays, and large fish. BV has managed to protect a large section of reef, known as Velondriake (see the boxed text, p88) which contains fringing, path, and barrier reefs. The white powder beaches are pristine, and there are some offshore islands to explore. Tourist infrastructure is limited, but sufficient. There are two excellent hotels, and a local dive shop to match. Local ecotourism includes pirogue trips for fishing, sailing, or whatever. If you are someone who wishes to engage and understand, as well as enjoy the outdoors, this is a place full of rewards.

Activities

Blue Ventures ECOTOURS, DIVING
(☎034 45 532 05; www.blueventures.org) Blue Ventures is an NGO working with the local community to create incentives for the sustaninable management of the the reef and its many resources. Staff hold daily lectures and guide visits to BV's bewildering array of community-based conservation and development initiatives. The organisation also offers a range of local ecotours, which further tie the community to the preservation of the natural world. Visitors can learn to line, spear, and net fish with the Vezo in Velondriake Marine Protected Area, to sail a pirogue to the island of Nosy Hao, or can take a tour of the spiny forest and its remarkable baobab trees. Call ahead or ask in person once you arrive; trips can be arranged with little advanced notice.

VELONDRIAKE MARINE PROTECTED AREA

The Vezo people who inhabit the southwestern coast depend on the sea for their livelihood and cultural identity. In order to achieve sustainable use of their natural resources, local people created Madagascar's first community-managed protected area, **Velondriake** (www.velondriake.org), in 2006. The protected area spans over 640 sq km – making it the largest locally managed marine reserve in the Indian Ocean – and is managed by 25 communities using *dina*, a traditional law recognised by the Malagasy government. Velondriake contains areas where traditional fishing activities continue, and others where it is temporarily or permanently forbidden. Conservation efforts even extend to aquaculture and family planning, in order to reduce dependency on natural resources. The program has been a great success, and is now being replicated elsewhere along the reef and in other parts of Madagascar by Blue Ventures and partner conservation groups.

Madablu DIVING
(☎034 38 192 36, 034 60 168 53; www.madablu.com; 2 dives €80) Italo and Nina, the dedicated Italian couple running this PADI operation, know everything about diving in this area, and are a pleasure to work with. Whale-watching trips are offered June to September.

Sleeping & Eating

Valahantsaka GUEST HOUSE €€€
(☎034 14 002 58; www.valahantsaka.com; full-board bungalows per person €100-145) The many Italians in Madagascar do wonders for the hospitality industry, and this small lodge is a prime example. There are three spacious high-end bungalows here, right on the sea, run by a classy older couple who have relocated for good and thrown everything into making this place sing, including the construction of a new restaurant with dreamy views. The homemade pasta is fabulous, and with 5km of private beach, you will have plenty of space for that after-dinner walk under the stars.

Manga Lodge LODGE €€€
(☎032 58 266 26; www.mangalodge.com; s/d/tr/q Ar60,000/90,000/110,000/130,000) Three cheers for the best entrance to a lodge on this coast: you arrive by pirogue on the resort's little white powder beach and sink your toes in the sand. The beachfront bungalows are suites that sleep four, while the kitchen offers fresh crabs and lobster (set menus Ar20,000). The prices here are a bargain, and will rapidly make up for any transfer cost. If you do stay somewhere else, take a pirogue here for dinner.

Coco Beach PIZZA €
(☎034 14 001 58; mains Ar5000, pizza Ar10,000) Unfortunately this set of very basic **bungalows** (d 70,000), which supports many Blue Ventures personnel, is charging twice what it is worth. The adjacent pizza restaurant is another story, however, and is a most pleasant place to spend an evening of conversation with interesting people from around the globe.

Getting There & Away

A taxi-brousse leaves from the central market in Morombé almost daily. It is also possible to take a pirogue from Morombé or Salary (Ar60,000, five to eight hours depending on wind) as long as you depart early in the morning.

MOROMBÉ

The northern end of the Great Reef peters out at Morombé, 280km north of Tuléar. Once cut off by the rough roads leading to it, Morombé has now cut itself off by air, too, as Air Madagascar has halted regular service (and you had to walk 2km into town from the strip anyway). There are few rewards for travellers who make it to Morombé, but it is a convenient stop if you're driving from Morondava to Tuléar. The **Pirogue d'Or** (☎032 02 147 24; www.piroguedormorombe.com) with basic bungalows on the sea, is probably the best place to stay, and arranges transfers. Somehow.

Southern Reef

There are some interesting places to visit on the reef south of Tuléar, including its best overall tourist destination, Anakao. But after that places of interest are fewer and farther between. Meanwhile the area inland contains a massive spiny forest of little or no interest to the traveller at all, once its basics have been digested. So really, the only sensible itinerary here is to continue hopping down the coast. How far you go simply depends on how much time you have. For those with limited time, a day trip to Sarodrano and St Augustine, or one or two days in Anakao, will suffice. For those wanting to unearth an unknown gem, in a more remote location, consider Ambola. Long-haulers have to decide between the inland route to Ampanihy, on the RN10, or the coastal route via Beheloka, Itampolo and Saodona, before continuing on to the cape. The latter is preferable, but only doable in the dry season between May and late October, as the Linta River becomes impassable. In reality, however, all bets are off in this area in the rainy season, as the roads have degraded substantially, and are subject to deep mud everywhere.

SARODRANO

Sarodrano is the first stop south of Tuléar, a fishing village of grass huts on a sandy peninsula that extends into the ocean beneath some cliffs. It's a short distance from the city, on a good road, but worlds away in every other respect.

The **Grotte de Sarodrano** (admission Ar2000), near la Mangrove, is worth a look (and swim). It's a bi-level natural pool jointly fed by tidal flow and freshwater springs, such that it contains both fresh and saltwater fish at different depths (and lots of them). From here you can take an interesting pirogue ride to Sarodrano village. If one isn't waiting, call Auberge de Pecheur.

Sleeping & Eating

Auberge de Pecheur BUNGALOW €
(☎032 42 903 90; d Ar20,000, without bathroom Ar12,000) You can rent a basic hut at this place right on the beach, and do nothing the rest of the day.

La Mangrove BUNGALOW €
(☎94 936 26; http://hotelchezalain-tuléar.com; d Ar30,000) For more midrange accommodation, try this place which appears on the right side of the road just before the peninsula. Putting the wobbly dock and muddy swimming hole aside, the bungalows are good value, and the grounds well-kept and shady.

Getting There & Away

From Sarodrano you can go on to Anakao by sail pirogue for only Ar15,000 – far less than the Ar50,000 boat trip from Tuléar – or back to Tuléar for the same amount. Either way it's 45 minutes to two hours, wind depending. Daily taxis-brousses from Tuléar are Ar3000.

ST AUGUSTINE

St Augustine lies at the mouth of the Onilahy River, on the other side of the cliffs from Sarodrano, along a good road. It's an excellent drive via switchbacks over the ridge and down into the lost valley beyond, the site of the very first English settlement in Madagascar in 1645. Only 12 people of 140 survived that brief stay; hopefully today's odds are a bit better. The little tropical town sits on a sandy former floodplain and is very scenic from above, with an alluring end-of-the-world feel that adds one hotel to our select list (see The Ends of the Earth, p167). **Longomamy** (☎94 914 29, d Ar15,000-20,000) is perched at the end of the Onilahy River, where local fishermen practice their timeless rhythm. It is a place where hours slip passed unnoticed, and perhaps that is a good thing, given that its French owner has been there 26 years. The hotel offers great seafood straight from the sea, and can arrange a pleasant **pirogue trip** (Ar8000) upriver to a crystal-clear natural pool. Daily taxis-brousses from Tuléar are Ar6000.

ANAKAO

Anakao is the best overall tourist destination on the Great Reef. It is blessed with an entrancing semicircle of white-sand beach, a slice of turquoise water, and a laidback ambiance. The best top-end hotel and the best budget hotel on the Great Reef are both here, among other strong options. In addition, there are two islands, **Nosy Ve** and tiny

DON'T MISS

CHOOSE ANAKAO

There are many points of access to the Great Reef, but if you only have time for one stop, our recommendation is Anakao. First of all, it's convenient and fun to reach. From Tuléar you take a zebu cart out to a boat that whisks you to Anakao in 45 minutes. There you'll find excellent lodging and dining options, in all price categories, and all the usual water activities found along this coast, including some good diving. And unlike Mangily, it's not overrun. It's the perfect place to end a journey before heading back home.

Nosy Satrana, to explore. Running water can be a problem, however, depending on the resort, and there are no ATMs.

Activities

Activities here are arranged through the hotels. One of the more robust centres is the **Anakao Club** (☎94 921 77), at the Anakao Ocean Lodge, which arranges boat excursions to the islands, mangroves, and whales (in season), diving, kite-surfing, windsurfing, and extensive quad excursions, the latter being a great way to see the area. **Longo Vezo** (☎94 901 27; www.longovezo.org), which has a CMAS-certified dive centre, also does much of the above, while adding 4WD trips that go as far south as Parc National de Tsimanampetsotse.

Sleeping & Eating

TOP CHOICE **Anakao Ocean Lodge** LODGE €€€
(☎94 921 76; www.anakaooceanlodge.com; d bungalow €130) This is the premier resort on the Great Reef. It's not that any of the elements are unique, but that each one is carried off to perfection. The bungalows are beautiful, with enormous cosmopolitan baths; the smiling uniformed staff are always there when you need them; the food (set menus €16) is a work of art. From the moment you step off the boat (transfers from Tuléar are €35), greeted with a drink, you descend into an ambiance of effortless laidback refinement, where attention to detail is of the highest calibre. Neither commerce nor mechanics are to be seen: just stone walkways, a light surf, a serene half-moon bay, and the sight of the pirogues sailing past.

TOP CHOICE **Auberge Peter Pan** BOUTIQUE HOTEL €
(☎94 921 40; www.peterpanhotel.com; r Ar15,000, d bungalows Ar25,000-40,000) This creative burst of liberal personality is the best budget hotel south of Tana. The young Italian owners, who have made this place their life's work, have crafted a funky selection of warmly eclectic bungalows, set in a playful yard of political art contained by a fence of enormous crayons. The dynamic bar within is a fusion of revolutionary and hip, with Che Guevara looking on while you sip a deadly rum drink from an enormous green coconut. And all of this on a beautiful beach. But apart from understanding the science of cool, these boys know how to cook. The spectacular ever-changing menu (mains from Ar13,000), a mixture of Italian and Malagasy, is precisely what is missing in hotels three times the price. The problem is that word has got out, and people are staying for weeks if not months. So book ahead, Che, and be careful of that Molotov cocktail. English spoken.

Longo Vezo BUNGALOW €€
(☎94 901 27; www.longovezo.org; d bungalow off/on beach Ar45,000/65,000) A secluded location overlooking the spiny forest to Nosy Ve, a private stretch of beach, bungalows discreetly hidden in the dunes, with hammocks and bucket showers, and convivial family-style dining all combine to form a casual beach camp ambience here that is unique. The shacks on the beach, which sleep five, are übercool.

Safari Vezo BUNGALOW €€€
(☎94 919 30, 032 50 385 20; www.safarivezo.com; d/ste with mandatory half-board €64/86) Lots of nice touches set these beach bungalows apart from the crowd, including stone steps, grass matte walls, drapes, shady terraces, and well-appointed bathrooms, the latter with seawater toilets. There's also a lively beach bar with Bahamian shutters for a bit of Caribbean vibe.

Lalandaka BUNGALOW €
(☎94 922 21; www.lalandaka.com; d bungalow Ar60,000-80,000) 'Upscale beach shack' sounds like a contradiction in terms, but this place manages to pull it off. The family versions are claustrophobic, but the doubles on the beach have a charming verandah where you can float in your hammock for hours, while the classy central lodge is just as attractive.

Chez Emile BUNGALOW €
(☎032 04 023 76; d bungalow Ar40,000, without bathroom Ar25,000) These bungalows are set back from the beach near the local village, in a well-kept sandy garden. The beach **restaurant** (mains Ar10,000) serves fast and cheap seafood.

Getting There & Away

Access is typically by sea or car from Tuléar (p83) although the latter currently requires a *very* long detour. If and when the new ferry begins operation it will cost Ar25,000 and save a full day of driving.

BEHELOKA

If you are thinking of staying here, either to access the reef or the Parc National de Tsimanampetsotse, we recommend pressing on the 20km to Ambola. The local hotel, **Canne à Sucre** (☎032 54 359 82; d Ar40,000, bungalow Ar70,000), has some decent accommodation, but cannot compete with the alternative to the south.

AMBOLA

Ambola is a town not found on many maps, so what a surprise it is to come upon a charming boutique hotel here in this remote part of the reef. One of our End-of-the-Earth picks (p167), **Le Relais d'Ambola** (☎032 43 555 74; www.ambola.net; d €30, f €70) is one of those special places that lingers in the mind for its serenity. The hotel sits up high on a bluff overlooking the reef, with pleasant breezes. It's also set apart by its design, which looks inspired by the Greek islands, all white walls and blue accents. The simply-furnished rooms are brightly coloured, with surprisingly tiled floors and distant views. The restaurant serves up great seafood fresh from the village. Perhaps most surprising is the resident dive operation, which gets high marks from customers who come a long way to use it. There is no pampering here, but if you want a few days of low-key charm in pristine surroundings, this is worth the trip from Tuléar. The hotel arranges return transfers for €65 per person.

PARC NATIONAL DE TSIMANAMPETSOTSE

This 43,200-hectare park makes a good day trip if you are in this area, but is not a generalist's first stop. There is a large and ancient salt lake with some part-time resident flamingos (April to October), which doubles in size during the rainy season; a cave pool, the **grotte mitoho**, with some endemic blind catfish; a smiling baobab tree; and most impressive of all, a large banyan tree full of parrots and ring-tailed lemurs whose tendrils fall several storeys into a flooded sinkhole. There are several circuits to choose from, but you can see all of the sights in two hours.

The **MNP office** is located in the town of Efoetse, 3km from Ambola. You can arrange a mandatory guide and itinerary here; a map of all the current routes is on display. The entry fee is Ar10,000, guide fees are Ar10,000. A good English-speaking guide is Laurent.

ITAMPOLO

The reef has already started to peter out by the time you get here, some 75km from Ambola. There are some very basic and dated bungalows available at **Gîte d' Etape Sud-Sud** (☎94 415 27; camping Ar10,000, r Ar25,000, bungalow Ar60,000, set menus Ar20,000) if you choose to stay. The main attraction is a gorgeous beach and decent diving.

THE CAPE

The south of Madagascar narrows to a wild cape which wraps around the tip of the island from Itampolo to Fort Dauphin. The sense of isolation here is palpable, and grows the further south you go, until you finally reach the cliff at Cap Sainte Marie, where there is nothing between you and Antarctica. Then it's back to civilisation – sort of. After many hours driving through dense spiny forest and one-zebu towns, the trail ends on the doorstep of lonely Fort Dauphin, a city isolated by hundreds of kilometres of tortuous roadway in all directions.

Itampolo to Fort Dauphin

Coming south from Itampolo you will need to drive through the Linta River (only possible during the dry season) to Saodona, on the river's eastern bank. There is an arduous roadway for about 85km to the northeast, where you join the RN10 at Ampanihy. Alternatively, check locally to see if you can cross the Menarandra River further south and continue along the coast to Lavanono.

AMPANIHY

POP 29,000

Ampanihy looks like it has suffered an air raid. The only reason to go here is to get gas and fix a flat, although if you must stay, the **Hotel Angora** (d Ar15,000) is surprisingly hospitable. The road is particularly bad between here and Tranoroa to the east. If you are driving straight to Fort Dauphin, it may be faster to turn northeast at Tranoroa towards Bekitro, then head southeast to Antanimora on the RN13, which rejoins the RN10 at Ambovombe.

LAVANONO

One of our End-of-the-Earth picks (p167) this secluded surfer paradise has some of the best waves in Madagascar, and no reef to interfere with them. The best place to stay in the area is the atmospheric **Tea Longo** (☎033 23 076 86; d bungalow without bathroom Ar20,000) right on the beach. Run by the hard-working Eveline, it has some tidy shacks that reverberate to the roar of the sea, and communal dining with fresh seafood and an interesting assortment of guests, as you don't end up here without a decent story.

RÉSERVE SPÉCIALE DE CAP SAINTE MARIE

Madagascar's southernmost tip, Cap Sainte Marie is a thoughtful climax to the 'eighth continent', a stark and windswept place that feels like the end of the Earth as well. There is an 18-hectare **reserve** (☎032 40 934 03) here partly created to protect radiated and spider tortoises, which ends at some cliffs. The road to the park is lightly trafficked except by these tortoises; you will need a local guide to find it. A small **MNP office** lets you know that you have arrived. Here you'll need to pick up a park guide (Ar15,000). A further drive takes you to the edge of the cliffs, where there is a lighthouse complex, a religious statue, and if you're timing is right, a memorable sunset beneath a huge sky. Whales are also visible offshore between July and November. A longer circuit takes you to a beach strewn with the eggshell fragments of the extinct elephant bird, *Aepyornis*. There are no hotels, but **camping** (sites Ar10,000) can be arranged at the park office. Otherwise the nearest accommodation is in Lavanono, a two-hour journey by 4WD.

FAUX CAP

If you thought there was only one end to Madagascar, and the Earth, guess again. As the name suggests, Faux Cap is another, even if it is a shade further north. Here you'll find a little lobster-fishing town hiding behind some windswept dunes; *Aepyornis* eggshell fragments littering an endless beach, the ever-present sound of the sea, and little else. But there is some decent accommodation. While a bit storm-ravaged in spots, **Libertalia** (☎032 07 560 41; madalibertalia@yahoo.fr; bungalows Ar45,000, mains from Ar5000), offers five solar-powered bungalows in stone buildings that are simple but not uncomfortable.

AMBOVOMBE

POP 76,500

Ambovombe is the junction for the rugged trip along the RN13 to the RN7 at Ihosy. As such, it is marginally better equipped than Ampanihy; we were able to find a Snickers bar in the gas station. One. So fuel up and move on. But do so carefully: the cratered road from here to Fort Dauphin is the worst in the south – and that's saying something.

RÉSERVE PRIVÉE DE BERENTY

This well-known private **reserve** (☎033 23 210 08; admission €18, d bungalow €48, set menus €10) contains nearly one-third of the remaining tamarind gallery forest in Madagascar, nestled between the arms of a former oxbow lake on the Mandrare River. It was one of Madagascar's first ecotourism destinations, and it has an international reputation, helped along by the friendly ring-tailed lemurs that greet you in the parking lot. Visitors can walk forest paths unguided in search of other lemurs. There is also an excellent **anthropological museum** that provides unique insights into local Antandroy culture.

THE ELEPHANT EGG

Elephant birds were a species of flightless birds unique to Madagascar that included the massive *Aepyornis*. Over 10m tall and weighing 400kg, it was the largest bird ever to walk the Earth. Scientists disagree as to the cause of its disappearance, which occurred sometime in the 17th century, but it seems clear that humans were responsible, either from eating the eggs or hunting the bird. Today the most poignant sign of these magnificent creatures is the shards of their eggshells, which litter the beaches of the cape. These were suitably enormous, with a circumference of a metre, and contained the equivalent of 160 chicken eggs. They have been made famous by David Attenborough, who featured his own reconstructed egg in his films on Madagascar. Complete eggs are also found. There is one at reception in Réserve de Nahampoana (p96) in Fort Dauphin, and one at the National Geographic Society which contains the skeleton of an unborn bird. Sensing commercial opportunity, people on the cape and elsewhere sell eggs made from various reconstructed fragments, usually using a great deal of plaster. It is not legal to remove these from the country, although it is said that the eggs seized at the airport are simply resold to the next tourist. The prohibition makes little sense, as the pieces will otherwise end up in the sea.

Times have changed, however. The worsening road from Fort Dauphin now means that half of a day's excursion is spent driving, leading 80% of visitors to stay overnight. Meanwhile, a similar reserve has opened in Fort Dauphin, Réserve de Nahampoana, while much of the wildlife here can be seen at other parks. The facilities too feel dated, giving it a sense of a reserve slowly becoming its own museum.

For many years Berenty would not allow admission unless you bought an expensive transfer from their own agent in Fort Dauphin. They have since widened their net to three locations: **Chez Gigi** (☎033 07 971 64) in Lavanono, **Croix Sud** (☎033 23 210 08) in Fort Dauphin and **Hotel Capricorn** (☎24 743 49) in Tuléar. Still, why not simply sell tickets at the entrance?

PARC NATIONAL D'ANDOHAHELA

This 76,020-hectare park protects some of the last remnants of rainforest in southern Madagascar, as well as spiny forest and 13 species of lemurs. It also boasts over 120 species of birds, as well as a variety of amphibians and reptiles, including crocodiles. Its boundaries encompass the Trafonomby, Andohahela and Vohidagoro mountains, the last of which is the source of numerous rivers and an important catchment area for the surrounding region.

The park currently maintains three main circuits for visitors. The most popular one is **Circuit Tsimelahy** (3.7km, two to 2½ hours), an excellent trail in the bird-rich transition zone between the humid east coast forest and the dry vegetation of the central region. There are campsites and some natural bathing pools. From Fort Dauphin, turn right at the signpost 48km along the RN13, then proceed 8km along a rough road.

Circuit Malio is a loop of 10km (four to five hours) through low-altitude humid forest. This is a bird and amphibian-rich walk with waterfalls and natural bathing pools, but it may be inaccessible during rainy season. From Fort Dauphin, turn right after 25km on the RN13, then proceed 13km on a dirt road (4WD advisable).

Circuit Mangatsiaka is a gentle loop of 4km (two hours) in bird-rich dry forest. From Fort Dauphin, follow the RN13 for 54km, then turn right and proceed 4km on a dirt road.

The park also has an **interpretation centre** along the RN13 at Ankazofotsy, about 40km west of Fort Dauphin. At the time of research this had been closed for six months due to lack of funding, but it may reopen by the time you read this.

To visit one of the three main circuits, go directly to the park entrance at those sites and purchase tickets there. Entry permits are Ar10,000 per day, and camping permits Ar8000 per day. Guide fees are time dependent. If you are interested in longer treks across the rainforest mountains visit the MNP office in Fort Dauphin.

With an early start, it is possible to visit the park on a day trip, but it is advisable to camp overnight.

Fort Dauphin (Taolagnaro)

POP 52,000

Fort Dauphin occupies a striking location between sea and mountains, as pictured on the back of the 5000 ariary note. The town is more prosperous than most, as a major mining operation is based here; after driving for days through the spiny forest, the sight of paved roads and streetlights is a wonder to behold. Apart from some great in-town beaches, the city proper has little to offer the traveller, but there is much to see in the surrounding area, particularly if you have a car. So while this isn't a tourist town, it is a good base of operations, with some decent accommodation. That said, the mining wealth is not trickling down, and crime is up. One has to be careful here, particularly when off on one's own.

PARC NATIONAL D'ANDOHAHELA

Best time to visit April–December, ie outside cyclone season

Key highlight Circuit Tsimelahy

Wildlife Three-cornered palm (only found here), spiny iguanas, harrier hawk

Habitats Humid forest, spiny forest, transitional forest

Gateway town Tsimelahy village

Transport options Rental 4WD (Ar150,000); taxi-brousse and hike in

Things you should know Best to stay overnight at Tsimelahy to give yourself enough time

Fort Dauphin

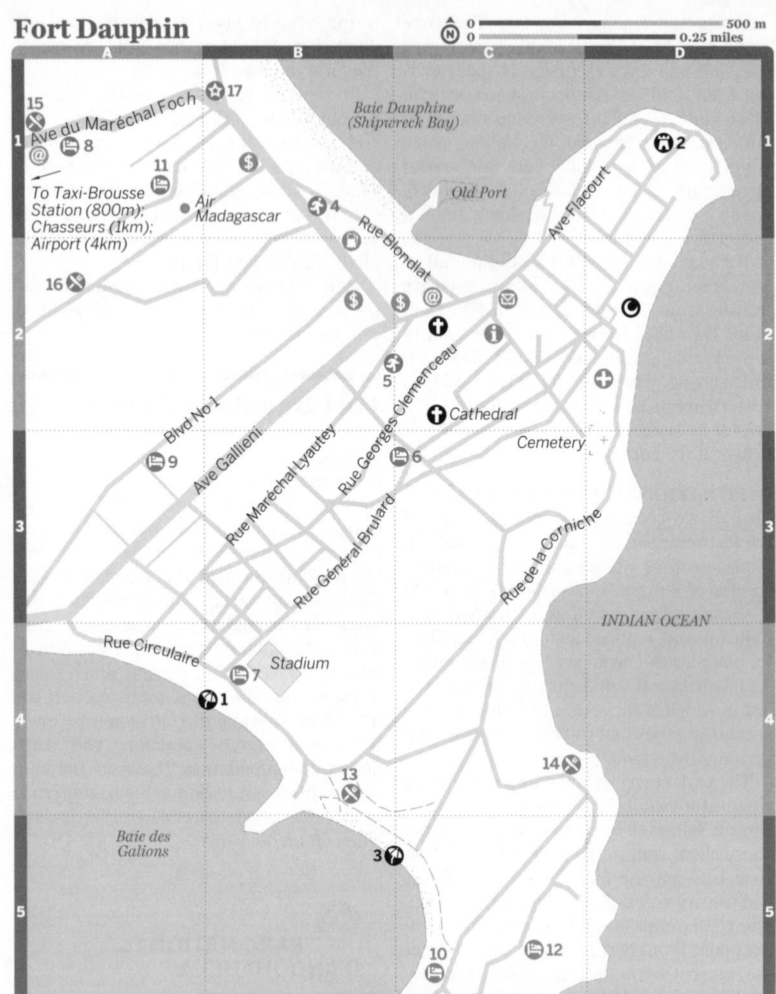

Sights & Activities

Libanona Beach & Ankoba Beach BEACH
These adjacent beaches have an exotic setting right in the city. The latter is known for its surfing, both board and wind.

Fort Flacourt FORTRESS
(admission Ar10,000; ⏲8-11am & 2-5pm Mon-Sat, 2-6pm Sun) This historic fort is currently used as a military base. The soldiers at the entrance endlessly discuss whether or not to let you in, how much it should cost, and who should get the money. There's not much to see except for a few cannons, so these negotiations are the highlight.

Ankoba Watersports SURFING
(☎92 215 15; www.ankoba.com; surfboard per hr €2, teacher per hr €2) Now's the time for those surfing lessons.

Tours

Lavasoa TOURS
(☎92 21 175; www.lavasoa.com) The Lavasoa hotel offers trips to Evatra and Lokaro (p97) including stays at its sister property Pirate Camp.

Fort Dauphin

Sights

1 Ankoba Beach B4
2 Fort Flacourt D1
3 Libanona Beach B5

Activities, Courses & Tours

4 Air Fort Services B1
5 Ankoba Watersports B2
Lavasoa .... (see 10)

Sleeping

6 Chez Anita C3
Chez Georges .... (see 13)
7 Chez Jacqueline B4
8 Hôtel-Restaurant Tournesol A1
9 La Croix du Sud A3
10 Lavasoa C5
11 Népenthès A1
12 Talinjoo C5

Eating

13 Chez Georges B4
14 Island Vibe C4
15 Mami Jo A1
16 Mirana Restaurant/Chez Bernard A2

Entertainment

17 Panorama Club B1

Goulzar Tours CAR & DRIVER
(☎033 12 516 14) Our top choice for a rental car with driver.

Flavien Razafimahatombo SURFING TOURS
(☎033 20 354 56, 034 66 854 21; flavinmad1@yahoo.co.uk) Drop the last name: Flav is the man to call if you want a surfing tour in the south, or just a private guide. Fluent English.

Air Fort Services VEHICLE RENTAL
(☎92 212 24; www.airfortservices.com; Ave du Maréchal Foch) Rents vehicles and arranges a variety of excursions in the southeast.

Sleeping

Many of Fort Dauphin's hotels have closed in the past few years as the omnipresent mining company has built its own housing.

TOP CHOICE **Lavasoa** BUNGALOW €€€
(☎033 12 517 03; www.lavasoa.com; d bungalow €40;) This friendly, well-run guesthouse has brightly painted bungalows in a superb location on the edge of a steep peninsula looking back over Libanona Beach and Pic St Louis; room No 6 has one of the best views in Madagascar. There is a variety of accommodation including a studio, and a pleasant deck for taking breakfast. The hotel also runs a tour company, and owns Pirate Camp on the Lokaro Peninsula (p97). Book in advance.

Talinjoo BOUTIQUE HOTEL €€€
(☎32 05 212 35; www.talinjoo.com; d incl breakfast €70;) This is the only stylish hotel in Fort Dauphin, with an attractive contemporary design and classy horizon pool. Located high on a hill overlooking Libanona Beach, it has a postcard view, too. Maddeningly, attention to detail is missing in some places, such as the use of cheap plastic shower curtains, but this is true all over the city. Rates include airport transfer.

Chez Georges GUESTHOUSE €€
(☎032 44 540 60; georgesliban@yahoo.fr; Libanona Beach; d/tr Ar45,000/65,000) There's only two rooms here, but they are right on Libanona Beach. The triple, a studio, is the town steal. The adjacent bar and restaurant (see p96), which share a log cabin ambiance, make this a mini-resort.

Chez Anita BUNGALOW €
(☎92 904 22, 033 12 679 83; anita@fort-dauphin.com; Bazarikely; d/tr bungalow Ar35,000/40,000) Somewhat worse for wear, but still comfy, these A-frame bungalows with attached restaurant, arranged around a quiet garden, are the best budget option in town. Pay the extra Ar5000 for a triple with loft.

La Croix du Sud HOTEL €€€
(☎032 05 416 98; www.madagascar-resorts.com; d Ar135,000-150,000) This is the sister hotel to the adjacent Le Dauphin, and the better choice. It's like a large plantation house, with a big metal roof and porches. At the same time glass is used to great effect, bringing in lots of light. Painted in solid colours, the rooms manage to be cheery, the best with baths and balconies, while an attractive lobby ties it all together.

Népenthès BUNGALOW €€
(☎034 60 832 54, 032 04 455 54; lenepenthes@yahoo.fr; Ampasikabo; d Ar52,000) These charming chalet-style cottages in their own compound

are clean, have hot water and are situated on spacious grounds.

Chez Jacqueline BUNGALOW €
(☎032 47 413 76; d Ar30,000) Jacqueline has cute little bungalows with high ceilings close by Libanona beach. The rooms are small and breezy and have hot water, and the manager is pleasant too.

Hôtel-Restaurant Tournesol BUNGALOW €€
(☎032 40 530 55, 033 12 513 16; Esokaka; d Ar50,000) These very clean, bright and good-value bungalows sitting behind an attractive **restaurant** (mains from Ar7000) have wonderful views of Pic St Louis. Choose the ones in the courtyard to avoid street noise.

Eating

Island Vibe BURGERS €
(mains from Ar12,000; ⏰lunch & dinner) This popular expat hangout run by two South African transplants occupies a large beach shack with sand floor and benches. Burgers, steaks, and chicken are the appropriate fare. The bar makes a mean mojito.

Chez Georges SEAFOOD €
(mains Ar8500-11,000; ⏰breakfast, lunch & dinner) This popular local eatery and adjoining bar enjoys a laid-back surf atmosphere in cabins overlooking Libanona beach. Catch-of-the-day and crab farci are house specialities, but expect a wait. People swim after putting in an order.

Chasseurs MALAGASY €
(mains Ar5000-10,000; ⏰lunch & dinner) Near the taxi-brousse station, this friendly neighbourhood institution offers traditional Malagasy fare, but is well above a *hotely*.

Restaurant Mirana/ Chez Bernard EUROPEAN €€
(mains Ar13,000; ⏰lunch & dinner Mon-Sat) This single room off a narrow side street is an insider spot known for its pizza, seafood and beef.

Mami Jo CHINESE/MALAGASY €
(mains from Ar4000; ⏰breakfast, lunch & dinner) The place to come for fried rice. Also offers great juices, yoghurt, and a pâtisserie.

☆ Entertainment

Panorama Club CLUB
(men Ar5000, women free) Locals, mining staff, and other expats mix in this disco, the only real nightlife in Fort Dauphin.

ℹ Information

Hotels Talinjoo, Lavasoa and Kaleta (in the centre) all offer free wi-fi. There are plenty of banks and ATMs sprinkled around the city.

Air Madagascar (☎92 211 22) Just off Ave Foch.

Mendrika Services (per min Ar60; ⏰8-11.30am & 2-5.30pm Mon-Fri) The best cyber cafe.

MNP office (☎92 904 85; Villa Dalia, Esokaka) Has information about Parc National d'Andohahela and other areas, but is hard to find; take a taxi.

Tourist Office (☎032 02 846 34; www.fort-dauphin.com; Rue Realy Abel) Useless except for a map – but you have one.

ℹ Getting There & Away

Air

Air Madagascar flies from Fort Dauphin to Antananarivo (Ar1,036,000, two hours), and Tuléar (Ar840,000, one hour) several times per week. These are ridiculously high fares, which may be cheaper to purchase in-country.

Car

Ask at the major tour providers (p94). See our advice on car hire first (p258).

Taxi-Brousse

Fort Dauphin's taxi-brousse station is in Tanambao, in the northwestern part of town along the road leading to the airport. For Fianarantsoa (Ar75,000, about 24 hours, dry season only) and Antananarivo (Ar90,000, 36 hours), the route goes via Ambovombe (Ar7000, three to four hours) and then north along the RN13.

It's not feasible to break the trip until Ihosy, as it is difficult to get onward transport from the smaller villages along the way. The roads are appalling and facilities almost nonexistent, so this isn't a trip for the faint-hearted. Nor is the daily *camion-brousse* to Tuléar (Ar30,000, two days). See our caution on p83.

ℹ Getting Around

The airport is 4km west of town. Taxis to/from the centre cost around Ar5000 to Ar10,000 per person. Taxis within town, including to the taxi-brousse station, cost Ar1800 per person.

Around Fort Dauphin

RÉSERVE DE NAHAMPOANA

This 67-hectare **forest reserve** (admission incl guide Ar22,000; ⏰sunrise-sunset) deserves much greater recognition. Its exotic tropical setting, with mountains for a backdrop, is prettier than Berenty, and it is certainly far more convenient, being a mere 7km north of the city, saving many hours of driving on bad roads. Add to this a robust and varied lemur population, including ringtail, sifaka, brown, bamboo, and mouse species, some with the same habit of dropping from trees to say hello; more humane crocodile pens; extraordinary bamboo groves; night walks; and a cooling sea breeze, and you wonder why so many people are driving west.

There are **bungalows** (Ar95,000) and a restaurant, too, making this a peaceful alternative to staying in Fort Dauphin itself. Just grab a taxi.

DOMAINE DE LA CASCADE

This gorgeous **park** (admission Ar12,000) about 9km from the Total station on the road to Ambovombe, is another easily overlooked gem. Almost 100 hectare in size, it consists of a nursery set in a paradise valley, with several walking trails, including one to a pretty waterfall where you can take a dip. If you are looking to park yourself in paradise for a day or two, the large **bungalow** (q Ar100,000), with kitchen, is absolutely ideal – you'll probably have the whole place to yourself.

PIC ST LOUIS

The summit of Pic St Louis (529m), which you can see around 3km north of Fort Dauphin, offers good views of the town and coast. From the base, allow 1½ to three hours for the ascent and 1½ hours for the descent. A dawn climb is ideal, before the going gets too hot or windy. You'll need a guide to show you the way – ask in town or contact one of the tour agencies (p94) – and you should travel in a group as there is a security risk here.

EVATRA & LOKARO PENINSULA

Lokaro Peninsula is a spectacular and well-preserved area of inland waterways, green hills and barrier beaches. It lies about 15km northeast of Fort Dauphin along the coast, or about 40km by road. Day excursions begin with a 3km drive from Fort Dauphin to the shore of Lac Lanirano then continue by boat to Lac Ambavarano and the tiny fishing village of Evatra. From here it is about 20 minutes on foot over the hills to a good beach.

Once at Evatra, you can arrange a pirogue to visit nearby Lokaro Island, or just stay and explore the peninsula itself, which has numerous opportunities for canoeing and walking. There are bungalows at **Pirate Camp** (d €25), run by Lavasoa (p95) in Fort Dauphin, which also has a camp site and hires equipment. If arriving on your own call ahead. To reach the Lokaro area by road, you'll need a 4WD; allow about two hours from Fort Dauphin. If you go by foot it will take a full day and require food and water. You should also walk with a group, as security is a problem along this route.

THE RN12

For information on the very difficult journey north from Fort Dauphin to Manakara on the RN12 see p162.

Western Madagascar

Includes »

Best Places to Eat

» Chez Madame Chabaud (p103)

» Mad Zebu (p109)

» Renala (p114)

» Les Bougainvilliers (p114)

Best Places to Stay

» Antsanitia Beach Resort (p105)

» Le Tropicana (p99)

» Orchidée du Bemaraha (p112)

Why Go?

Madagascar's western region – divided in two, with no roads linking the south and north – is a country of extremes: hot and arid during the dry season but so muddy the rest of the year that much of it is inaccessible. Off-road fanatics take note: here the 4WD is king. The region is famous for its bizarre-looking *tsingy* (karst) that rise in spikes and crippled spires and create the kind of landscapes described in sci-fi novels. It is also prime baobab country, with some of the most iconic specimens, looking every bit like their folk nickname 'roots of the sky' with their crooked, spindly branches.

Relief from the hot and dusty plains comes in the form of rivers, natural swimming pools and idyllic remote resorts, all the most unexpected and wonderful surprises in such a harsh environment.

When to Go

Majunga

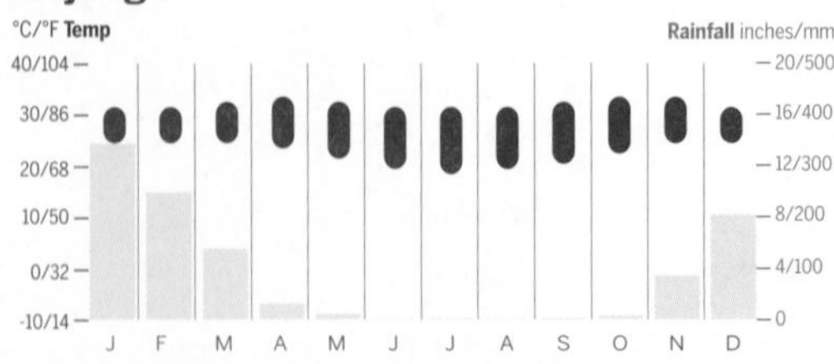

Apr–Oct The region's dry season and only time to see Parc National des Tsingy de Bemaraha.

Nov Fossa mating season at Réserve Forestière de Kirindy and your best chance to spot one.

Oct–Jan Diving at its best around Belo-sur-Mer.

Getting There & Around

With the exception of the well-maintained Route Nationale 4 (RN4) between Antananarivo (Tana) and Majunga (Mahajanga), and the RN35 between Antsirabe and Morondava, there are no sealed roads in this region so 4WD is imperative to explore sights off the RN network.

The only way to get from Morondava in the south to Majunga in the north is to backtrack through Antananarivo. Unfortunately, there are no flights between Morondava and Majunga.

MAJUNGA (MAHAJANGA)

POP 209,000

Majunga is a sprawling and somnolent port town with a palm-lined seaside promenade, shady arcades and walls draped with gorgeous bougainvillea. With its large Comoran and Indian populations, and historical connections with Africa, it is one of the most colourful and ethnically diverse places in Madagascar.

The city has long been a favourite holiday destination for Malagasies (it gets particularly busy from July to September), with its easy access from Tana, lovely climate and seaside location.

History

Majunga and the bay of Bombetoka have been occupied since the 9th century. Arab traders established a number of trading posts along the coast in the 13th and 14th centuries, and the area became a thriving commercial crossroads between the Malagasy highlands, East Africa and the Middle East.

Swahili and Gujarati traders settled in Majunga and the nearby town of Marovoay in the 19th century; these communities were known for the exquisitely carved wooden doors that adorned their houses, and a few can still be admired in Majunga and Marovoay.

Because of Majunga's strategic location, the French selected it as the base for their military operations in 1895, which ended with Madagascar becoming a French colony.

Sights & Activities

La Corniche NEIGHBOURHOOD

Majunga is all about the Corniche, the palm-lined promenade bordering the sea made up of Blvd Poincarré and Blvd Marcoz. In the evening, residents come here to enjoy a stroll under the setting sun, sip a soft drink or nibble kebabs from the dozen street carts. During school holidays (July to September), it has a fair-like atmosphere, with makeshift (and slightly scary-looking) Ferris wheels, horses to ride on and families having a great time.

At the T-junction with Ave de France, there is an enormous **baobab tree** (circumference: 21m!) thought to be well over 700 years old. It is considered *fady* (taboo) to touch it.

Hôtel La Piscine SWIMMING

(Blvd Marcoz; admission Ar10,000; ⌚8am-5pm) If you want to sunbathe in style, there is no better stop than the Olympic-size swimming pool of the aptly named Hôtel La Piscine. It's popular with families at the weekend and during school holidays.

Tours

The following travel agencies can organise excursions to all regional attractions, from half-day to all-inclusive camping trips, week-long circuits and fun days out on quad bikes or boats.

La Ruche des Aventuriers ADVENTURE TOUR

(☎62 247 79; www.laruchedesaventuriers.net; Rue Richelieu) This travel agency organises affordable excursions to all the main sights around Majunga (€52 per day for 4WD, fuel is extra), including three-day camping trips to the hard-to-reach Lac Kinkony.

Aventure & Découverte ADVENTURE TOUR

(☎62 934 75; www.aventure-decouverte.com; 401 Rue Ampasika) Specialises in quad bike (€130) excursions to nearby attractions; also organises 4WD and pirogue trips.

Maderi Tour ADVENTURE TOUR

(☎62 023 34; www.maderi-tour.com; Rue Jules Ferry) Catamaran excursions (€210 per day for up to eight people), and pricey 4WD circuits across the region.

Sleeping

TOP CHOICE **Le Tropicana** BUNGALOW €€€

(☎62 220 69; www.hotel-majunga.com; Rue Administrateur Lacaze; d/f Ar90,000/130,000;) The Tropicana is an oasis of lush greenery right in the heart of Majunga. The lovely bungalows are small but full of character (and often full of guests – reserve ahead), set around a gorgeous pool. It's a peaceful and homey place, where guests can enjoy a quiet read in the garden loungers or catch up on news in the TV lounge-cum-restaurant-bar. Wi-fi works mostly in common areas.

Western Madagascar Highlights

1 Follow the sensational *via ferrata* mountain route in the Grands Tsingy at **Parc National des Tsingy de Bemaraha** (p110)

2 Travel through regions where no road goes during a boat trip on the **Tsiribihina River** (p110)

3 Admire the sunset at the photogenic **Allée des Baobabs** (p117)

4 Splash about in the emerald-green water of the natural swimming pools at **Grottes d'Anjohibe** (p109)

5 Spend a couple of days in the remote and otherworldly village of **Belo-sur-Mer** (p117)

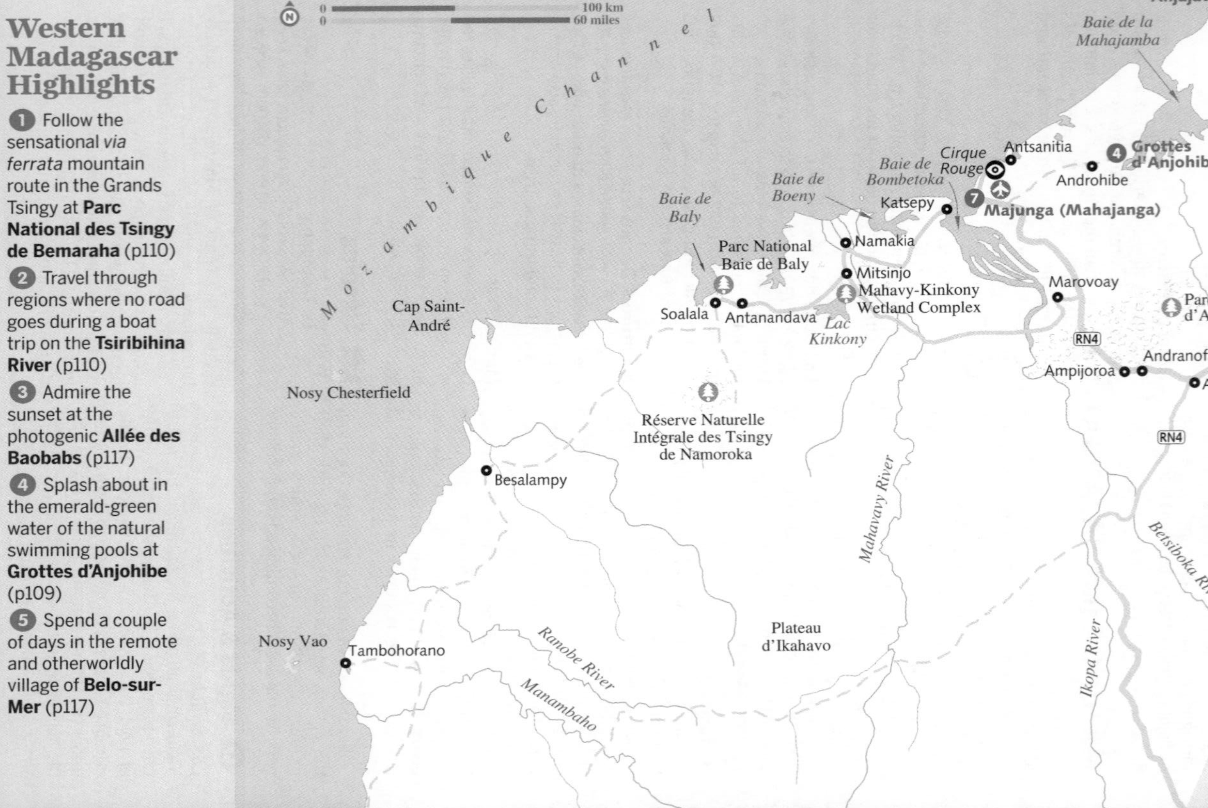

6 Go on a night walk at **Réserve Forestière de Kirindy** (p116) to see nocturnal lemurs

7 Dine at the delicious **Chez Madame Chabaud** (p103) in Majunga (Mahajanga) and enjoy a mean caipirinha

8 Put your bags down for a few days of remote idyll on the **Anjajavy Peninsula** (p106)

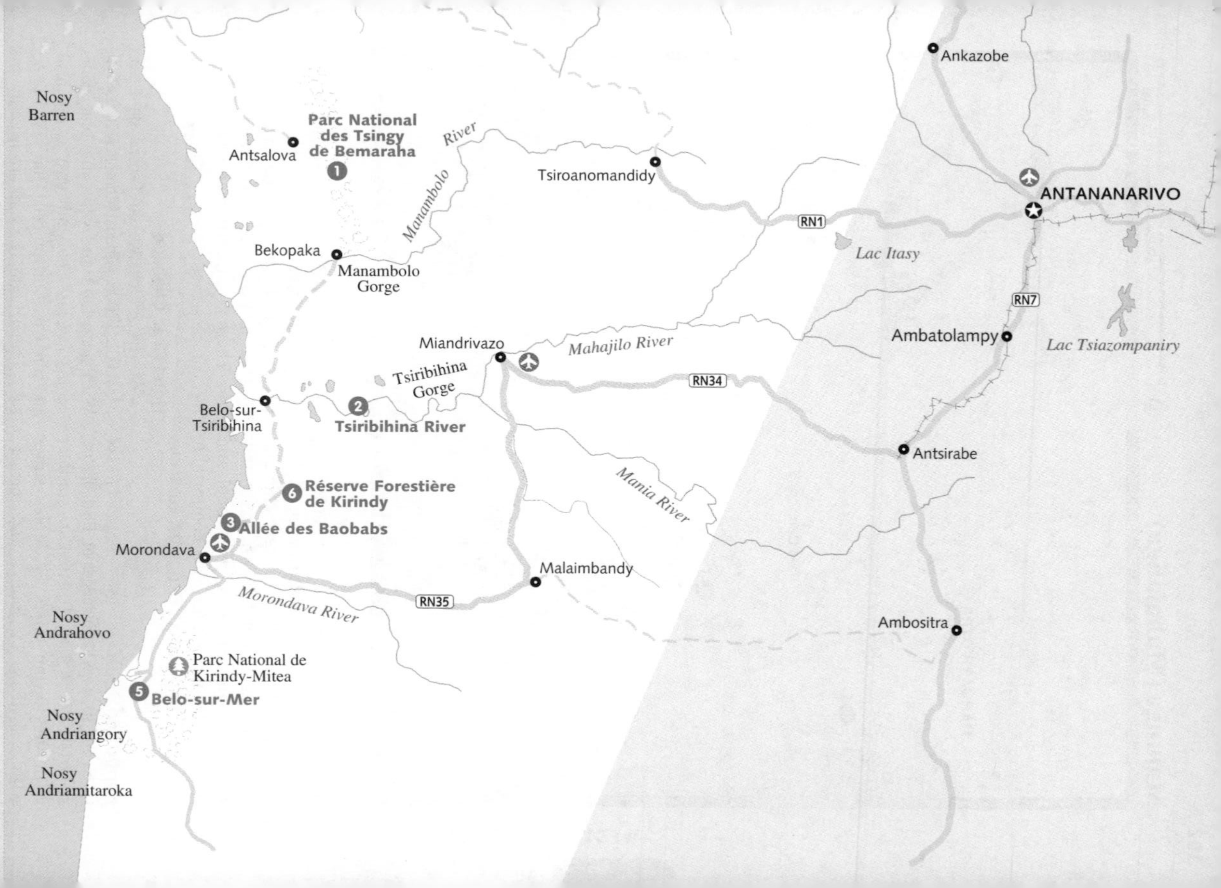

Majunga (Mahajanga)

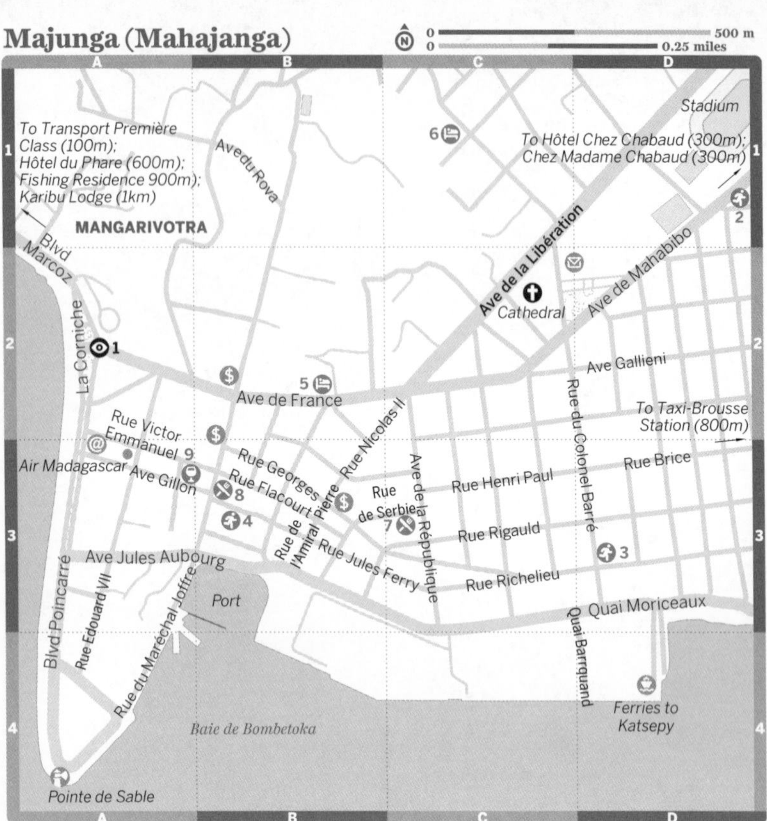

Coco Lodge BOUTIQUE HOTEL €€€
(☎62 230 23; www.coco-lodge.com; Ave de France; d Ar135,000;) A very chic and well-designed little hotel with pretty pink buildings built around a small pool and bar. The rooms are huge, very comfortable and individually decorated, with gorgeous bathrooms.

Karibu Lodge LUXURY HOTEL €€€
(☎62 247 10; www.karibulodge.net; Blvd Marcoz; ste Ar140,000;) Opened in summer 2011, the Karibu offers 15 duplex suites with sea views, TV lounge and terrace/balcony. The rooms have been furnished to very high standards and the infinity pool and bar-restaurant overlooking the sea are prime spots to enjoy the sunset.

Hôtel du Phare HOTEL €€
(☎62 235 00; hotelduphare@moov.mg; Blvd Marcoz; r Ar44,000-58,000;) Overlooking the Corniche, next to Majunga's lighthouse, is this friendly establishment. Rooms are simple but very spacious and spotless. Rooms at the back are equipped with fans, those at the front (with sea views) have air-con. There is a nice garden where breakfast can be served.

Hôtel Chez Chabaud HOTEL €
(☎62 233 27; off Ave du Général de Gaulle; r Ar21,000-36,000, without bathroom Ar16,000;) With neon light and white-and-blue walls, rooms at Chez Chabaud have as much atmosphere as a prison cell. That said, the hotel is immaculate, the staff are friendly and you won't find better value anywhere else. The cheaper rooms have fans and shared facilities.

Eating

Besides the places listed here, you'll find many of the hotels we've listed have quality restaurants.

Majunga (Mahajanga)

TOP CHOICE **Chez Madame Chabaud** FUSION €€
(62 233 27; off Ave du Général de Gaulle; mains Ar11,000-16,000; Wed-Mon) Small, intimate and oh-so-delicious, Chez Madame Chabaud is an institution in Majunga. Christiane (the original Mme Chabaud's daughter) prepares a divine fusion cuisine mixing Malagasy, Creole and European influences that befit the city's heritage. Try the *camaron* (large freshwater prawn) or the *ouassous* (a huge crayfish) and the mean cocktails. The dining room is small, so booking is recommended.

Parad'Ice CAFE €
(Rue du Maréchal Joffre; mains Ar5000-9000; 8am-9.30pm Tue-Sun) This cheerful cafe-restaurant serves simple but well-prepared meals, including salads you can tuck into without hesitation, and rotating *plats du jour* such as *ravitoto* (pork stew with manioc greens), zebu stew etc. It also does burgers and *croque-monsieurs* (ham-and-cheese grilled sandwiches), excellent home-made ice creams and breakfasts.

Fishing Residence SEAFOOD €€
(www.fishingresidence.com; Blvd Marcoz; mains Ar13,000-16,000) This hotel-restaurant is well known for its exquisite seafood, such as calamari and prawns in *combava* (wild lemon) sauce or grilled swordfish. There is also a good selection of meat dishes, including game in season. The dining room is in a large thatched hut by the hotel's swimming pool and is particularly atmospheric in the evening.

Boulangerie Zapandis BAKERY €
(Rue de Serbie; snacks & coffees Ar1000-5000; 6am-noon & 4-6pm Fri-Wed) A true French patisserie that doubles up as a cafe serving wonderful cakes, pastries, croissants and creamy ice cream.

Marco Pizza PIZZERIA €€
(Ave d'Amborovy; pizzas from Ar10,000) This friendly joint with street seating churns out excellent – and absolutely huge – pizzas with a variety of meat, fish and vegetarian toppings.

LOCAL KNOWLEDGE

CHRISTIANE CHABAUD

One of Madame Chabaud's two daughters, Christiane runs the delicious Chez Madame Chabaud restaurants in Majunga and Katsepy. Her sister runs the hotel of the same name.

Majunga for Foodies

Majunga is a prime hunting area and there is a lot of game meat in season (May to October): *roussette* (fruit bat), porcupine (with a taste similar to pork but fattier), comb duck, partridge and *potamochère* (wild boar). Thanks to the coast and the estuary we also get excellent seafood, including *ouassous* (huge crayfish) and *camarons* (large freshwater prawns): they are delicious grilled or stuffed.

Favourite Place Around Majunga

The natural swimming pools at the Grottes d'Anjohibe are magical: when I go there, I feel like I'm in a film. There is a small basin for children, a big one for adults...and the colour of the water and the plants – God must have come this way. I also flew to Soalala recently and saw Katsepy and the flat Tsingy of Namoroka: it was really special to see all this from above.

Time Out

I like going for a drink at Karibo Lodge in the evenings: it's got postcard sunset views.

TAXIS-BROUSSES FROM MAJUNGA

DESTINATION	COST (AR)	DURATION (HRS)	DEPARTURE TIME (APPROXIMATE)
Antananarivo	30,000	10	8am & 5pm
Ambanja	40,000	12	5pm
Diego Suarez	60,000	17	5pm

It's a couple of kilometres from the centre but every taxi knows where it is so you won't have trouble finding it.

Drinking

Majunga's main socialising spot in the evenings is the seafront promenade, La Corniche.

L'Ouvre-Boîte BAR
(Ave Gillon; ⊙11am-midnight) This funky bar, with its eclectic decor, dozens of plants and French radio playing, is popular with local *vazaha* (foreigners) and a nice place to unwind. It also serves simple meals.

Karibu Lodge BAR
(Blvd Marcoz; ⊙11am-11pm) With its west-facing location right by the water's edge, the bar of the Karibu Lodge hotel is one of the most atmospheric places for sundowners in Majunga.

Information

Bank of Africa (BOA; cnr Rue Georges V & Rue Nicolas II) Changes money; ATM.

BFV-SG (Cnr Rue du Maréchal Joffre & Ave de France) Changes money and travellers cheques; ATM.

BNI-CA (Rue du Maréchal Joffre) Changes money; ATM.

Cyber de l'Alliance Française (Cnr La Corniche & Rue Victor Emmanuel; per hr Ar1800; ⊙7.30am-10pm)

Espace Médical (☎62 248 21; Magarivotra; ⊙24hr) The best place for medical treatment.

Post Office (Rue du Colonel Barré)

Tourist Office (www.majunga.org; 14 Ave Philibert Tsiranana) Can recommend excursions, arrange guides and help with all manners of bookings. Also sells city maps.

Getting There & Away

Air

Air Austral (☎62 227 65; www.air-austral.com; Airport) Flies three times a week between Majunga and Dzaoudzi, Mayotte (55 min, €180).

Air Madagascar (☎62 224 61; www.airmadagascar.com; Ave Gillon) Flies several times weekly to Antananarivo (one hour, €187) and once a week to Diego Suarez (€187).

Bus

To travel in luxury, **Transport Première Class** (☎033 07 601 67; www.malagasycar.com; Blvd Marcoz) runs comfortable, air-con vehicles between Tana and Majunga (Ar78,000, 10 hours, daily). They sit just two people to a row and include lunch. Departure is at 7am close to the CNAPS; drop-off is at Hôtel Le Grand Mellis in Tana. Booking is essential.

Another good alternative to standard taxi-brousse (bush taxi) is **Transpost** (Post Office), run by Madagascar's postal service. It has minibuses between Majunga and Tana (Ar25,000, 10 hours, Tuesday, Thursday and Saturday); pick-up and drop-off is at the central post office in both cities. Departure is at 7.30am sharp. Booking essential.

Taxi-Brousse

There are two taxi-brousse stations in Majunga: one on Ave du 14 Octobre near the town hall and the other, much bigger, one on Rue George Ranaivoson, close to the Jovenna petrol station.

For Nosy Be, change at Ambanja for Ankify (Ar5000, 30 minutes), where you'll find boats for Nosy Be. The road between Majunga and Tana is excellent; the road between Majunga and Ambanja has been rehabilitated and is now very good.

Getting Around

To/From the Airport

The airport is 6km northeast of town. A taxi to/from town costs Ar15,000. Taxis-be (Ar800) stop about 300m from the airport.

Car

Upmarket hotels and tour companies in Majunga can arrange car or 4WD rental. Expect to pay Ar150,000 to Ar200,000 per day for a 4WD and around Ar80,000 for a regular car. Petrol is extra.

Taxi

The standard rate for a taxi ride in town is Ar3000.

AROUND MAJUNGA

Apart from the relatively close attractions north of the city, other regional highlights require a couple of days to get there and back (more for Lac Kinkony), or one long day with a lot of driving (Ankarafantsika and Grottes d'Anjohibe).

North of Majunga

Attractions in this area are very accessible: not only are they close to Majunga, but you don't need a 4WD to get there. If you don't have your own vehicle, travel agencies in Majunga can organise half-day trips taking in Cirque Rouge and Lake Mangatsa. Another great way to see these sights is with Aventure & Découverte's quad bike excursions (p99), which can also take in beaches and other local scenic spots.

CIRQUE ROUGE

The Cirque Rouge is one of western Madagascar's most famous sights. This amphitheatre of eroded rock is tinted in a rainbow hue of colours, including red, pink, ochre and white. A stream runs along the bottom of the valley and through a small ravine down to the sea (a lovely 10 minutes' walk). New developments have unfortunately started encroaching on the site, however.

Cirque Rouge is 12km north of Majunga; a charter taxi will cost around Ar50,000 for the return trip, including waiting time.

LAC MANGATSA

This tiny **lake** (admission Ar1000), also known as Lac Sacré, is about 16km northeast of Majunga. Locals come here to give thanks to or petition the help of royal ancestors, with whom it is believed possible to communicate through the huge tilapia that inhabit the crystal-clear waters. Two large trees on the lake's shore are covered with strips of material and zebu horns, gifts honouring fulfilled requests.

West of Majunga

KATSEPY

Katsepy *(kah-tsep)* is a small, sleepy fishing village across the Bombetoka Bay from Majunga with a couple of swimmable beaches. It used to be a favourite Sunday outing thanks to the twice-daily ferry, but since the economic crisis, the ferry now only makes one guaranteed trip a day, forcing visitors to either sleep in Katsepy or rely on the private (and unreliable) boat shuttles instead.

Most visitors are likely to go *through* Katsepy on their way to Kinkony, but there are a couple of low-key sights to visit, and an excellent hotel-restaurant.

Located about 8km southwest of Katsepy, **Katsepy's Lighthouse** (admission Ar5000) has sweeping views of Bombetoka Bay and Mozambique Channel. The lighthouse is now powered with solar energy, but before the panels were put in place, the keeper had to get up three times a night to rewind the pulley that kept the light turning. It's a two-hour walk through a very hot landscape to get here from Katsepy; otherwise you can charter a taxi-brousse to take you there and back (Ar40,000, with a half hour at the site).

Some 20km south of Katsepy is the **Celestine Mines** (admission Ar5000). You can visit the mine and buy gemstones (pale-blue) or beautiful geodes. It takes 1½ hours to drive from Katsepy; a half-day trip from Katsepy including the lighthouse and the mines should cost around Ar160,000.

ANTSANITIA BEACH RESORT

Located about 40 minutes north of Majunga on an isolated stretch of coast, **Antsanitia Beach Resort** (☎62 023 34; www.antsanitia.com; bungalows from Ar145,000;), pronounced 'An-tsan-tee', is a fantastic resort. As well as creature comforts – lovely bungalows with wood and raffia furniture, a gorgeous pool, open-air bar and fabulous restaurant – and a wonderful setting, guests will be able to enjoy a plethora of activities, from sailing to trekking, snorkelling, pirogue trips and cultural excursions.

The hotel has put sustainability at the heart of everything it does, so many of the activities on offer involve trips to local villages or outings with local fishers. The resort also employs and trains a number of people from the area, and it donates part of the fees from activities to the local communities' fund. Antsanitia is also doing its bit for the environment: hot water comes courtesy of the sun, 'air-con' courtesy of the sea breeze.

The hotel can arrange transfers (Ar50,000 one way).

If you do come to Katsepy, having to sleep and/or eat at the wonderful **Chez Mme Chabaud** (62 233 27; mains Ar10,000-14,500, bungalows Ar30,000) is no hardship. Run by the same family as the eponymous restaurant in Majunga, it serves the same delicious blend of Malagasy and French cuisine with fresh, local ingredients. The seven pretty bungalows have been built and decorated with local materials and are right by the beach, in a lovely garden. To preserve the site's peacefulness, the hotel has eschewed generators in favour of wind and solar energy.

The Majunga–Katsepy ferry (passenger/car Ar2500/30,000, one hour) leaves Majunga at 7.30am daily. It then leaves Katsepy around 9am. If there are many cars and/or trucks waiting in Katsepy, it sometimes does a second trip in the afternoon. If the ferry doesn't come back, private motorboats (Ar3000, 30 minutes) ply the crossing between Majunga and Katsepy in both directions several times a day until about 3pm. They work like a taxi-brousse and only leave when full (14 to 18 passengers). You're pretty much guaranteed to get wet; life jackets are available.

MAHAVY-KINKONY WETLAND COMPLEX

The Mahavy-Kinkony Wetland Complex gained temporary protection status in 2007; it incorporates a diverse and fragile ecosystem consisting of marine bays, river and river delta, and 22 lakes, including Madagascar's second-largest, Lac Kinkony. The reserve is also home to dry deciduous and gallery forest, savannah, marshland, mangrove, caves and lots of wildlife.

What most people come to Lac Kinkony for however, are the birds. There are 143 species, and it is the only place where all of western Madagascar's species of waterfowl can be seen in the same location.

Getting to Lac Kinkony is virtually impossible under your own steam since there is no tourism infrastructure. Travel agencies in Majunga organise all-inclusive

ANJAJAVY'S FLY-IN RESORTS

For those looking for something truly off the radar, the remote resorts on the Anjajavy Peninsula are the answer. Each is unique and about as close to paradise as one finds in Madagascar, but they come at a price: getting there alone costs an eye-watering €200 to €600.

Anjajavy LODGE €€€

(France 33 1 44 69 15 03; www.anjajavy.com; s/d incl meals €265/420;) Part of the prestigious Relais & Châteaux network, Anjajavy is the quintessential desert-island idyll. The guest villas are luxurious, with polished wood, fine linen and their own private terrace. There are myriad activities, many of them free: snorkelling, swimming, guided walks through the forest and to local villages. Massages, fishing or boat excursions are also available. The hotel leases 450 hectares of native dry deciduous forest and protects it as a nature reserve. It is also actively involved in working with local communities, employing people from surrounding villages and supporting local enterprise. A three-day minimum stay is required; transfer is by private plane from Antananarivo.

Lodge des Terres Blanches LODGE €€€

(032 05 151 55; www.lodgeterresblanches.com; per person full-board €70, bungalows incl meals €140) This is the most reasonably priced of the three resorts. There are six basic but comfortable bungalows in a gorgeous location – a white beach backed by lush forests that are home to lemurs and geckos. The hotel can arrange drop-offs for picnic hikes, boat trips to hidden coves and baobab-rich islands, and quad bike excursions. It's also popular with sports fishers. Transfer is by boat or private plane from Majunga.

La Maison de Marovasa-Be LODGE €€€

(032 07 418 14; www.marovasabe.com; d all-inclusive from €500; Mar-Jan;) The exquisite Marovasa villa offers beautiful suites and bedrooms, all with balconies. The house has a 1930s retro feel about it. The surrounding environment is more arid than in other Anjajavy resorts, but Marovasa is involved in local reforestation projects; the hotel is also powered by wind and solar energy rather than generator. Access is by private plane from Antananarivo, Majunga or Nosy Be.

camping trips, but you'll need at least three days (the roads are *very* rough) and a minimum of Ar1 million for the 4WD, fuel and guide (for two to four people).

Parc National d'Ankarafantsika

Ankarafantsika (130,026 hectares) is the last strand of dry western deciduous forest in Madagascar, and the need for its protection is obvious: as you drive to Ankarafantsika, whether from Tana or the north, there isn't a tree in sight for hundreds of miles.

The park straddles the RN4 and is therefore easily accessible, even by public transport.

The driest time to visit Ankarafantsika is between May and November, but October and November can get very hot. Wildlife-viewing is often better during the early part of the December-to-April wet season, when rainfall is still relatively light.

Ankarafantsika is home to eight lemur species, many easily seen, including Coquerel's sifaka and the recently discovered *Microcebus ravelobensis*. You're also likely to see brown lemurs and four nocturnal species: sportive, woolly, grey mouse and fat-tailed dwarf lemurs. More elusive is the rare mongoose lemur, which is observed almost exclusively here.

Birdwatchers will be rubbing their hands in anticipation: Ankarafantsika is one of Madagascar's finest birdwatching venues, with 129 species recorded, including the rare Madagascan fish eagle and the raucous sickle-bill *vanga*. There are over 70 species of reptiles, including small iguanas, a rare species of leaf-tailed gecko and the rhinoceros chameleon (the male sports a large, curious-looking bulblike proboscis).

Vegetation consists of low and scrubby deciduous forest with pockets of such dry-land plants as aloe and *Pachypodium* (or 'elephant's foot') plus baobabs and orchids.

Park Fees & Guides

Park permits (1/2/3/4 days Ar25,000/37,000/40,000/50,000) must be bought at the **MNP office** (☎62 780 00; www.parcs-madagascar.com; ⏲7am-4pm). **Guides** (Ar15,000-40,000 depending on the circuit) are compulsory and must be booked here too. Most speak excellent English.

PARC NATIONAL D'ANKARAFANTSIKA

Best time to visit Year-round.

Key highlight The profusion of birdlife and scenic landscape.

Wildlife Birds, birds, lemurs, more birds!

Habitats Dry deciduous forest.

Gateway towns Ampijoroa.

Transport options Taxis-brousses or private vehicle.

Things you should know Ankarafantsika makes an ideal stopover to break the journey between Tana and Majunga.

Activities

Hiking is the name of the game here. There are eight **short circuits** in the park, some of which can be combined into a half-day hike. Circuits in the western half of the park go through dense forests on a sandy plateau and are great for lemur-spotting (sifakas and brown lemurs in particular) and birdwatching. There is also a breathtaking canyon that is well worth the trek in baking heat across the grassland plateau.

The northern half of the park is all about the lake and the baobabs. The birdwatching is excellent here, too (and completely different from the south), and there are more reptiles, including crocodiles. If you have time, try to see both sides.

Park guides also organise one-hour **night walks** (Ar25,000). Unfortunately, visitors are no longer allowed in the park at night, so the walk simply follows paths along the RN4. That said, night time is still your best chance to see the tiny mouse lemur, and chameleons are easier to spot by torchlight too.

Sleeping & Eating

Gîte d'Ampijoroa HOTEL €€
(☎62 780 00; akf.parks@gmail.com; camping Ar6000, r without bathroom Ar35,000, bungalows Ar80,000) The national park offers several types of accommodation, all of which are adequate but not particularly great. The camping facilities are good, but the pitches, close to the road and a little exposed, are not that enticing. The rooms are more sheltered, but the shared facilities are really scraping the barrel. As for the bungalows (which sleep up

SURVIVAL OF THE FITTEST

The ploughshare tortoise has long been endangered in Madagascar. The tortoise's vulnerability comes in part from its unusual mating habits – in order to mate, the male tortoise must become aroused by fighting with other males. Males fight by locking together the front of their shells, which are shaped like a plough, before trying to tip each other over. If no other males are available to fight with, the male is unable to copulate and thus numbers drop. More details on the ploughshare's bizarre sexual habits can be found in the book *The Aye-Aye and I* by Gerald Durrell, whose estate runs the **Durrell Wildlife Conservation Trust**.

This trust has been operating a very successful captive breeding programme in Parc National d'Ankarafantsika for 25 years. Although it took many years of trial and error in the sex-therapy department, the world's rarest tortoise is now breeding here so successfully (400 have been bred over the last 25 years) that 45 have been reintroduced in the wild.

The Durrell project has had such success with the ploughshare that it's expanded its breeding program to the flat-tailed tortoise and the highly-endangered side-necked turtle living only in Madagascar's western lakes.

Because of the extra security it takes to ensure the safety of these very rare species, you'll only be able to watch the tortoises through a chain-link fence.

to four), they are certainly very spacious, if not luxurious.

The redeeming feature of this motley assortment of sleeping options is the park's restaurant, which serves delicious three-course meals for a bargain Ar10,000. (Note that some of the guides' families run little eateries in the area and guides might try to get you to eat there instead of the park's restaurant).

Getting There & Away

The entrance to the park is just off the RN4, about 114km southeast of Majunga and 455km from Antananarivo, close to the village of Ampijoroa. If you don't have your own vehicle, catch a taxi-brousse to Majunga from Tana (Ar30,000, eight hours) or a taxi-brousse towards Andranofasika from Majunga (Ar5000, three hours) and ask to be dropped off at the park. You'll have no problem flagging a taxi-brousse to go to Majunga whatever the time of day, but you may have to go to Majunga to find a taxi-brousse to Tana as many are likely to be full by the time they drive past the park.

TSIRIBIHINA RIVER REGION

This region, between Antsirabe and Morondava, is home to the beautiful Tsiribihina River and spectacular Parc National des Tsingy de Bemaraha, a Unesco World Heritage Site. Tours of the park are often combined with boat trips down the Tsiribihina River.

Miandrivazo

Miandrivazo *(Mee-an-dree-vaaz)*, which lies along the main road, Route Nationale 34 (RN34), between Antsirabe and Morondava, is the starting point for boat trips down the Tsiribihina River to Belo-sur-Tsiribihina. Unless you're joining one of these popular trips, there's really no reason to stop here.

The family-run **Gîte de la Tsiribihina** (☎95 936 88, 032 52 163 31; d without bathroom Ar13,000-16,000, mains Ar7000), may have rickety beds in the rooms and distressed plumbing in the bathrooms, but it's in a beautiful old building and has oodles of charm (with a wide balcony replete with loungers), leafy surroundings and very friendly hosts. The hotel serves food, and the staff can help you organise pirogue trips down the Tsiribihina River if you haven't already organised your own. Room rates include breakfast.

There are daily taxis-brousses to Antananarivo (Ar24,000, nine hours), Antsirabe (Ar10,000, six hours) and Morondava (Ar20,000, six hours). Road conditions are good. Taxis-brousses from Antananarivo leave the capital around 5pm or 6pm and reach Miandrivazo in the middle of the night.

Belo-sur-Tsiribihina

POP 25,000

Belo-sur-Tsiribihina, lost in the marshes and mangroves of the Tsiribihina Delta, is a dusty collection of two-storey buildings. It is located halfway between Morondava and the Parc National des Tsingy de Bemaraha. It's often referred to as 'Belo', and is not to be confused with the coastal village of Belo-sur-Mer, which lies further south.

There is nothing to do or see in Belo, but there are two excellent sleeping and eating options, which come in very handy for those on their way to/back from the Tsingy de Bemaraha or the Tsiribihina.

Sleeping & Eating

Hôtel-Restaurant du Menabe HOTEL €
(☎032 42 635 35; http://hoteldumenabe.free.fr; d/tr Ar25,000/30,000) In an old, colourful colonial building, Hôtel du Menabe offers some grand rooms with huge double beds. Most have bathrooms and all are impeccably clean. The hotel is run by a friendly Frenchman, Bruno, and there is a great atmosphere, notably in the evenings when the dining room fills up with travellers swapping stories of Tsingy ascents and Tsiribihina descents.

TOP CHOICE **Mad Zebu** INTERNATIONAL €€
(☎032 07 589 55, 032 40 387 15; restaurantmadzebu@yahoo.fr; mains Ar12,000-16,000) The 'crazy zebu' is the most incongruous find in dusty Belo: dishes seem to come straight out of a Michelin-starred restaurant (the chef trained in prestigious kitchens in Madagascar and Europe), with exquisite creations such as pan-fried shin of zebu with roast cherry tomatoes or Nile perch in coconut sauce, all elaborately presented. Every travel agent in Madagascar books its clients here for lunch on their way between Morondava and the Tsingy de Bemaraha, so it's a good idea to book ahead.

Information

There is no bank or internet access in Belo. The nearest facilities are in Morondava.

Getting There & Away

Boat

Belo is on the northern side of the Tsiribihina River so vehicles (and passengers) coming from Morondava need to use the ferry (passenger/vehicle Ar500/20,000, 45 minutes, 6am to 7pm).

Taxi-Brousse

There are daily taxis-brousses between Belo-sur-Tsiribihina and Morondava (Ar10,000, four hours). Departures are from the Morondava side of the river. The road is unsealed but in good condition.

WORTH A TRIP

GROTTES D'ANJOHIBE

These **caves**, about 73km east of Majunga, are some of the most impressive in Madagascar. A series of subterranean rooms and galleries, some of them the size of buildings, adorned with stalactites and stalagmites stretch over five kilometres. Shafts of light penetrate every room from passageways and holes in the ceiling, giving the caves an eerie feel. In a clearing close to the opening chamber, vegetation has reclaimed its rights and there are excellent creepers from which to swing Tarzan-like.

What most people now come to Anjohibe for, however, are not the caves, but the stunning **natural swimming pools** (admission Ar10,000). Of a deep emerald-green colour, and framed by luxuriant vegetation and *ravinala* trees fanning their leaves like parading ostriches, they are the most improbable find in an otherwise arid landscape. The first pool is shallow, while the second pool, at the foot of a spectacular waterfall, is deep and wonderful for swimming.

It takes a good 3½ hours to get to Anjohibe from Majunga, so spend the night there to make the best of the pools and caves (to do it as a day trip, you'll need to leave at first light to be back by sunset). Local guide **Rivo** (☎032 45 839 28), who speaks basic English, can organise a two-day visit, with a night's camping by the pool (Ar5000 per person). The facilities are basic (tent, bush toilet, no shower) and the meals (Ar12,500 each for lunch and dinner, Ar7000 for breakfast), prepared by locals, are simple. The campsite is right by the pools, so you'll have plenty of time to swim; it's also a favourite of local lemurs, who come here in the hope of food. At night, Rivo will get the campfire going.

The track to the Grottes d'Anjohibe is passable only between April and October and requires a 4WD. If you don't have your own vehicle, Rivo can help you rent one.

Camions-brousses

These huge, 4WD army-style trucks go to Bekopaka (for Parc National des Tsingy de Bemaraha) every few days in the dry season (May to October). The trip (Ar20,000) takes anything from 10 to 24 hours and is extremely rough.

Parc National des Tsingy de Bemaraha

Parc National des Tsingy de Bemaraha is a Unesco World Heritage Site, and its highlights are the jagged, limestone pinnacles known as *tsingy* and the impressive infrastructure – *via ferrata* (mountain route equipped with fixed cables, stemples, ladders and bridges), rope bridges, walkways – that the park has put in place to explore them. Formed over centuries by the movement of wind and water, and often towering several hundred metres into the air, the serrated peaks would definitely look at home in a Dalí painting.

Park visitors will stay at the small village of **Bekopaka**, at the entrance of the gorges of the Manambolo River. It is a ramshackle collection of huts with bright green paddy fields stretching under immense skies.

TSIRIBIHINA RIVER BOAT TRIPS

Drifting down the Tsiribihina *(Tsi-ree-been)* has become a popular organised tour, and for good reason: the trip between Miandrivazo and Belo-sur-Tsiribihina allows you to see a bit of the country where life is ruled by the river, not the roads, and at a pace more in tune with local life than hectic Western schedules. It is a rare moment of utter relaxation, where admiring the landscape, reading a book, chatting with the crew or sitting in quiet contemplation by the campfire are the main occupations.

The Trip

Trips generally start close to Miandrivazo and cover 146km of lazy bends all the way to Belo-sur-Tsiribihina. It takes about 2½ days to cover the distance at a leisurely pace. The scenery is beautiful and varied: the river is in turns broad in the plains and narrow through the Tsiribihina Gorges, with vast sandbanks converted to paddy fields alternating with tall, red cliffs and beautiful deciduous forest. There is excellent birdwatching along the river, as well as lemurs, crocs and chameleons. You'll also see Malagasies going about their daily life: men fishing or attempting to cross the river with their loaded zebu carts, women washing clothes by the riverside, and children playing and swimming.

Day One generally finishes with a visit to lovely waterfalls, where you can have a paddle (this will be your shower for the day). Camp is set on sandbanks every night, complete with campfire and prime viewing of the Milky Way; most operators will organise short walks and visits to local villages. In some cases, they'll invite local musicians and dancers to provide entertainment one evening, which can turn into quite a party if villagers join the festivities!

Most trips arrive at Belo-sur-Tsiribihina by lunchtime on Day Three.

Packages: Pirogue or Motor Boat?

The main time for river descents is from April to November. Travel operators have been running trips on the Tsiribihina for some years now and the packages are generally very well organised. They include all camping equipment, food, (nonalcoholic) drinks, a guide and, of course, the boat. You have two options: traditional wooden pirogue or motorised boat.

Purists argue that traditional wooden pirogues are the genuine experience. Their big advantage is their quietness: except for the splash of the paddle, silence reigns. Pirogues also only take three to four people (including the *piroguier*, or paddler), offering a very intimate experience. The downside is comfort: once you've boarded the pirogue, you're stuck in that position until your next stop and you are very exposed to the beating sun. Allow about €300 for a group of three or four.

The *chaland* (or motor boat) is a narrow, barge-like boat with two decks. The lower deck has the engine room, kitchen, dining area and storage, whilst the upper deck is basically a viewing platform with loungers, seats and an awning for shade. They generally fit eight to

Park Fees & Guides

Guides (Ar12,000-40,000 for up to five people) are compulsory. They must be booked at the **MNP Office** (☎034 49 401 30; www.parcs-madagascar.com; ⏰6-11am & 1-4pm) at the entrance of Bekopaka, where you must also pay your **park fees** (per 1/2/3/4 days Ar25,000/37,000/40,000/50,000) and pick up your harness if applicable. Most guides now speak English and Italian.

Top tip: during peak season (July and August), there are not enough guides and harnesses so arrange everything the day before to avoid disappointment. This also allows you to depart around 5am and avoid the human jams along the *via ferrata* (seriously).

Activities

Much of the walking in the *tsingy* area of the park is pretty strenuous – gaps between the rocks are very narrow, bridges are high and the caves under the pinnacles are cramped and dark. Anyone with a low level of fitness or vertigo might find exploring the *tsingy* challenging, particularly the Grands Tsingy where hauling, squeezing, crawling and pulling are all part of the fun. It is worth noting that visitors of stout

12 people. Obviously the biggest downside is the noise of the engine, but they make up for it in comfort and conviviality by allowing you to move around and chat with fellow passengers. Most operators will stop the boat for lunch so that you can eat in peace. Trips generally cost €160 to €200 per person.

Either way, note that you'll need a bladder of steel to hold it between stops, and anti-diarrheals at the ready should you need them.

Packages generally include the transfer from Miandrivazo to the boarding point on the river; trips finish at Belo-sur-Tsiribihina. Motor boats arrive at the ferry landing in Belo, but pirogues generally stop 40km upstream and travellers finish the last stretch either by zebu cart or 4WD.

Tour Operators

The following tour operators are very reputable and organise excellent trips; if you would like to do the trip by motor boat, you'll have to go through one of them, although they can also organise pirogue trips. Most agencies will offer to combine the Tsiribihina with a visit to Parc National des Tsingy de Bemaraha (well worth doing), with a 4WD coming to pick you up from the landing and delivering you in Morondava three days later. These trips cost around €900 per person on the basis of two people, but around €500 per person with four people (the biggest cost is the 4WD).

Mad Caméléon (☎22 630 86; www.madcameleon.com)

Espace Mada (☎22 262 97; www.madagascar-circuits.com)

Remote River Expeditions (☎95 523 47; www.remoterivers.com)

You'll also find plenty of hotels and local operators in Miandrivazo and Antsirabe that can organise pirogue trips. Do try and inspect the camping equipment before setting off and make sure you confirm what is included, the kind of food you will be served and how much water will be available.

For security reasons, you must visit the police station in Miandrivazo with your passports and your *piroguier* before setting off; at the end of the trip, the *piroguier* will ask you to sign a discharge confirming that the trip went well, which he will hand back at the police station.

Treading Lightly

The increased traffic on the river has taken its toll: trash and improper burial of human waste are real issues in this fragile ecosystem. Many operators are, sadly, not as strict as they should be on the issue of toilets so take responsibility for yourself: make sure you bury any waste in a hole at least 15cm deep and 30m from the river.

PARC NATIONAL DES TSINGY DE BEMARAHA

Best time to visit April–October.

Key highlight The dramatic, dark grey, serrated pinnacles of the Tsingy.

Wildlife The park's main draw is its geology rather than wildlife, although you're bound to come across some of the park's eight species of lemurs.

Habitats Humid and dry forests, grassland, limestone rock formations.

Gateway towns Bekopaka

Transport options Access to Bekopaka is possible by 4WD between April and October from Morondava.

Things you should know It is *fady* to smoke, go to the toilet outside designated areas, or point at the *tsingy* with your finger outstretched.

build may not be able to go through the tight passages inside the caves – the guides know the trails inside out and will let you know if they foresee a problem. They have also developed an arsenal of tricks to coax even the most vertigo-struck trekkers across the rope bridges.

The **Petits Tsingy**, near Bekopaka, is the most accessible section of the park. There are seven hiking circuits in this area, ranging from an easy 1½-hour walk with walkways and easy bridges, to a pretty serious six-hour circuit requiring you to abseil a 30m cliff. Many involve a section by pirogue through the stunning Manambolo River Gorges.

The much larger **Grands Tsingy** lie 17km north of Bekopaka and are the most impressive. Most visitors drive to the start of the two circuits (four hours each), which follow a fantastic *via ferrata* – no climbing experience required, you just wear a harness, which you clip to cables and ladders as you go.

Having come all the way to Bekopaka, you should spend at least a day in the Petits Tsingy and a day in the Grands Tsingy – more, of course, if time allows.

Sleeping & Eating

There isn't a huge amount of choice for accommodation in Bekopaka so book ahead. If you'd like to get out of your hotel, head to the ferry crossing for a cold beer in one of the atmospheric *gargotes* (cheap restaurants).

Orchidée du Bemaraha HOTEL €€€
(☎032 50 898 79; www.orchideedubemaraha.com; Bekopaka; camping per tent Ar35,000, r Ar60,000-100,000;) With beautiful grounds, a pool and a lovely bar, this is a fantastic place to come back to after scaling the pinnacles of the Tsingy. Both the tents and rooms are good-value and well-appointed. There are half- and full-board options (Ar35,000/55,000).

Tanankoay BUNGALOWS €€
(☎034 18 251 93; www.tanankoay.com; Bekopaka; camping Ar5000, d Ar40,000-68,000, without bathroom Ar15,000) This super-friendly hotel offers everything from camping to plush and spacious ensuite bungalows. There is a lovely garden, and the restaurant serves excellent food in the evening (the Ar19,000 three-course meal is great value) – although it must be said that the packed lunches are rather sorry-looking. It is very popular so make sure you book in advance. Tanankoay is 900m north of Bekopaka on the road to the Grands Tsingy.

Camp Croco CAMPGROUND €€
(☎22 630 86; www.madcameleon.com; s/d/tr Ar40,000/45,000/60,000) This lovely tented camp, run by the reputable tour operator Mad Caméléon, has an atmospheric location with epic sunsets on the southern banks of the Manambolo River. The large canvas tents are mounted on decks; inside you'll find proper beds and basic furniture. They are comfortable but considering you have to share bathrooms and toilets, definitely overpriced. Travellers rave about the food, however (Ar24,000 for a three-course meal).

Information

Bekopaka lacks mains electricity, and hotels generally switch on their generators between 5pm and 10pm. The only mobile phone network that works is Telma; there is no internet access. There are no banks so make sure you have enough cash before setting off from Morondava.

For more planning advice, author recommendations and insider tips on Parc National Des Tsingy de Bemaraha, head to www.lonelyplanet.com/madagascar/western-madagascar/parc-national-des-tsingy-de-bemaraha.

Getting There & Away

You need a 4WD to access the Tsingy: there is no way round it. Bekopaka and the national park are on the north side of the **Manambolo River ferry crossing** (passenger/vehicle free/Ar5000; 6.30am-noon & 2-6pm); the crossing is about 80km of very rough track north of

Belo-sur-Tsiribihina (four hours) and passable only from April to October. The village of Bekopaka is about 3km from the ferry crossing.

A car and driver in Morondava will set you back around Ar180,000 per day including fuel. Alternatively, hotels in Bekopaka, tour operators in Morondava and those running trips on the Tsiribihina can organise trips to the park (allow €400 to €500 for two people for a four-day trip).

In the dry season, there are infrequent **camions-brousses** from Bekopaka to Belo-sur-Tsiribihina (Ar20,000, 10 to 24 hours) and Maintirano (Ar50,000, one to two days) in the north.

MORONDAVA & AROUND

Morondava

POP 36,000

Morondava is a terminally laid-back seaside town with sandy streets and gently decaying clapboard houses. There is not much to do or see in the town itself, and most people come here on their way to/from Parc National des Tsingy de Bemaraha or the Tsiribihina River. It's also the base from which to explore Réserve Forestière de Kirindy and the famous Allée des Baobabs.

Tours

The following can help you organise trips to Belo-sur-Mer (three days, from €150 per person), Parc National des Tsingy de Bemaraha (four days, from €400 per person) and Réserve Forestière de Kirindy (€40 for the day trip), as well as deep-sea fishing trips and sailing excursions (€150, plus fuel for motorboats).

François Vahiako ADVENTURE TOUR
(95 521 63, 034 04 338 54; Les Bougainvilliers, Rue de l'Indépendance) Vahiako is the head of the Morondava Guides Association and the best person to go to for affordable vehicles (4WD with driver) for trips to the Tsingy de Bemaraha, Belo-sur-Mer or anywhere in the area.

Chez Maggie ADVENTURE TOUR
(95 523 47; www.chezmaggie.com; Rue de l'Indépendance) Chez Maggie is an agent for **Remote River Expeditions** (www.remoteriver.com), which runs sustainable-travel-focused trips down the little-explored Mangoky, Mahavavy and Manambolo Rivers. The hotel also organises trips to local attractions.

Couleur Café SAILING
(95 935 02, 032 43 666 54; Rue de l'Indépendance) This cafe-restaurant has a catamaran that can take up to eight people. It runs trips to Belo-sur-Mer (one-way/return Ar90,000/150,000) as well as excursions along the coast.

Jean le Rasta ADVENTURE TOUR
(95 527 81, 032 04 931 60; L'Oasis, Rte de la Plage) Charismatic Jean le Rasta, or Rasta Jean, speaks English, is reliable and owns a 4WD. He runs a range of tours in the region and across southern Madagascar. Look for him at l'Oasis.

Sleeping

TOP CHOICE **Trecicogne** GUESTHOUSE €
(95 924 25; www.hoteltrecicogne.com; Rue de l'Indépendance; d Ar45,000, without bathroom Ar20,000;) This Italian-run guesthouse, right at the end of Nosy Kely peninsula, is a lovely place. The rooms all have polished wooden floors, whitewashed walls, blue curtains and are absolutely spotless. The cheaper ones share bathrooms and only have fans. The restaurant is in a verandah overlooking the mangrove canal at the back. The hotel can organise trips to most regional attractions, including pirogue trips to Belo-sur-Mer.

Renala BUNGALOW €€€
(032 04 976 88; www.renala.net; Rue de l'Indépendance; r/bungalows from Ar55,000/80,000;) Renala's pretty rooms and clapboard bungalows, with their brightly coloured bedspreads and curtains, have a girly quality to them. There's an excellent two-storey restaurant right on the beach and a nice TV/internet lounge. The hotel can help you organise trips to the Tsingy and Belo-sur-Mer.

Chez Maggie BUNGALOW €€€
(95 523 47; www.chezmaggie.com; Rue de l'Indépendance; r Ar80,000-140,000;) Whether you sleep in the atmospheric captain's cabin with its marine-themed decor, the well-appointed bungalows or the superb mezzanine 'chalets', Chez Maggie is a delight. You could spend many hours reading in the garden, lounging by the pool or admiring the ocean.

Hôtel Maeva GUESTHOUSE €€
(95 944 49; www.hotelmaeva-morondava.com; Rue de l'Indépendance; d/tr/q Ar60,000/80,000/100,000;) A charming whitewashed house with a colonial feel and friendly management, Maeva offers seven simple but spacious rooms. It's right on the beach so even

Morondava

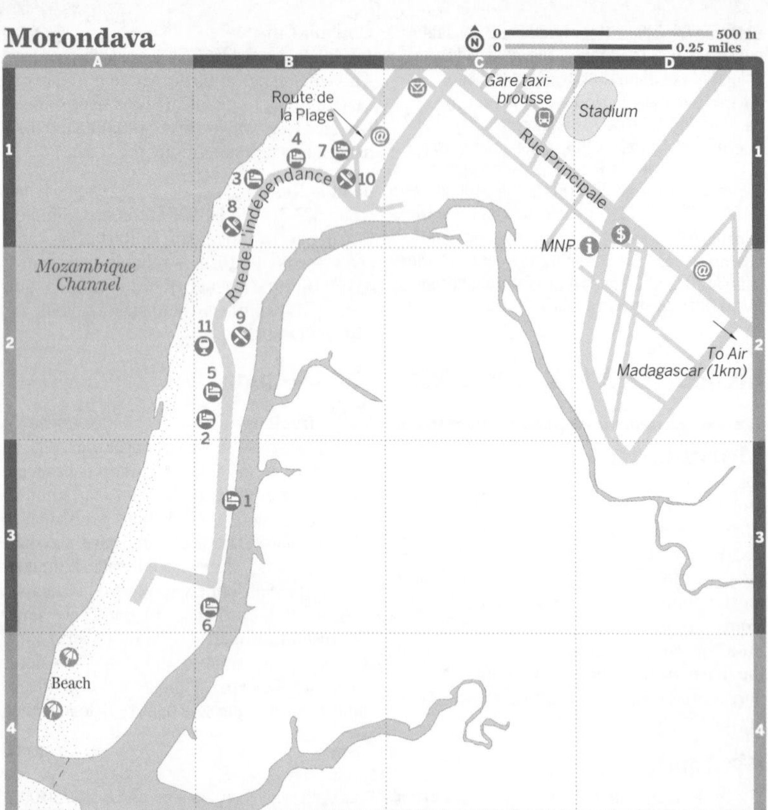

though air-con is available, you will hardly ever need it thanks to the night sea breeze.

Baobab Café HOTEL €€€
(☎95 520 12, 032 02 440 71; baobabtours@blueline.mg; Rue de l'Indépendance; r from Ar80,000; ❄@📶🏊) This option has smart but rather plain rooms with fridge and satellite TV. Twin rooms have two double beds, and there's a pool, snooker table and game room. It doubles as the French consulate for Morondava.

Les Bougainvilliers HOTEL €€
(☎95 521 63; bol_nd@yahoo.fr; Rue de l'Indépendance; r/bungalows Ar20,000/40,000) The bungalows, right on the beach, are good value, but the rooms are pretty basic. There is an atmospheric restaurant overlooking the sea that serves great food.

Zoom Hôtel HOTEL €
(☎032 44 942 03, 032 46 298 35; Rte de la Plage; r Ar24,000) Basic, clean rooms with fan but no mosquito nets (a concern in Morondava). It is across the road from the popular Oasis bar-restaurant.

Eating & Drinking

TOP CHOICE **Renala** EUROPEAN €€
(Rue de l'Indépendance; mains Ar13,000-18,000) In a tall wooden building on stilts overlooking Morondava's beach, the Renala serves delicious Franco-Malagasy cuisine. Seafood is the name of the game: try the *camaron*, the crab or whatever fish is on offer that day. All the side dishes are beautifully crafted, too, including delicious sautéed potatoes if you fancy a change from rice.

Les Bougainvilliers MALAGASY €€
(Rue de l'Indépendance; mains Ar10,000-15,000; ⏰breakfast, lunch & dinner) The Bougainvilliers has made a name for itself by serving excellent Malagasy dishes and therefore attracting travellers as well as locals. You'll

Morondava

Activities, Courses & Tours

Sleeping

Eating

Drinking

find traditional dishes such as *ravitoto*, *romazava de la mer* (a seafood stew) and coconut crab. The three-course *menu du jour* (Ar20,000) is excellent value. The breakfast (Ar6500) also includes very good croissants.

L'Oasis EUROPEAN €

(Rte de la Plage; mains Ar8000-12,000) Presided over by an affable local guy called Jean le Rasta, or Rasta Jean, l'Oasis has the best atmosphere in town. There is live music every night, including drums and reggae performed by Rasta Jean and other local musicians. The food is also pretty good, although fairly standard with grilled meat and fish, coconut chicken etc.

Couleur Café CAFE €

(Rue de l'Indépendance; mains Ar7000-10,000; breakfast, lunch & dinner) In a beautiful traditional building made of local wood and thatch, Couleur Café serves simple meals such as crêpes, sandwiches and grilled meat or fish. It's a lovely spot for lunch thanks to its beach location; there is also a great bar, with a nice selection of flavoured house rums.

Le Masoandro EUROPEAN €€

(Chez Maggie, Rue de l'Indépendance; mains Ar11,000-15,000; breakfast, lunch & dinner) The atmosphere at Chez Maggies's thatch-roof restaurant is a tad formal, but you can't fault the service, or the food. The house speciality is grill: be it steak, jumbo shrimp or the catch of the day, everything comes out cooked to perfection. The bar has a wide selection of scotch, whiskey and delicious homemade coconut rum.

La Capannina ITALIAN €€

(Rue de l'Indépendance; mains Ar11,000-14,000; lunch & dinner Thu-Tue) Run by an Italian and Malagasy couple, this place serves consistently yummy Italian food – think lots of pastas and different sauces, and pizzas straight out of the wood-fired oven. Sit outside on the attractive terrace or in the thatched dining room overlooking the river.

My Lord CLUB

(Tue-Sun) This dive of a nightclub attracts a pretty young crowd; music is a mix of R & B and Malagasy sounds.

SAKALAVA EROTICA

The western part of Madagascar has traditionally been the area with the strongest African influence. The language of the dark-skinned western peoples contains many words taken from mainland African languages. The dominant tribe in the area is the Sakalava, who venerate the relics not of their own ancestors, but of their ancient royal families. This belief, plus the use of spirit mediums to communicate with dead royalty, also has an African base (Bantu).

The Sakalava are perhaps best known for covering the tombs of their dead with elaborate, erotic carvings, often depicting oral sex or other acts considered *fady* (taboo) in life. Although Sakalava tombs were once visible throughout the entire western region, many were pillaged for their valuable carvings. Following this desecration, the Sakalava now understandably keep the location of those burial grounds still containing intact tombs top secret. It's important to respect their privacy. If you are lucky enough to see these erotic artworks, please take only photos.

TAXIS-BROUSSES FROM MORONDAVA

DESTINATION	COST (AR)	DURATION (HRS)	FREQUENCY
Antananarivo	45,000	15	Daily
Antsirabe	35,000	12	Daily
Miandrivazo	20,000	6	Daily
Belo-sur-Tsiribihina	10,000	3	Daily
Tuléar	60,000	48	several times weekly Apr-Oct
Belo-sur-Mer	30,000	4	several times weekly Apr-Oct

Information

BFV-SG (Rue Principale) Changes money; ATM.

Cycern (Rue Principale; per min Ar100; ⏲Mon-Sat) Woefully slow internet.

Espace Cyber (Rte de la Plage; per min Ar100; ⏲8am-12.30pm & 2.30-7.30pm Mon-Sat) Zebu-cart slow internet.

Getting There & Around

To/from the airport

Taxis between town and the airport cost Ar10,000; taxis within town cost Ar2000.

Air

Air Madagascar (☎95 920 22; www.airmadagascar.com; Mamahora) Flies several times weekly between Morondava and Antananarivo (one hour, €187) and once a week between Morondava and Tuléar (one hour, €187).

Boat

Morondava is connected with the villages to the south, including Belo-sur-Mer, by pirogue and *boutre* (single-masted dhow used for cargo). Boats depart regularly for Belo-sur-Mer and Morombé, although journey times depend entirely on wind and sea conditions. Safety is a concern on these boats, and there are no facilities; if you do decide to travel by sea, bring sun protection and all the food and water you will need.

Taxi-Brousse

The road between Morondava and Tana is now in good condition, save for 20km outside Morondava. The road between Morondava and Tuléar (Toliara) is a very rough track that is only passable in the dry season (April to October); the taxis-brousses that do the route are 4WD *bâchés* (small, converted pick-up trucks) or *camions-brousses* – even worse in comfort than normal taxis-brousses. Taxis-brousses leave in the morning as and when they fill up.

Réserve Forestière de Kirindy

This reserve, 60km northeast of Morondava, covers about 12,500 hectares and was established in the late 1970s as an experiment in sustainable logging and forest management. It is now a protected area, popular with scientists and travellers for its amazing wildlife.

Kirindy is one of the few places in Madagascar where you are very likely to see the fossa *(Cryptoprocta felix)*, the country's largest predator, a puma-like creature with oversize ears and a strangely elongated body, the size of a large cat. The best time to see them is in the mating season (September to

RÉSERVE FORESTIÈRE DE KIRINDY

Best time to visit Year-round.

Key highlight The profusion of wildlife, including some of Madagascar's rarest mammals.

Wildlife Fossa, giant jumping rat, lemurs, tortoises and many birds.

Habitats Deciduous dry forest.

Gateway towns Morondava.

Transport options Private vehicle or taxi-brousse, plus a 5km walk.

Things you should know Kirindy is probably the best place in Madagascar to do a night walk since the place teems with wildlife and you are allowed to go right in the reserve (unlike in national parks).

DON'T MISS

ALLÉE DES BAOBABS

One of the most photographed spots in Madagascar is this small stretch of the RN8 between Morondava and Belo-sur-Tsiribihina: flanked on both sides by majestic *Adansonia grandidieri baobabs*, it is a sight that has become symbolic of Madagascar. The trees here are as old as 1000 years, with huge, gnarled branches fanning out at the top of their trunks: it's easy to see why they've been nicknamed 'roots of the sky'.

The best times to visit Allée des Baobabs are at sunset and sunrise, when the colours of the trees change and the long shadows are most pronounced, although bear in mind that every vehicle driving down from Parc National des Tsingy de Bemaraha aims to get here around sunset and that it can therefore be very busy, particularly during the park's high season (July to September).

If you don't plan to see the Allée on your way to/from attractions north of Morondava (Tsingy, Tsiribihina or Réserve Forestière de Kirindy), a taxi from Morondava town costs about Ar50,000 return. All tour operators in Morondava can also help you out.

November), although your chances are good year-round since they tend to hang around the camp in the hope of stealing goodies from the kitchen.

If you don't get to see the fossa, you might be lucky enough to see one of Madagascar's most charming rodents, the giant jumping rat (its only jump is to come out of its burrow, otherwise it's very much a scurrying kind of creature).

In any case, you're guaranteed to see at least a couple of the six species of lemurs, mainly nocturnal, including the fat-tailed lemur and the tiny mouse lemur, believed to be the world's smallest primate.

There are also 45 bird species and 32 reptile species, including the rare Madagascan flat-tailed tortoise. Keep in mind that some animals hibernate during the winter months of June to August.

Park Fees & Guides

Entry permits cost Ar20,000 per person. A **guide** is compulsory and costs Ar12,000/20,000 for a two-hour day/night visit for up to four people.

Sleeping & Eating

Ecolodge de Kirindy LODGE €€
(☎032 40 165 89, 95 928 65; cfpfmva20051@yahoo.fr; bungalows Ar52,000, without bathroom Ar42,000, camping Ar12,000) Kirindy has something for every budget, from comfortable bungalows to dorms and camping pitches. All beds come with bedding and mozzie nets; lullabies are courtesy of the forest residents. There is a small on-site restaurant serving good meals (mains Ar5000 to Ar20,000) and cold beer. Bring a good torch.

Getting There & Away

Kirindy is about 60km northeast of Morondava, signposted off the Belo-sur-Tsiribihina road. If you're travelling by taxi-brousse (Ar10,000, two hours), this is as far as they will take you. The forest camp and office are 5km into the reserve, which you'll have to walk if you don't have your own vehicle.

Belo-sur-Mer

Few places will make you feel so far away from anywhere than Belo-sur-Mer. The village, sitting on the edge of a small lagoon, seems to have been swallowed up by the dunes and in the heat of the midday sun, time literally seems to stand still.

The village is a regional ship-building centre, and huge cargo vessels are still constructed on the beach in the same manner they were four centuries ago. It's also one of the country's main salt-producing areas, with vast salt marshes a few kilometres inland from the village.

Sights & Activities

As the name of the village suggests, life in Belo is all about the sea, so spend a morning or an afternoon wandering along the beach. Watch fishermen prepare their gear or bring their catch, admire the craftsmanship of pirogue- and *boutre*-builders or look for beautiful shells on the beach.

Nosy Andrahovo SNORKELLING
Belo-sur-Mer's star attraction is this string of coral-fringed islands, some semi-submerged. The islands are uninhabited and offer fabulous snorkelling. All hotels in Belo can organise

trips to Nosy Andrahovo with local pirogues; allow around Ar15,000 per person for a half-day, Ar35,000 for a full day with picnic lunch.

Menabe Plongée DIVING
(☎033 09 436 32; www.menabelo.com; 1/2 dives €50/75; ⊙Oct-Jun) The diving around Belo is excellent thanks to the proximity of a deep passage through the Mozambique Channel (humpback whales are not uncommon) and the coral reefs of Nosy Andrahovo. This dive centre, operated by the owners of Ecolodge du Menabe, operates largely outside the dry season, when transfers to Belo are done by boat from Morondava.

Sleeping & Eating

Ecolodge du Menabe LODGE €€€
(☎033 09 436 32; www.menabelo.com; d Ar75,000) Remote, scenic and peaceful, the Ecolodge is Belo's best accommodation option. The nine bungalows are simple but comfortable and right on the beach. Meals (fixed menu, Ar25,000) are served under a large canopy, and the food is good, with plenty of fresh fish, although travellers have complained about stingy portions and high prices. The hotel can organise boat trips as well as boat transfers to/from Morondava (Ar580,000 one-way for up to 10 people) when the road is impassable (October to June). The Ecolodge is right at the end of the peninsula.

Dorohotel BUNGALOWS €
(☎033 01 863 54; r without bathroom Ar15,000-25,000) The small bungalows here sit so close to each other that they look like a row of terraced houses, but they are spotless, as are the toilets and shower rooms, and good-value. There is a good atmosphere in the restaurant in the evening. Dorohotel is right in the centre of the village.

Corail BUNGALOWS €€
(☎033 20 326 87; r Ar60,000) A handful of haphazard but coquettish bungalows, the Corail is a family-run outfit right by the beach. There are some nice touches throughout, such as the hammocks on the porch, open-roof showers and raffia-decorated mirrors, and the home-cooked food is delicious.

MASONJOANY

In many areas of western and northern Madagascar, you will see women with their faces painted white. This facial mask, known as *masonjoany*, is supposed to protect skin from the sun, make it softer and suppler and remove blemishes. It's applied during the day and usually removed at night.

Masonjoany is made by grinding a branch from a tree of the same name against a stone with a small amount of water to form a paste. The *masonjoany* tradition persists in the Comoros, where the paste is made from ground sandalwood and coloured a startling canary yellow.

MORONDAVA TO TULÉAR

The coastal road from Morondava to Tuléar may look like a short cut compared to backtracking all the way to Antsirabe, but make no mistake: this is not the easy option. This road is only passable in the dry season (theoretically from April to October, although you should always check conditions with locals) and it takes three bone-shaking days on dreadful tracks. The reward is an adventure that'll be worth telling the grandkids, with beautiful landscapes, interesting villages, makeshift ferries and heavenly beaches. The journey goes like this:

» Day 1: Morondava to Belo-sur-Mer, four hours. Head off in the morning and spend the afternoon in the atmospheric village of Belo. Go on a pirogue trip to the coral islands, laze on the beach or visit the lovely Parc National de Kirindy-Mitea.

» Day 2: Belo-sur-Mer to Morombé. This is a long, punishing day of off-road driving. You'll have to set off at first light, stop in Manja for lunch and you'll arrive in Morombé just before it gets dark.

» Day 3: Morombé to Tuléar, along the coast. This splendid stretch of coastline hugs Madagascar's Great Reef. There are a number of gorgeous hotels and lots of good snorkelling and diving to do, so you may well want to split this in two days. For more info on this bit of the coast, see p84.

Information

There are no banking facilities in Belo – the nearest bank is in Morondava – nor is there electricity apart from that generated by the hotels. The only working mobile phone network is Airtel.

Getting There & Away

Boat

From November to May, the only way to access Belo-sur-Mer is by sea. Local pirogues ply the route, but journey times are entirely dependent on winds: many travellers have reported being left stranded, so bring plenty of food and water and allow plenty of time. It is much faster (2½ hrs) but also more expensive to arrange a motor boat transfer with one of the tour operators in Morondava or Ecolodge du Menabe in Belo.

Car

Access to Belo-sur-Mer by road is only possible by 4WD from May to November. There are irregular taxis-brousses (Ar25,000, four hours) between Belo-sur-Mer and Morondava in 4WD *bâchés*.

Parc National de Kirindy-Mitea

Not to be confused with the Réserve Forestière de Kirindy, the Parc National de Kirindy-Mitea, which surrounds the village of Belo-sur-Mer, is one of Madagascar's newest parks. It is remote, beautiful, with little infrastructure, and for that reason, seldom visited. What this means for visitors is that those making the effort to get here will be rewarded with an intimate experience in an environment rarely disturbed by visitors.

Park Fees & Guides

The park is still developing its infrastructure, so **admission fees** (per 1/2 days Ar10,000/15,000) are low, as are guiding fees: there are two **guides** (Ar5000) who speak French and English. Because the park is remote, it is best to organise your visit in Morondava. The friendly staff at the **MNP Office** (☎95 921 28; www.parcs-madagascar.com; Ny Havana Bldg, Morondava; ⏰7.30am-noon & 2.30-6pm Mon-Fri) will issue you with entry tickets and arrange a guide. They can also help you arrange transport.

There is also a small park **office** in Belo-sur-Mer, between the church and Dorotel: the building is unmarked, so ask people to point it out. Staff are often out and about; if that's the case, Dorotel is generally well informed as to their whereabouts.

PARC NATIONAL DE KIRINDY-MITEA

Best time to visit Year-round.

Key highlight The park's brackish water lakes and the sand dunes.

Wildlife Birdlife, including flamingos.

Habitats Dry deciduous forest.

Gateway towns Belo-sur-Mer

Transport options By boat year-round; by 4WD from May to October.

Things you should know It is easier to arrange a visit of the park from Morondava where the MNP office has admin staff. In Belo, ask at Dorotel.

Activities

The main draw at Kirindy-Mitea is the birdlife – 47 species in total, 33 of which are endemic – although there are lemurs and reptiles too. The park has two two-hour hiking circuits: one focusing on the birdlife along the lake and the coast, and the other on the park's forest. There is also the possibility of doing a pirogue trip (Ar30,000) along the estuary and the mangrove; the park staff can help you arrange it.

Getting There & Away

You will need your own transport to access Kirindy-Mitea. The park can be reached by road between May and October (it's on the rough Morondava–Belo-sur-Mer road). Access is by boat for the rest of the year, which must be arranged with the park.

Northern Madagascar

Includes »

Best Places to Eat

- » La Table d'Alexandre (p133)
- » Le Melville (p141)
- » Les Bungalows d'Ambonara (p128)
- » Chez Mama (p131)

Best Places to Stay

- » Eden Lodge (p137)
- » Camp Two, Parc National de Marojejy (p153)
- » Le Grand Bleu (p132)
- » Tsara Komba (p134)

Why Go?

If you're unable to decide between a discovery trip and a 'lace up your boots and forge a new trail' kind of trip, you'll love travel in Northern Madagascar. Activity junkies will be spoilt for choice with everything from diving to kitesurfing, while all travellers will revel in the region's diverse landscapes.

The area around Nosy Be is Madagascar's premier beach destination, with exquisite lodges, more sea-based activities than you'll have time to try, excellent seafood and idyllic scenery. It couldn't be more different from the mainland, where arid plains, strange geological formations and wind-battered coastline lend the place a frontier feel. As for the SAVA region, those who make it to this isolated part of the country will be rewarded with world-class trekking through primordial rainforest.

The region also hosts Madagascar's flagship cultural events, the Donia and Zegny'Zo – unique chances to discover Malagasy artists.

When to Go

Hell-Ville

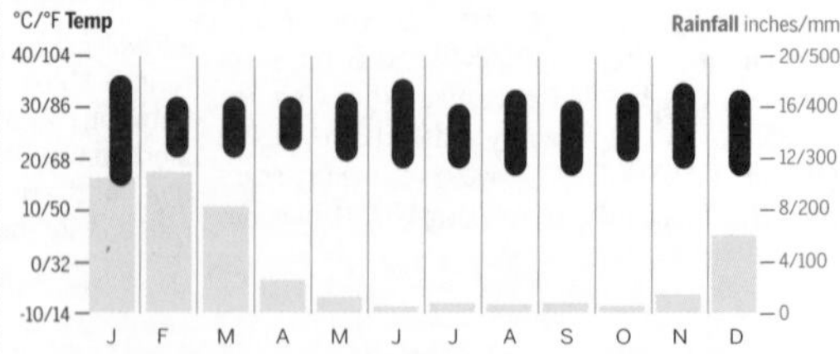

May–Jun The Donia and Zegny'-Zo festivals bring together artists from across Madagascar.

Jul–Sep Humpback whales make their annual visit to Madagascar and can be seen around Nosy Be.

May–Nov Access to the western part of Parc National de l'Ankarana is guaranteed.

Getting There & Away

Nosy Be is the only airport outside Antananarivo (Tana) to have direct flights to France (with Air Madagascar) and Italy (charter flights). There are also direct flights from Nosy Be and Diego Suarez (Antsiranana) to the neighbouring islands of the Comoros and Réunion.

Air Madagascar (☎82 211 93; www.air-madagascar.com) flies daily from Nosy Be and Diego Suarez to Antananarivo.

Sailing yachts regularly come into Nosy Be, and many are prepared to take passengers. Their principal destinations are the Comoran island of Mayotae, Mozambique and South Africa.

The road journey from Diego Suarez to Antananarivo (Ar50,000, 24 hours) is a long and arduous one. To/from the east, expect a day of potholes between Vohémar (Iharana) and Ambilobe.

NOSY BE

Despite being Madagascar's number-one beach destination, the island of Nosy Be remains relatively low-key. It's the most expensive destination in Madagascar, and rooms can cost twice as much here as on the mainland. Still, compared to Europe, prices are competitive (except for the most exclusive resorts), and many visitors find the lack of major development and *mora mora* (literally, slowly slowly) lifestyle worth the extra euros.

The climate is sunny year-round, and Nosy Be is paradise for water-based activities. Diving is the island's top draw, but there is plenty of swimming, snorkelling and sailing for those keen to stay close to the surface.

Once you've had enough of seascapes, head for the rolling landscapes of the little-explored hinterland: as well as the brilliant Réserve Naturelle Intégrale de Lokobe, there are cocoa, ylang-ylang and vanilla plantations, crater lakes and waterfalls, and miles of dirt tracks accessible only by foot or quad bike.

Despite all these assets, Nosy Be can have a bad name as the capital of sex tourism. It's true that Ambatoloaka is seedy in places but it is by no means representative of the whole island, and definitely not of the surrounding islands, which are all tiny, remote and heavenly.

It's also worth knowing that tourism operators and the authorities in Nosy Be have come down hard on prostitution and that perpetrators face heavy prison sentences.

History

Nosy Be's first inhabitants are believed to have been 15th-century Swahili and Indian traders. Later, the island served as a magnet for refugees, merchants and settlers of all descriptions.

In 1839, the Sakalava queen Tsiomeko fled to Nosy Be and turned to the French for help in resisting her Merina enemies. In 1841, the Sakalava ceded both Nosy Be and neighbouring Nosy Komba to France.

In recent years, with increasing tourism development and local environmental pressures, deforestation has become a problem on the island, as has destruction and damage of offshore coral reefs.

Dangers & Annoyances

The biggest scam in Nosy Be is the sale of so-called 'direct transfers' from Nosy Be to Diego Suarez. Touts and agencies will claim that after the boat trip from Nosy Be to Ankify, you will be whisked away in a comfortable minibus, all for a mere Ar80,000. Don't fall for it: standard taxis-brousses (bush taxis) are all you'll find in Ankify. So resist all offers on Nosy Be, take the boat to Ankify (Ar10,000) and once in Ankify, choose your taxi-brousse (Ar30,000) as you would at any taxi-brousse station (the one in best condition and/or the fullest).

Activities

Nosy Be has a plethora of activities. Most are sea-based (diving, snorkelling, day trips to islands etc), but operators have also started to offer activities to explore the island's beautiful hinterland.

Diving

Nosy Be and the surrounding islands are home to a rich diversity of marine life and offer world-class diving. Boxfish, surgeonfish, triggerfish, damselfish, clown fish, yellowfin tuna, barracuda, eagle rays, manta rays and humpback whales (July to September only) can all be spotted. Around Nosy Sakatia you're likely to see clown fish, barracuda, turtles, and perhaps dolphins and whale sharks.

On average, visibility on dives is about 15m year-round – much more on good days. The best months are April to December. July and August can be windy, especially to the north around Nosy Mitsio. The best months for seeing whale sharks are October and November, while manta rays are more prevalent from April to June and October to November.

Most operators run daily morning trips long enough for two dives, with boats leaving around 8am and getting back in time for lunch. Prices are about €40 for a *baptême* (first dive), €40/70 for one/two dives with

Northern Madagascar Highlights

1. Witness turtles nesting or hatching at the remote and ecofriendly **Eden Lodge** (p137)
2. Locate the silky sifaka in **Parc National de Marojejy** (p152)
3. Assault your senses with a visit to the **Millot Plantations** (p135), where cocoa and spices are grown
4. Go **sailing** to some of the small islands around Nosy Be (p133)
5. Watch black lemurs, boa constrictors, owls and more in Nosy Be's stunning **Réserve Naturelle Intégrale de Lokobe** (p130)
6. Marvel at geology's work of art at the **Tsingy Rouges** (p151)
7. Trek along **Les Trois Baies** (p144)
8. Snorkel off the tiny island of **Nosy Tanikely** (p134)
9. Take a self-guided walk through the history-filled streets of **Diego Suarez** (p137)

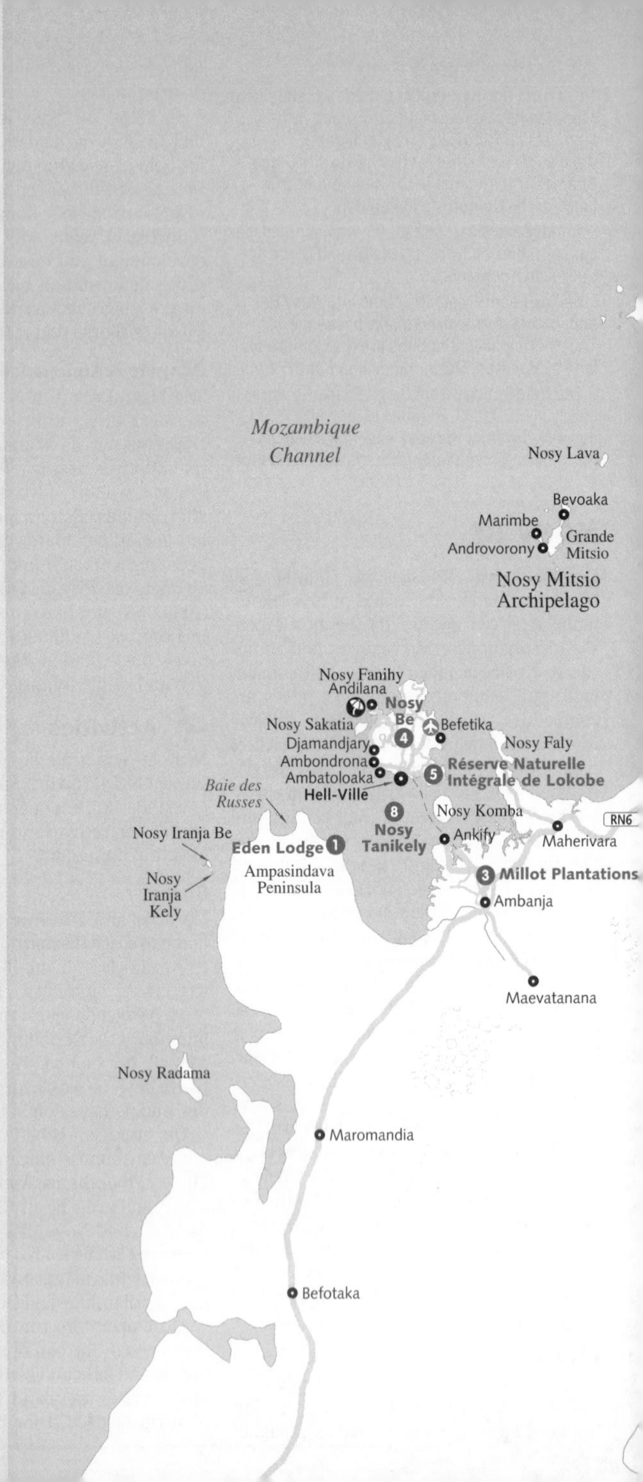

Mozambique Channel

Nosy Lava
Bevoaka
Marimbe
Grande Mitsio
Androvorony
Nosy Mitsio Archipelago
Nosy Fanihy
Andilana
Nosy Be
Nosy Sakatia
Befetika
4
Djamandjary
Nosy Faly
Ambondrona
5 Réserve Naturelle Intégrale de Lokobe
Ambatoloaka
Baie des Russes
Hell-Ville
8 Nosy Tanikely
Nosy Komba
RN6
Nosy Iranja Be
Eden Lodge 1
Ankify
Maherivara
Nosy Iranja Kely
Ampasindava Peninsula
3 Millot Plantations
Ambanja
Maevatanana
Nosy Radama
Maromandia
Befotaka

Cap d'Ambre
(Tanjon'ny Bobaomby)
Bobahala
(235m)
0
40 km
0
20 miles
Le Coq
(273m)
Anjiabe
Baie du Courrier
Windsor
Castle
(371m)
Mer d'Emeraude
Nosy Hara
Cap Miné
Ramena
Diego Suarez
(Antsiranana)
9
7
Les Trois Baies
Montagne
des Français
(426m)
Baie
d'Befotaka
Réserve
Forêt d'Ambre
Nosy
Tendro
RN6
Joffreville
(Ambohitra)
Parc National
Montagne
d'Ambre
Montagne
d'Ambre
(1475m)
Tsingy
Rouges
6
Nosy Lowry
Irodo
INDIAN
OCEAN
Lac Antanavo
Parc National
de l'Ankarana
Andrevo River
Lokia
Mahamasina
RN6
Ambilobe
RN5A
Vohémar (Iharana)
Milanoa
Tanambana
Lac
Andranotsara
Andrahary
(1785m)
Bemarivo
River
Sambava
Antohamaro
Parc National
de Marojejy
2
Mt Marojejy
(2132m)
Réserve Spéciale
d'Anjanaharibe-Sud
Andapa
Marojejy
Massif

equipment, and €50 for a night dive. Many also run all inclusive, catamaran sailing trips (from two to five days) to surrounding archipelagos such as Nosy Iranja, Nosy Mitsio and Nosy Radama, with two dives a day (€400 to €850, depending on the number of people on the boat, the length of the trip and the number of dives).

Courses are conducted in French or English, with many staff also speaking Italian. A PADI course costs around €300 to €400; it's best to book certification courses in advance.

Nosy Be & Surrounding Islands

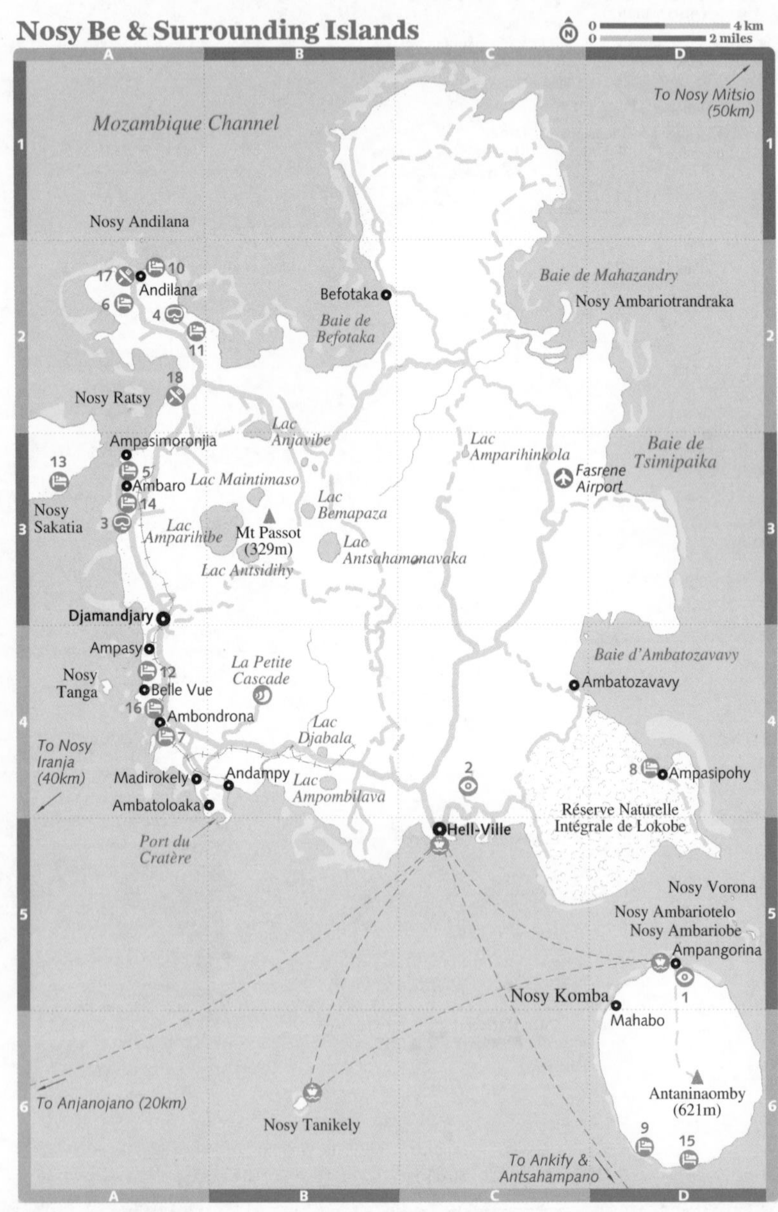

Océane's Dream DIVING
(☎032 07 127 82; www.oceanesdream.com; Ambatoloaka) One of the most well-established and recommended operators on the island, it offers single and introductory dives along with diving cruises to Nosy Mitsio, Nosy Iranja and Nosy Radama. A minimum of two people (previous certification required) is needed. It also does CMAS and PADI dive courses.

Plongée Toukoul DIVING
(Map p124; ☎032 53 847 98; www.plongeetoukoul.com; Andilana) A fairly new operator, Plongée Toukoul offers PADI courses as well as diplomas from the French Federation of Marine Sports (FFESSM). It is one of the few operators to offer dedicated courses for children (from the age of eight).

Madaplouf DIVING
(Map p124; ☎033 14 248 33; www.madaplouf.com; Bemoko) A small operator, Madaplouf runs PADI and CMAS courses in Spanish, German and Italian as well as French and English.

Tropical Diving DIVING
(☎032 49 462 51; www.tropical-diving.com; Hôtel Coco Plage, Ambatoloaka) Offers a good range of PADI-CMAS courses and a variety of diving excursions to nearby islands, including a one-day trip to Nosy Iranja, and two- or three-day trips to Nosy Mitsio and the Radama islands.

Forever Dive DIVING
(☎032 07 125 65; www.foreverdive.com; Madirokely) A small operator, Forever Dive is run by the friendly Sylvia, who's been living in Nosy Be since 1999. It delivers NAUI courses.

Snorkelling

Snorkelling is best at Nosy Tanikely, Nosy Mitsio and Nosy Sakatia. All tour operators on Nosy Be run trips to Nosy Tanikely, generally combined with a visit to Nosy Komba. Madaplouf also arranges half-day snorkelling outings to Nosy Sakatia (€30).

Fishing

The best time for fishing is March to June and October to December. Fishing excursions aren't cheap – expect to pay at least €400 per day per boat, including equipment, for up to four people. The hotels **Le Grand Bleu** (Map p124; ☎86 920 23; www.legrandbleunosybe.com; Andilana) and **Sakatia Passions** (Map p124; ☎032 41 325 49; www.sakatia-passions.com; Nosy Sakatia) specialise in sports fishing.

Quad Biking

Quad bikes are a great way to explore Nosy Be. Popular routes include a circuit around the crater lakes, remote beaches in the north and cocoa plantations to the south. The following are dedicated operators; a number of hotels also have their own quads and offer excursions to their guests. Excursions generally cost €60/100 for a half/full day.

Tsanga Tsanga Tour DRIVING TOUR
(Map p124; ☎033 14 334 20; isoal@moov.mg; Ambaro)

Madaquad DRIVING TOUR
(Map p124; ☎032 65 657 13; www.madaquad.net; Andilana)

Black & White DRIVING TOUR
(☎034 61 183 07; Ambatoloaka)

Nosy Be & Surrounding Islands

Sights
1 Lemur Park D5
2 Ylang-Ylang Distillery C4

Activities, Courses & Tours
Le Grand Bleu .... (see 11)
3 Madaplouf A3
Madaquad .... (see 10)
Nosy Be Original .... (see 14)
4 Plongée Toukoul A2
Sakatia Passions .... (see 13)
Tsanga Tsanga Tour .... (see 14)

Sleeping
5 Chanty Beach A3
6 Chez Eugénie A2
7 Domaine de Manga Be A4
8 Jardin Lokobe D4
9 Jardin Vanille D6
10 Le Belvédère A2
11 Le Grand Bleu A2
12 Nosy Be Hôtel A4
13 Sakatia Passions A3
14 Sambatra A3
15 Tsara Komba D6
16 Tsara Loky A4
Vanila Hôtel .... (see 14)

Eating
Chez Eugénie .... (see 6)
17 Chez Loulou A2
18 La Table d'Alexandre A2

NOSY BE ON A BUDGET

Nosy Be is expensive compared to the rest of Madagascar. Accommodation is particularly pricey, with the bulk of hotels falling squarely in the top-end category. There are, however, a number of ways to come to Nosy Be on a budget and still enjoy the very best of the island.

» **Accommodation** The only budget options are in Hell-Ville. True, they're not on the beach, but being in town means you'll be spoilt for choice for dinner and save the taxi fare. And you can still swim, snorkel and sunbathe to your heart's content during the day.

» **Eating** Food is generally good value in Madagascar, and Nosy Be has a couple of excellent budget eating options, including fabulous bakeries. The market in Hell-Ville is also a good place to pick up picnic supplies.

» **Transport** Use shared taxis between Hell-Ville and Ambatoloaka, and for touring the rest of the island, rent a motorbike rather than a car: they're super cheap (Ar20,000 per day and about Ar3000 of petrol for a day's riding) and ideal for exploring Nosy Be.

Tours

Nosy Be is home to dozens of tour companies, some specialising in sailing trips to explore the surrounding islands, others providing day trips of all kinds on and around the island, such as Nosy Komba and Nosy Tanikely (Ar90,000), Nosy Be (Ar90,000), Lokobe (Ar95,000), Nosy Sakatia (Ar120,000) and Nosy Iranja (Ar130,000).

MadaVoile TOUR
(☎86 065 55; www.madavoile.com; Ambatoloaka) One of the best sailing operators on Nosy Be, with a superb fleet of sailing boats, offering highly recommended cruises – from day trips to Nosy Sakatia or Nosy Komba to five-day trips to Nosy Mitsio or Nosy Radama including diving and fishing. Find it at the top of the hill in Ambatoloaka, opposite Coucher du Soleil bungalows.

Nosy Be Original TOUR
(Map p124; ☎032 48 587 55; www.nosybe-madagascar.com; Vanila Hôtel, Ambaro) A tip-top operator organising a range of excursions on and around Nosy Be, including lovely sailing trips on an 18m catamaran. It is also one of the few organisations to run whale-watching trips during the humpback whale migration (July to September).

Kokoa Travel TOUR
(☎86 932 51; www.kokoa-nosybe.com; Ambatoloaka) This agency mainly caters to Italian travellers; it runs all the usual suspects for day trips, as well as circuits in northern Madagascar. It's on Ambatoloaka's main street.

Evasion Sans Frontière TOUR
(☎86 062 44; www.mada-evasion.com; Hell-Ville) This tour operator, one of the biggest in Madagascar, specialises in the north; it's a well-oiled machine, and their Diego–Nosy Be circuits take in all the highlights. They also organise excursions on Nosy Be, including a day trip around the island and excursions to Lokobe.

Getting There & Away

Be aware that the offers of 'direct' transfer from Nosy Be to Diego Suarez are a scam (see p121). For onward travel from the mainland port of Ankify, see p136.

Air

Air Madagascar (☎86 613 60; www.airmadagascar.com; Rte de l'Ouest, Hell-Ville) Flies daily to/from Antananarivo (one hour, €184) and several times a week to/from Majunga (Mahajanga; one hour, €150) and Diego Suarez (25 minutes, €123).

Air Austral (☎86 612 32; www.air-austral.com; Blvd de l'Indépendance) Flies direct to Réunion (2½ hours) and Mayotte (45 minutes).

Boat

Small speedboats shuttle between the mainland port of Ankify and Hell-Ville on Nosy Be (Ar10,000, 30 minutes, 5.30am to 4pm). They work like taxis-brousses and leave when full. Trade winds pick up in the afternoon, so the crossing is smoother in the morning and therefore more popular, which means you'll never have to wait long for your boat to depart. Life jackets are provided.

If you're travelling with a vehicle, the Fivondronana Ferry sails between Anstahampano port, near Ambanja, and Hell-Ville in Nosy Be (Ar20,000, two hours, daily). Departure times vary according to the high tide.

Getting Around

Nosy Be's main road, which goes all the way around the island and takes in the airport, Hell-Ville, Ambatoloaka, the west coast and Andilana, is sealed and in good condition.

To/From the Airport

Nosy Be's Fasrene Airport is on the island's east side, about 12km from Hell-Ville. Taxi fare from the airport to Hell-Ville is around Ar30,000. It is about Ar40,000 to Ambatoloaka and Andilana.

Boat

For the ultimate freedom to explore Nosy Be's shores and the surrounding islands, you can charter one of the speedboats doing the Hell-Ville–Ankify transfer for around Ar200,000 a day.

Car & Motorcycle

The best way to get around Nosy Be is by motorcycle (helmets are compulsory): roads are good, traffic is light, distances are short and the weather is lovely – perfect conditions to ditch the car, which rules on the mainland. If you'd rather have a vehicle, however, don't worry about a 4WD: a sedan (saloon) car is perfectly adequate.

Moto Mada (☎032 02 680 25; Ambatoloaka; ⏲7.30am-6pm) Rents Chinese motorbikes in very good condition (Ar20,000). They can deliver and pick up the motorbike from your hotel for another Ar5000.

Location Jeunesse (☎032 59 055 26; Ambatoloaka; ⏲7am-6pm) Rents out motorbikes (Ar20,000) and mountain bikes (Ar15,000).

Nosy Easy Rent (☎033 11 611 00; www.nosyeasyrent.com; Ambonara, Hell-Ville) Rents Dacia Logan/Mitsubishi pick-ups for €65/90 per day, with a 150km mileage. Find it as you exit Hell-Ville in the direction of Ambatoloaka, on your left hand side, about 300m after the *centrale électrique* (power station).

Taxi

Collective taxis (Ar2000) travel between Hell-Ville and Ambatoloaka (20 minutes) and between Hell-Ville and Dzamandzar (25 minutes) from 6am until 7pm. Pick them up near the market in Hell-Ville, and flag them on the main road of Ambatoloaka as they cruise (and beep) for customers.

A chartered taxi between Hell-Ville and Ambatoloaka costs Ar10,000, between Hell-Ville and Andilana Ar50,000. From Hell-Ville's centre to the jetty, it is Ar2000 to Ar3000.

Hell-Ville (Andoany)

POP 22,000

Despite the off-putting moniker (named for Admiral de Hell, a French governor of Réunion), Nosy Be's main town is anything but hellish. Rather, it's an upbeat, if rather dishevelled, place where frangipani and bougainvillea frame crumbling ruins of old colonial buildings, sidewalk cafes bustle with tourists and expats sip strong espresso.

Sleeping

TOP CHOICE **Les Bungalows d'Ambonara** BUNGALOW €€€

(☎86 613 67; www.nosy-be-holidays.com; off Route de l'Ouest; bungalows Ar75,000;) In a former coffee plantation, the bungalows of Ambonara are scattered in a luxuriant garden, with a small green pool sitting in the middle of it all like an emerald in its case. The whole place has been beautifully built and decorated using local materials such as wood, stone, bamboo and raffia. Owner Jean-Michel is also a dab hand at *rhum arrangé* (homemade rum with fruit inside) – he exports his creations across Madagascar – and you can sample and buy his products here. To find it, head out in the direction of Ambatoloaka; it is signposted on your right hand side, just before the Air Madagascar office.

YLANG-YLANG

The low, gnarled ylang-ylang (e-lang-e-lang) tree is seen in plantations all over Nosy Be. Its scented green or yellow flowers are distilled to make oil, which is exported to the West for perfume. The trees are pruned into low and rather grotesque shapes to make picking the flowers easier.

Distillation at the large **ylang-ylang distillery** (Map p124; admission Ar15,000; ⏲8am-3.30pm Mon-Fri, 7.30am-2.30pm Sat), 3km east of Hell-Ville, takes place on Monday, Wednesday and Friday only.

The distillery is now also home to a small zoo, including a large lemur park. It's a shame to see these animals in cages or confined to tiny islands (lemurs can't swim) when they can be viewed in their natural environment just a few kilometres down the road at Lokobe.

To reach the distillery head east from Hell-Ville along the Route de Marodokany for 3km. All taxi drivers know where the place is (Ar20,000 for the return trip, including an hour waiting time).

Hell-Ville (Andoany)

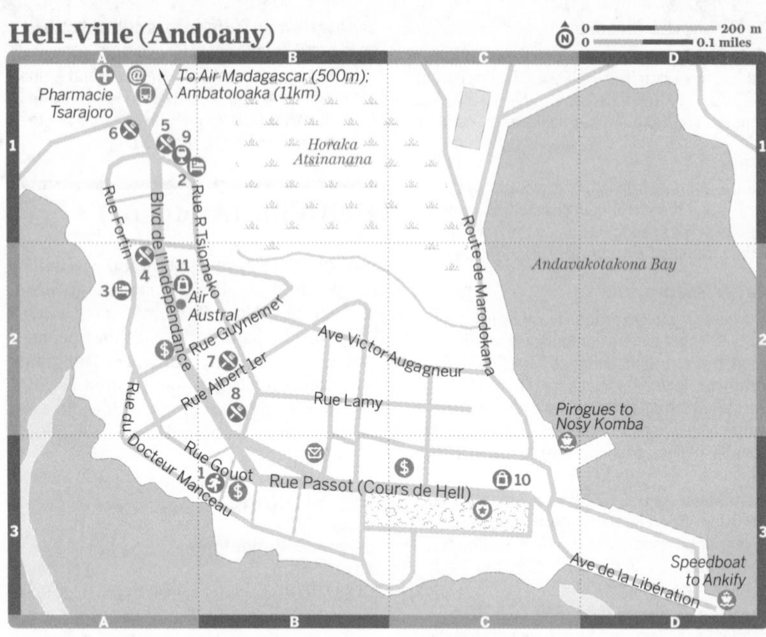

Hell-Ville (Andoany)

Activities, Courses & Tours

1 Evasions Sans Frontière B3

Sleeping

2 Hôtel Belle Vue A1
3 Hôtel Plantation A2

Eating

4 La Case de Moffe A2
5 Le Manava A1
6 Marché de Hell-Ville A1
7 Nandipo B2
8 Oasis Café B2

Drinking

9 La Porte Rouge A1

Shopping

10 Le Village C3
11 Société de Rhum Arrangé A2

Hôtel Plantation HOTEL €€
(☎032 07 934 45; plantation_b@yahoo.fr; Rue Fortin; r Ar35,000-65,000; ❄📶) In a beautiful old colonial mansion, this is a charming little place. Ask to see a few rooms before you settle as the cheaper ones can be a little dark, while the nicest have beautiful parquet floors and sea-facing balconies. The restaurant serves good food and is equipped with wi-fi.

Hôtel Belle Vue HOTEL €€
(☎86 613 84; bellevuehotel-nosybe@yahoo.fr; Rue R Tsiomeko; d Ar40,000, with shared toilet Ar25,000; ❄📶) The Belle Vue is an excellent budget option right in the centre of Hell-Ville, with very friendly management. Cheaper rooms have fans and share a toilet, but all are immaculate and cheerful. The ones at the back of the building are the best – brighter, airier and with nice views. Wi-fi is only available in the reception area.

Eating & Drinking

TOP CHOICE **Les Bungalows d'Ambonara** FUSION €€€
(www.nosy-be-holidays.com; off Route de l'Ouest; mains Ar16,000-18,000; ⊙Tue-Sun) The speciality at Les Bungalows d'Ambonara is zebu steak: Jean-Michel knows where to source the most tender meat and cooks it to perfection, with a vegetable gratin and melt-in-your-mouth sautéed potatoes. If meat doesn't float your boat, the menu changes regularly and features plenty of fish and seafood, all cooked exquisitely with local spices. Finish your dinner with one of the restaurant's 20 *rhums arrangés*, another speciality.

TOP CHOICE **Le Manava** MALAGASY €€

(Rue R Tsiomeko; mains Ar11,000-15,000) On the top floor, Le Manava is an unexpected gem. The fare is simple but incredibly tasty, with grilled meat or fish with seasonal vegetables, and rice or chips. The balcony terrace is an atmospheric place to people-watch, and there is always a good atmosphere at the bar, with people playing pool and live music several times a week.

Nandipo PIZZERIA €€€

(Rue Albert 1er; mains Ar16,000-20,000; breakfast, lunch & dinner;) This very cool place, done up as a Spanish bodega (the owner is from Barcelona), is the yachtsmen's and expats' hangout of choice. It serves good (if pricey) wood-oven pizzas and has good music, a great selection of drinks and the best ambience in town.

La Case de Moffe CAFE €

(Blvd de l'Indépendance; cakes & sandwiches Ar1000-5000; 7am-1pm & 3-7pm Mon-Sat, 7am-1pm Sun) La Case de Moffe is an endearing Franco-Malagasy name that means 'the bread's house'. This little bakery does scrumptious bread and croissants (courtesy of a French baker). There is a lovely patio where you can enjoy your pastries with an espresso or devour baguette sandwiches with fresh fruit juices. The éclairs are to die for.

Oasis Café CAFE €

(Blvd de l'Indépendance; mains Ar6000-12,000; breakfast, lunch & dinner Mon-Sat) Oasis' sidewalk seating is prime people-watching territory. The cafe serves food all day, but it does breakfast best, with excellent baguettes, good pastries and proper coffee, including espresso.

Marché de Hell-Ville MARKET €

(Place du Marché; 6am-5pm) Hell-Ville's market is a good place to pick up fruit and veggies for picnics, as well as spices.

La Porte Rouge BAR

(Rue R Tsiomeko; 11am-11pm) Next to the Hôtel Belle Vue, La Porte Rouge is a social watering hole popular with locals. The ambience is animated and amiable. There is sometimes dancing and live music at the weekend.

Shopping

Société de Rhum Arrangé DRINK

(Blvd de l'Indépendance; 8am-6pm Mon-Sat) If you'd like to take a taste of Madagascar home with you, why not plump for a bottle of *rhum arrangé*? There are more than 20 flavours to choose from at this little place, from vanilla to cinnamon, liquorice to coconut. The half-litre bottles (Ar12,000) make perfect presents.

Le Village HANDICRAFTS

(www.maquettesdebateaux.com; Rue Passot; 8am-6pm Mon-Sat) This boutique sells exquisitely crafted model boats; each is unique and handmade at Le Village's workshop in Antananarivo using precious woods. Prince Albert of Monaco and the King of Spain have shopped at Le Village; prices start at around €80.

Information

For more reviews, insider tips and planning advice on Nosy Be, head to www.lonelyplanet.com/madagascar/northern-madagascar/nosy-be.

Bank of Africa (BOA; Blvd de l'Indépendance) ATM, Western Union.

BFV-SG (Rue Gouot) ATM (Visa) changes travellers cheques.

BNI-CA (Rue Passot) ATM (Visa and MasterCard).

Espace Médical (Rte de l'Ouest; 86 925 99; 24 hrs) About halfway between Hell-Ville and Ambatoloaka. French, Italian and some English spoken.

Kelly Services (Gallerie Ankoay, Blvd du Général de Gaulle; internet per min Ar80; 7am-10pm) Very fast and reliable connection; wi-fi is cheaper.

Pharmacie Tsarajoro (Blvd du Général de Gaulle) Well-stocked pharmacy.

Post Office (cnr Blvd de l'Indépendance & Rue Passot)

THE DONIA

Every year around Pentecost (late May or early June), Nosy Be holds a week-long music festival known as the **Donia** (www.festival-donia.com). Groups from Madagascar, neighbouring islands such as the Comoros, Réunion and Mauritius, and France perform a wonderful mix of rock, reggae, Creole and pop. There are also a number of fringe events, including a carnival, sporting events and seminars. Around 50,000 people attend every year, and the island is at its most effervescent. The main venue is Hell-Ville, although there are events across the island.

DON'T MISS

RÉSERVE NATURELLE INTÉGRALE DE LOKOBE

The **Réserve Naturelle Intégrale de Lokobe** (www.parcs-madagascar.com) protects most of Nosy Be's remaining endemic vegetation. The reserve is home to the black lemur (the male is dark brown, almost black, while the female is a lovely chestnut colour with white tufts around its ears and cheeks) and several other lemur species. You're also likely to spot boa constrictors, owls, chameleons and many wonderful plants, from ylang-ylang trees to vanilla orchids, traveller's palms and more.

You will need a guide to visit Lokobe (only the periphery of the reserve is actually accessible to visitors). The best guide is **Jean Robert** (☎032 02 513 85). As well as knowing the reserve intimately and being a mine of information on all things fauna and flora, Jean is a real character, who will get you to sing the national anthem before you set off but then insist on silence during the visit to minimise disruption to Lokobe's wildlife (he'll just whisper the names of the animals as you go). Jean organises lovely day trips to Lokobe that cost Ar80,000 per person. They include taxi between your hotel and Ambatozavavy, transfer in pirogue from Ambatozavavy to Ampasipohy (the starting point for walks), a two-hour walk in the forest, lunch, drinks and admission fees to the reserve. Most tour operators in Nosy Be organise similar packages, often through Jean Robert.

If you would like to spend the night in Lokobe, **Jardin Lokobe** (Map p124; ☎86 938 11, 032 59 700 36; d half board incl breakfast & dinner €110) is a little slice of paradise in the tiny village of Ampasipohy. The bungalows seem to come straight out of the glossy pages of an interior-design magazine, with warm colours, local materials and stunning bathrooms. Didier, the owner, is great company and his dizzying array of *rhum arrangé* (homemade rum with fruit) is guaranteed to keep the conversation flowing until the wee hours. The beach in front of the hotel is not great for swimming, but Didier organises a night walk in the reserve for guests.

Ambatoloaka

Nosy Be's southernmost beach is one of the island's most touristy, but definitely not its best. Its popularity with foreign men of a certain age in search of young Malagasy love is what gave Nosy Be a bad name. Many travellers will feel uneasy about the sleazy atmosphere, particularly in bars and restaurants. That said, Ambatoloaka can be fun: the nightlife is good by Malagasy standards, and the village comes into its own on Sundays when locals come en masse to enjoy a day at the beach. A number of hotels have also taken a very firm stand against sex tourism and their efforts deserve to be supported.

The village of Ambatoloaka basically stretches along one long street, with most of the hotels, bars and restaurants clustering at the beach end of it. The beach itself, which becomes Madirokely at its northern end, is pretty, but the constant flow of touts, diving boats coming in and out and noise from the seafront establishments means it's no good for an afternoon of R&R; head north if that's what you're after.

Sleeping

Places are often full, so it's best to reserve in advance. Lots of places quote in euros.

TOP CHOICE **L'Heure Bleue** BOUTIQUE HOTEL €€€
(☎86 060 20; www.heurebleue.com; Madirokely; bungalows €100;) On a hill overlooking the beach of Madirokely, this gorgeous hotel has a terrace with great views and a sensational saltwater pool just above the sea. The bungalows are made of polished wood and come with smart linen bedclothes and giant sliding-glass doors, which open on to balconies with distant ocean views and armchairs for private sunbathing. Rates include breakfast.

Hôtel Gérard et Francine GUESTHOUSE €€€
(☎032 07 127 93; www.gerard-et-francine.com; d €55;) A beautifully decorated family guesthouse with bright-yellow walls, wooden floors and a verandah overlooking the beach. The rooms come in all shapes and sizes – some are in the main house and some in the garden. The hotel uses solar power for hot water, and the owners are very involved in initiatives to preserve Nosy Be's environment.

They also lobby actively against sex tourism in Nosy Be. Rates include breakfast.

Hôtel Benjamin BUNGALOW €€€
(☎86 927 64; www.hotelbenjamin-nosybe.com; bungalows €36) Situated in a beautiful garden and quiet location back from the main road, this is a pretty good deal for Nosy Be. The bungalows are furnished simply, but each comes with a petite verandah. Some have hammocks.

Villa Razambe APARTMENT €€€
(☎86 927 64; www.hotelbenjamin-nosybe.com/villa_razambe.html; villa €200) If you're planning a family reunion or just have a lot of friends, you can rent the villa. It has four bedrooms, a lovely terrace, a kitchen and a magnificent pool. And it's only 150m from the beach.

Coco Plage HOTEL €€€
(☎032 40 680 96; coco.plage@moov.mg; d Ar135,000-157,000; wi-fi) If you're interested in diving, this is a good choice. The long established Tropical Diving (see p125) is based here. There are 12 rooms right on the beach and another six facing a pretty garden at the back. All are well appointed, and the sea breezes provide natural air-con at night.

Le Coucher du Soleil BUNGALOW €€
(☎86 928 42; coucherdusoleil@wanadoo.mg; bungalows Ar50,000-65,000) This is the best budget option in Ambatoloaka. The bungalows come with or without running water; those without running water actually have more charm than the more modern ones, but you'll have to content yourself with bucket showers. It's signposted from the main street in Ambatoloaka.

Eating

TOP CHOICE **Chez Mama** HOTELY €
(mains Ar5000-10,000) For a true Malagasy eating experience, try Chez Mama, located on Ambatoloaka's main street. Mama buys her ingredients at Hell-Ville's market every morning, and everything she cooks is fresh, tasty and incredibly cheap. Try some of the local staples such as *romazava* (beef and vegetable stew) or *poulet sauce* (chicken in tomato sauce). Half portions are available.

Chez Papa Bebetto HOTELY €
(mains Ar5000-10,000; Mon-Sat) Another excellent hotely that's popular at lunchtime, it specialises in simple meals such as zebu steak, pan-fried calamari with garlic or grilled chicken, all served with rice or chips. The homemade juices are delicious.

Chez Teresa ITALIAN €€
(mains Ar10,000-13,000; Wed-Mon) Run by the ebullient Teresa, this Italian restaurant is an eye-catching place, with its candy-colour decor and fairy lights. The menu features plenty of pizza and pastas that make good use of the plentiful supply of seafood. The house Limoncello is a delight.

Drinking & Entertainment

Le Taxi-Be BAR
(Wed-Mon) This lively bar is very popular with local *vazaha* (foreigners) and young Malagasy women. For all that, it's not a creepy place, with live music every night and a cut-out Renault 4L decorating the stage.

Djembe Disco CLUB
(admission Ar3000; Thu-Sun) This is Nosy Be's favourite nightclub, located at the end of the village on the road leading to Madirokely town. It's the place to be seen in the evenings – popular with local couples, expats and foreign men on the prowl. Besides a dance floor, Djembe regularly hosts live music events. There are also pool tables.

Information

BNI-CA ATM accepting MasterCard and Visa.

Baobab Kafé (per min Ar100; 10am-6pm; wi-fi) Internet.

Pharmacie Nourdine (8am-noon & 2-6pm Mon-Sat)

The West Coast

With its lovely beaches and postcard sunset views, it's no surprise most hotels on Nosy Be have decided to set up shop on this bit of the island. It stretches from Madirokely to Andilana in the north. The further north you go, the more isolated and quieter it gets, so you'll need to eat where you sleep (or take a taxi to go out) if you stay up there. If you yearn for company, you'll be happier in Ambatoloaka or Hell-Ville.

Beaches

Andilana BEACH
Far and away Nosy Be's best beach, Andilana, at the island's northwest tip, is a long stretch of pearly white sand, with water that's true turquoise and clear as gin. It's

ideal for swimming and chilling for an afternoon, with gorgeous sunsets.

Andilana ignites on Sundays, when French expats and Malagasy from around Nosy Be come for a lazy day in the sun. Families lay out picnics on a shaded bit of sand, tuck into a crate of beers, bring their stereo, swim and dance until the sun goes down.

Ambondrona BEACH

On a small bay just north of Madirokely, Ambondrona is more tranquil than its southern neighbours, with lovely views of the mainland hills across the sea.

Sleeping

Accommodation on this bit of the coast is almost exclusively top end.

TOP CHOICE **Le Grand Bleu** GUESTHOUSE €€€

(Map p124; ☎86 920 23; www.legrandbleunosybe.com; Andilana; d €30-65; ❄≋) On a hill overlooking the sea, Le Grand Bleu has spectacular views from its terrace restaurant, where you can curl up on a pillowed chair and read a book or chow on wood-fired pizza. The star attraction is the dazzling infinity pool (with infinity views); the hotel is also three minutes' walk from a lovely beach. The bungalows are very pretty, with blue-and-white walls, wood floors and four-poster beds with mosquito net. Each also has its own little terrace and hammock. Half- and full-board plans are available. Simpler bungalows (no air-con) are also available for €30 a night.

Le Grand Bleu offers all sorts of excursions and activities (Guillaume, the owner, is a seasoned fisherman), including sailing, scuba diving (they work with diving club Plongée Toukoul), canoeing and quad bike outings. The hotel is about 3km from Andilana.

Le Belvédère GUESTHOUSE €€€

(Map p124; ☎032 76 751 99; www.hotel-nord-madagascar.com; Andilana; d Ar125,000) Perched on a bluff overlooking the wonderful Andilana beach (a mere five minutes' walk away), this is a small and simple hotel – there are no TVs, minibars or fridges. But it's the lack of modern amenities that makes Belvédère so charming: you won't get enough of the sunsets and tranquillity. The decent-size rooms each come with a front porch – complete with sun chairs and tables – overlooking the ocean. Rates include breakfast.

Vanila Hôtel RESORT €€€

(Map p124; ☎86 921 01; www.vanila-hotel.com; Ambaro; d/ste €109/295; ❄@≋) The pick of the top-end beach hotels on this bit of the coast, it caters more to couples and families than tour groups, and its design – small buildings with thatched roofs, and lots of local art such as batiks and baobab sculptures – gives the Vanila a boutique feel. Rooms are charming, with salmon-colour walls and wooden furniture. As well as the pools and beach, there is a sensational (but pricey) spa. Vanila also organises a range of excursions in Nosy Be and nearby islands, and excellent talks on whales during the whale migration season (July to September).

Sambatra GUESTHOUSE €€€

(Map p124; ☎86 921 90; www.sambatra.com; Ambaro; d €50) With a handful of simple but cheerful rooms right on the beach, Sambatra is overpriced by Malagasy standards but not bad for Nosy Be. The sunsets and views of Sakatia are gorgeous and the restaurant serves excellent food (breakfast is included in the rates). The hotel also runs quad company Tsanga Tsanga Tour, which organises excellent excursions in the island's hinterland.

Domaine de Manga Be APARTMENT €€€

(Map p124; ☎86 060 88; www.domainemangabe.com; Ambondrona; d/tr/q €40/50/60) A rather stylish and original self-catering complex aimed predominantly at families. The beautifully decorated studio apartments, villas, rooms and bungalows come in all shapes and price ranges, but all have kitchens or kitchenettes, nets and fans. If you pay a supplement you can hire an apartment with a cook to prepare your meals.

Nosy Be Hôtel RESORT €€€

(Map p124; ☎86 061 51; www.nosybehotel.com; Ampasy; d €60-100; ❄≋) The Nosy Be Hôtel stands out from the competition thanks to its highly original decor – including stunning wooden furniture made on Nosy Komba and lots of local artwork – and lush garden on the edge of the beach. The hotel offers various plans, from B&B to all inclusive. There is an on-site dive centre, and quad bike and island-hopping trips can be arranged.

Chanty Beach GUESTHOUSE €€€

(Map p124; ☎86 928 16; www.chantybeach-hotel.com; Ambaro; r/bungalows incl breakfast €66/82; ❄) This German-run place is a charming, if slightly staid, white colonial-style guesthouse in a neat garden on the beach facing Nosy Sakatia. Some of the bungalows have their own kitchenettes, and there's a small restaurant/bar serving mostly seafood. Activities include sailing trips and boat rentals. Diving and island excursions can be arranged. There is snorkelling nearby.

Chez Eugénie GUESTHOUSE €€€
(Map p124; ☎86 923 53; www.chez-eugenie.com; Andilana; d €40) There are just five rooms at this little hotel and restaurant owned by a French and Malagasy couple. It's an unusual structure, with two separate wings joined under one big thatched roof to form a dining room. Abodes are small, but pretty, with firm mattresses and high-quality linens. The hotel is about 200m from beautiful Andilana beach.

Tsara Loky PENSION €€
(Map p124; ☎032 04 853 97; Ambondrona; d Ar60,000) This laid-back hotel offers small, wonky bungalows in the village of Ambondrona. It's a little cramped and overpriced for the comfort level, but you won't find cheaper this close to the beach (a mere 50m). There's also a good atmosphere, with locals often meeting up in the parking lot to play *pétanque* (a French game similar to bowls or bocce). To get here, turn at the Manga Be signpost from the main road, take a sharp right after the railway track and follow the sign to 'Snack Flo'; turn left when you get to Snack Flo.

Eating

TOP CHOICE **La Table d'Alexandre** FRENCH €€€
(Map p124; ☎033 14 247 22; Ambaro; mains Ar16,000-22,000; ⏱lunch, dinner by reservation only) For a decadent lunch on a day trip around the island, stop at Alexandre's. The debonair French chef here serves exquisite cuisine in a dining room that wouldn't have looked out of place in the set of *Out of Africa*: a gazebo perched on a low hill overlooking mangroves and Nosy Sakatia, decorated with traditional china and 19th-century paintings. Splendid.

Chez Loulou SEAFOOD €€€
(Map p124; ☎032 40 439 92; Andilana; set menus Ar35,000) Right on the beach, with tables in the sand, this casual restaurant and bar is best known for its gargantuan Sunday seafood buffet lunch (Ar40,000). Seafood also gets pride of place in the daily three-course meal. If you want to linger after dessert at lunch, grab a sun chair and an ice-cold THB and kick back with a good book. Booking is essential for the Sunday buffet.

Chez Eugénie MALAGASY €€€
(Map p124; www.chez-eugenie.com; Andilana; set menus Ar25,000) Chez Eugenie offers three-course set menus that rotate daily, with a delightful blend of Malagasy and French influences. Everything is cooked fresh, in an open kitchen at the end of the big dining room.

Mt Passot & Crater Lakes

Mt Passot (329m), Nosy Be's loftiest point, lies about 15km northwest of Hell-Ville (somewhat further by road). It's a good spot for watching the sunset and the sweeping panorama. It's also one of the best places to see Nosy Be's crater lakes. Unfortunately, the viewing area is now packed with souvenir stalls, which somewhat detracts from the experience.

If you have your own wheels, the summit is easily accessible by car or motorbike (allow 45 minutes from Ambatoloaka); otherwise you could charter a taxi from Hell-Ville or Ambatoloaka: allow Ar80,000 for the return trip, including time at the top.

There have been muggings in the area so if you're on your own or on a motorbike, ensure that you drive back before it gets dark.

ISLANDS AROUND NOSY BE

If money is no object, the islands surrounding Nosy Be – particularly Nosy Iranja and Nosy Mitsio – are home to some idyllic resorts, ideal for a few days of remote tranquillity. If you're on a tighter budget, take a day trip to check out the palm-fringed white beaches and do some excellent snorkelling.

Nosy Komba

This **island** (www.nosykomba.com) rises off the ocean floor midway between the mainland and Nosy Be in an almost perfect cone shape and looms above the turquoise sea: its summit reaches a mighty 622m (much higher than that of Nosy Be).

Most people visit Nosy Komba on an organised tour from Nosy Be: these generally combine Nosy Komba and Nosy Tanikely, with just a couple of hours at the village of **Ampangorina**, so the best way to experience the island is either to sleep there or to hire your own pirogue (dugout canoe) for the day.

Sights & Activities

Ampangorina Craft Market MARKET

Ampangorina is Nosy Komba's main village; it doubles up as an interesting craft market, with everything from multicoloured raffia bags to embroidered bed sheets and table linen spilling out of every house in the village.

Nosy Komba Trails HIKING

Nosy Komba's interior has been remarkably well preserved and is prime hiking territory. It takes about five sweaty hours to walk from one side of the island to the other or up to the summit from Ampangorina and back down. It is recommended you take a guide (Ar20,000): ask for Yvonne at any of the shops or enquire at Chez Jojo.

Lemur Park ZOO

(Map p124; admission Ar2000) This isn't a zoo so much as an attraction: the lemurs are wild, but locals feed them bananas so that the animals will eat off your hand or jump on your shoulder for that perfect photo op. The practice is detrimental to the animals but generates substantial revenues for the village, which has helped protect the forest. So if you'd like to support the village, pay the admission fee to admire the lemurs, but decline the offer to feed them.

Sleeping & Eating

TOP CHOICE **Tsara Komba** LODGE €€€

(Map p124; ☎86 921 10; www.tsarakomba.com; s/d full board €330/500; wi-fi) With just eight bungalows, this stunning lodge is about as exclusive and secluded as you get. The polished wooden rooms come with king-size beds and a porch looking out to the sea. The garden is a work of art, as is the food served in the dining room with panoramic views. Tsara Komba has a fantastic program of activities, including walks on Nosy Komba, visits of the cocoa plantations in Ambanja, day trips to Nosy Be and all the usual sailing and snorkelling trips in the area.

Jardin Vanille LODGE €€€

(Map p124; ☎032 07 127 97; www.jardinvanille.com; d with half/full board Ar440,000/520,000) This lovely lodge offers cute and comfortable Malagasy-style bungalows located on Nosy Komba's lovely Anjiabe beach. The restaurant serves a rotating, and very fine, menu and overlooks the sea. Numerous excursions, including snorkelling, diving and fishing trips, can be arranged, along with Nosy Be transfers.

Chez Jojo HOTELY €€

(Ampangorina; mains Ar7000-20,000; ⊙lunch) Right at the western end of Ampangorina village, in a dining room overlooking the sea, Chez Jojo serves simple but copious dishes, with excellent grilled fish and calamari.

Getting There & Away

Organised tours to the island are available from most tour operators in Nosy Be (see p126) and cost around Ar90,000 in combination with Nosy Tanikely. A chartered pirogue from Hell-Ville costs around Ar120,000 for the day, a speedboat Ar210,000.

Nosy Tanikely

Nosy Tanikely is 10km west of Nosy Komba. It is a protected **marine reserve** (admission Ar10,000; ⊙8am-5pm) and one of the best snorkelling sites in the area, with coral, numerous fish and sea turtles.

Snorkelling is best in the morning, before the wind picks up. Although the reserve officially opens at 8am, you are allowed to come earlier – just stick around until the reserve officials arrive so that you can pay your admission fees. Snorkelling equipment is available from the reserve's cabin for Ar10,000.

Most organised day tours combine Nosy Tanikely with Nosy Komba, using the beach on Nosy Tanikely for a lunchtime picnic.

Nosy Sakatia

At just 3 sq km, Nosy Sakatia, just off the west coast of Nosy Be, is quiet and tiny. It's famous for its orchids and it's an easy place to wander around. There is also good snorkelling and a couple of good diving sites off the island.

Sakatia Passions (Map p124; ☎032 41 325 49; www.sakatia-passions.com; bungalows €75; air-con) is a convivial lodge with 12 bungalows nestled in a coconut plantation. The bungalows are done up with dark polished wood and rough-hewn porches; all have sea views. A raft of activities – sailing, snorkelling, walking, fishing (the hotel's speciality) and diving – can be arranged, making it ideal for families.

On Sundays, the hotel organises a scrumptious seafood buffet (Ar45,000) that is open to all; there is generally live music and a great atmosphere. Booking is recommended.

To get to Sakatia, make your way to the Nosy Be beach of Ambaro, next to the Chanty Beach hotel, where you'll find pirogues that can do a transfer (Ar15,000) or take you on a tour of the island (price negotiable depending on the length of the excursion).

Nosy Mitsio

Nosy Mitsio is a small, beautiful archipelago about 55km northeast of Nosy Be where the main attractions are the still relatively virgin dive sites and the picture-perfect beaches.

Most diving and tour operators in Nosy Be (p121) organise multiday diving trips or cruises to Nosy Mitsio (€400–850, depending on the number of people on board, the number of dives and number of days).

If you'd like to treat yourself to a few nights of remote idyll, stay at the relaxed **Tsarabanjina** (reservations +230 402 27 77; www.tsarabanjina.com; bungalows full board €500; wi-fi). There are no TVs or phones here (the only concession to modern living is wi-fi in the communal areas) – just the sea, the beach and the hills, in which the thatched rosewood bungalows effortlessly blend. Snorkelling, sailing and waterskiing are included in the price, although most people come here to dive: Tsarabanjina has a PADI and NAUI-certified club. A three-night minimum stay is required. The boat transfer from Nosy Be or Ankify takes an hour and a half.

Nosy Iranja

The gorgeous Nosy Iranja, southwest of Nosy Be, actually consists of two islands: the larger and inhabited Nosy Iranja Be (about 200 hectares) and the tiny Nosy Iranja Kely (13 hectares). The islands are connected by a 1.5km-long sand bar, negotiable on foot at low tide. Sea turtles regularly lay their eggs on the beaches.

Nosy Iranja is a popular sailing day trip from Nosy Be (Ar130,000; check tour operators in Nosy Be, p126); the excursion generally includes snorkelling, swimming and a good lunch on board the boat.

Hôtel Nosy Iranja (033 37 111 50; www.iranjalodge.co.za; bungalows full board €400; wi-fi), on Nosy Iranja Be, has chic bungalows with decks, hammocks and loungers. Inside, a four-poster bed and a wood-and-stone bathroom await. An array of excursions can be arranged. There's a three-night minimum stay (book in advance). Transfer is from Nosy Be or Ankify.

AMBANJA & AROUND

Ambanja

POP 30,000

Ambanja is a small, tree-lined town on the Sambirano River, and the junction for overland travel to and from Nosy Be. It is famous for its large cocoa, spice and vanilla plantations, some of which can be visited.

TOP CHOICE Millot Plantations FARM

(www.cananga.fr; 4hr tours €10) Madagascar is famed for its vanilla and its spices but did you know that it also produces one of the world's finest cocoa? This beautiful plantation, established in 1904, is a leading producer of organic cocoa, spices and essential oils, and a visit to this little slice of paradise is not only highly informative but a true festival of the senses: with a backdrop of stunning scenery, the formidable Mado, your guide, will invite you to taste or smell every plant on the farm, from the lychee-like raw cocoa beans straight out of their husk to potent green peppercorns soaking in brine and vinegar. You'll also poke your nose in the distillery, where ylang-ylang essential oils or freshly picked vetiver roots will fight for your olfactory attention.

The plantation's main products are cocoa, spices (combava, or wild lemon; four spice; pepper; chilli etc) and perfume plants (ylang-ylang, vetiver, lemongrass, palmarosa, patchouli etc), and over the course of the visit, you'll see how each plant is grown, picked and processed (distillery for perfume plants and preparation areas for cocoa and spices). Millot is entirely organic and employs more than 800 people, the majority of them women. The plantation also supports the village school, which most of the employees' children attend.

At the end of the visit, you can have lunch at the gorgeous old **farmhouse** (3-course meal incl drinks €15), where you'll be served dishes prepared with products from the plantation, including a wondrous chocolate cake with a vanilla cream. Make sure you try Mado's exquisite chocolate-flavoured rum (made with the plantation's cocoa, of course) before you head off.

Because the plantation spreads over 15 sq km, you'll need a vehicle. If you don't have your own, you can hire the plantation's for the length of your visit (€50). It is also possible to sleep at the farmhouse, where there are simple and atmospheric rooms (d €50, including dinner).

Getting There & Away

From Ambanja there are regular taxis-brousses to Ankify (Ar2000, 30 minutes), where you'll find the ferry to Nosy Be. Taxis-brousses also go to Diego Suarez (Ar30,000, five hours), Majunga (Ar40,000, 13 hours) and Tana (Ar50,000, 18 hours).

Ankify

Ankify is the main port for boats and ferries between the mainland coast and Nosy Be. If you arrive too late for the crossing to Nosy Be (4pm) or the last taxi-brousse to Diego Suarez (noon), there are a couple of nice but expensive places to stay.

Sleeping & Eating

Le Dauphin Bleu BUNGALOW €€€
(☎032 45 334 61; www.ledauphinbleu.eu; s/d Ar126,000/140,000) Nestled in a tropical garden with stunning views of Nosy Komba and the mainland's hills, the bungalows here are delightful. Each has its own terrace to make the best of the fine setting, and there is a small beach below with crystal-clear water. The hotel is about 3.5km from the port of Ankify.

Les Baobabs BUNGALOW €€€
(☎033 07 208 87; bungalows Ar100,000) About 500m from the ferry landing, Les Baobabs has quaint round bungalows on a gorgeous beach with superb views across to Nosy Komba. The restaurant is on an atmospheric verandah.

Getting There & Away

For information on boats to Nosy Be, see p126.

The road between Ankify and Diego Suarez is sealed (although deteriorating fast between Ambilobe and Diego) and serviced by dozens of taxis-brousses every day.

Ambilobe

POP 56,000

Ambilobe is a junction town for transport between the northeast coast (Vohémar, Marojejy, Sambava) and Madagascar's north (Diego Suarez) and northwest coast (Ambanja). As with junction towns the world over, it is neither attractive nor interesting but if you need to stay the night, **Noor** (☎82 061 95; r Ar30,000), near the Jovenna petrol station, is your best bet.

You'll find vehicles to Diego Suarez (Ar15,000, three hours) and Ambanja (Ar15,000, 1½ hours) throughout the day; taxis-brousses for Vohémar (Ar30,000, eight hours) leave daily. There are also vehicles to Sambava (Ar40,000, 12 hours).

DIEGO SUAREZ & AROUND

Madagascar's northernmost region is an alluring place: it's remote, host to weird and wonderful geological sights, and has two oceans – the Mozambique Channel and the Indian Ocean – and a disarming contrast of very wet and very dry.

Diego Suarez (Antsiranana) is the main gateway town, although by no means the only place in which to base yourself to explore the region. There is plenty of excellent hiking to do in the two national parks of Montagne d'Ambre and Ankarana, and a growing niche of more adventurous sports to try, such as rock climbing, quad biking and kitesurfing.

Some travellers decide to base themselves in Diego or Joffreville (Ambohitra) and do day trips from there; others will prefer to do a couple of days in Diego and then work their way down (or up) the RN6, sleeping in Joffreville for Montagne d'Ambre and in Parc National de l'Ankarana to minimise travelling time.

History

The history of the area around Diego Suarez is intimately linked to its bay: the second largest in the world (after Rio de Janeiro in Brazil), its

TAXIS-BROUSSES FROM ANKIFY

DESTINATION	PRICE (AR)	DURATION (HRS)	DEPARTURE TIMES
Ambanja	2000	½	All day
Ambilobe	20,000	2	Morning
Diego Suarez	30,000	5	Morning

strategic location on the Indian Ocean trade routes and the natural shelter it provides have been prized by generations of pirates, slave traders, merchants and navies.

The earliest evidence of human settlement in Madagascar was found here. The bay was frequently visited by East African and Arab traders, but it wasn't until the 16th century that Portuguese explorers landed here. In 1885, France, which had gradually increased its presence on the big island, signed a treaty with Madagascar granting France the right to occupy the territories of Diego Suarez and Nosy Be, a precedent which eventually led to colonial occupation.

In 1942, during WWII, British forces seized Diego Suarez from the French, fearing that Vichy-supporting troops (who had capitulated to Hitler) might support the Japanese navy, allied to Germany. The area was handed back to the French at the end of the war in 1946. Madagascar finally obtained independence from France in 1960, but the French foreign legion retained a base in Diego until 1975.

Dangers & Annoyances

There have been a number of muggings in isolated areas popular with travellers such as Montagne des Français and the Trois Baies. To minimise chances of things going wrong, never go alone. Even if you're part of a couple or small group, take a guide, tell your hotel where you're going and don't take valuables with you.

ANKIFY TO DIEGO SUAREZ IN 4WD

The popular northern circuit from Diego Suarez (Antsiranana) to Nosy Be offered by travel agents means that a number of 4WD often drop their clients in Ankify for the final leg of their trip and head back to Diego Suarez empty. As a result, **Evasion Sans Frontière** (☎86 062 44; www.mada-evasion.com; Hell-Ville) accepts passengers on the way back for Ar40,000 per person (a mere Ar10,000 more than the taxi-brousse and so much more comfortable). Just ring ahead to find out when a vehicle might be available.

Diego Suarez (Antsiranana)

POP 75,000

With its wide streets, old colonial-era buildings, and genteel air, Diego is a lovely base from which to explore Madagascar's northern region. It is a slow-moving place where nearly everything shuts between noon and 3pm, and the residents still indulge in long afternoon naps.

Diego is an important port in Madagascar; the town notably exports tinned fish and soft and alcoholic drinks – there is an

EDEN LODGE, MAINLAND PARADISE

On a remote peninsula of the mainland only accessible by boat, **Eden Lodge** (☎034 86 931 19; www.edenlodge.net; Anjanojano; d full board €460; wi-fi) is everyone's desert island fantasy.

Designed to minimise its impact on the environment, the lodge effortlessly blends with the surroundings: lemurs roam the garden, birds nest in the baobabs at the back of the dining hut and resident green turtles lay their eggs on the beach in front of the tents. Seeing these marine giants labour over their nests or witnessing the eggs hatching is a once-in-a-lifetime experience.

The eight luxury tents, inspired by East Africa's famous tented camps, are equipped with beautiful mahogany beds, colourful fabrics, and, wait for it, private massage cabins. Meals are served in the atmospheric communal thatched dining room–lounge (complete with fairy lights in the evenings); the menu changes daily and makes the best of the hotel's vegetable garden and the abundant seafood.

There is plenty to do around the lodge: snorkelling off the beach is a must, sailing, canoeing and windsurfing (with or without a guide). The resident guide can also take you on walks around the peninsula and of course, the lodge can organise excursions to Nosy Be and other islands. Sociable types shouldn't miss the opportunity of a game of soccer with local villagers on the bumpy pitch, or try a game of *pétanque*: a word of warning, the locals are *very* good!

The lodge is powered by solar energy and the staff only use organic cleaning products. Transfer to Eden Lodge (40 minutes) is by boat from Nosy Be or Ankify.

important Star (THB) bottling plant on the outskirts of town. Thanks to its deepwater anchorage, Diego has also become a firm favourite of cruise ships, which visit between December and March. The ships are a magnificent sight as they cross the bay, although the outpouring of thousands of visitors for just one day turns the usually sleepy Diego into a bit of a madhouse.

There are no beaches in Diego itself, but plenty of amazing views of the bay, and the town has recently got its act together to encourage visitors to explore its fascinating architecture and history.

Sights & Activities

TOP CHOICE A La Découverte de Diego Suarez WALKING TOUR

Diego's tourist office and local heritage association, Ambre, have designed four self-guided walking tours of Diego Suarez (Colonial Sights; Architecture and History; The Port and Seafront; Markets and Artisans) that take in the main historical and architectural highlights of the city. Each itinerary (1½ to two hours) has a dedicated leaflet (Ar3000), complete with map, photos and detailed explanation about each highlight of the itinerary. Leaflets are available from the tourist offices in Diego.

Le Grand Hôtel SWIMMING

(Rue Colbert; per person per week/weekend Ar15,000/20,000) The hotel's pool has been beautifully landscaped, with tropical plants all around and an attractive deck for loungers.

Tours

The following companies offer a variety of activities and excursions to Ankarana, Montagne d'Ambre, Trois Baies, Tsingy Rouges and Mer d'Emeraude. They're also the best place to go to if you'd like to hire a 4WD to explore the region under your steam, notably between Diego and Nosy Be, and to explore the vanilla coast (Vohémar, Sambava and Antalaha). Allow Ar180,000 to Ar220,000 per day for a 4WD with driver and fuel, depending on the distance.

Diego Raid DRIVING TOUR

(☎032 40 001 75; www.diegoraid.com; Rue Colbert; tours per day Ar270,000-460,000) This operator organises highly recommended quad bike excursions to areas such as Les Trois Baies, Windsor Castle and La Montagne des Français. As well as taking in the main sights, the trips tend to leave the tarmac well behind and take the scenic route instead.

New Sea Roc ROCK CLIMBING

(☎82 218 54; www.newsearoc.com; 26 Rue Colbert) New Sea Roc specialises in climbing and camping trips (€40 per person per day, minimum four days) on the remote Nosy Hara archipelago, a marine park. New Sea Roc also offers climbing in the Montagne des Français area, fishing, snorkelling and trekking excursions.

Evasion Sans Frontière TOUR

(☎82 230 61; www.mada-evasion.com; Rue Colbert) This well-respected company runs day trips to all the main regional sights, including Mer d'Emeraude.

Paradis du Nord TOUR

(☎82 235 06; www.leparadisdunord-diego.com; Rue Villaret Joyeuse) Run by the affable Eric, this agency has a large fleet of quality vehicles and offers the cheapest rates in town. Find it behind the Tsena (covered market).

Cap-Nord Voyages TOUR

(☎82 235 06; www.cap-nord-voyages.com; 51 Rue Colbert) Offers excursions to all the usual suspects, with transfer by 4WD; also specialises in fishing trips.

King de la Piste TOUR

(☎82 225 99; www.kingdelapiste.de) A German-run company, King runs excursions along the Diego–Nosy Be corridor. It has its own hotel in Ankarana and one on the outskirts of Diego. It also does car hire.

Sleeping

There are few budget hotels in Diego, but the midrange category has a couple of great options.

Le Jardin Exotique BOUTIQUE HOTEL €€

(☎82 219 33; http://jardinexotique.hotel-diegosuarez.com; Rue Louis Brunet; r Ar65,000-75,000; ❄📶) Rooms at this quirky boutique place all come with parquet floors, four-poster beds, mosquito nets, bold and creative paint jobs and Italian showers in the bathrooms. The cheapest just have fans, but no less character. The rooftop terrace has picnic tables, and the views over the bay of Diego Suarez are awesome (bring a few cold beers up with you – there's a fridge in all the rooms). The garden area, with its marble statues and tumbling bougainvilleas, is wonderful.

La Belle Aventure GUESTHOUSE **€€€**
(☎032 44 153 83; www.labellaventure-diego.com; 13 Rue Freppel; d Ar55,000-85,000; ❄📶) Gilles and Elisabeth built their Beautiful Adventure in a great neighbourhood of Diego: quiet, yet close to the centre, and with good views of the bay. Because the building is so new (it opened in 2011), everything is bright, fresh and impeccable, with colourful sheets and lemur and baobab friezes on the walls. Gilles and Elisabeth are lovely hosts and will bend over backwards to ensure you have a good time.

La Terrasse du Voyageur HOTEL **€€€**
(☎82 240 63; www.terrasseduvoyageur-hotel.com; Rue du Mozambique; s/d/tr Ar50,000/65,000/110,000; ❄📶) Right in the centre of Diego's market district, La Terrasse du Voyageur is not exactly in a postcard location, but what the hotel is offering is conviviality and a chance to be a little closer to the local community. As well as having nice but slightly noisy rooms (simple, colourful, with old-fashioned bathrooms), the building has become an important community focus point: neighbourhood associations have their offices there, there is a kids' club on Wednesdays, movie nights on Thursdays, live music on Fridays on the terrace; the list goes on. The hotel also uses solar panels for hot water.

Villa La Baie de Diego Suarez GUESTHOUSE **€€**
(☎032 44 153 83; www.baiedediegosuarez.com; Rue Richelieu; d Ar60,000, without bathroom Ar40,000; 📶) The Villa probably has the most jaw-dropping view of the Bay of Diego Suarez in Diego: breakfast or a sundowner on the balcony really takes some beating. You can sometimes spot dolphins, and watching container ships or cruise ships come in is majestic. The rooms are sparsely furnished but spacious and light (opt for one upstairs). Some share bathrooms.

Hôtel Belle Vue HOTEL **€€**
(☎82 210 21; 35 Rue François de Mahy; d Ar45,000, without bathroom Ar20,000) A lively hotel that is the only budget option with charm in Diego. The rooms are simple, but clean, with fan and net. The ancient bathrooms and terminal plumbing do need some TLC, but what really does it at Belle Vue is the view of the bay from the terrace, the relaxed atmosphere, and the bar, ideal for sundowners.

Allamanda Hôtel BOUTIQUE HOTEL **€€€**
(☎82 210 33; www.hotels-diego.com; Rue Richelieu; d from Ar216,000; ❄@📶🏊) The swanky Allamanda is just steps from the sea and has all the luxuries you would expect from a top-end hotel. The exterior of the building itself is a bit bland and boxy, but the rooms are spacious and elegantly decked out in a nautical-themed decor.

LOCAL KNOWLEDGE

MARCO TARQUINIO

Marco founded La Terrasse du Voyageur after being inspired by the work of his brother Flavio, who runs the sustainable tourism agency Tany Mena Tours in Antananarivo (p31). He wanted to build a hotel that would bring travellers and Malagasies closer together.

The Zegny'Zo Festival

This is the highlight of the year in our neighbourhood: **Zegny'Zo** (www.zolobe.com/festival-zegnyzo) is an international street arts festival that takes place every year during the last two weeks of May, and Diego's inhabitants have really made it their own: as well as clowns, musicians, mural painters, giant puppets etc, there was a parade of Renault 4L's (the main car used by taxis in Diego), for instance, in 2011 to celebrate the 50th anniversary of the car. Artists stay with us, and the energy and creativity are incredible.

Diego's Market District

Much of the tourism infrastructure in Diego is around Rue Colbert, but I would encourage travellers to venture further out and explore the market district (the tourism office has self-guided walks). It is a vibrant place, with small restaurants and bars opening up.

Favourite Place Around Diego

I love the Trois Baies and the Mer d'Emeraude, they are very unspoilt.

Le Grand Hôtel HOTEL €€€
(☎82 230 63; www.grand-hotel-diego.com; Rue Colbert; r Ar276,000; ❄@🛜≋) With its imposing facade, this hotel lives up to its moniker. The rooms are plush but devoid of charm. Where the Grand Hôtel scores points is with its pool and tip-top location in the centre of town.

Hôtel Fiantsilaka HOTEL €
(☎82 223 48; dom.bigot@wanadoo.fr; 13 Blvd Etienne; d Ar35,000, without bathroom Ar22,000) A basic option in the centre of town; rooms are ageing but kept clean. The French manager is very friendly.

Diego Suarez (Antsiranana)

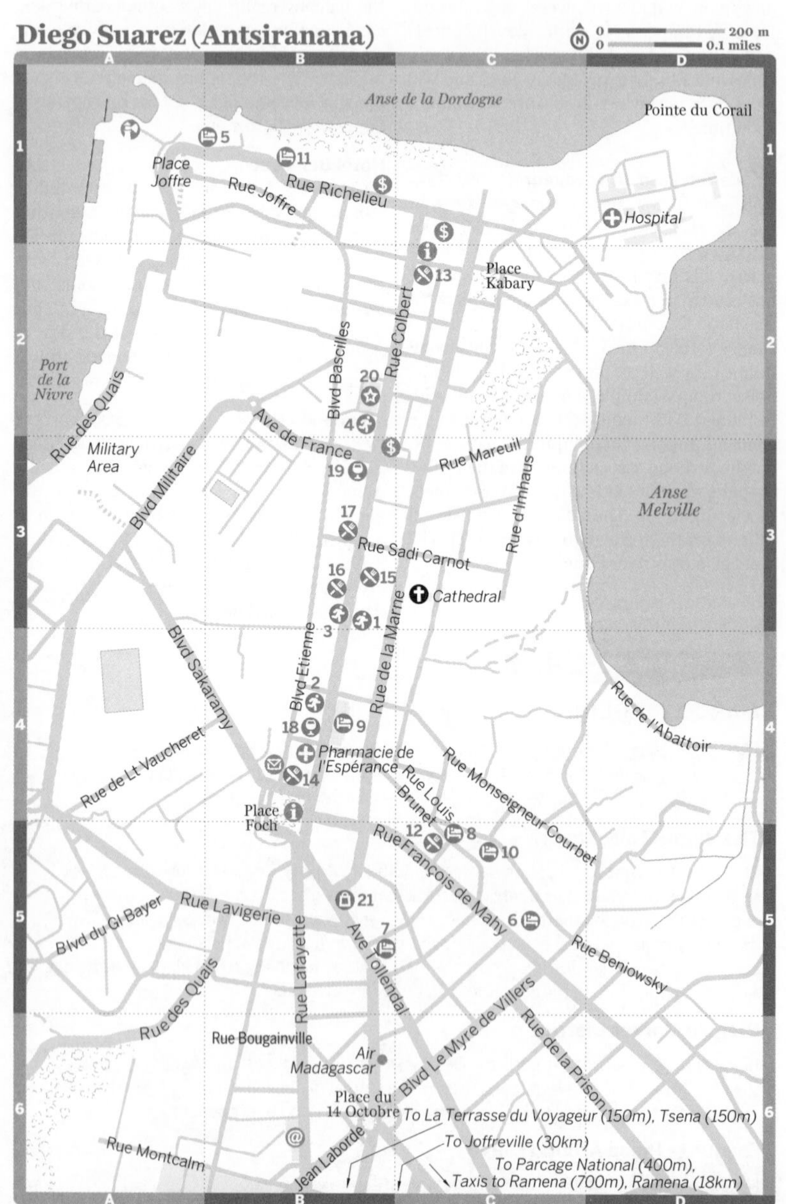

Eating

Diego has some excellent restaurants, but as with accommodation, they're not the cheapest in Madagascar. In the early evenings, there are good **street-food stands** along Rue Colbert.

TOP CHOICE Le Melville FRENCH €€€
(☎032 05 606 99; www.hotels-diego.com; Allamanda Hôtel, Rue Richelieu; mains Ar15,000-23,000; ⊙breakfast, lunch & dinner) Right by the sea, with a fabulous patio that's particularly alluring at sunset, the atmosphere at Melville is romantic and sophisticated without being stuffy. The food is absolutely delicious: the fat zebu steak with vanilla mash is sumptuous, and seafood- and fish-lovers will be spoiled for choice. Service is also top-class, with wine recommendations from staff. Booking is recommended for weekends.

La Bodega FUSION €€€
(cnr Rue Colbert & Rue Flacourt; mains Ar15,000-18,000; ⊙Mon-Sat) The name suggests Spanish influence, but owner Cyrille is from France and the colourful restaurant is in Madagascar, so it's hardly surprising the menu is a mix of all three nationalities. We loved the tapas à la Malagasy, the grouper carpaccio with avocado and lime mousse, and the amazing rum cocktails. It's always busy, too, and has a great atmosphere.

Balafomanga INTERNATIONAL €€
(18 Rue Louis Brunet; mains Ar12,000-15,000; ⊙Mon-Sat) The big menu at Balafomanga offers a bit of everything, although the delicious food definitely has a big French and Malagasy influence, with dishes such as grouper in pink peppercorn sauce, barbequed prawns and garlic calamari. It's a funky dining environment, with Chinese lanterns and multicoloured walls and tablecloths. A faux flame burns in a dangling cast-iron pot, and rows of home-brewed fruit-flavoured rum sit in big plastic pots on the low-lit bar.

La Gourmandise FRENCH €€
(Cnr Place Foch & Blvd Etienne; mains Ar10,000-18,000; ⊙Fri-Wed) Run by the formidable Nicolas, Frenchman, bon vivant and globe-trotting chef, La Gourmandise serves dishes true to its owner's origins: tripe *à la mode de Caen* (stewed tripe), prawns *à la Provençale* (in garlic and tomato sauce) or zebu steak with blue cheese sauce. Service can be slow, but the food is worth the wait.

La Terrasse du Voyageur MALAGASY €€€
(☎82 240 63; www.terrasseduvoyageur-hotel.com; Rue du Mozambique; set menus Ar20,000; ⊙dinner) The restaurant at La Terrasse du Voyageur sits on the eponymous terrace with sweeping views of Diego. It's a cosy and convivial space, with a TV lounge, a library, a bar and live music every Friday. The food is a set taster menu of Malagasy dishes; portions are gargantuan and the food delicious, and the menu is good value. The restaurant is only open for dinner and you must book (by lunchtime at the latest).

Diego Suarez (Antsiranana)

Activities, Courses & Tours
1 Cap-Nord Voyages ... B3
2 Diego Raid ... B4
3 Evasion Sans Frontière ... B3
Le Grand Hôtel ... (see 9)
4 New Sea Roc ... B2

Sleeping
5 Allamanda Hôtel ... B1
6 Hôtel Belle Vue ... C5
7 Hôtel Fiantsilaka ... B5
8 La Belle Aventure ... C5
9 Le Grand Hôtel ... B4
10 Le Jardin Exotique ... C5
11 Villa La Baie de Diego Suarez ... B1

Eating
12 Balafomanga ... C5
13 La Bodega ... C2
14 La Gourmandise ... B4
15 La Rosticceria ... B3
Le Melville ... (see 5)
Pâtisserie Le Grand Hôtel ... (see 9)
16 Score ... B3
17 Street-Food Stands ... B3

Drinking
18 Boîte Noire ... B4
19 Vahinée Bar ... B3

Entertainment
20 Alliance Franco-Malgache ... B2

Shopping
21 Ateliers d'Artisanat ... B5

TAXIS-BROUSSES FROM DIEGO SUAREZ

DESTINATION	PRICE (AR)	DURATION (HRS)	DEPARTURE TIMES
Ramena	2000	1	All day
Joffreville	3000	1½	All day
Ambilobe	15,000	3	All day
Ankify	30,000	5	All day
Sambava	50,000	15	All day
Majunga	50,000	18	Afternoon
Antananarivo	50,000	24	Afternoon

La Rosticceria ITALIAN €€
(47 Rue Colbert; mains Ar12,000-18,000) Mmm, this Italian restaurant has a fantastic selection of risottos, gnocchi, lasagne and fresh-made tagliatelle and spaghettis with pesto, cream, meat or seafood sauces. The ambience is as delicious as the food, with owner Adelio singing his heart away to Italian hits. The restaurant decor follows a nautical theme, with intricately carved wooden vessels and old maps for decoration. Outside tables sit on the sidewalk. Save room for coffee and dessert: both the real espresso and the creamy gelato are marvellous.

Pâtisserie Le Grand Hôtel BAKERY €
(Le Grand Hôtel, Rue Colbert; cakes & sandwiches Ar1000-Ar10,000; ⌚6am-9.30pm) This excellent bakery doubles up as a cafe that's popular with tourists. It's a great choice for an economical and light breakfast or a cheap lunch of salad or sandwich. There are some lovely pastries, too, which you can devour with real espresso.

Score SUPERMARKET
(Rue Colbert; ⌚8.30am-1pm & 3-7.30pm Mon-Fri, 8.30am-7.30pm Sat, 8.30-11.30am Sun) Very well-stocked supermarket.

Drinking & Entertainment

Diego has good nightlife by Malagasy standards, so make the best of it!

Vahinée Bar BAR
(Rue Colbert) A local favourite, Vahinée has something for everyone: a wide-screen TV showing football and rugby, a pool table, and live music every night. The atmosphere is excellent, and there is a range of drinks, from beer to cocktails.

La Terrasse du Voyageur BAR
(www.terrasseduvoyageur-hotel.com; Rue du Mozambique) With such fabulous views of Diego, this rooftop bar is a prime spot for sundowners. The bartender makes some mean cocktails (hello, caipirinha!), and there is live music on Fridays and poetry slam sessions on Saturday afternoons.

Boîte Noire LOUNGE
(Rue Colbert) With big faux-leather couches, pool tables and intimidating bouncers, this is Diego's fanciest disco. It attracts a chic, wannabe crowd (and a few prostitutes).

Alliance Franco-Malgache PERFORMING ARTS
(www.alliancefr.mg; Rue Colbert) The Alliance Franco-Malgache is housed in a magnificently restored art deco–style building, which is worth a look on its own. There are regular art exhibitions here, along with film screenings, concerts and shows.

Shopping

Ateliers de l'Artisanat ARTS & CRAFTS
(Ave Tollendal) This boutique has a huge selection of handicrafts and artwork from all over Madagascar.

Information

All banks have ATMs and money-changing facilities. For more planning advice, author recommendations and insider tips on Diego Suarez, head to www.lonelyplanet.com/madagascar/northern-madagascar/diego-suarez-and-around.

Bank of Africa (BOA; Rue Colbert)

BFV-SG (Rue Richelieu) Changes travellers cheques.

BNI-CA (cnr Ave de France & Rue Colbert)

Housseni.com (Ave Tollendal; per hr Ar1700; ⌚8am-9pm Mon-Sat, 3-8.30pm Sun) The fastest internet option in town.

Post Office (Place Foch)

Pharmacie de l'Espérance (Rue Colbert)

Tourist Office (www.office-tourisme-diego-suarez.com; Place Foch; ⌚8am-noon & 3-6pm Mon-Fri, 8.30-11.30am Sat) Sells four self-guided itineraries taking in Diego's historical and architectural highlights; it can also help you find a hotel or a tour operator for popular excursions. There is a second branch that's located at the corner of Rue Colbert and Rue Flacourt.

 Getting There & Away

Air

Air Madagascar (☎82 214 74; Ave Sourcouf) links Diego with Antananarivo (1½ hours, €187) daily and has weekly flights to Sambava (35 minutes, €125), Nosy Be (25 minutes, €123) and Majunga (55 minutes, €188).

Taxi-Brousse

Diego Suarez has several taxi-brousse stations: **Parcage National**, next to the French cemetery, serves Majunga and Antananarivo. **Gare Routière d'Ambilobe**, 6km south of town, next to the airport, has taxis-brousses to Joffreville, Ambilobe, Ankify and the northeast coast. Taxis for Ramena leave from the stop on Blvd Duplex. All taxi drivers in Diego Suarez will know which station to take you to if you tell them your final destination.

For destinations on the northeast coast, it can be quicker to get a taxi-brousse to the junction town of Ambilobe and change to a vehicle heading east. The road from Ambilobe to Vohémar is unsealed, and in the rainy season, the journey can take much more than 12 hours.

 Getting Around

To/From the Airport

Diego's Arrachart Airport is 6km south of the town centre. Taxis charge Ar10,000 to get from there to town; otherwise, you can walk out to the main road and catch a taxi-be (Ar200).

Taxi

Taxi journeys in Diego cost a flat Ar1000, Ar1500 at night. Tuk-tuks (motorised rickshaws) are Ar700.

A popular alternative to expensive 4WD is to charter a taxi to the Trois Baies (Ar60,000) and Parc National Montagne d'Ambre (Ar80,000).

Diego to Ramena

The road between Diego and Ramena hugs the coastline of the Baie des Français, part of the immense Baie de Diego Suarez. The sea is an ethereal turquoise colour that contrasts beautifully with the ochres and browns of the towering Montagne des Français.

The bay and mountain were named so in memory of the Malagasy and French forces killed in 1942 in Allied resistance to the pro-German Vichy French forces. The **Montagne des Français** is now a protected area, with abundant birdlife; it's a hot, two-hour climb to the summit, with spectacular views for reward. Unfortunately, there have been repeated muggings on the trail so guides and agencies have stopped offering the excursion for now; check with operators for the latest on security.

Sleeping & Eating

Le Suarez BOUTIQUE HOTEL **€€€**
(☎82 901 28; Rte de Ramena; s/d Ar110,000/160,000; ❄🏊) This is a true country boutique joint with an absolutely gorgeous pool that has a small waterfall and lovely thick padding on the sun chairs around it. The 12 bungalows have thatched roofs and redbrick-and-stone walls. Inside you'll find a breezy space with whitewashed walls and wooden beams on the ceiling; there's more local wood in the dark polished floors and matching four-poster beds. There is a large open-air restaurant, and excursions can be arranged. It is about 4km from Diego's centre on the road to Ramena.

La Note Bleue Park Hotel BOUTIQUE HOTEL **€€€**
(☎032 07 125 48; www.diego-hotel.com; Rte de Ramena; d/ste €125/190; ❄🏊) The Note Bleue is big and brash. You do get a lot of space in the rooms (each has a balcony or terrace with a swing), but the freakish blue furniture and tiles are overwhelming. There is a restaurant with fabulous food and house rum, however, and a huge pool

NOSY LONJA

The small island of Nosy Lonja in the middle of the Baie des Français is known in French as Pain de Sucre (Sugar Loaf) for its supposed resemblance to the much larger Sugar Loaf Mountain in Rio de Janeiro harbour in Brazil. It's off-limits to foreigners and considered sacred by the Malagasy, who use it for *fijoroana* (ceremonies invoking the ancestors).

with two waterslides (the hotel is very kid-friendly). La Note Bleue has its own dock and boat and runs loads of excursions. It also has a free shuttle to Diego Suarez for hotel guests. It is about 3km from Diego's centre on the road to Ramena.

Ramena

A sleepy fishing village for most of the week, Ramena (located 18km northeast of Diego) wakes up on Sundays, when seemingly half the population of Diego Suarez comes here for a knees-up on the beach: restaurants fill up for the traditional Sunday buffet and the beach at the northern end of the village becomes picnic central (complete with stereos, crates of beer and some quality dancing!).

For visitors, coming here on Sundays is a great opportunity to partake in Malagasy fun. But staying in Ramena is also a good alternative to staying in Diego, particularly if you're after some beach time.

Sleeping & Eating

La Case en Falafy BUNGALOW €€

(Chez Bruno; ☎032 02 674 33; www.case-en-falafy.com; bungalows Ar40,000, mains Ar8500-11,000; @) One of the best value options in the Diego Suarez area, La Case en Falafy is about 200m from the beach, up a small hill. It is a convivial place, with a great bar, two pools and an open-air restaurant. The thatched-roof bungalows sit in a lovely garden. Try for one situated at the back of the property – they are a bit more spread out and quiet. Tours and excursions can be arranged.

Badamera GUESTHOUSE €

(☎032 07 733 50; www.hotel-nord-madagascar.com; r from Ar20,000) A few hundred metres up a hill from the beach, this popular and laid-back budget place has a stylish terrace and restaurant that gets good reviews for its food (the musical Sunday buffet, Ar30,000, is particularly popular). The rooms and bungalows are spread out in the exotic garden; though basic, they're clean and come with nets.

Villa Palm Beach PENSION €€

(☎032 02 409 04; palmbeach@gmail.com; r Ar45,000) A clean and homey pension just one row back from the beach, it offers well-kept rooms in a family house. Accommodation is simple, with nets, fans and wood floors, but it has a lovely feel and there are sea views from the upstairs rooms.

Le 5 Trop Près SEAFOOD €€

(☎032 07 740 60; www.normada.com/5trop; mains Ar12,000-15,000) Ramena is a fishing village so it's hardly surprising that seafood is plentiful. Le 5 Trop Près (pronounced like St Tropez, a wink to the glitzy French Riviera town) does a great job of preparing it in all its guises: fried, grilled, in sauces – everything is delicious. It is especially popular on Sundays, when booking is recommended.

L'Emeraude SEAFOOD €€

(mains Ar13,000-15,000) This rather smart restaurant, with its lovely deck on Ramena's beach, has a great reputation for its excellent food and Saturday-night disco. It follows a nice formula of fish, crab or calamari, offered either in sauce, curried, fried or grilled.

Getting There & Away

Taxis-brousses make several runs between Diego Suarez and Ramena (Ar2000) each day – although you sometimes have to wait a while for the vehicle to fill. Chartering a taxi is an easier option, but will cost about Ar60,000 return.

Les Trois Baies (The Three Bays)

On the eastern side of the peninsula that juts into the bay east of Diego is a series of beautiful bays with stunning beaches. There are many coves and inlets along this stretch of the coast, but the area is named after three majestic bays: **Baie de Sakalava** (Sakalava Bay), the **Baie des Pigeons** (Pigeons Bay) and the **Baie des Dunes** (Sand Dunes Bay). It's a wild, harsh but starkly beautiful environment, with not a village in sight, strong winds from April to November and baking heat from December to March.

Activities

TOP CHOICE **Les Trois Baies Circuit** HIKING

The **walk** from Baie de Sakalava (the southernmost of the three bays) to Ramena has become a popular excursion. It takes roughly half a day to walk from one end to the other, more if you include stops for swimming and/or a picnic. Many tour operators in Diego offer it as a package, with transfer from Diego in 4WD, drop-off at one end and pick-up at the other, a guide and a picnic on the way.

If you're staying in Diego, a cheaper way of doing it is to charter a taxi for the day (Ar80,000), have it drop you off at Baie de

LIBERTALIA

The first mention of the Pirate Republic of Libertalia was in a 1726 story by Daniel Defoe. According to Defoe, Libertalia was founded around the Baie des Français by Captain Misson, a French adventurer with a Robin Hood bent who sailed the seas freeing slaves and avoiding bloodshed whenever possible. He teamed up with a defrocked Dominican priest, Father Caraccioli, to set up a communist Utopia.

They began building with the help of assorted freed African slaves and British, French, Dutch and Portuguese pirates. A parliament was formed, a printing press was started, crops were planted, stock was reared and a new international language was established.

All seemed to be going well until the Malagasy people living around the 'International Republic of Libertalia' descended en masse from the hills and massacred the Libertalian population. Caraccioli was killed, but Misson escaped. His eventual fate remains a mystery.

As yet, there is no physical evidence of Libertalia, and some historians have relegated it to the realms of fantasy. Sceptics argue that Robinson Crusoe's creator could easily have invented a pirate republic.

Sakalava and then pick you up in Ramena (or vice versa). It's also recommended you take a guide (Ar50,000; ask at your hotel or the tourist office), as the route is not always obvious and there have been muggings in the area.

Between December and March, when the wind has died down, **swimming** in the three bays is blissful: beaches are deserted and the sea is calm, with a translucent, pale turquoise colour that contrasts with the dark blue of the depths. There is good **snorkelling** too. Baie des Dunes is the most sheltered of the three main bays.

Around the lighthouse at **Cap Miné**, you'll come across rusting military installations (cannons, bunkers, buildings in ruins) dating back to WWII. The cape dominates La Grande Passe, the entrance of the bay of Diego Suarez, and waves crash below the cliffs with thunderous might.

The area between Cap Miné and Ramena is a military base and you'll need to pay an admission fee (Ar5000) at the main gate.

Kitesurfing EXTREME SPORTS

From April to November, when the winds blow so strong you'll struggle to retain ownership of your hat, the Baie de Sakalava is a prime kitesurfing spot. The two hotels based in the bay offer equipment rental and courses.

Sleeping & Eating

The only accommodation in the area is on Baie de Sakalava, right by the beach.

Sakalava Lodge BUNGALOW €€€

(☎82 921 52; www.sakalava.com; Baie de Sakalava; bungalow full board €75-95) There are two types of bungalows at the Sakalava Lodge: the garden bungalows are 'hard' structures, with whitewashed walls and colourful soft furnishings. The seaside bungalows, however, are completely different – made of local materials and with lots of polished wood, pebbles and stone for decoration. Both have bags of charm, and the whole place has a languid beach feel to it. With regards to activities, kitesurfing rules (equipment and lessons are available); excursions can also be organised.

Royal Sakalava BUNGALOW €€€

(☎82 926 36; www.royalsakalava.com; Baie de Sakalava; r with half/full board €96/108) The concrete bungalows at Royal Sakalava are functional but devoid of charm, which shouldn't matter too much if you're here to make the best of the wind and surf. Royal Sakalava's French kitesurfing instructor is IKO-affiliated (International Kiteboarding Organisation), and the hotel offers courses from beginners to advanced (€35 per hour). If you know what you're doing, you can rent equipment. The hotel has a nice communal area/dining room, with sofas, a pool table and a TV, where you can relax in the evenings.

La Mer d'Emeraude

On the northern side of the entrance to the Baie de Diego Suarez lies the gorgeous **Mer d'Emeraude** (Emerald Sea), a sheltered bay of the Indian Ocean the colour and translucence of a rare gemstone. The shelter is provided by a series of small islets, which make ideal picnic stops and have good swimming and snorkelling.

Thanks to this idyllic setting, the Mer d'Emeraude has become a popular day trip from Diego Suarez for some R&R. Standard packages include transport to Ramena, the sailing from Ramena to Mer d'Emeraude (generally in a local sailing boat), three hours on an islet to sunbathe, swim and snorkel (equipment is normally included) and a lunch that includes alcoholic drinks. It's worth knowing that the package from Ramena onwards normally only costs about Ar60,000 per person, yet many agencies charge around Ar250,000 for two because of the 4WD transfer from Diego to Ramena; so if you're on a budget, tell the tour operator you'll arrange transport to Ramena yourself (and take a taxi-brousse or charter a taxi for the day).

The sailing from Ramena to the Mer d'Emeraude can be very rough between May and November when trade winds are strong, and you're pretty much guaranteed to get wet. Make sure you arrange this excursion with a reputable agency (see p138).

Joffreville (Ambohitra)

Joffreville (Ambohitra), established in 1902, was once a pleasure resort for the French military. Today it's a sleepy but incredibly atmospheric place, with crumbling colonial buildings, ever-changing weather and gorgeous views of the valleys and mountains.

Most people use the town as a jumping-off point to visit the fabulous and adjacent Parc National Montagne d'Ambre, but Joffreville has some lovely hotels, which would make a brilliant base from which to explore northern highlights such as the Tsingy Rouges, Diego, Ankarana, Les Trois Baies etc. Joffreville has a couple of small grocery stores but you'll find better supplies in Diego.

Sleeping & Eating

The village store sells a few basics, but if you plan on camping in the park you'll need to get food and other supplies in Diego. All the hotels do meals.

Nature Lodge LODGE **€€€**
(☎034 20 123 06; www.naturelodge-ambre.com; bungalows Ar200,000) A couple of kilometres before you reach Joffreville, Nature Lodge boasts magnificent views of the valley and lovely wooden safari-lodge-style cottages. The interiors are very chic, with colourful batiks, original sculptures and raffia matting on the

WORTH A TRIP

WINDSOR CASTLE & BAIE DU COURRIER

Windsor Castle is a 391m-high rock formation about three hours' drive (about 50km) northwest of Diego Suarez. The mountaintop is flat and served as a French fort and lookout, which was taken by the occupying British in 1942; you'll understand why it was fought over when you get to the summit: the 360-degree views, including Diego and the Bay of Diego Suarez to the east, Baie du Courrier to the west, the archipelago of Nosy Hara to the southwest and Cap d'Ambre to the north, are breathtaking.

Although Windsor Castle is impressive, what really makes the trip worthwhile is the journey there. The site is remote and can only be accessed by 4WD; you'll pass beautiful and varied scenery along the way and get a fascinating insight into the local economy and what life is like in remote areas.

After driving through Diego's industrial estate, you'll reach the salt marshes run by the Compagnie Salinière de Madagascar. This is one of Madagascar's most important salt-producing areas, with an annual production of 80,000 tons destined for consumer (food) and industrial markets. You'll also drive through paddy fields (some producing three crops a year thanks to irrigation, others relying on the rain for their annual crop), forests of mango trees (reputed to be the best in the country) and miles of arid bushland with wandering zebus. The villages on **Baie du Courrier** live from fishing; a pick-up truck takes the catch to Diego daily and if you get to the bay before lunchtime, you'll get a chance to see the weighing and negotiating of the goods by the waterside.

Since this trip is all about local knowledge and anecdotes, the key is a good guide. One of the best ways of doing the excursion is by quad bike with Diego Raid (p138) as the terrain is fun and varied. All tour operators in Diego can also organise the trip with a 4WD, driver and guide (Ar270,000 for up to three people): shop around and ask to meet the guide before you go.

walls. Meals are served in the large thatched dining room and bar (meals Ar35,000).

Le Relais de la Montagne d'Ambre PENSION €
(☎032 88 475 06; r without bathroom Ar30,000) Sisters Henriette and Louise run this lovely pension from their atmospheric 1932 colonial house. The rooms are no-frills, with just a bed and a wardrobe, but it's the service people enjoy most at the Relais: meals in the big dining rooms at night, crêpes for breakfast, reading in the beautiful garden or cosying up inside on rainy days. The three-course lunch (Ar15,000) is the best deal in town.

Le Domaine de Fontenay LUXURY HOTEL €€€
(☎82 908 71; www.lefontenay-madagascar.com; r €181) This grand hotel has a rustic charm to it. It has eight grand bungalows with stone floors, huge wood-and-marble bathrooms and four-poster beds. The restaurant in the old farmhouse (dating to 1904) features a chimney designed by Gustave Eiffel, of Tower fame. It also has an orchid garden, giant tortoises and a private nature reserve that has most of the wildlife you can see at Montagne d'Ambre, as well as views over Diego's bay.

Information

There is no electricity in Joffreville; hotels generally turn on their generators from 5pm to 10pm. The nearest bank is in Diego Suarez.

Getting There & Away

It is easy to catch a taxi-brousse to Joffreville (Ar3000, 1½ hours) from Diego. Vehicles depart from the Gare Routière d'Ambilobe, next to Arrachart Airport. It is unlikely you'll find a vehicle back to Diego after 4pm.

Parc National Montagne d'Ambre

This wonderful **national park** (www.parcs-madagascar.com) is literally a breath of fresh air from the arid northern plains: at 1000m, it is generally 10 degrees cooler than in Diego or Ankarana, even more so in winter, and its luxuriant forests could not contrast more with the mineral beauty of the lower grounds.

It rains almost every day in Montagne d'Ambre, and the park (182 sq km) and adjacent massif act as Diego's water reservoir: hydrologists have calculated that the area contributes 50 million cubic metres of water annually to northern Madagascar, enough to support 700 sq km of rice paddies.

PARC NATIONAL MONTAGNE D'AMBRE

Best time to visit Year-round.

Key highlights Beautiful waterfalls and streams, the world's smallest chameleon (if you manage to see it!).

Wildlife Lemurs, amphibians, birds, wild orchids.

Habitats Humid forest.

Gateway towns Joffreville.

Transport options 4km from Joffreville by foot or private vehicle.

Things you should know It rains almost every day at Montagne d'Ambre, and temperatures can drop to a nippy 3°C at night and just 10°C or 15°C on winter days (June to September), so take some warm clothes and a waterproof jacket.

For visitors, the park provides lovely walks in gorgeous forests, with plenty of waterfalls and lakes to rest by. The summer season (December to April) is the best for seeing reptiles and amphibians, but birdwatching and views from the summit are better in winter months. One day is enough to get a good sense of what the park and the wildlife are like, but two days would give you time to trek to the summit and discover many lakes and waterfalls dotting the park.

Park Fees & Guides

The park's **headquarters** (☎82 213 20; www.parcs-madagascar.com; ⏰7.30am-4pm), at the park entrance, 4km southwest of Joffreville, can help with information, **permits** (per day Ar25,000) and **guides** (Ar25,000-50,000 for up to five people, depending on the circuit), which are compulsory. Most guides speak French and English.

Wildlife

Of the seven species of lemurs found in the park, the most notable are the crowned lemur and Sanford's lemur. Others include the rufous mouse lemur, the dwarf and northern sportive lemurs, the aye-aye (rarely seen) and the local Montagne d'Ambre fork-marked lemur. Among other mammals, the ring-tailed mongoose is probably the most frequently observed.

Reptile and amphibian life thrives in the park's humid conditions, and Montagne d'Ambre is where you'll find the diminutive Brookesia chameleon, the world's smallest. It lives in leaf litter and you'll need your guide's well-trained eyes to find it.

Activities

There are six hiking trails in Montagne d'Ambre ranging from easy one-hour walks to more strenuous eight-hour treks. Many can be combined to tailor your own circuit: ask your guide to recommend the best itinerary.

Highlights include the **Voie des Mille Arbres** ('Path of A Thousand Trees'), a majestic alley planted with tall exotic species (Montagne d'Ambre was an important research centre for forestry and tree plantations during the 20th century), the **Petit Lac**, a small crater lake also known as Lac de la Coupe Verte, and **Cascade Antankarana**, a beautiful waterfall flowing into a tranquil pool surrounded by fern-covered cliffs. Nearby is the path known as **Jardin Botanique**, a forest track lined by orchids, palms, lianas and bromeliads. Not far away, another trail leads to the small **Cascade Sacrée**, a sacred waterfall where locals often make offerings.

A longer track leads to the viewpoint over **Cascade Antomboka** (or Grande Cascade), a narrow waterfall that plunges 80m into a forest grotto.

The summit of **Montagne d'Ambre** (Amber Mountain; 1475m) is reached via an 11km trail heading south from the park entrance. From the campsite it's a relatively easy three- to four-hour hike, and less than an hour from the base to the summit. On clear days (sadly, a rare event), there are wonderful views of the lush forests. Just below the summit is **Lac Maudit**, where local *fady* (taboo) prohibits swimming, and to the southeast is the larger **Grand Lac**, where you are allowed to camp.

Sleeping

The following places must be booked through the national park headquarters.

Gîte d'Etape CABIN €

(dm Ar6000) Run by the park, this cabin has a kitchen and a sitting area. It's located near the Cascade Sacrée, in a beautiful clearing.

Campsites CAMPGROUND €

(camping per tent Ar2000) There are three campsites in the park, all in gorgeous locations. The campsite near the Cascade Sacrée has the best facilities, with picnic tables, showers and water. The other two sites, near Grand Lac and Lac Maudit, only have pit toilets.

Getting There & Away

The park entrance is about 4km southwest of Joffreville. There are no taxis-brousses from Joffreville to the park entrance so if you don't have a private vehicle, you'll have to walk. A chartered taxi for the day from Diego costs Ar80,000.

Parc National de l'Ankarana

Parc National de l'Ankarana is a striking and undeveloped fantasyland that's home to uniquely Malagasy sights: psychedelic fields of spiky *tsingy* (limestone pinnacle formations) sitting next to dry forests. Running through and under the *tsingy* are hidden forest-filled canyons and subterranean rivers.

The **park** (www.parcs-madagascar.com) is famed for its bat-filled grottoes and mysterious caves steeped in legend and history, where the Antakarana (the predominant ethnic group in northern Madagascar) took refuge from the Merina (the traditional ruling elite from the highlands) during the 18th-century tribal wars.

Park Fees & Guides

The park's **headquarters** (⏲7.30am-4pm) is located at the eastern entrance of the park in the village of Mahamasina on the RN6.

Entry **permits** (per 1/2/3 days Ar25,000/37,000/40,000) and **guides** (Ar25,000-50,000 for up to 5 people, depending on the circuit), which are compulsory, must be arranged here.

There are no park offices at the western entrance of Ankarana so make sure you make all arrangements in Mahamasina.

Wildlife

The dry *tsingy* are full of strangely shaped succulents such as Euphorbia and Pachypodium, while the sheltered intervening canyons are filled with leafy cassias, figs, baobabs and other trees typical of dry deciduous forest.

Of the area's more than 10 species of lemurs, the most numerous are crowned, Sanford's and northern sportive lemurs. Tenrecs and ring-tailed mongooses are also common, the latter particularly around campsites where they come in search of food (make sure you pack everything away).

Parc National de l'Ankarana

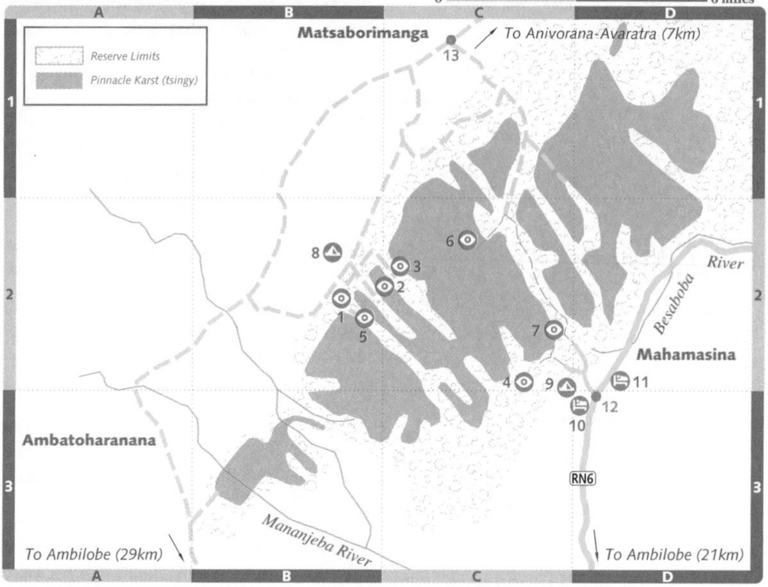

Parc National de l'Ankarana

Sights

1	Canyon d'Andohalambo	B2
	Grands Tsingy	(see 6)
2	Grotte Cathédrale	C2
3	Grotte d'Andrafiabe	C2
4	Grotte des Chauves-Souris	C2
5	Grotte Squelette	B2
6	Lac Vert	C2
7	Perte des Rivières chasm	C2
	Petits Tsingy	(see 4)

Sleeping

8	Campement d'Andrafiabe	B2
9	Campement du Prince	C2
10	Chez Aurélien	D3
11	Le Relais de l'Ankarana	D2

Information

12	Main Park Entrance	D3
	Park headquarters	(see 12)
13	Western Park Entrance	C1

Over 90 species of birds have been identified in the reserve, including the orange-and-white kingfisher, crested *coua*, Madagascan fish eagle, crested wood ibis and banded kestrel. Many of the park's guides are keen birders and will relish the opportunity to tell you about them.

Fourteen of Madagascar's 33 species of bats live here, of which you're bound to see at least half a dozen (no vampires!) in the park's numerous caves. And finally, one animal you're very likely to see, even though you'd probably rather not, is the scorpion: they thrive in Ankarana, living under rocks and logs. To make sure that you find them rather than them surprising you, don't leave your bag on the forest floor and check where you sit. Campers will have to be especially careful with their shoes and when packing their tent.

Activities

Ankarana is best known for its serrated, dark-grey *tsingy* and its caves, and there are a variety of circuits to take in the highlights. The park is split in two halves, which are distinct and not easily linked, so ideally you should set aside two days to visit both sides.

The eastern half is the most accessible, via the village of Mahamasina, and the best place to admire the strange-looking *tsingy*. The easiest way to see these surreal pinnacles is to do the two- to three-hour **Grotte des Chauves-Souris** (Cave of Bats) circuit. This impressive

PARC NATIONAL DE L'ANKARANA

Best time to visit June to December, when both the eastern and western parts of the park are accessible (the west is cut off in the rainy season).

Key highlights Dark-grey *tsingy* (limestone pinnacle formations) and magnificent caves.

Wildlife Bats, birds and lemurs.

Habitats Dry deciduous forest.

Gateway towns Mahamasima

Transport options Taxi-brousse to Mahamasima (between Ambilobe and Diego), or private vehicle.

Things you should know Most lakes and rivers are sacred in Ankarana, so bathing and swimming are not permitted. Bring a torch for visiting the caves. Guides are compulsory.

cave has superb stalactites, stalagmites and thousands of bats hanging from the walls, and nearby is a small viewpoint from where you can look over the **Petits Tsingy**.

The route to the **Grands Tsingy** is a longer walk –five hours return – with some interesting sights on the way, including **Perte des Rivières**, a massive rock chasm in which three of the park's rivers plunge during the rainy season (they come out 20km later in the Mozambique Channel). There are some good viewpoints and a rope bridge to cross. The hike to the pretty **Lac Vert** is the longest circuit (nine hours in total) and takes in all the main sights in the eastern half of the park.

The western half of Ankarana is different and only accessible from June to December. Here the focus is on three sets of caves, **Grotte Squelette** (Skeleton Cave), **Grotte Cathédrale** (Cathedral Cave) and **Grotte d'Andrafiabe**, which you can visit through a subterranean circuit (if this doesn't appeal, another circuit links two of the caves via a 'normal' path). There are beautiful canyons along the way, including **Canyon d'Andohalambo**.

Sleeping & Eating

TOP CHOICE **Le Relais de l'Ankarana** GUESTHOUSE €€€
(☎032 02 222 94; http://relaisdelankarana.unblog.fr; Mahamasina; r Ar80,000) Run by the hospitable Hobaya family, the Relais is a wonderful halt on the Diego–Nosy Be route. The guesthouse was built in 2008 (this was, apparently, their retirement plan), and the rooms are comfortable and elegant, with exquisite wood-clad sloped ceilings featuring geometric patterns. The garden has been carefully landscaped with drought-resistant plants to make the best of the limited water resources. The food is superb, too (three-course meals Ar22,000). At night, views of the stars and Milky Way are one of a kind. The Hobayas speak English and Spanish as well as French.

Chez Aurélien BUNGALOW €
(☎032 40 630 14; aurelien_ank@yahoo.fr; Mahamasina; bungalows Ar20,000, without bathroom Ar10,000) A brilliant option for independent budget travellers. It's located right next to the park entrance on the RN6 – perfect for those travelling by taxi-brousse. Bungalows are very basic (bucket showers, and shared facilities for the cheapest ones) but clean, and the restaurant is excellent, with a lovely dining room in a small thatched shelter. The *menu complet* (a three-course meal with a choice of mains; Ar10,000) is the best value in town.

Ankarana Campsites CAMPGROUND €
(camping per tent Ar5000; Parc National de l'Ankarana) Campement du Prince (Grottes des Chauves-Souris) Campement d'Andrafiabe (Andrafiabe) The two campsites are basic, with pit toilets and no drinking water. Watch out for scorpions. Campsite booking must be arranged at the park headquarters in Mahamasina.

Information

The only mobile phone network that works in Mahamasina and around the park is Orange. There is no electricity in Mahamasina or in the park; hotel generators generally work from 5pm to 10pm. The nearest bank is in Ambilobe.

For more tips and author reviews of Parc National de l'Ankarana, head to www.lonelyplanet.com/madagascar/northern-madagascar/reserve-speciale-de-lankarana.

Getting There & Away

Mahamasina village is approximately 100km southwest of Diego Suarez and about 40km north of Ambilobe along the RN6. The main park entrance at Mahamasina is accessible year-round and easily reached by taxi-brousse; drivers can drop you off at your hotel or at the park entrance and you won't have problems flagging a vehicle for your onward journey. Be aware that you'll likely have to pay the whole Diego–Ambilobe fare (Ar15,000).

DON'T MISS

TSINGY ROUGES

About 65km south of Diego, between the turn-off for Joffreville and Parc National de l'Ankarana, lies one of Madagascar's most awesome natural wonders, the **Tsingy Rouges** (Red Tsingy; admission Ar10,000). These scraggly pinnacles, erosion's work of art, are made of laterite, an iron oxide–rich soil with an intense red-brick colour.

These surreal formations stand on the edge of beautiful canyons: it's a fragile environment, and local authorities have thankfully stepped in to protect the site. There are three areas you can access, including a breathtaking viewpoint. The most stunning site is at the bottom of a small ravine, where *tsingy* (pinnacle formations) line an entire bank like an army of sentinels. If you're here with a guide, ask him or her to show you the three natural pigments found in the soil – ochre, vermilion and magenta – which northern Malagasies use for face paints and natural dyes.

Because of its colour, the Tsingy are best admired early in the morning (around 7am or 8am) or late in the afternoon (around 4pm), when the light is low and warm.

You will need a 4WD to access the Red Tsingy: the turn-off on the RN6 is 45km south of Diego and signposted. It's then 20km along a dirt track that's pretty good in places, dismal in others. En route, you'll cross a number of eucalyptus plantations destined for charcoal production. (The majority of Malagasies use charcoal for cooking and its production is a leading cause of deforestation, so these plantations help preserve primary forests). You'll also be treated to sweeping views of the Indian Ocean. The dirt track can be impassable during the rainy season (December to April).

To reach the western half of the park, you'll need your own vehicle. All tour operators in Diego Suarez can arrange 4WD hire to Ankarana, as well as multiday excursions or day trips from Diego.

SAVA REGION

The SAVA region (known for its four principal towns, Sambava, Antalaha, Vohémar and Andapa) is disconnected from the rest of the country, with the exception of a single airport (Sambava) and one rough road to Ambilobe on the RN6 (which continues to Diego Suarez and Ambanja).

The only overland route from Maroantsetra is by foot, requiring several days of trekking. Having said that, the airport makes the region's principal attraction, the superb Parc National de Marojejy, easily accessible. The area is also better off economically than most, as its principal crop is the valuable vanilla bean, and you can pull together a decent beach break here, too. So this is a pleasant place to be marooned, particularly as there are very few tourists to be found.

Sambava

POP 38,000

Sambava is one of those places that is not set up for tourism but contains a good weekend if you know where to go. There's a nice secluded part of town just two blocks off the main street with good accommodation just steps from the beach. The beach itself is very long, and nearly unoccupied, with enormous crashing waves. Take care with currents (and, some say, sharks). If you have been travelling hard, Sambava is an inexpensive place to recharge your batteries, particularly after a tough trek in Marojejy. It is also the best place to stay prior to visiting the park, as it can be reached by taxi from Sambava with an early start; you don't need to overnight in Andapa.

Tours

For Nosianna river trips, plantation tours, pirogue trips, or simple transportation, call **Dylan** (☎032 04 059 05, 033 04 779 15; randria.dylan@yahoo.fr), a professional driver and guide who speaks English. **Bruno** (☎032 07 610 28) at Mimi Hotel, on the road to the taxi-brousse station, can also help plan tours.

Sleeping & Eating

Staying on the beach is highly recommended. Otherwise there is some very inexpensive budget accommodation nearby.

TOP CHOICE **Hôtel Orchidea Beach II** HOTEL €€€
(☎88 923 24, 032 04 383 77; http://orchideabeach.marojejy.com; Plage des Cocotiers; d Ar70,000, bungalows Ar37,000, mains Ar9000; ❄) This is a charming, quiet and leafy hotel with whitewashed

KHAT: LEGAL HIGH?

The area between Ambilobe and Diego is a big *khat*-growing area. This small flowering shrub produces a compound that is an amphetamine-like stimulant. Chewed, the plant's leaves cause hyperactivity and euphoria and are a popular drug, particularly among taxi-brousse drivers who often work very long hours.

Although the authorities largely turn a blind eye to *khat* production and consumption, it is worth knowing that it is has not actually been legalised. Before the political turmoil hit in 2009, there had been talk of the government taking a stand to either legalise *khat* so that its trade could be included in the formal economy (*khat* adds welcome revenue to poor rural households), or make it illegal and encourage growers to focus their energy on other crops. Unfortunately, the political crisis has left the matter unsettled for now.

buildings and a manicured courtyard tucked away on a pleasant side street across from the beach. The brightly painted rooms have nice tiled baths (but no nets), and the amiable staff serves up good food. The two beachfront bungalows are a steal, with crashing surf right outside your door.

Villa Scheridanne GUESTHOUSE **€**
(☎032 69 687 10; d Ar30,000-40,000) Next to Orchidea Beach, this new pastel guesthouse has upper-storey rooms with beautiful balconies, and a cosy warmth. If it weren't for the caged lemurs, we would make this our top choice.

Las Palmas BUNGALOW **€€**
(☎88 920 87, 032 40 073 72; laspalmas.hotel@gmail.com; bungalows with air-con Ar52,000; set menus Ar18,000; ❄) Another well-manicured property in a great location across from the beach, offering nice rooms with great bathrooms and some bungalows.

For the budget-minded, there are two clean and incredibly cheap hotels near the large Hotel Victoria on the main street, just two blocks from the beach. **Hotel Flamboyant** (☎032 40 639 20; d Ar12,000) has no sign, but is down the alley to the right of the Victoria, past the gate, while **Hotel Florencia** (☎032 02 466 21; d Ar14,000-28,000) is one block closer to town. **La Terrasse** (⏲8am-1am), the Polynesian hut 200m from Victoria, has good Malagasy seafood and fun karaoke at night. **Boule d'Or** (⏲4pm-9m Tue-Sun), the mustard building down the street opposite La Terrasse, is the only pizzeria.

Information

There are several banks with ATMs at the northern end of town. Internet access is available at BIC for Ar50 per minute.

Getting There & Around

Air

Air Madagascar (☎88 920 37; Rte Principale) flies from Sambava several times weekly to Antananarivo (€184, one hour), sometimes via Maroantsetra (€88, 30 minutes). There are also flights to Diego Suarez (€122, 30 minutes). The Sambava airport is about 2km south of town. A taxi is Ar5000, or you can walk.

Taxi-Brousse

Taxis-brousses to Antalaha (Ar15,000, three hours) depart from the southern taxi-brousse station in the market. The northern taxi-brousse station handles transport to Andapa (Ar7000, 2½ hours), Vohémar (Ar8000, six hours) and Diego Suarez (Ar50,000, 17 hours).

A private car to Andapa will cost you Ar60,000, so buying the two front seats in a brousse is a far less expensive while still comfortable proposition.

Parc National de Marojejy

This is one of Madagascar's great undiscovered parks, a fact all the more astonishing because it is one of the best managed and easiest to get to. You can fly from Antananarivo to Sambava, jump in a taxi, and 2½ hours later you are off on a world-class trek.

The park consists of over 550 sq km of pristine mountainous **rainforest** – an often thick, steep, and root-filled jungle with numerous streams and **waterfalls**. It is a primordial place, where the astonishing 'angel of the forest', the silky sifaka, inhabits misty mountains, and spectacular views of the Marojejy Massif peek through the canopy. For naturalists, the area is noted for its extraordinary biodiversity, including 2000 types of plants, 147 species of reptiles and amphibians, 118 species of birds, and 11 species of lemurs, about 70% of which are endemic to Madagascar. It also ascends through four levels of forest, enhancing the variety of experience. In 2007 the park was designated a Unesco World Heritage Site.

The local MNP office here is to be applauded. Assisted by American researcher Erik Patel, whose **Simpona** (www.simpona.org) organisation works to protect the silky sifaka, they have constructed three quality camps at different altitudes, each set in an attractive location. Trained guides, cooks, and porters provide excellent service. Cabins are cleaned regularly. Revenue is distributed to local communities, helping turn conservation into a winning enterprise. There is also an excellent interpretation centre at the park office (with signs in English), a model for parks elsewhere. For more information see www.marojejy.com.

Park Fees & Guides

The **MNP office** (☎88 070 27; mjj.parks@gmail.com) is located near the 66km post on the main Sambava–Andapa road, just before Manantenina, and arranges **entry permits** (per 1/2/3/4 days Ar10,000/15,000/20,000/25,000). Guide/cook fees are Ar15,000/9000 per day if you provide the guide's food, Ar18,000/12,000 otherwise. Porters are Ar4000 to Ar7000 per day depending on the length of the hike. Camping is Ar6000 a day per bed. An excellent English-speaking guide is Mosesy, the head of the local guide organisation. To maximize your chance of seeing a silky sifaka, an additional specialist guide may be necessary.

Activities

The park has a single trail ascending through three camps to the summit of Mt Marojejy. The trail officially begins at the park boundary, about a 1½-hour walk from the park office. If you want to cut down your trekking time, you can arrange for a ride to the trailhead, but it is a beautiful walk to get there, along a dirt road through lush mountains, small villages, and rice paddies. **Camp One (Mantella)**, at 450m, takes about two hours to reach, and has six cabins (wooden frames with canvas walls) and a campground. This is an area of lowland rainforest.

Camp Two (Marojejia), at 775m, takes an additional two hours and a bit more work to reach. It has four cabins with fully made beds, and a large covered kitchen and dining area. This is a transition area between lowland and montane rainforest and is the best place to see wildlife, including colourful millipedes the length of your hand (a lot more enjoyable than it sounds), leaf-tailed geckos, and paradise flycatchers. It is also a wonderful place to hang out with a cup of coffee, surrounded by the sounds of the forest and the rush of a nearby stream.

Camp Three (Simpona), at 1250m, is the base camp for ascents to the summit, and has two cabins with a sheltered dining area. It is a very steep and strenuous climb to get there, requiring both hands and feet as you surmount one root after another, a challenge magnified when it is wet. The final leg to the summit, 2132m high, stretches 2km and can take up to four or five hours to traverse.

Note: the trek from the park boundary to the second camp is a nature expedition. The trail from Camp Two is a climbing expedition. If you prefer the former, there is no need to go past Camp Marojejia, which anyone in decent shape can reach. Beyond it you must be very fit, and prepared for cold weather.

Sleeping

If you have to stay outside the park, Sambava is recommended. The only other option is Andapa, a small town nestled in the hills some 40km away on the way to Réserve Spéciale d'Anjanaharibe-Sud. It is closer to the park. but further from Sambava (where you must return), lacks the appeal of the beach, and has little accommodation.

If you do choose Andapa, the best place to stay is the surprising **Hotel Beanana** (☎88 072 20; http://hotel-beanana.no-ip.com; d Ar35,000, breakfasts Ar7000), a bright-white drive-in motel that is new, clean, and inexpensive, with hot water and decent Chinese food. **Hotel Vatosoa** (☎88 070 78; d Ar16,000, mains Ar5000) offers more basic rooms.

PARC NATIONAL DE MAROJEJY

Best time to visit August to November: it's dry season, and birding is best.

Key highlight Silky sifaka.

Wildlife Massive millipedes, paradise flycatcher, mantella frog.

Habitats Four levels of forest: low altitude, dense montane, high montane, high altitude.

Gateway towns Sambava and Andapa.

Transport options Taxi from Sambava or Andapa (Ar60,000).

Things you should know Minimum four days' trek to scale the summit.

RÉSERVE SPÉCIALE D'ANJANAHARIBE-SUD

The entry permit for Marojejy also provides entry to the Réserve Spéciale d'Anjanaharibe-Sud. This 182.5-sq-km area to the southwest is little visited. It is 20km from Andapa by rutted dirt road, has no facilities, and offers much of the same vegetation and wildlife as Marojejy. That said, it is a place of outstanding beauty and solitude, where the wail of the indri can be heard. More information is available at the park office.

Getting There & Away

Taxis-brousses go daily between Andapa and Sambava (Ar7000, 2½ hours) and will drop you off at the park office en route.

Antalaha

POP 40,000

A relatively affluent city, thanks to the vanilla bean, Antalaha surprises with its street lights, proper drainage and excellent roads. The airport closed in 2011 for renovations, however, leaving the town marooned at the end of the paved road from its sister vanilla town, Sambava. Beyond lies the Masoala Peninsula (p183), which can only be crossed by foot. Consequently, Antalaha is the starting point for some treks into Masoala, but the majority begin in Maroantsetra, which offers better access to the coastal lodges and Nosy Ve, as well as the relative calm of the Baie d'Antongil.

Tours

Bureau de Liaison de Parc National de Masoala HIKING
(☎032 41 800 81; Ave de l'Indépendance) Arranges treks into Masoala park, including permits and guides. Fees are the same as entering from Maroantsetra.

Pharmacy Kam-Hyo TOUR
Marie-Hélène, at this pharmacy in the centre of town, arranges tours of the local vanilla plant, or anything else you may happen to need. Definitely a new take on the tourist information centre.

Sleeping & Eating

Hazovola HOTEL €€
(☎032 41 287 11; www.hotelantalaha.com; d incl breakfast Ar70,000, mains from Ar11,000; ❄✉) The best hotel in town. Rooms have nice tiled baths, balconies, and flat-screen TVs. Locals praise the restaurant.

Hôtel Florida HOTEL €
(☎032 41 555 12; d from Ar18,000, with hot water Ar23,000; ❄) Your best budget option. On the main road opposite Pharmacy Kam-Hyo. Some more expensive rooms with air-con are also available.

Hôtel Océan Momo BUNGALOW €€
(☎032 02 340 69; www.ocean-momo.com; d Ar70,000, mains Ar12,000) This comfortable hotel about 100m south of the port has imposing white bungalows, in rows beside the beach, with tiled floors, dark wood furniture and four-poster beds. The restaurant is large and tastefully decorated, with a range of seafood on offer.

Jeannick Gargotte MALAGASY, EUROPEAN €
(pizzas Ar9000-13,000; ⏲dinner) This expat hangout is a popular spot for pizza and a range of Malagasy/European food. It's on the main road to the pharmacy.

Information

There are banks and ATMs in town, and an internet cafe at Orange, next to Pharmacy Kam-Hyo.

Getting There & Around

Boat

Cargo boats sail regularly on the rough and sometimes dangerous journey between Antalaha and Maroantsetra, sometimes also stopping near

DON'T MISS

A SCREAMING BARGAIN

Sometimes when comparing prices in terms of ariary, we forget how inexpensive things really are in Madagascar. But consider this: for Ar70,000 a day, two people can hire a porter, a guide, a cook, and lodging at Camp Two in Parc National de Marojejy, one of Madagascar's top national parks and a Unesco World Heritage Site. Meanwhile, the entry fees alone to an East African game park are *four times that*. So if you arrive in Tana with Mother Nature on your mind, we suggest getting on the next plane to Sambava, and hailing a taxi.

WORTH A TRIP

CAP EST

Remote and beautiful Cap Est is Madagascar's easternmost point. You can get here by hiring a car or taking a four-hour taxi-brousse ride south from Antalaha. Hotels here are routinely destroyed by cyclones, but at the time of writing the basic **Hotel du Voyageur** was still standing. The nearby town of Ambodirafia has an MNP office that can provide you with all the necessary information and support (guides, porters) for treks down the peninsula's east coast. The walk from here to the very tip of the peninsula, Cap Masoala, takes about four days, camping along the way, with numerous rivers that must be crossed by pirogue. From there you have to either return, or continue around the peninsula to Maroantsetra, a hard but adventurous slog that could take another four to six days. Cargo boats also leave intermittently from Cap Masoala for Maroantsetra.

Cap Est. There are no set schedules; inquire at the port about sailings. There are also cargo boats to other areas along the east coast, including Tamatave (Toamasina), Sambava and Vohémar.

Taxi-Brousse

Heading north, there are usually several taxis-brousses each day between Antalaha and Sambava (Ar15,000, three hours). Departures are from the taxi-brousse stand about 2km north of town.

Heading south, two taxis-brousses daily go to Cap Est (Ar15,000, four hours) in the dry season. Taxis-brousses towards Cap Est depart from the taxi-brousse station on the airport road. If you're taking a mountain bike to Cap Est, the taxis-brousses can tie it on top.

Eastern Madagascar

Includes »

Best Places to Eat

- Le Bateau Ivre (p170)
- Piment Banane (p170)
- La Pirogue (p173)
- Idylle Beach (p179)

Best Places to Stay

- Princesse Bora Lodge & Spa (p180)
- Chez Sika (p181)
- Masoala Forest Lodge (p189)
- Ony Hôtel (p166)
- Le Bon Endroit (p182)

Why Go?

Eastern Madagascar is travel the way it used to be. There is a wildness here of primordial allure, from the misty mountains of Masoala, down the huge coastline with its pounding sea and overhanging palms, to the lush alleyways of the Pangalanes Lakes. When you arrive back home, it all has the quality of a dream. This part of the country is largely cut off from the rest, and from itself, by a degraded transportation network, including some roads out of an engineer's nightmare. Travelling here requires a combination of plane, car, 4WD, dirt bike, scooter, pirogue (dugout canoe), ferry, cargo boat, taxi-brousse (bush taxi), and motorboat. This inaccessibility results in isolated communities and, for the traveller, a constant sense of coming upon undiscovered locales, including entire national parks. There's no doubt it can be frustrating at times, but Eastern Madagascar produces more traveller's tales than anywhere else. If you value that, come here first.

When to Go

Tamatave (Toamasina)

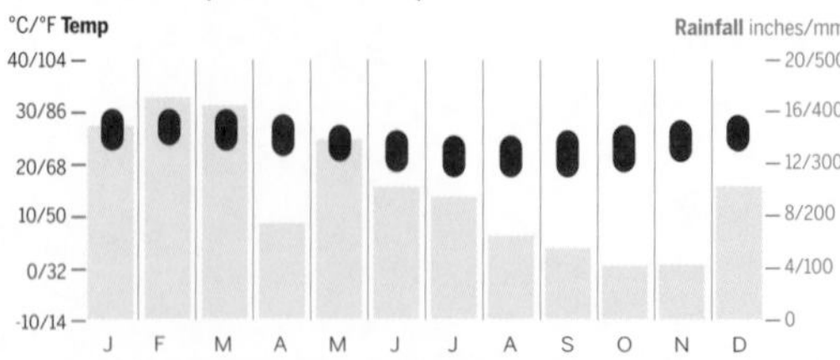

Jun–Oct Vanilla season. Flights can be full in the northeast.

Jul–Sep Whale-watching in the Baie d'Antongil

Dec–Mar Hold onto your hat, it's cyclone season

Eastern Madagascar Highlights

1. Hear the wail of the indri in **Parc National d'Andasibe** (p159)
2. Take a cargo boat through the **Pangalanes Lakes** (p162)
3. Drive the infamous **RN5** (p175) from Soanierana-Ivongo to Maroantsetra
4. Watch the elusive aye-aye eat a coconut during a night walk on **Aye-Aye Island** (p184)
5. Camp out on the tropical jungle island of **Nosy Mangabe** (p188)
6. See breaching humpbacks on a **whale-watching trip** (p180)
7. Explore the island of **Ile Sainte Marie** (p177) by quad or dirt bike
8. Stay in an ecolodge at **Parc National de Masoala** (p189)
9. Do absolutely nothing on **Ile aux Nattes** (p181)

Getting There & Away

Air Madagascar (www.airmadagascar.com) serves Tamatave (Toamasina), Sambava, Maroantsetra, and Ile Sainte Marie, largely in a circuit from Antananarivo (Tana). In 2011 the airport at Antalaha closed for at least two years of renovations. Air Madagascar and Air Austral both fly to Tamatave from Réunion.

Almost all land access to Eastern Madagascar is via a single road, the RN2 from Antananarivo. It is possible to drive up the coast from Fort Dauphin (Taolagnaro), but this is 4WD adventure travel, not transportation.

There is an unreliable train service running every Monday that leaves at 7am from Moramanga to Tamatave. The vintage Michelin train also has limited service from Tana to Andasibe (p34).

Head to **Lonely Planet** (www.lonelyplanet.com/madagascar/eastern-madagascar/antananarivo-to-toamasina) for reviews and advice on the trip from Antananarivo to Tamatave.

MORAMANGA TO BRICKAVILLE

Moramanga

POP 32,000

The first major stop in the east after leaving Antananarivo on the RN2, this commercial centre has little tourism value of its own, but you'll have to pause here if you're heading to the Andasibe Parks on public transport. Take a *pousse-pousse* (rickshaw) around.

Sights

Musée de la Gendarmerie Nationale MUSEUM
(Police Museum; ☎56 821 39; Camp Tristany; admission Ar5000; ⊙9-11am & 2.30-5pm Sat, Sun & holidays) Exhibits cannons, police uniforms, a vintage taxi-brousse, and an enormous bunch of dried marijuana.

Sleeping & Eating

Bezanozano HOTEL €€€
(☎56 825 98, 033 12 083 24; d Ar80,000;) This sprawling complex is your best choice in this town, even if it isn't finished. The rooms are new and large, with balconies, and the restaurant is excellent: try the *pasta de la maison*. Management is helpful, and a huge pool is most welcome in summer. Prices negotiable.

Hotel Nadia HOTEL €
(☎56 822 43; s/d/tr Ar20,000/30,000/40,000) A basic budget option in the middle of the busy market, with its own cafeteria. Serviceable but could be cleaner.

Hôtel Restaurant Espace Diamant HOTEL €
(☎56 823 76; d Ar30,000) A short walk west of the *gare routière* (station), this spic-and-span hotel has new tiled rooms, big beds and a large restaurant.

Le Coq d'Or CHINSE, MALAGASY €
(☎56 820 45; mains from Ar6000; ⊙lunch & dinner Mon-Sat, lunch Sun) A neat painted cafe off the main road, serving *soupe chinoise* (noodle soup with fish, chicken or vegetables), fried chicken and other Malagasy meals. Highly rated by locals.

La Sirène Dorée PIZZERIA €
(mains from Ar6000; ⊙breakfast, lunch & dinner) Just a tad smarter than its rivals, with mirrored windows concealing the restaurant, pizzeria, patisserie and *salon de thé*.

Information

The **Regional Tourism Office** (☎033 11 413 21) is located above the Bezanozano restaurant and covers Moramanga, the Andasibe Parks, and Lac Alaotra.

Getting There & Away

Taxi-Brousse

Taxis-brousses leave regularly from Antananarivo's eastern taxi-brousse station for Moramanga (Ar5000, 2¾ hours).

There are direct taxi-brousse connections from Moramanga to Andasibe (Ar2000, 1½ hours) every few hours. To get to Tamatave (Ar15,000, five to seven hours), you may need to wait until a vehicle coming from Antananarivo arrives with space.

Train

A slow passenger train departs Moramanga every Monday at 7am, arriving at Tamatave at 5pm. It returns Tuesday at 8.20am, arriving at Moramanga at 6.55pm. It also departs Moramanga every Thursday at 3pm, but only goes as far as Ambila-Lemaitso, arriving at 10.30pm. It returns Friday at 8am, arriving in Moramanga at 4pm.

It is always wise to check the schedule with **Madarail** (www.madarail.mg) ahead of time, either through your hotel, at the station (best), or online. Oddly, either route is the same price (Ar10,000).

Andasibe Area Parks

The small town of Andasibe is surrounded by several parks and reserves whose unique wildlife and close proximity to the capital have made this area extremely popular with travellers. The largest is the Parc National Andasibe-Mantadia. This is actually the organisational union of two separate parks, the northern **Parc National de Mantadia** (16,000 hectares) and the much smaller **Parc National d'Andasibe** (810 hectares), previously known as Réserve Spéciale d'Analamazaotra, or Périnet. To these are added **Parc Mitsinjo**, **Réserve de Torotorofotsy**, **Vohimana Forest**, **Réserve de Maromizaha**, and the latest addition, **Mahay Mitia Ala (MMA)**.

Thankfully, accommodation is more or less centralised along a single main road. Bring warm clothing in winter, and enough cash to see you through, as the nearest banks/ATMs are in Moramanga.

LAC ALAOTRA & AROUND

The trip from Antananarivo via Moramanga to Lac Alaotra, Madagascar's largest body of fresh water, has historically been of interest to Malagasy and other visitors. However, major environmental damage around the lake, difficult access, negative feedback on the Route des Contrabandiers hiking trail from Lac Alaotra to the East Coast, and the underdevelopment of the nearby Parc National de Zahamena, reduce the attractiveness of this area for most visitors.

PARC NATIONAL D'ANDASIBE

As it's easiest to access, Parc National d'Andasibe gets the most visitors, and tends to fill up from July to October, Madagascar's tourist high season. The entrance is 2km along a sealed road from the town of Andasibe. Because the reserve is small, most of it can be covered in short walks, including two small lakes, **Lac Vert** (Green Lake) and **Lac Rouge** (Red Lake). The best time for seeing (and hearing) indris is early in the morning, from 7am to 11am.

PARK FEES & GUIDES

The **MNP office** (⌚6am-4pm) is located at the entrance and contains a helpful interpretation centre. Entrance permits are Ar25,000/37,000 per person for one/two days and valid at Parc National de Mantadia as well. For guide fees see the individual circuits below.

Sights & Activities

The real draw here is the rare indri, Madagascar's largest lemur, whose unforgettable wail can be heard emanating from the misty forest throughout the day, most commonly in the early morning. There are about 60 resident family groups of two to five indris each. You may also see woolly lemurs, grey bamboo lemurs, red-fronted lemurs, black-and-white ruffed lemurs and diademed sifakas. In 2005 the Goodman's mouse lemur was discovered here and identified as a distinct species. Eleven species of tenrec, the immense and colourful Parson's chameleon and seven other chameleon species are also found here. Over 100 bird species have been identified in the park, together with 20 species of amphibian. The park is also home to the endemic palm tree *Ravenea louvelii*, found nowhere else on the island.

There are three organised walking trails, all of which are generally easy going. The most popular trail is the **Circuit Indri 1** (Ar15,000, about two hours), which includes the main lakes and the territory of a single family of indris. The slightly longer **Circuit Indri 2** (Ar25,000, two to four hours) visits the lakes and encompasses the patches of two separate families. The **Circuit Aventure** (Ar35,000, up to six hours) does all of the above, plus some moderately more strenuous walking.

Night walks (Ar10,000) take place along the road on the perimeter of the reserve, and are not permitted in the forest itself. You will probably be able to see tenrecs and mouse and dwarf lemurs on this walk. Bring a torch (flashlight).

Behind the MNP office is the small **Parc à Orchidées** (Orchid Park; ⌚7.30am-noon & 2-5.30pm), which is at its most attractive in October. By late summer it's almost completely dried up. There's no signage so you need a good guide to fully appreciate it.

PARC NATIONAL DE MANTADIA

Parc National de Mantadia, located about 21km north of Parc National d'Andasibe, was created primarily to protect the indri, and also hosts the black-and-white ruffed lemur. A quiet, beautiful area with numerous

ANDASIBE AREA PARKS

Best time to visit October to November when orchids are blooming

Key highlight Indris

Wildlife Diadenem sifaka, Parson's chameleon, leaf-tailed gecko, paradise flycatcher

Habitats Primary and secondary mid-altitude rainforest

Gateway town Andasibe

Transport options Taxi-brousse or car

Things you should know Bring a raincoat at any time of year

waterfalls, it is undeveloped and seldom visited compared with its popular neighbour to the south, so if you're here in high season it's well worth the detour to escape the crowds. If the weather has been wet (which it often is), watch out for leeches on the trails. Established circuits include **Circuit Rianasoa** (Ar15,000, one hour), **Circuit Chute Sacrée** (Ar15,000, about 1½ hours) and **Circuit Tsakoka** (Ar40,000, about three hours). For more of a challenge, you can also embark on an **Adventure Circuit** of two to three days, camping in the park (Ar50,000 per day).

Permits and guides can be obtained at the MNP office in Parc National d'Andasibe. Entrance permits are for one/two days, cost Ar25,000/37,000 per person and are good for both parks. You'll need all your own camping equipment if you're planning to stay the night; the MNP **camp site** (tent sites free), just outside the park, has no facilities. To get to Mantadia from the MNP office, you will most likely need your own vehicle or bicycle. Transport can usually be arranged with park staff, or sometimes through guides and local hotels.

PARC MITSINJO & RÉSERVE DE TOROTOROFOTSY

Located on the main road 150m from Parc National d'Andasibe, **Parc Mitsinjo** (☎033 14 414 89, 034 15 854 24; http://mitsinjogooglepages.com; ⏰7am-9pm) is a private reserve run by Association Mitsinjo, an association of guides set up to promote conservation and community tourism. It's a great idea to add this to your itinerary before or after visiting the main park. There are three circuits, a **short circuit** (Ar25,000), a **medium circuit** (Ar35,000) and a **long circuit** (Ar50,000). An excellent **night hike** within the actual forest (60 to 90 minutes, Ar10,000 to Ar15,000, available 6.30pm to 9pm), gives you a much better chance of seeing the smaller nocturnal lemurs, sleeping chameleons and rare leaf-tailed lizards, while a **full-day trek** covers both forest and wetlands (Ar80,000). **Camping** (sites Ar5000) and pirogue trips (Ar10,000) are also available, and a new canopy tour will begin in 2012. There's no separate entry fee.

Mitsinjo also manages the **Réserve de Torotorofotsy**, a varied and attractive landscape of wetlands, forests and small villages known for its greater bamboo lemurs and excellent birdwatching. For more information on these parks visit Mitsinjo's small handicrafts shop in Andasibe itself, opposite the post office.

RÉSERVE DE MAROMIZAHA

This 10,000-hectare ecotourism reserve, about 8km southeast of the Parc National d'Andasibe-Mantadia, offers good **camping**, numerous **walking tracks**, stands of **rainforest** and **panoramic views**. The area is home to 11 lemur species, although you probably won't see many of them. They include diademed sifakas and black-and-white ruffed lemurs, both of which are also found at Parc National de Mantadia. Visits here can be organised with the guides at Parc National d'Andasibe. The reserve is accessible from the park gate via an easy trail. No permit is necessary.

VOHIMANA FOREST

Established as a private reserve in 2001, this crucial forest corridor links the Andasibe area parks with the forests of the south, and is administered by the NGO **Man and the Environment** (MATE; ☎Tana 22 674 90; www.mate.mg), which is developing it as an ecotourism site in conjunction with their conservation work. At present facilities include around 20km of **walking trails**, three **picnic areas** and a **botanical garden**, and local guides have been trained in some interesting specialist circuits highlighting such things as medicinal plants. Contact MATE for all details on access, tariffs and facilities; volunteer placements are also available.

MAHAY MITIA ALA (MMA)

This park opened in 2011 and is managed by local people who have come together for the sake of conservation and local development. The same species are here as in other parks, including the indri and the elusive aye-aye.

The main benefit appears to be accessibility. The trails are clear and wide, allowing clearer views of wildlife, and there are no steep hills as exist elsewhere. The park entrance is one kilometre north of the MNP office in Parc National d'Andasibe, where guides can be found. There is a **small circuit** (Ar20,000) and a **large circuit** (Ar30,000). **Night hikes** are Ar12,000.

Sleeping & Eating

Hotels are spread from one end of the main road to the other. Andasibe village is a muddy outpost of wooden shanties that offers little to the traveller.

Vakôna Forest Lodge LODGE €€€
(☎033 02 010 01, 034 15 705 80; www.hotelvakona.com; d Ar190,000, mains from Ar14,000;) This forest resort has everything – a lake with an island full of lemurs (entry Ar6500), an equestrian centre, a beautiful lodge, racket sports, private airstrip, crocodile park (entry Ar12,500) – except great bungalows. They're the only thing average about it, however, and the forest drive in is worth the trip alone. Be aware of the location 2km north of Andasibe: you are a long hike from the park office and will need a vehicle or transfers (Ar15,000).

Andasibe Hotel HOTEL €€€
(☎034 14 326 27; www.andasibehotel.com; d Ar175,000;) Where Vakôna Forest Lodge fails, this hotel on the west side of the village shines: it has the best double rooms around, with split levels, bold Asian styling, and knockout views across a verdant rice paddy. The **restaurant** (mains from Ar14,000) has equally creative French cuisine, and there's a nice pool deck. Located on a jungle lake, the hotel offers many activities, and rents bikes so you can get around on your own. Half-board (Ar45,000) is optional.

Hôtel Les Orchidées HOTEL €
(☎56 832 05, 034 36 024 49; d Ar30,000-40,000) This wooden hotel-restaurant in the centre of Andasibe village seems intent on proving that you can't judge a book by its cover. Once you get past the rough exterior, it feels like a charming cabin, with cosy rooms upstairs. The great surprise is the large brick annexe out back that triples its size. The pole in the **restaurant** (mains Ar7000) adds a welcome structural element.

Vohitsara Guest House GUESTHOUSE €
(☎034 60 089 69; vohitsara@hotmail.com; d/f Ar20,000/30,000) This family-run operation on the outskirts of the village offers a varied selection of clean budget rooms with external showers and Malagasy food on request. Reception is in the Mitsinjo building.

Mikalo BUNGALOW €€
(☎56 832 08, 033 11 817 85; new bungalow d Ar94,000) This hotel on the south side of the village has a showpiece roadside **restaurant** (set menu Ar19,000) offering the usual suspects – zebu, seafood, pasta – that gets high marks for design. But you need to sort carefully through the bungalows, which come in three levels of varying quality and attention to detail. Pass on the old chalets near the train station in favour of the new wooden bungalows in the forest with balconies and occasional fireplaces.

Hôtel Feon'ny Ala BUNGALOW €€
(☎56 832 02, 033 05 832 02; d bungalow Ar38,000-64,900, camping Ar8000) Whoever named this charming garden hotel 'Song of the Forest'

THE WAILING INDRI

The wondrous indri has been described as looking like 'a four-year-old child in a panda suit' and is famous for its eerie cry, a whooping siren that can be heard over a mile away. It is used mainly to define a particular group's territory, though there are also distinct mating and alarm calls. Indris are active on and off throughout the day, beginning about an hour after daybreak, which is usually the best time to see them. Despite the incredible cacophony of sound that comes out of the forest, each individual only calls for about four or five minutes per day.

Indris eat complex carbohydrates, and therefore need to spend much of their day in a sedentary manner digesting their food. They spend most of their time high in the forest canopy, feeding, sleeping and sunning themselves. Their powerful hind legs make them capable of 7m horizontal leaps from tree to tree, perfectly balanced despite their stump-like tails. Indris are also very sensitive to any change in environment, which is the main reason for their endangered status – not only does deforestation threaten their habitat, but no indri has ever survived in captivity, as they simply stop eating and die.

was pretty much on the money: the site is virtually part of the forest near Lac Rouge in Parc National d'Andasibe, so close that you can hear the indris at breakfast. The thatched bungalows are rather close together but very comfortable, with hot showers. A couple of basic bungalows with shared bathroom are also available (Ar17,700). The restaurant does all meals well and can provide picnic lunches for walkers.

MNP Campsite CAMPGROUND €
(camping per tent Ar5000) Camping is available behind the MNP office.

Getting There & Away

From Tana, the best way to reach Andasibe is to take a taxi-brousse to Moramanga first, then another to Andasibe. Ask the driver to drop you at your hotel. Otherwise, you can take any taxi-brousse along the RN2 to the Andasibe junction, then walk or hitch the 3km to the village itself.

If you're leaving Andasibe, you either have to return to Moramanga first, or wait for a taxi-brousse on the RN2. This can de difficult going east as brousses from Tana tend to be full. If you hire a car or taxi from Tana, keep in mind that you'll have to leave by 6am in order to hear the indris. If you hear a clickety-clack, it's the tiny Moramanga–Brickaville passenger train, which passes through Andasibe every Tuesday and Saturday.

Brickaville

Brickaville, reached by train (Ar3500) or taxi-brousse (Ar6000, three hours) from Moramanga or taxi-brousse from Tamatave (Ar5000, three hours), is a ramshackle transit point. From here you can transfer to Ambila-Lemaitso or Manambato in the Pangalanes Lakes, or direct to Tamatave. There are two taxi-brousse stations, north and south, both of which serve the same destinations, with the exception that only the north station serves Andasibe. Contrary to what you may hear, there is no bank here.

PANGALANES LAKES

For travellers, the most popular section of the extensive Pangalanes Canal (see p166) is the region between Ambila-Lemaitso and Tamatave, where the canal links several large lakes together.

This is one of Madagascar's lightly visited natural wonders, where half the fun is getting around. Travel here is done largely by long and narrow metal canal boats, which ply the waters from end to end, leaking all the while. Some carry tourists to the lake hotels, others cargo, villagers, and the occasional off-the-beaten track traveller. Cruising in this placid freshwater network is a fascinating journey through time and history, not to mention luxuriant vegetation. In the villages of the Betsimisaraka people, which spot the banks, traditional life goes on as ever. People throw cast nets, paddle by in pirogues, dry eels in the sun, and invariably wave a greeting. Fishing weirs appear at intervals, like gates across the waterway. The lakes themselves are very placid and picturesque, with nice beaches and no development apart from a handful of beach bungalows. The canal creates an interesting topographical effect, too, a long

THE DEAD ZONE

With the exception of Manakara, the southeast coast of Madagascar is basically a dead zone for travellers, unless you want pure 4WD adventure. Heading south from Brickaville, Vatomandry, Mahanoro, and Nosy-Varika offer virtually no sights or attractions with the exception of some waterfalls. In Mananjary the beach is used as a latrine and the market floods in heavy rains. After Manakara (p65), the RN12 is paved as far as the frontier town of Vaingaindrano, and easily traversed save for a 30km stretch of unpaved road north of Farafangana. However, the unpaved 220km between Vaingaindrano and Fort Dauphin (Taolagnaro) is notoriously treacherous and should only be attempted in dry season with a trustworthy 4WD. The route contains 10 ferry crossings, five motorised and five hand-powered, and two nature reserves. Parc National de Midongy Sud, located 100km inland of Vaingaindrano, requires a difficult trip through dense jungle, and is only for specialists. Manombo Reserve, 30km to the south of Farafangana, is the only worthwhile stop, home to a rare patch of coastal forest and the rare white-collared brown lemur. Swimming is dangerous along the entire coastline due to sharks and strong currents.

Pangalanes Lakes

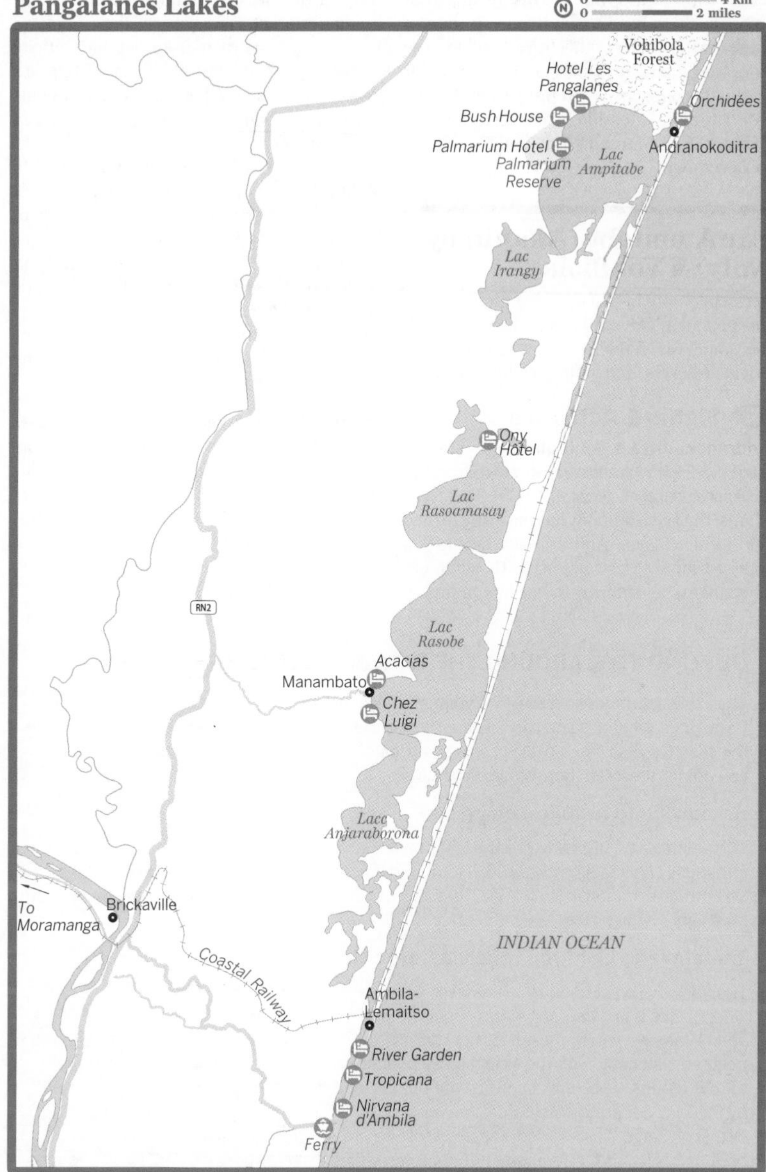

and very narrow outer beach that separates it from the Indian Ocean, such that a brief walk takes you from placid lake to tempestuous sea. Oddly, for such extensive wetlands, there are few animals of any kind to be seen from the water, not even birds.

Bear in mind, when you enter the lakes, you enter the eurozone, too. For the most part, this is a destination supported by European travellers who come on tours. As a result, prices have risen, and there is no regularly scheduled transport system. Boats come with tour groups. This means that solo travellers have to find space in one of these boats, or hire an entire boat for the ride. Never fear, if you are a single traveller or small group, check out our tips and make reservations if possible. The best times to visit are from March to May and September to December.

Lac Ampitabe (Akanin'ny Nofy) & Vohibola

Accessible only by boat, Lac Ampitabe is the most popular lake, with several hotels (including some well-hidden budget options), two private reserves, and an interesting village.

Sights & Activities

Andranokoditra & Vohibola VILLAGE

(MATE; ☎22 674 90 in Antananarivo; www.madagascar-environnement.com; circuit Ar18,000) The NGO Man & the Environment has basically turned the local village, Andranokoditra, into a tourist-friendly destination, with such improvements as signage to various points of interest (like an essential oils distillery) and a small market for local jewellery. Some of this certainly detracts from the authenticity of the experience, but at the same time it's done as well as possible, and definitely helps the local economy: you will run into a lot of visitors here.

The village is also the centre for tours into **Vohibola**, one of the last remaining pieces of littoral forest in the country, which contains a nursery. There are two hiking trails, the Discovery Trail, a half day immersion in forest conservation, and the Wetlands trail, a 2½-hour tour that includes a pirogue journey. Visits (and accommodation) are arranged through the MATE office near the entrance to the village.

Palmarium Reserve PARK

(☎033 14 847 34; admission Ar13,000; ⊙dawn-night) This private reserve next to Palmarium Hotel is a great place to test your inner guide. There are 50 hectares of dense forest cut with wide trails and seven species of lemur to spot, including Coquerel's sifaka and some tame black-and-white ruffed lemurs.

GETTING TO & AROUND THE PANGALANES LAKES

The easiest, but not necessarily cheapest, way to get to the lakes is to arrange a transfer through your hotel. If you can find a seat on a tour group's boat this should greatly reduce the cost. Calypso Tours (p167) can also arrange this. The other way is to do it yourself. If you opt for the latter, here are your options.

Brickaville to Ambila-Lemaitso

The southern point of entry to the lakes begins at Ambila-Lemaitso, 13km from Brickaville. Either call Nirvana d'Ambila (p166) for a transfer, or ask around for a private car at the taxi-brousse station in Brickaville. Take this option if you intend to stay in Ambila-Lemaitso overnight.

Tamatave to Lac Ampitabe via Cargo Boat

The northern point of entry to the lakes is the *gare fluviale* (river station) in Tamatave, where canal boats carrying cargo depart daily around 10.30am. Any *pousse-pousse* (rickshaw) can take you there, but do not confuse the cargo boat dock, which is midway down a polluted waterway, with the empty canal boats at the very end of it, as the latter are rented to tour groups. If you can, confirm your departure the afternoon prior, otherwise show up by 9.30am. For around Ar16,000 you will be given space to occupy, although it may mean sitting on cargo. The river odyssey that follows is a *National Geographic* photo op, with a boatload of locals for company, although you should bring a raincoat, and visit a bathroom first. It takes all day to reach Andranokoditra village, from where you can walk or take a pirogue (dugout canoe) to a hotel.

Brickaville or Tamatave to Manambato

It is possible to reach the lakeside village of Manambato, 30km north of Ambila-Lemaitso, by car. There's a turn-off from the RN2 about 11km north of Brickaville, and a 7km track thereafter. A two-wheel drive is sufficient if there is no mud. From Tamatave, the best way

Sleeping

Bush House BUNGALOW €€€
(☎22 530 70; www.bushhouse-madagascar.com; d bungalow with half board per person €42) These quality German-run bungalows with cheery porches have a nice elevated location that affords views across the lake, with stairs winding down to the beach. The hotel also owns a great viewpoint on the top of a hill from where you can see the interesting landscape of lakes, peninsula, and sea around you. Activities are well managed, with lots of options to chose from. Free kayaks are a plus. Also sponsors a local village school.

Hotel Les Pangalanes BUNGALOW €€
(☎032 04 618 44, 034 74 583 48; d bungalow Ar58,000) Everything is done well at Hotel Les Pangalanes. There's a nice lodge, good food (set menu Ar20,000), attentive management, and clean bungalows, all at a very attractive price. Half-board is required.

Palmarium Hotel BUNGALOW €€€
(☎033 14 847 34; www.palmarium.biz; d bungalow Ar110,000, set menu Ar25,000) The bungalows are expensive at this package-tour destination, but the lemurs that crash dinner are great company, and there is a nice bar to hang out in that finally knows how to make a decent mojito. Tents are available if rooms are full.

For budget travellers, the only options are some accommodation in or near the village of Andranokoditra.

Chez L'Habitant (Ar11,000), run by MATE, has six bungalows located in the middle of the village; inquire at the MATE office at the village entrance. **Orchidées** (d Ar35,000, set menu Ar12,000) has five new bungalows a short walk from the village, and an office within it. Ask directions when you get there or call **Edouard** (☎034 37 523 68, 033 08 529 62).

is to buy two front seats in a taxi-brousse to Brickaville (Ar10,000 total), and ask the driver to take you on to Manambato (another Ar35,000). Barring that, you'll have to hire a taxi. From Manambato you have to charter a boat to your hotel. Talk to the men at the beach. They will start negotiating at Ar150,000 and will go as low as Ar50,000. Alternatively, wait until the next tour group shows up and see if they are going your way, as a single seat will be *much* cheaper.

Train

An inexpensive, if infrequent, possibility is the passenger train. The train departs Tamatave every Tuesday at 8.20am, travels down the barrier beach past the lakes, stopping at various villages along the way, and continues inland to Moramanga. Ask for the stop nearest your destination. Conversely, one can take the train from Moramanga on Monday at 7am and expect to reach the lakes by mid-afternoon. The total fare is Ar10,000. Alternatively, the same train departs Moramanga every Thursday at 3pm, but only goes as far as Ambila-Lemaitso, arriving at 10.30pm. It returns Friday at 8am, arriving Moramanga at 4pm. The cost of this shorter journey is, inexplicably, also Ar10,000. It is always wise to check the schedule with **Madarail** (www.madarail.mg) ahead of time, either through your hotel, at the station (best), or online.

Getting Around

Once you are in the lakes, getting around can be expensive unless you are careful. You can walk around any single lake easily enough, but you'll need a boat between them, unless you want to hike down the barrier beach. If hiring a boat, it is best to deal with the locals, not the hotels, who quote in euros for transport; negotiations are best done in the local village or on the beach. For example, an entire canal boat from Manambato to Lac Ampitabe can be had for Ar50,000 direct from the operator, whereas hotels charge Ar150,000 for the same journey. A boat from Manambato to Ambila-Lemaitso should be about the same.

Lac Rasoamasay

Our top choice in this entire region, **Ony Hôtel** (☎53 983 37, 033 11 587 25; http://onyhotel.free.fr; d Ar65,000, q Ar85,000), occupies an interesting location in the middle of three different lakes. This is a very family-friendly place, with nice thatched log cabins on the beach, plenty of hot water, and a very kind and diligent staff that gets high marks from guests. It's also the most secluded and private of the lake hotels, giving it a very peaceful ambience. The surprise is how much there is to do here, including forest walks, village visits, swimming, pirogue trips, and hikes to the sea (only 40 minutes away) – more than enough to keep you busy for several days. This conscientious hotel sponsors local conservation efforts.

Lac Rasobe & Manambato

This pretty lake has a beautiful white-sand beach and two places to stay. Of these, **Acacias** (☎033 12 338 35; www.acaciasbungalows.com; d bungalow Ar50,000) is the much better choice, with cute bungalows on the beach connected by sandy paths, and management that pays attention to the details. Picnics packed on request. **Chez Luigi** (☎033 20 552 55; d bungalow Ar40,000) has some colourful bungalows steps from the beach, but meals are overpriced and at the time of research there had been no running water for some time; clients are handed a bucket of water from the lake. The prices did not reflect this.

Ambila-Lemaitso

The main attraction in this sleepy region is **Nirvana d'Ambila** (☎033 15 017 78, 033 11 016 60; lenirvanadambila@moov.mg; d bungalow Ar60,000), one of our choice end-of-the-Earth hotels, which faces the ferry crossing at the end of the Brickaville road. The hotel enjoys a captivating location astride the barrier beach, with its canal dock on one side, the roaring ocean on the other, and barely 50m in between. The clean and basic bungalows, with private bathrooms and hot water, have all been renovated, and the atmospheric **restaurant** (breakfast Ar6000, set menu Ar30,000), with its great fresh seafood and jazz playing in the background, will lull you into relaxation, assisted by an attentive and friendly staff bearing bottles of wine.

Be forewarned: this is a place that slowly steals your heart. There is something special about it, a tranquillity that grows over time, such that its name becomes entirely appropriate. Half-board obligatory.

From the ferry crossing, it's another 4km north along a sandy track to Ambila-Lemaitso, where you can inquire about boats heading up or down the canal. Less expensive, but more run-of-the-mill accommodation includes **Tropicana** (☎036 11 044 56; d bungalow Ar30,000) and **River Garden** (☎033 07 909 98; rivergarden16@yahoo.fr; d bungalow Ar30,000) both of which offer similar riverfront bungalows. The most incongruous sight is the three large French **canal boats** (☎033 12 257 18) at Tropicana, straight from the Canal du Midi, which are rented out for Ar250,000 per half day, Ar500,000 per full day.

THE PANGALANES CANAL

The Canal des Pangalanes is one of the quiet wonders of Madagascar, a collection of natural and artificial waterways that stretches over 645km along the east coast from Foulpointe to Farafangana. It was constructed between 1896 and 1904, during the French colonial period, in an effort to create a safe passage for cargo boats to Tamatave; one look at the waves on the nearby Indian Ocean explains why. Since then the navigability of the canal has ebbed and flowed like the tide. After WWII the canal was expanded and 30-ton barges could travel the 160km from Tamatave to Vatomandry. After a long period of silting in, renovations began in the 1980s, including a new barge network. Today the canal is slipping backwards again. Sections north of Tamatave, between Vatomandry and Mahanoro, and south of Mananjary have grown in. The remains of the old barge network are rotting by the pier in Tamatave. During research we had to get out of the boat in order to push it over a growing *pangalane* (sill) between Lac Rasobe and Lac Rasoamasay, even though the boat only drew a few inches of water. It all makes one wonder: could the depth of the canal be an economic barometer for Madagascar?

TAMATAVE (TOAMASINA)

POP 240,000

Tamatave is very much like its cousin on the western coast, Tuléar (Toliara). It is a hot, dusty and chaotic port town full of decaying colonial buildings, roadside markets and throngs of *pousse-pousse* carts. The emphasis is on commerce, not tourism, apart from being an important transit point. There are also some bright spots amid the fading grandeur if you know where to find them, meaning that you can have a good time here for a day or two. It's a convenient spot to break the journey between Antananarivo and Ile Sainte Marie, or to organise a trip down the Canal des Pangalanes. Avoid walking at night, however, particularly alone, and don't leave articles where they can be snatched.

Sights & Activities

Place de Colonne & Place Bien Aimé PLAZA

For the one-two punch on Malagasy independence, first go to the Place de Colonne, a monument to those killed in the 1947 uprising against the French, which is in a sad state of disrepair; then walk down Amiral Pierre to the Place Bien Aimé, where you will find the remains of a once grand park. A dozen magnificent banyan trees weep before a crumbling colonial mansion.

Musée du Port MUSEUM

(admission by donation; ⌚9am-4pm Mon-Sat) The small University Museum constitutes barely 2½ rooms of farming tools, fishing implements, archaeological finds and tribal charms, along with poster displays on deforestation and local conservation projects. Some of the captioning is in English, including translations of some typically cryptic Malagasy proverbs.

Bazary Be & Bazary Kely MARKET

Tamatave's colourful **Bazary Be** (Big Market) sells fruit, vegetables, spices, handicrafts and beautiful bouquets of flowers (should you feel the need to brighten up your hotel room). The **Bazary Kely** (Little Market) sells fish and produce in the ruins of a commercial complex on Blvd de la Fidelité, west of the train station.

Swimming Pools SWIMMING

For around Ar3000 you can swim at various hotels, including **Hôtel Neptune** (Blvd de la Libération) and **Sharon Hotel** (Blvd de la Libération), but the big pool at Le Bateau Ivre (p170) is more fun, and free if you eat there.

DON'T MISS

THE ENDS OF THE EARTH

The end of the Earth: it's a term you'll hear used to describe many a place in Madagascar. But what does it mean? There seems to be several factors: isolation, natural beauty, the sea, and a distant horizon, forming a reflective place where the world appears to stop, and the spirit deepens. With that in mind, here are our favourite end-of-the-Earth hotels in Madagascar:

» Le Relais d'Ambola, Ambola (p91)

» Club Vanille, Manakara (p66)

» Nirvana d'Ambila, Ambila-Lemaitso (p166)

» Tea Longo, Lavanono (p91)

» Longomamy, St Augustine (p89)

» Eden Lodge, Nosy Be (p137)

» Tsarabanjina, Nosy Mitsio (p135)

» Ecolodge du Menabe, Belo Sur Mer (p118)

» Anjajavy, Majunga (p106)

Tours

Calypso Tours BOATING

(☎032 40 247 78, 032 04 628 82; http://calypstour.skyrock.com; Hôtel Eden, Blvd Joffre; tour incl lunch Ar70,000) Day-long (10am-5pm) tours of the Canal des Pangalanes from Tamatave. Located in Hôtel Eden.

Tropical Service CRUISES

(☎53 336 79; www.croisiere-madagascar.com; 23 Blvd Joffre) Top-end local tours, cruises, car hire, transfers and travel services.

Sleeping

Tamatave has a lot of hotels but, with rare exceptions, mediocrity rules.

Calypso Hotel & Spa HOTEL €€€

(☎53 304 59, 032 07 131 33; www.hotelcalypso.mg; Rue Lt Noël; d Ar270,000, ste Ar420,000) As the price suggests, this is the top hotel in the city, and the only one with this level of finish. Only a year old, it offers elegantly appointed rooms with glass showers and an attractive island-style decor, a beautiful indoor pool, a gym, a spa, and a posh restaurant. Clients are a mix of business people and high-end tour groups.

Tamatave (Toamasina)

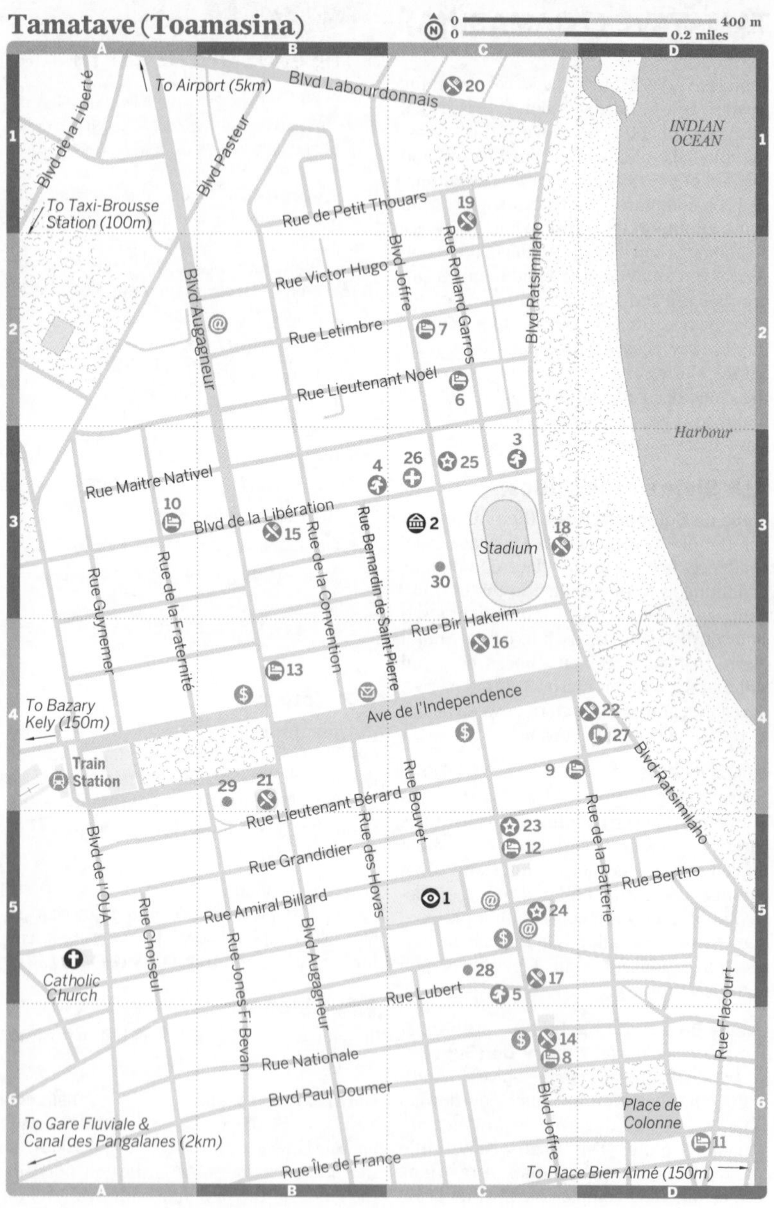

Le Palais des Isles GUESTHOUSE €€€
(☎53 314 33, 032 77 356 13; tsarisland@moov.mg; d Ar120,000, f Ar150,000) Finally, the logical move we've been waiting for – a colonial mansion turned into a guesthouse, with a swank restaurant to boot. This white architectural gem from the 1930s has two floors with a huge wrap-around balcony, and three nice rooms with large bathrooms and euro-mattresses. Too bad on our visit the staff raised incompetence to the same high level.

Tamatave (Toamasina)

Sights
1 Bazary Be ... C5
2 Musée du Port ... C3

Activities, Courses & Tours
Calypso Tours ... (see 8)
3 Hôtel Neptune ... C3
Le Bateau Ivre ... (see 18)
4 Sharon Hotel ... B3
5 Tropical Service ... C5

Sleeping
6 Calypso Hotel & Spa ... C2
7 Génération Hôtel ... C2
8 Hôtel Eden ... C6
9 Hôtel Fréderic ... C4
10 Hôtel Les Flamboyants ... A3
11 Hotel Toamasina ... D6
12 Java Hotel ... C5
13 Le Palais des Isles ... B4

Eating
14 Adam & Eve Snack Bar ... C6
15 Chez Bruno ... B3
16 La Terrasse ... C4
17 La Véranda ... C5
18 Le Bateau Ivre ... C3
19 Piment Banane ... C1
20 Restaurant Labourdonnais ... C1
21 Score ... B4
22 Shoprite ... D4

Entertainment
23 City Pub ... C5
24 Ibiza Club ... C5
25 Queen's Club ... C3

Information
26 Espace Médical ... C3
27 Honorary Consulates for Norway, Denmark & the UK ... D4

Transport
28 Air Austral ... C5
29 Air Madagascar ... B4
Air Mauritius ... (see 28)
30 Loulou Bike Rentals ... C3

Génération Hôtel HOTEL €€
(☎57 220 22; Blvd Joffre; d Ar65,000; ❄) This slightly cluttered but genial hotel is greatly helped by a resident group of local mining company employees, who rate it highly. Rooms cleaned daily, English spoken, good food, and laundry are some of the benefits.

Hôtel Eden HOTEL €
(☎53 312 90; calypsotour@netcourrier.com; Blvd Joffre; r Ar25,000, without bathroom Ar16,000) This popular backpackers' hotel is a good budget choice, with a mix of shared and private bathrooms and helpful staff. Calypso Tours (p167) is based here, so it's a good place to organise a tour of the Canal des Pangalanes.

Hôtel Fréderic HOTEL €
(☎53 347 40; Rue Lt Bérard; d Ar34,000; ❄) This good budget option on a quiet corner has a mixture of tiled and parquet rooms with some fridges but no nets. Corner rooms 101 and 201 are easily the best seats in the house, with lots of light and great balconies. A pizza restaurant and cabaret/piano bar are helpful additions.

Hôtel Les Flamboyants HOTEL €€
(☎53 323 50, 032 71 093 51; hotelflamboyants@gmail.com; Blvd de la Libération; r with fan/aircon Ar41,000/55,000; ❄) This is your typical concrete box hotel done moderately well, with air-conditioning that is welcome in summer but sold to the unsuspecting when unnecessary. Rooms are large, with decent balconies, but hot water struggles at times, as does the staff.

Java Hotel HOTEL €€€
(☎53 316 26, 034 12 252 53; http://javahotel.wifeo.com; 34 Blvd Joffre; d Ar140,000; ⓦ) An antiseptic business hotel, but given the competition, a bit of mouthwash feels refreshing. Rooms and hallways sparkle, while the brand new elevator leaves the hardened traveller dumbstruck. Interior parking is another welcome touch, particularly in Tamatave.

Hotel Toamasina HOTEL €€
(☎53 335 49; www.hotel-tamatave.com; 13 Rue de la Colonne; d Ar59,000-65,000, ste Ar77,000-89,000; ❄) Facing Place de la Colonne, this hotel's rooms are a mixed bag of shapes, sizes and styles; the suites in particular are good value, with satellite TV for the homesick. Attached is the reasonable **Pousse-Pousse restaurant** (mains Ar6000) which serves a mixture of Malagasy, Italian, and Oriental fare.

Eating

TOP CHOICE Le Bateau Ivre INTERNATIONAL €€
(☎53 302 94; Blvd Ratsimilaho; mains Ar9000-18,000; ⏱breakfast, lunch & dinner;) This sprawling beachfront enterprise manages to do everything well – and we do mean everything. There is a central restaurant and bar, a beach bar with BBQ, a hamburger bar, a pizza oven, a stage, a 25m swimming pool, and even beach volleyball. Beneath the central big top, you'll find a diverse mix of clientele, from miner expats to Malagasy families; charmingly cluttered rooms full of statuary, fossils, and parasols; excellent seafood, creative drinks, and nightly music; and a broad view of the port's commercial dock. This eclectic mix is not only stimulating, it manages to define a vibe for the whole city that seems entirely appropriate, like a Cotton Club for Tamatave. If you're only in town one night spend some time here, although given the options, there is little reason to leave. Very busy on weekends.

TOP CHOICE Piment Banane FRENCH €€
(☎034 08 043 09; Rue de L'Ourd; mains from Ar10,000; ⏱lunch & dinner Mon-Sat;) You wouldn't generally find a sophisticated brasserie next to a ruined police station, but we are in the land of exceptions. And exceptional is how to describe this welcome addition to the city, from the stylish decor to the creative cuisine ('neo-gastro' as the chef calls it) to the extensive wine list, all of which has garnered rave reviews from those pickiest of culinary travellers, the French. 'Monsieur, I implore you, try the *tornedos rossini*!'

La Terrasse PIZZA €
(Blvd Joffre; mains Ar9500; ⏱breakfast, lunch & dinner) This hopping streetside bistro with tasty pizza and grills is the go-to lunch spot for people on the move.

Chez Bruno CAFE €
(Blvd de la Libération; snacks from Ar500; ⏱breakfast) A handy patisserie-cafe near Hôtel Les Flamboyants, known for its above-average coffee.

Adam & Eve Snack Bar CREPERIE €
(Blvd Joffre; mains from Ar2000; ⏱breakfast, lunch & dinner Tue-Sun) A popular budget option, the open bar and terrace has a loyal following for the Malagasy dishes, juice, ice cream and crêpes.

La Véranda FRENCH €
(☎53 334 35; off Blvd Joffre; mains Ar4000-9000; ⏱lunch & dinner Mon-Sat) A popular choice for French expats and visitors thanks to its wide-ranging menu and very reasonable prices. The three-course set menu (Ar13,000) changes daily, and is far too tempting to settle for less.

Restaurant Labourdonnais FRENCH €
(Blvd Labourdonnais; mains from Ar6000; ⏱lunch & dinner) Next door to the French consulate, this unflashy green-and-white establishment sits discreetly in its walled compound, providing refined French cuisine with indoor and outdoor seating.

Self-caterers and treat-seekers should try the **Score** (Ave de l'Independence; ⏱8.30am-1pm & 2.30-7pm Mon-Sat, 8.30am-12.30pm Sun) or check out **Shoprite** (Ave de l'Independence) supermarkets.

Entertainment

Apart from hotel restaurants, bar-restaurants, and the Bateau Ivre, Tamatave's surprisingly dynamic nightlife centres on a few swinging discos. A poll of their popularity, courtesy of those who know best (eg pousse-pousse drivers) yields the following pecking order: 1) **City Pub** (Blvd Joffre; ⏱Mon-Sat); 2) **Pandora Station** (Rte de l'Aéroport); 3) **Ibiza Club** (Off Blvd Joffre; ⏱Mon-Sat) and 4) **Queens Club** (Blvd Joffre). In our opinion, the large and well-ventilated Ibiza Club, which is only six months old, may soon push its way up the list.

Information

There are many banks in the centre with ATMs; BNI-CA takes MasterCard.

Butterfly Cybercafé (Blvd Joffre; per hr Ar1800; ⏱8.30am-noon & 2.30-6pm Mon-Sat)

Cyber Sky (Blvd Joffre; per min Ar30; ⏱8am-8pm Mon-Sat)

Espace Médical (☎53 315 66; Blvd de la Libération; ⏱24hr)

Librairie GM Fakra (Rue Joffre; ⏱closed Mon morning) Some English newspapers and magazines, plus maps of the region and postcards.

MNP (☎53 327 07; Rte d'Ivoloina) General information about national parks in the region, a kilometre out of town on the road to the airport.

Speed Net (Blvd Augagneur; per min Ar15)

Getting There & Away

Air

Air Madagascar (☎53 323 56; Ave de l'Independence) flies most days between Tamatave and Antananarivo (€150, 45 minutes), and Ile Sainte Marie (€150, 30 minutes). Other services connect Tamatave with Sambava (€200, 30 minutes) and Maroantsetra (€150 to €200, 30 minutes). Prices can change depending on whether you purchase tickets abroad or domestically (much cheaper). Be forewarned that during the vanilla season (June to October), flights in the northeast can be full.

Air Madagascar and **Air Austral** (☎53 300 26; Rue de Lattre de Tassigny) each fly several times a week to St-Denis on Réunion for around €400 return.

Boat

If you are heading to Ile Sainte Marie via Soanierana-Ivongo, your boat company will provide a shuttle service from Tamatave. If you are heading to the Pangalanes Lakes, see p164 for transportation information.

Cargo boats without set schedules also ply the waters of the northeast. This type of travel is generally slow and uncomfortable, and potentially dangerous, particularly during cyclone season (December to March); always check forecasts and ask local advice before travelling. Those prone to motion sickness should not attempt it. Standards vary widely; cabins are sometimes available, but on most boats you can expect to be bedding down on deck, and you will need to bring your own food and water. If you're still interested, ask any *pousse-pousse* driver to take you to the bureau of boats going to Mananara or Maroantsetra. This is an obscure shed by the port that you will never find on your own.

Taxi-Brousse

The taxi-brousse station at the northwestern edge of town serves Antananarivo as well as points north as far as Soanierana-Ivongo (Ar8000, four hours) and south as far as Mahanoro (Ar8000, four hours). Minibuses and coaches run along the RN2 throughout the day to Moramanga (Ar12,000, seven hours) and Antananarivo (Ar15,000 to Ar19,000, at least seven hours). It is best to leave early to ensure that you reach your destination during daylight.

If road conditions permit, you may be able to find a *camion-brousse* (truck) or similar large vehicle heading towards Mananara or Maroantsetra (Ar70,000, two to three days). A 4WD to Mananara will likely cost Ar150,000 (two days).

Private 4WD

Taxi-brousse company **Kofifen** (☎033 11 640 95) also rents private 4WDs for travel on the RN5. Published prices for car and driver from Tamatave include Mananara (Ar1.25 million) and Maroantsetra (Ar1.48 million) but aggressive bargaining can cut this in half.

WORTH A TRIP

BY SEA TO RÉUNION & MAURITIUS

For an interesting itinerary twist, consider this ocean voyage. The mixed cargo and passenger ships **MS Mauritius Trochetia** and **Mauritius Pride** (www.croisiere-madagascar.com/en/indian-ocean-cruise.html) depart Tamatave once every two weeks or so for the islands of Réunion and Mauritius. One-way fares to Réunion are €264/232 per adult for a 1st-/2nd-class cabin (based on two people sharing), and €303/282 to Mauritius. More expensive deluxe cabins are also available. Tickets are available from Tropical Service (p167).

Train

A slow passenger train departs Moramanga every Monday at 7am, arriving in Tamatave at 5pm (Ar10,000). It returns on Tuesday at 8.20am, arriving in Moramanga at 6.55pm. It is always wise to check the schedule with **Madarail** (☎22 345 99; www.madarail.mg) ahead of time, either through your hotel, at the station (best), or online.

Getting Around

Taxis between town and the airport (5km north of town) should cost around Ar25,000, though drivers will demand Ar10,000 at arrivals. Taxi rides within town are Ar3000.

Some local minibuses shuttle passengers around town for Ar300, if you can work out the routes; service No 4 goes to the Bazary Kely and the port.

With its wide, flat avenues, Tamatave is ideal for cycling. For bike rental try **Loulou Bike Rentals** (☎032 04 414 83; Blvd Joffre; per day Ar6000; ⏲7.30am-6pm), which is located opposite the stadium.

To hire a car locally, inquire at any hotel, restaurant or travel agency, or ask around at the taxi-brousse station. It may be more expensive if you want to take the vehicle beyond Foulpointe.

Pousse-pousse drivers charge from Ar1000 per trip within the town centre. The drivers are fairly friendly but some travellers have reported being hassled for more money when it comes time to pay the bill.

NORTH OF TAMATAVE

Parc Zoologique Ivoloina

The **Parc Zoologique Ivoloina** (☎53 012 17; www.seemadagascar.com; admission Ar10,000; ⏲9am-5pm) is a very well-run zoo and botanical garden set on a lovely lake just north of Tamatave. The beautiful grounds cover 282 hectares and contain more than 100 lemurs from a dozen different species, both caged and semi-wild, as well as chameleons, radiated tortoises, tree boas and tomato frogs. The botanical garden contains more than 75 species of native and exotic plants, and a model farm designed to demonstrate sustainable agricultural methods. Visitors can enjoy four walking trails with booklets in English, pirogue trips around the lake (Ar6000), a snack bar, and an education centre. An optional guide is Ar10,000.

The park is run by **The Madagascar Fauna Group** (☎53 308 42; www.savethelemur.org; Rte de l'Aéroport), located 4km north of Tamatave. It's a worldwide conservation association headquartered in St Louis, USA. In addition to hosting tourists, there are captive breeding programmes for endangered species and a halfway house for animals being reintroduced into the wild. The park also raises local awareness of wildlife and conservation issues – around 70% of the estimated 14,000 annual visitors are Malagasy.

To reach the park from the city, take the RN5 north, go 9km past the airport, and turn left on the unpaved road in front of the Ivoloina Bridge. Continue on until you see the park entrance sign (the trip takes half an hour). A charter taxi from town costs around Ar30,000; taxis-brousses to Ivoloina village (Ar1500) leave every hour or two. From Ivoloina village it's a scenic 4km walk to the park entrance.

Foulpointe (Mahavelona)

Foulpointe (fool-*pwant*) is a nondescript town with some nice white-sand beaches along with a strip of decent accommodation and dining, certainly enough for a weekend. If you're looking for a quick sun 'n' fun escape from Tamatave this is a worthy option.

Sights

Fort Manda FORTRESS

Ruins of this 19th-century Merina fort, built for Radama I, are about 500m north of Foulpointe. Its walls, which are 8m high and 6m thick in places, are made from coral, sand and eggs.

Sleeping & Eating

Génération Hôtel Annexe BUNGALOW €€

(☎57 220 22; www.generation-hotel-foulpointe.com; d or bungalow Ar36,500, q bungalow Ar 81,500; ❄) This garden site towards the southern end of the strip offers a choice between standard concrete rooms and nicer thatched bungalows, some two-tier models sleeping up to six people. It's not directly on the beach but the big terraced restaurant, which serves Chinese and French food, is only 20m away.

Le Grand Bleu BUNGALOW €€

(☎57 220 06, 032 02 311 61, 033 08 080 69; www.hotel-grandbleu.com; d bungalow Ar68,000, 6-person villa Ar124,000; ❄) The 'Big Blue' has a similar set-up to the Génération, with two main differences: the complex fronts directly onto the beach, and here it's the rooms that come better equipped, though if you're any judge of character you'll forego air-con for the subtler breezes of the cute wickerwork bungalows.

Manda Beach Hôtel HOTEL €€

(☎57 220 00; www.mandabeach-hotel.com; d Ar40,000, bungalow Ar77,000; 🏊) With its central pool, concrete rooms, tennis courts, Western music, and long stretch of parasols on the sand, not to mention the nearby golf course, this place feels more like an upscale beach motel in Florida than a hotel in Madagascar. Choose the beachfront bungalows over the industrial rooms. Airport transfers for one to three people cost Ar90,000.

Getting There & Away

Foulpointe lies 58km north of Tamatave. Minibuses depart from the Tamatave taxi-brousse station daily, generally in the mornings (Ar5000, 1½ hours). For short hops, such as to Mahambo or Fenoarivo-Atsinanana, you can try flagging down just about any vehicle going in the right direction; hotel vehicles may be able to take you all the way to Tamatave, but you'll have to pay at least the equivalent of the taxi-brousse fare.

Several vehicles daily pass Foulpointe on their way between Tamatave and Soanierana-Ivongo. Heading south, the time they pass Foulpointe depends on what time the ferry from Ile Sainte Marie arrives at Soanierana-Ivongo. Heading north, wait by the road side before 9am to get to Soanierana-Ivongo in time for the best boats.

Mahambo

Mahambo is a coastal village with a safe swimming beach and luxuriant vegetation that comes right down to the shore in some places. For the moment it's much quieter and generally more enticing than Foulpointe, primarily because it's further from the main road, and while facilities are already expanding it should still be some time before resort life starts to take over in the same way.

Sleeping & Eating

TOP CHOICE **La Pirogue** LODGE €€€
(☎57 301 71, 033 08 768 10, 033 08 768 18; www.pirogue-hotel.com; r Ar55,000-79,500, bungalows Ar93,500-295,000) This elegant resort rises well above Foulpointe to become one of the top choices on the East Coast. It has a fascinating reef-front location, and lots of creativity on display, from the delicate sea urchins on the menu to the local wood carvings and fossils in the bungalows to the safari fishing trips to the nearby reef. The charming and sophisticated French-American owners, who also run a guesthouse on the Côte d'Azur, have worked carefully on every detail, and attract a diverse clientele, including many families. A great range of accommodation helps, beginning with a very reasonable double room, and ending with the spectacular *bungalow de luxe*.

Zanatany BUNGALOW €
(☎57 301 35; d bungalow Ar25,000, f bungalow Ar40,000) Resplendent in its bright-blue paint job, this little restaurant located in the centre of the village also has the cheapest digs in town, if you don't mind finding Jennifer Lopez in your bungalow. Her poster, that is.

Ylang-Ylang BUNGALOW €
(☎57 300 08, 033 09 380 39; mamitina@wanadoo.mg; bungalow Ar20,000-25,000) If you can't be on the beach, then this wonderfully scented garden with its well-kept row of wooden cottages is a fine substitute.

Getting There & Away

Mahambo is 30km north of Foulpointe (Ar1500) and about 90km from Tamatave (Ar4500) on the RN5. If taking a taxi-brousse, ask the driver to drop you at the intersection (you'll see the hotel signs), then walk about 2km down the sandy track heading east.

Fenoarivo-Atsinanana (Fénérive Est)

POP 24,000

Unless you have a great interest in cloves, or the need for a bank, there's really no reason to come to this agricultural market town (usually just called 'Fenoarivo' or 'Fénérive'), but if you're driving through and want to exercise your legs a bit, it's fun to track down the remains of the **pirate fort** 2km to the south, in Vohimasina, although you'll need local help to find it. It's a large circular stone wall atop a hill with a commanding view in all directions, screaming for an archaeologist. Look for the modern observation tower adjacent.

If you must stay, the best place is the new ensuite bungalows behind the restaurant and disco **Mimi Club** (☎033 20 425 87; d bungalow Ar50,000; ⏲breakfast, lunch, dinner; ❄), which you can't miss: it's behind the long red wall on the main road. The **disco** (entry Ar2000) hops Friday, Saturday and Sunday, though, so either bring earplugs or put on your dancing shoes.

Soanierana-Ivongo

POP 44,000

The riverside shanty port of Soanierana-Ivongo is the most practical of places: you go there to get a boat to or from Ile Sainte Marie, and if you get stuck, to stay overnight.

The latter can occur for three reasons: 1) you arrive late, because the trip down the RN5 from Mananara takes longer than you expected, or because you take a slow taxi-brousse; 2) you arrive on time but the boat is full; or 3) you arrive on time but the trip has been cancelled due to weather conditions. This typically occurs when there has been a weather cancellation the previous day, creating a backlog of passengers.

Careful planning avoids problem one, and a reservation avoids problem two, but a weather delay is always a possibility, particularly during winter, and can even last more than a day. If that happens, the only alternative is to hire a car to take you to the airport in Tamatave, assuming there is a flight with empty seats to Ile Sainte Marie. Thus our warning: travellers on a tight schedule, who are not otherwise driving the coast road, should seriously consider flying from Tamatave to Ile Sainte Marie just to be safe, even if it is more expensive. Otherwise you risk spending several days in what is definitely not paradise.

In addition, the crossing here is dangerous, as the boats exit a shallow river mouth with incoming breaking waves. In 2011, a boat capsized killing a government minister and 13 others, largely because they could not swim. Before that there was a fatal accident in 2006.

The danger is particularly pronounced between June and September, when water levels are low. Having said that, if the weather complies, it is a pretty and inexpensive trip. Some travellers choose to fly one way between Tana and Ile Sainte Marie and then travel back by shuttle and private car, stopping off along the way.

Sleeping & Eating

All the hotels here are basic and on the main road, although some are a long walk from the port with luggage. There is no internet connection anywhere.

Charme de la Mer HOTEL €
(☎033 72 025 78; d Ar25,000, without bathroom Ar20,000) This small budget gem, hidden behind Relais on the left as you walk out of town, is worth the trip and the bucket shower. The secluded double room in back, facing the sea, is the best in town, with its own little porch and waves breaking on your pillow (or so it sounds). If you want a private bathroom, the room opposite will do. There is a small cook-to-order restaurant, or you can eat in Relais.

Relais HOTEL €€
(☎033 72 025 78; d Ar30,000) This hotel has basic rooms and the best restaurant in the neighbourhood.

Hôtel Les Escales HOTEL €
(☎033 08 486 38, 033 17 403 03; bungalows without bathroom Ar16,000) This is the obvious choice, as it is located right next to the boat jetty, with a tiny porch where you can have a beer and watch the madness when the boats arrive.

Getting There & Away

Boat

There are four main shuttle boats from Soanierana-Ivongo to Ambodifotatra on Ile Sainte Marie. All have offices on the waterfront in Ambodifotatra and Soanierana-Ivongo. On average boats leave Ambodifotatra around 6am and Soanierana-Ivongo around 10am. Crossing time is 1¼ hours for the fastest boat, *Melissa Express*. Transfers from Tamatave take another hour and cost Ar10,000 each way for all companies. You can often negotiate a price reduction of Ar10,000 on a return ticket. Before sailing out to the island, passengers are asked to go to the nearby police station to register.

If you have no reservation, make sure you know when the boats leave, as they all leave in the morning based on the changing tides. Arrive early to get your pick of the litter. There's not a lot to discriminate between them except when they depart (departures take place over an hour or so) and how long they take (*Melissa Express* saves a half hour on the slowest alternative). The important thing is to assess which boat will arrive first.

Cap Sainte Marie (☎Soanierana-Ivongo 57 404 06, 57 400 36, Tamatave 53 351 48, 032 05 218 08, one way Ar90,000, return Ar130,000) Shuttle from Tamatave leaves from Tanambao V, next to Jesosy Mamonjy church.

Gasikara (☎Soanierana-Ivongo 034 43 856 13, Tamatave 033 24 354 58, 032 62 870 99; one way Ar70,000, return Ar120,000) Shuttle from Tamatave leaves from Gare Routière Transport Vatsy.

Melissa Express (☎Soanierana-Ivongo 033 18 732 64, Tamatave 032 18 732 72; one way Ar70,000, return Ar140,000) Shuttle from Tamatave leaves from Valpinson, near the baker. The *Melissa Express* also offers a weekly service from Soanierana-Ivongo to Mananara (Ar60,000) and Maroantsetra (Ar100,000). This is the only service of its kind on this coast, and inexpensive, but is subject to interruptions, particularly from June to September.

Rozina V (☎Soanierana-Ivongo 033 19 200 82, 034 61 970 63, Tamatave 034 76 301 89; one way Ar70,000, return Ar120,000) Shuttle from Tamatave leaves from Tanambao V, next to Telemorefo school.

Taxi-Brousse

Taxis-brousses depart Tamatave for Soanierana-Ivongo (Ar8000, three to four hours) around 6am every morning. However, they are not necessarily coordinated with boat departures, so you could end up getting stuck. It makes more sense to book a transfer with your boat company. Returning to Tamatave, vehicles wait for the arrivals from Ile Sainte Marie, so a taxi-brousse makes more sense. For taxis-brousses going north, inquire at the station.

Private 4WD

The RN5 north from Soanierana-Ivongo to Mananara and Maroantsetra is a Pandora's box of potential delays, as well as a tremendous 4WD adventure. Taxi-brousse company **Kofifen** (☎033 11 640 95) rents private 4WDs for this journey. They quote a price of Ar1.45 million including driver but this can be cut in half with heavy bargaining.

Manompana

This small coastal village 38km north of Soanierana-Ivongo is where to head if you want to ditch beach tourism in favour of rural isolation. Nearby attractions include the scenic **Point Tintingue**, the protected **Ambodiriana forest** (www.adefa-madagascar.org) and the even smaller fishing village of **Antanambe**.

A French charity, **Marmaille a la Case** (http://marmaillealacase.free.fr), has also set up an education and cultural centre here, staffed partly by volunteers. **Au Bon Ancrage/Chez Wen Ki** (☎53 957 72, 033 19 746 41; d bungalow Ar15,000) offers basic bungalows on the beach, with bucket showers, and a convivial restaurant with fresh seafood.

ILE SAINTE MARIE

The best thing about Ile Sainte Marie is that it contains all the ingredients for a great vacation *and* great travel. This is a very long (57km), thin, lush, and relatively flat tropical island surrounded by beaches and reef, and spotted with thatched villages, with the port of Ambodifotatra, a quarter of the way up the western coast, being the only sizable town. South of here, the shore is lined with a great variety of hotels and resorts, but without overpowering the setting, culminating in the small island of Ile aux Nattes, a postcard for tropical paradise, where one can easily imagine pirates coming ashore with treasure chests in tow. In contrast, the upper half of the island is quite wild, and its great length means that there is plenty of room for exploration. There is a fantastic adventure to be had by buggy, quad or dirt bike through remote villages and along beautiful paradisiacal shoreline, culminating in the natural pools at the island's northern tip. So if you just sit on the beach, you have greatly missed out.

Some key dates: July to September is whale-watching season, and December to March is cyclone season. There are many times (mid-December to mid-January, April to May, July to October, as well as weekends

THE INFAMOUS RN5

Depending on how you look at it, the RN5 from Soanierana-Ivongo to Maroantsetra is either the worst road in Madagascar, or the best 4WD adventure in the country. The very idea of calling it a 'National Route' is so hysterical that only the sight of your 4WD being floated across a river on a few oil drums will stop you laughing.

The trip has two legs, Soanierana-Ivongo to Mananara, and Mananara to Maroantsetra, of which the first one is the most difficult. There are sections of sheer rock, sections of deep sand, and everything in between, particularly mud. In January/February the entire route is impassable. At the same time, much of the trip is adjacent to, and sometimes even on, an endless stretch of paradisiacal coastline, with bright white sand and overhanging palms.

Best of all are the numerous river crossings, some with dilapidated bridges that require close inspection – walk across these *before* the car – and others with ferries both real or home-made, where you get out and everyone pulls a rope to get across. At one end or the other you'll find a rickety village where you can pick up dried fish, bread, and soda. With luck, the entire adventure takes two days, with an overnight in Mananara, leaving time to do a night walk on Aye-Aye Island.

As you can imagine, the drivers who do this 240km journey day in and day out are some of the most talented 4WD captains anywhere. Our choice is **Toni** (☎033 06 366 48) who should really be driving professional rallies. Otherwise, search out a **Kofifen** (☎033 11 640 95) kiosk or 4WD at any taxi-brousse station from Tamatave to Maroantsetra, or call them there. The published rate for this stretch is Ar1.45 million, including fuel, but some hard bargaining can cut this in half. The price can be further defrayed by taking on extra passengers. By the time we reached the end, we were running an impromptu taxi-brousse with 10 people on board.

Ile Sainte Marie

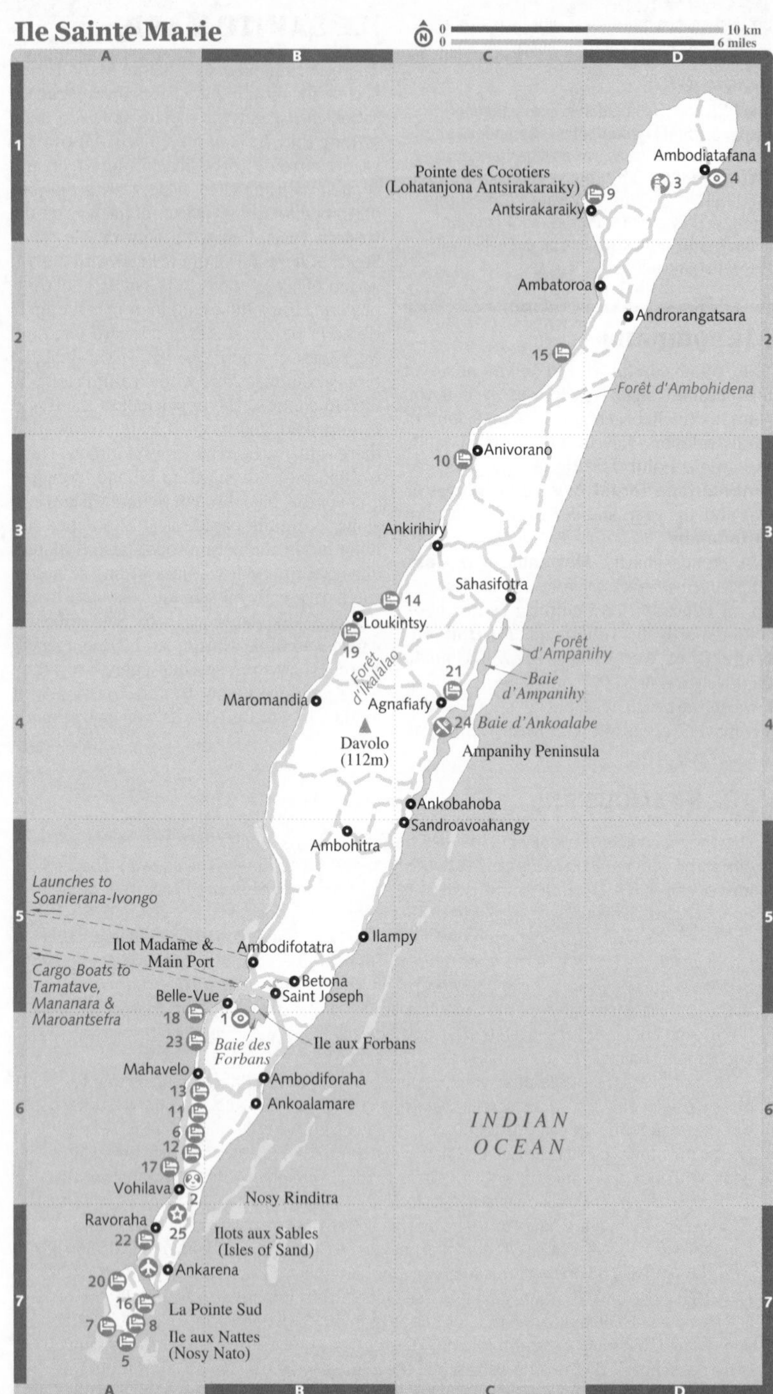

Ile Sainte Marie

Sights

1 Cimetiére des Pirates ... B6
2 Endemika ... A6
3 Fanilo Albrand Lighthouse ... D1
4 Piscine Naturelle d'Ambodiatafana ... D1

Sleeping

5 Analatsara ... A7
6 Chez Pierrot ... A6
7 Chez Sika ... A7
8 Chez Tity ... A7
9 Cocoteraie Robert ... D1
10 Eden Bé Guest House ... C3
11 Hôtel Lakana ... A6
12 Hôtel Soanambo ... A6
Jardins de Eden ... (see 1)
13 La Baleine ... A6
14 La Crique ... B3
15 Le Bon Endroit ... C2
16 Le Petit Traversé ... A7
17 Les Villas de Vohilava ... A6
18 Libertalia ... A6
19 Masoandro Lodge ... B4
20 Meva Paradis ... A7
21 Paradis d'Ampanihy ... C4
22 Princesse Bora Lodge & Spa ... A7
23 Vanilla Café ... A6

Eating

24 Mangrove Le Gourmand ... C4

Entertainment

25 Case a Nono ... A7

and Malagasy holidays) when it would be wise to make reservations. There is also a tourist tax of Ar10,000 per person per stay, and up to Ar5000 per room per night, although sometimes this is included in the quoted room rate.

Getting There & Away

Air

Air Madagascar (☎57 400 46) flies daily between Ile Sainte Marie and Antananarivo (€184, one hour) and six times weekly to/from Tamatave (€150, 30 minutes). Flights to Maroantsetra and destinations further north usually involve a stopover at Tamatave. Flights up the northeast coast are often full; in the vanilla season (June to October) book as far in advance as possible, and reconfirm all bookings.

Boat

For shuttles to/from Soanierana-Ivongo, see p174. Boats leave Ambodifotatra as early as daybreak. Cargo boats leave from a different port on Ilot Madame, the tiny island at the entrance to Baie des Forbans, sailing to Mananara, Maroantsetra and Tamatave. There are no set schedules; departures from Ile Sainte Marie are often in the evening or at night, depending on the tides, and you will likely have to wait several days for something to turn up.

Getting Around

There is a good paved road between Loukintsy and the airport, and between Ambodifotatra and Ilampy. Work is proceeding on Ankirihiry to Ilampy, in order to complete a paved circuit of the central island. The remaining roads are dirt, rock, or sand.

To/From the Airport

The airport is located at the southern tip of the island, 13km south of Ambodifotatra. Hotel transfer prices range from Ar2000 to Ar40,000 one way, depending on distance. If you can find one, taxis-brousses usually charge Ar5000 between the airport and Ambodifotatra. A private taxi costs Ar20,000.

Bicycle

Virtually every hotel and all kinds of other places have bikes of varying quality for hire. The going rate is around Ar10,000 per day. Once off the paved road you need a mountain bike, and even then going will be difficult in stretches.

Car & Motorcycle

The whole food chain of motorised vehicles – including cars, buggies, quads, motorcycles and scooters – is available for hire. If you wish to travel in a group, you can hire a car and driver through any high-end hotel; negotiations start at a too-high Ar300,000 per day.

At the Total station, **Flash Tour** (☎032 04 760 20) rents a minibus. A much better option is a buggy or quad, which also comes with a driver/guide. The well-run **Quad Sainte Marie** (☎032 40 745 39, www.quadsaintemarie.com) starts negotiations at a high Ar400,000/300,000 per day for a buggy/quad, but the experience of open-air driving around the island is priceless. That same experience, and perhaps even better, can be had *much* more cheaply by renting a dirt bike for a mere Ar50,000 per day plus petrol from the rental agent near the Bank of Africa in Ambodifotatra. If you know how to ride a motorcycle, and have the right insurance, you can handle this upgrade, but you must be careful of sudden sand traps in the road.

SHIVER ME TIMBERS

In the late 17th and 18th centuries Ile Sainte Marie was the headquarters of the world's pirates, who enjoyed its proximity to maritime trade routes, its protected harbour (a great place to hide), its abundant fruit, and its women. Legendary brigands like William Kidd once brought their boats here for repairs, and set up house on Ile aux Forbans, near Ambodifotatra. At one point the pirate population topped 1000. Today the remains of several pirate ships still lie within a few metres of the surface in the Baie des Forbans, including Kidd's *Adventure*, and Captain Condent's famous *Fiery Dragon*, while the skull and crossbones can be seen engraved at the nearby pirate cemetery.

Finally, for those who wish to putt-putt along sealed surfaces, you can pick up a scooter for around Ar15,000 per day, which is a lot of fun too. If your hotel doesn't have any, you'll see them for rent along the main road in Ambodifotatra, or call **Nicole et Véronique** (☎034 74 362 67).

Taxi & Taxi-Brousse

There are a few taxis-brousses on Ile Sainte Marie. Most run along the route between the airport and Ambodifotatra (Ar5000); a few travel north along the road from Ambodifotatra up as far as Loukintsy (Ar2500). Private taxis are more common, though disproportionately expensive. They usually hang out by the harbour in Ambodifotatra. You have a reasonable chance of flagging one down along the airport road during the day, or call **Faustin** (☎032 44 867 46) at night. Tariffs are fixed and posted at the tourist office and hotel receptions: it's Ar20,000 to the airport, Ar35,000 to Loukintsy, and Ar120,000 for a full day's hire.

Ambodifotatra

Ambodifotatra (am-bodi-*foot*-atr) is Ile Sainte Marie's only real town and has all the island's practical facilities. You'll find everything you need to organise your stay, plus some interesting restaurants.

Activities

Most activities on the island are offered by hotels; diving is one exception. The season runs from July to January; the best time is from October to December. Dive centres are often closed between February and May.

Il Balenottero DIVING
(☎57 400 36, 032 05 501 25; www.il-balenottero.com; Small Boat Harbour) A large operation with five boats. It also offers whale-watching, yacht cruises and fishing trips.

Le Lémurien Palmé DIVING
(☎57 040 15, 032 04 816 56; www.lemurien-palme.com, Ave La Bigorne) Dives start at Ar80,000. It also offers dive training, sea excursions, and whale-watching.

Tours

AT-SM Agency TOURS
(☎032 40 084 43, 034 01 793 81; atsm11@live.fr) If you are looking to put together any type of itinerary on the island, the best person to call is Orpheu (or-*fay*), the former head of the island's tourism office. This dynamic young gentleman speaks fluent English, makes things happen and knows everyone. He now runs his own agency.

Sleeping

If you're looking for beach accommodation, you're in the wrong place. Ambodifotatra is generally good for inexpensive hotels near the port and standalone restaurants (which may close by 9pm.)

Hotel Freddy HOTEL €€
(☎57 907 03, 032 83 079 50; Rue Belgique; d Ar 40,000, without bathroom Ar30,000; ❄) This brand-new midrange hotel, conveniently-located in the town centre, does all the basics right. Rooms are clean and sizable with hot water, a shared balcony, lots of light, and even air-con. Try the corner room first.

Les Palmiers BUNGALOW €
(☎57 402 34, 032 04 960 94; hotel-palmiers@yahoo.fr; d/tr bungalows Ar26,000/30,000; @) A little compound with smart, good-value bungalows with fans, up a path from the centre of town. The studio triples are a bargain.

Hotel Hortensia HOTEL €
(☎57 403 69; d Ar21,000; breakfast Ar5000) Nice large balconies face the ocean at this spacious and reasonable two-storey hotel.

Ambodifotatra

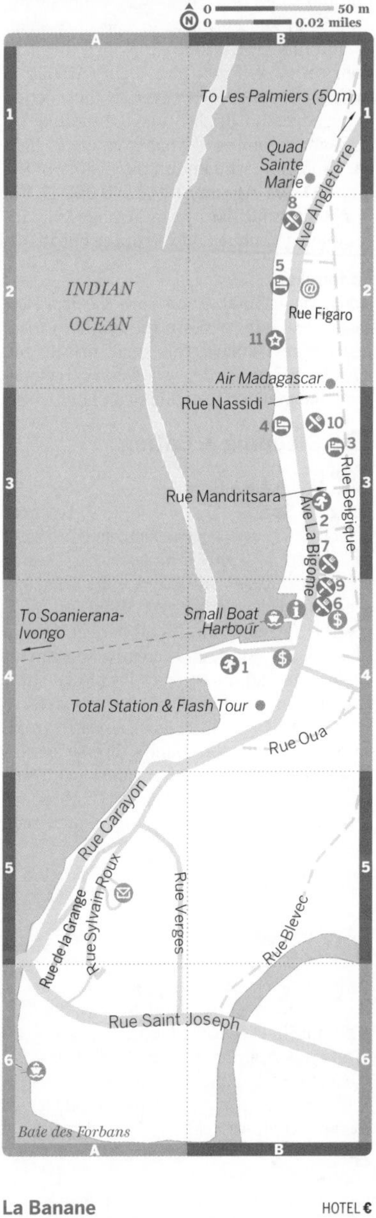

0 50 m
0 0.02 miles

To Les Palmiers (50m)
Quad Sainte Marie
Ave Angleterre
INDIAN OCEAN
Rue Figaro
Air Madagascar
Rue Nassidi
Rue Belgique
Rue Mandritsara
Ave La Bigorne
To Soanierana-Ivongo
Small Boat Harbour
Total Station & Flash Tour
Rue Oua
Rue Carayon
Rue Sylvain Roux
Rue Verges
Rue de la Grange
Rue Blevec
Rue Saint Joseph
Baie des Forbans

La Banane HOTEL €
(☎032 02 280 26; dm Ar3000) Backpackers take note: a dorm bed in this decent hotel by the sea is a rare find. The bar is a lively expat hangout, too.

Ambodifotatra

Activities, Courses & Tours

1 Il Balenottero B4
2 Le Lemurien Palmé B3

Sleeping

3 Hotel Freddy B3
4 Hotel Hortensia B3
5 La Banane B2

Eating

6 Du Quai B4
7 Food Stalls B3
8 Idylle Beach B2
9 La Paillote B4
10 Pizza Mama Santa B3

Entertainment

11 Baramix/La Polina B2

Eating

TOP CHOICE **Idylle Beach** EUROPEAN €€
(mains from Ar10,000; ⏲10am-10pm, closed Tue; ⏲lunch & dinner) This casual yet sophisticated bar-restaurant is done just right. Eat under the umbrellas on the white sand, or retreat into the shadows of the multicoloured verandah – either way the creative menu, a rare treat, will entice you from its southwest salad to its strawberry-banana juice.

La Paillote EUROPEAN €
(mains from Ar8000; ⏲breakfast, lunch & dinner) This *vazaha* hangout entices with its very attractive open-air floor plan, street-front location great for people-watching, and broad menu, from pizza to langouste. Try the thick zebu fillets. Eight rooms forthcoming in 2012. English spoken.

Du Quai CHINESE, MALAGASY €
(mains from Ar9000) The food here is way above average, but the prices aren't.

Pizza Mama Santa PIZZERIA €
(pizza Ar8000-12,000) Great oven-fired pizza. For the cheapest eats on the island, try the food stalls that appear in the market area around 6pm daily. There are some small food stores facing the harbour with limited supplies.

Entertainment

Nightlife is best found at **Baramix/La Polina** (admission Ar4000; closed Tuesday), a disco that starts up after 8pm.

Information

There are banks and ATMs in the centre of town. Internet access is available at **Alex Papurus** (per min Ar50) on the main road. The **Office Régional du Tourisme** (☎034 57 901 47; ⏰8am-noon & 2-6pm Mon-Sat), facing the port, has forgotten its mission.

South of Ambodifotatra

The area between Ambodifotatra and the airport contains most of the island's hotels, making it easy to reach various restaurants. The beach is narrow on this western shore, but on the other side, facing the Ilots aux Sables (Isles of Sand), lies a beautiful unspoiled stretch of tropical coastline. Walk across the small hill to the east of the airport.

Sights

Cimetière des Pirates CEMETERY

This is a fascinating spot from which to contemplate the history of the island. The scenic cemetery overlooks the Baie de Forbans, which, as a quick look at the map will tell you, was the perfect pirate hangout, and smells of a very different era. Ironically, most of the gravestones are actually missionaries, but you can clearly see the skull and crossbones on the grave of one young English pirate. The crumbling piers where they dragged their ships out of the water for repairs are visible from here, as is the small island of **Ile aux Forbans**, where many pirates lived, and a lookout point. Access is via an isolated foot track, which crosses several tidal creeks and slippery logs about 10 minutes south of the causeway. Guides hang around at the entrance to collect a small community fee (Ar2000), to which they add their own fee if you hire them (Ar5000 is more than ample). However, as their actual knowledge and English may be limited, we strongly recommend that you come here with someone who knows the history of the area. **AT-SM Agency** (☎032 40 084 43, 034 01 793 81; atsm11@live.fr) can arrange this. It's completely unique and worth the effort.

Endemika ZOO

(admission Ar15,000; ⏰8am-noon & 2-5pm Mon-Sat) About halfway down the southern road, just before Vohilava, this small private zoo and botanical garden showcases regional flora and fauna. It takes about an hour to see.

Sleeping & Eating

TOP CHOICE **Princesse Bora Lodge & Spa** LODGE €€€

(☎57 040 03; www.princessebora.com; d half board per person in low/high/whale-watching season Ar230,000/270,000/310,000; 🏊❄@) This one is easy to review: it has everything you could possibly imagine, and it's all perfect. One of Madagascar's top resorts, creative touches include an extraordinary spa with pirogue tubs and its own essential-oil laboratory, extensive wine cellar with private label, a nearby tropical nursery with the island's diverse species on display, huge round bungalows with suspended wooden beds and enamel bathrooms, serpentine corridors reminiscent of a reef,

HUMPBACK SEASON

Every year several hundred humpback whales make their way from the Antarctic northward to the warmer Malagasy waters around Baie d'Antongil, where they spend the winter months breeding and birthing before the long journey back. En route they swim past Ile Sainte Marie, where they are often sighted between July and mid-September. Getting to see these amazing creatures close up can be a highlight of a visit to Madagascar.

Humpbacks can measure up to 15m in length and weigh as much as 35,000kg. Despite their size, they are exceptionally agile, and capable of acrobatic moves such as breaching (launching themselves out of the water). These whales are also renowned for their singing, which is presumed to be related to mating patterns. Humpback songs can last up to an hour, and are considered the most complex of all whale songs.

During humpback season you can go on 'whale safaris' around the island for about €40 for a half-day trip. Inquire at the dive centres (p178) and shuttle-boat companies, as hotels without their own boats often arrange trips through them. The business is informally regulated by **Cétamada** (☎033 65 656 56; www.cetamada.org), a Madagascar conservation organisation that promotes responsible whale watching. Participating hotels agree to respect a code of approach, assure security protocols on board, and have a qualified guide. You can help by hiring a boat with a Cétamada sticker on it.

and on and on. There's also more normal offerings, like an artsy pool, a nice beach with comfortable sun beds and outdoor showers, and an elegant restaurant. None of this comes cheaply, but this is one high-end property where you really do get what you pay for. The secret is the extraordinary Swiss family behind it, for whom the lodge is not just a business but a ruling passion extending well beyond the normal boundaries of tourism. The same philosophy has also made their Café de la Gare in Antananarivo a great success.

TOP CHOICE **Libertalia** BUNGALOW €€€
(☎57 903 03, 032 02 763 23; www.lelibertalia.com; d Ar94,000) The lascivious whistles of the house parrot welcome you to this popular hotel named after the mythical pirate kingdom. The setting is unique, with a small private island connected to the lovely beach, and a great swimming dock. A sophisticated kitchen, with large breakfasts, lively staff, and special touches like a band and dancing, are all part of a winning personality that keeps clients returning.

Jardins de Eden BUNGALOW €€€
(☎034 09 265 76; lesjardinsdeden@moov.mg; d bungalow Ar70,000) If you want to be away from the main coastal road, and enjoy some cooler weather, the only option, and a good one, is this new guest house with five bungalows high up on a hill overlooking the pirate cemetery, with grand views at reasonable rates. Botano-philes will be particularly pleased with the grounds. Clients arrive by pirogue and gain free access to the pirate cemetery (p180).

Les Villas de Vohilava VILLA €€€
(☎57 900 16, 032 04 757 84; www.vohilava.com; villa €65-105) These five large and very well-done beachfront villas, with two to three rooms, a kitchen, and a chef, are designed for groups of six to 10 people. The attentive owner ensures a quality stay. You can hire bikes and scooters, and kayaks are free.

Vanilla Café BUNGALOW €€
(☎032 40 239 43; d incl breakfast Ar50,000) A small place with basic bungalows, all with bathrooms and hot water. A bit pricey, but it has some very pleasant waterfront dining.

Chez Pierrot BUNGALOW €€
(☎57 401 43, 034 01 060 91; chezpierrot@moov.mg; d/f Ar60,000/120,000) These spic-and-span, mismatched bungalows with bright bedcovers and deckchairs are arranged in a neat garden next to the sea, but there's no real beach, just an elevated artificial replacement.

Hôtel Lakana BUNGALOW €€€
(☎032 07 090 22; www.sainte-marie-hotel.com; d bungalow Ar110,000-120,000) This hotel and restaurant is known for its bungalows on stilts over the sea, each with its own bathroom back on land. Smarter rooms (with bathrooms) are clustered in a well-tended garden.

Hôtel Soanambo HOTEL €€€
(☎57 401 37; www.hsm.mg; s/d €159/222; P ❄ 🏊 @) This large package-tour resort has been newly renovated to nice effect, but there is nothing here unique to Sainte Marie or Madagascar. If you want a generic high-end beach hotel with pool, tennis, and modern architecture then here you are. Accepts credit cards.

La Baleine BUNGALOW €
(☎032 40 257 18; lantoualbert@moov.mg; d/tr/f bungalow Ar30,000/40,000/60,000; @) Basic beachfront bungalows with the world's most rickety dock.

☆ Entertainment

The main night spot is **Casa à Nono** (⊙Thu & Sun), near the airport.

Ile aux Nattes (Nosy Nato)

What a lovely place this is. Ile aux Nattes is a classic tropical island, with curving white beaches and overhanging palms, a turquoise sea with waves breaking over the reef, a gentle breeze, and a lush green interior. While only a brief pirogue ride (Ar5000 return) from the tip of Sainte Marie, or a mere walk at low tide, there's a palpable sense of isolation and adventure. Numerous sand pathways (beware the crab holes!) open the way for exploration without the possibility of getting too lost in an area only 2km across. Surprisingly, there is also some great, wonderfully quirky accommodation. So if you are suffering from visions of tropical paradise, here is your medicine.

Sleeping

TOP CHOICE **Chez Sika** BUNGALOW €
(☎032 04 607 74; azafadysica@yahoo.fr; d Ar30,000) Wow. If you are looking for inexpensive accommodation, look no further: this one outperforms places two or three

times its cost. The hotel is like an open park beneath the palms, with an absolutely gorgeous location on a fringing reef. For Ar50,000, the family bungalow is the best value anywhere on Sainte Marie, with two large rooms, a thatched porch, a hammock with dreamy views, and the clever use of pirogues as shelving. Only breakfast is served, but there is a kitchen for guests (and plenty of other hotels nearby). Best of all, management has not crafted a system for extracting as much money from you as possible. They actually *lend you* snorkel equipment, and spearfishing trips are free. A refreshing choice from every perspective.

TOP CHOICE **Analatsara** BUNGALOW €€€
(☎57 906 11, 032 02 127 70; lebaronjpbriois@gmail.com) The owner of Analatsara has crafted a high-quality mini-resort basically for the love of sharing it. For Ar120,000 per person you get an open bar, laundry, half-board, and a double bed with loft. A six-person house with housekeeper, chef, and 24-hour electricity is €600 per week. The standout option is the treehouse, replete with trapdoor entry.

TOP CHOICE **Le Petit Traversé** BUNGALOW €€€
(☎57 905 62, 032 42 360 52; www.madxperience.com; tr Ar105,000) This is one of the island's wonderfully personable offerings. The ongoing project of castaway South African Ockie Snyman, it is uniquely aimed at an English-speaking audience (no French is spoken), and feels more like a community than a hotel, including family-style dining, and music and movies at night. The menu changes constantly, from lasagne to fish and chips, with seafood a recurring theme, and also pizza, made in an oven built into the prow of a beached boat. Ockie's aquarium bar is another creative first, and there is a glass-bottomed boat forthcoming. It's not cheap, but not easily forgotten, either. Beware the wandering lemurs!

Meva Paradis BUNGALOW €€
(☎032 02 207 80; www.mevaparadis.com; d with breakfast Ar70,000; mains from Ar16,000) There's nothing remarkable about these ensuite bungalows, all of which have cold water, but they are sitting on a great stretch of beach.

Chez Tity BUNGALOW €
(☎034 04 065 80; cheztity@gmail.com; d without bathroom Ar25,000) This is a friendly Malagasy-owned place, popular with backpackers, with a bit of wisdom thrown in: all the bungalows are named after philosophers.

North of Ambodifotatra

Sometimes it's easy to forget, but north of Ambodifotatra lies three quarters of the island. In terms of accommodation, almost all is on the west coast, which is more sheltered from cyclones. There is a good paved road to Loukintsy, after which the road gets rough, and the real adventure begins.

It will take several enjoyable hours, but you can drive all the way to the **Piscine Naturelle d'Ambodiatafana** (admission Ar2000) a natural swimming pool at the northeastern tip of the island, where there are some basic bungalows. The **Fanilo Albrand lighthouse** lies to the southwest. From the ridge Maroantsetra and Baie d'Antongil are sometimes visible.

Sleeping

TOP CHOICE **Le Bon Endroit** GUESTHOUSE €
(☎57 906 62, 033 09 624 38; lebonendroit.sm@gmail.fr; d/f Ar30,000/45,000) This newly-renovated guesthouse is off the beaten track, but an absolute bargain. The simple ensuite bungalows occupy a rugged coral beach, with a central **restaurant** (mains Ar8000-15,000). There is a full range of activities (deep-sea fishing, snorkelling, kayaking, spearfishing, and more) almost all of which are free or offered at cost of fuel (bikes are Ar10,000 per day). You could easily stay here a week and have plenty to do. Transfers arranged. Highly recommended.

Eden Bé Guest House GUESTHOUSE €€
(☎034 19 059 52; www.eden-be-guest-house.com; per person incl breakfast €22-30; @) This tasteful guest house on a large piece of waterfront is a big step above the competition, with a charming ambience that is part safari lodge and part piano bar. The simple rooms are very comfy, with thick euro-mattresses and balconies overlooking the sea. A delightful verandah is the perfect breakfast spot. The owners have paid great attention to the details, with sophisticated touches throughout. Quads and other activities available, English is spoken.

Masoandro Lodge LODGE €€€
(☎57 910 43, 032 05 416 15; www.hsm.mg; standard bungalow with half board €112; ❄) This beautiful wooden lodge is located on a hillside with great long-range views, and has a fantastic pool area at the tip of a peninsula, with an adjacent waterfall. It's well situated

WORTH A TRIP

AMPANIHY BAY

If you look at the map of Saint Marie, you'll see a long narrow bay on the east side of the island, and a peninsula to match. Baie d'Ampanihy is a wild and untouristed place, where village life goes on as it has for centuries. It makes for a great day trip, or even an overnight, assuming you have hired a vehicle. The typical route is to drive north from Ambodifotatra to Loukintsy, where you can cross the island to Agnafiafy. Here you'll see a sign for **Mangrove Le Gourmand** (☎57 901 98), a bungalow restaurant in a clearing overlooking the bay. The food here is fresh from the sea, and fabulous. By fresh, we mean they have wicker baskets of live fish and mangrove crabs in the nearby creek, while the morning's catch of shrimp is still kicking. Ask for coconut milk, and the cook will climb the adjacent palm tree to get you one. Call ahead to book fresh food.·

After lunch, you can hire a pirogue to take you across the bay to the peninsula (Ar5000). You'll probably see local women wading up to their necks as they fish for shrimp.

Now consider this: the locals report that every year from mid-November through December enormous sharks, larger than your pirogue (dugout canoe), enter the mostly shallow bay through a very deep channel in order to give birth. They never attack anyone, although their young are sometimes netted by accident, while the sight of a huge dorsal fin can prompt an early bathroom break. Once you reach the peninsula, you can walk across to the ocean, where you can look for miles in either direction, probably seeing no one. You can spend as much time as you'd like beachcombing here before returning.

If you'd like to stay overnight, **Paradis d'Ampanihy** (fax 57 402 78; d bungalow Ar20,000) offers basic bungalows near Agnafiafy; fax Hèléne ahead, and the staff at Mangrove Le Gourmand can direct you. They also have another surprisingly good restaurant, with some very tasty dishes with coconut sauce, and guides available for exploring the nearby forest.

at the end of the good road heading north, so you can reach town or adventure equally. The deluxe bungalows are much larger than the standard ones, but the latter are easier to get to, and half the price. Multiple excursions available.

La Crique BUNGALOW €€€
(☎57 902 45; d/f bungalow Ar89,000/149,000) The rooms at La Crique have verandahs with deckchairs from which you can look out over a rose garden and a magnificent stretch of beach. Most bungalows are en suite.

Cocoteraie Robert BUNGALOW €€
(☎57 901 76, 034 29 666 98; d bungalow Ar50,000) This long-established hotel has rebuilt itself after the tragic cyclone that struck here several years ago; at the time of research they were finishing the restaurant. The beach is the main selling point, one of the best in Sainte Marie, with sweeping horizon views encompassing miles of shoreline. The downside is that it's rather difficult to get to; the hotel will arrange a transfer from Loukintsy or the airport.

BAIE D'ANTONGIL & MASOALA PENINSULA

North of Soanierana-Ivongo lies the remote Baie d'Antongil, a place that seems better known to humpback whales than to humanity. Its boundaries stretch from Mananara around Maroantsetra to the Masoala Peninsula, forming a deep blue U teeming with fish and surrounded by mountainous forest. Cut off from easy road access to the south, and with nothing but hiking trails elsewhere, this is a place whose only reliable contact with the outside world is the intermittent flights into Maroantsetra. As a result, there is a captivating sense of timelessness here, as if one has been flung back into 1950s Madagascar. Disconnected from the wheels of progress, one turns to the mountains, the sky, and the sea.

Mananara

POP 46,000

Mananara is a small and very out-of-the way town set in a clove- and vanilla-producing area at the southern entrance to Baie

Baie d'Antongil & Masoala

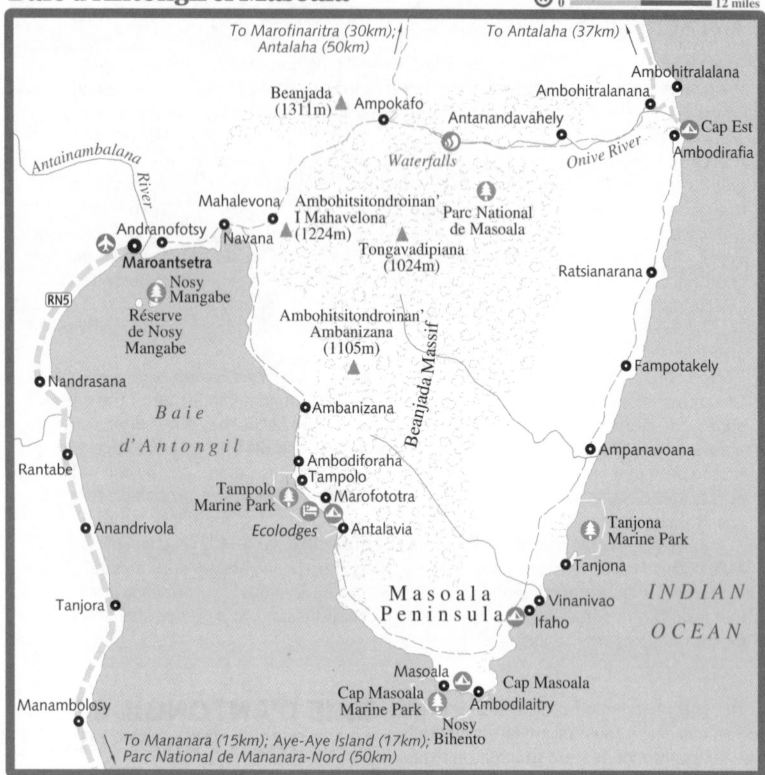

d'Antongil. If you're heading down the RN5, you'll probably stay here the night. If so, don't miss the night walk at Aye-Aye island, the easiest way to see Madagascar's most reclusive and bizarre lemur. Reserve ahead. Otherwise, this is the place to stay if you wish to explore the nearby Parc National de Mananara-Nord. There's also some decent snorkelling off the peninsula behind the airport, and internet access at the Boutique Orange.

Sights & Activities

Aye-Aye Island PARK

(night tours Ar20,000) The patron of Chez Roger also owns this small island in the middle of the Mananara River and offers night tours including transport (car and pirogue) and guide. The prize: caught in the beam of a flashlight, the aye-aye sits up in the leaves of a palm tree digging out the meat from a coconut with its bizarre bony finger. Call **Chez Roger** (☎032 52 329 87) to book ahead.

Parc National de Mananara-Nord PARK

The very remote Parc National de Mananara-Nord (23,000 hectares) encompasses some of the last remaining lowland rainforest in Madagascar. An additional 1000 hectares of offshore islets and their surrounding reefs are protected as a marine national park. The largest of these islets is Nosy Atafana. While lemurs are not always seen by visitors, Mananara-Nord contains indris, brown lemurs, ruffed lemurs and aye-ayes, and is the only known habitat of the hairy-eared dwarf lemur. There is also a variety of geckos, including the endemic uroplatus and day geckos. Offshore there are dugong.

The **MNP office** (☎033 12 692 60, 033 12 768 97; mananara_nationalpark@yahoo.fr) is in Sahasoa, about 30km south of Mananara. Come here first to arrange your visit. The park entry fee is Ar10,000. Guide and porter fees start from Ar10,000/15,000 per half/full day. Many guides speak some English. They will print out a map upon request.

The park has two main circuits, one terrestrial and the other marine. The **terrestrial circuit** begins 6km south of the park office by foot. It takes two hours to get there, two to do the circuit, and another two to get back. The **marine circuit** includes a trip to Nosy Atafana, and costs an additional Ar120,000-150,000 for boat and fuel. The cost per person thus declines with the size of the group (max eight). For any trip in the park, you'll need to be self-sufficient with food and water, and if trekking, in good shape. **Camping** is Ar8000 per day. A limited amount of camping equipment is for hire at the park office.

Mananara-Nord saw only 100 tourists in 2011. This region is not only difficult to reach, but the park itself is not great value. The two-hour terrestrial circuit requires four hours of hiking to get there and back. The marine circuit is a quick 15 minutes to Nosy Atafana, but the circuit is only an hour – not long for the price.

If you are coming from Maroantsetra, the large, mountainous and lush Nosy Mangabe (700 hectares) offers a lot more than the small and flat Nosy Atafana (23 hectares).

Sleeping & Eating

Sahasoa Bungalows BUNGALOW €
(033 19 671 81; d/f without bathroom Ar15,000/30,000, set menu Ar5000) These new, clean bungalows on a tropical-paradise beach in Sahasoa are close to the park office, and dirt cheap.

Chez Roger BUNGALOW €
(032 52 329 87; d Ar20,000) This is the best place to stay if you want to visit Aye-Aye Island. The big and comfortable bungalows in back have bathrooms (bucket showers), there are reasonable rooms available, and the restaurant does decent meals.

Hôtel Aye-Aye BUNGALOW €
(032 95 883 96; d Ar25,000; pool) This hotel near the airport is also a good budget option, with basic ensuite bungalows among the palm trees, a small pool and a restaurant. Cold water.

Entertainment

Mananara is, surprisingly, a bit of a party town. For that Malagasy beat, try Volume 5 near the Boutique Orange.

Getting There & Around

Boat

The **Melissa Express** (Maroantsetra 032 05 733 58, Mananara 032 46 001 71, Ile Sainte Marie 033 18 732 69) passenger boat offers a weekly service between Mananara and both Maroantsetra (Ar40,000) and Soanierana-Ivongo (Ar60,000). This is the only service of its kind on this coast, and inexpensive, but is subject to interruptions, particularly from June to September.

Cargo boats sail occasionally between Mananara, Ile Sainte Marie, Maroantsetra and Tamatave. There are usually several departures, depending on the weather, although there are no set schedules. This journey is only really safe between September and March, due to sea conditions. Inquire at the small port in Mananara. Boats often come in and leave again fairly quickly, so you'll have to return often. Fares between Mananara and Ile Sainte Marie or Maroantsetra average about Ar50,000; the trip takes at least eight hours, often sailing through the night. Occasional cargo boats go as far as Antalaha, Sambava or even Diego Suarez (Antsiranana) in the north. There are no facilities of any kind on the boats, so bring sun protection (an umbrella is handy), food and water.

Taxi-Brousse

Taxis-brousses heading south or north along the RN5 all stop here, so go to the station to inquire, on the main road near the town hall. You will definitely want to read up on the RN5 before you do (p175).

Private 4WD

Taxi-brousse company **Kofifen** (033 11 640 95) also rents private 4WDs. They quote Ar685,000 including driver to Maroantsetra, and Ar1.25 million to Tamatave, but in our experience hard bargaining can cut these prices nearly in half.

Maroantsetra

POP 27,000

If you were going to make a movie about old Madagascar, this would be the place to film it. Set at the apex of the Baie d'Antongil, near the mouth of the Antainambalana River, Maroantsetra is full of languid charm, enjoying both river scenery and ocean views. Locals will tell you that very little has changed here in 30 years. And yet there is a lot for the visitor to do. This is the perfect base for exploring the entire bay, including the forests of Masoala, the island of Nosy Mangabe, and the humpback whales that visit and give birth from July to September. Just be aware that Maroantsetra's climate is one of the wettest in Madagascar, particularly from May to September, and there are no ATMs.

Tours

Madagascar National Parks TOURS
(☎032 41 944 46) The local MNP has trained English-speaking guides with great local knowledge who can organise any itinerary you want to the Masoala Peninsula, Nosy Mangabe, or Parc National de Mananara-Nord for a reasonable price. A great example is **Augustine** (☎34 16 490 32; vitimbary@yahoo.fr).

Relais du Masoala BOAT TOURS
(☎032 07 901 84; relais@cortezexpeditions.mg) Maroantsetra's most upmarket hotel has several boats, and organises quality excursions with English-speaking guides, including overnight stays. Options include a river cruise; trips to the Masoala Peninsula; Navana (a beautiful wild creek and beach) and Nosy Mangabe; and trips in whale-watching in season. The price per person depends on the size of the party.

Hippocampe TOURS
(☎032 64 418 99; madahippocampe@live.fr) Another quality hotel-run operation offering quads, 4WD tours, and boat trips to the parks, personally run by the French owner (no English). The boat is a beautifully restored cabin cruiser.

Mada Expeditions WALKING, KAYAKING
(☎032 40 377 77; http://mada-expeditions.com) Offers extensive trekking and kayaking trips around Masoala, requiring advance notice.

Sleeping

The properties on the canal benefit from a sea breeze, making them cooler than the inland options. Be careful of the hand-sized spiders that spin webs on hotel paths at night.

TOP CHOICE **Relais du Masoala** LODGE €€€
(☎032 07 901 84, Antananarivo 22 632 53; relais@cortezexpeditions.mg; d bungalow €76, dinner €12; P) This is the best lodge in the Baie d'Antongil, with an interesting location at the end of a canal, and a bridge across to the ocean beach, affording dreamy views of Nosy Mangabe. The luxury bungalows have enormous bathrooms and porches, while the kitchen serves the finest cuisine in the area. The lodge is owned by the Grand Dame of Madagascar, Monique Rodriguez, who also serves as the country's honorary consul, handling the most difficult visa issues. The opportunity to share a glass of wine with her on the verandah while listening to stories of Madagascar past is not to be missed. At the time of research the lodge was about to break ground on an important new sister property on the Masoala Peninsula, facilitating dual accommodation arrangements for guests.

Le Coco Beach BUNGALOW €€
(☎57 702 06; d Ar60,000, with air-con Ar81,000, without bathroom Ar20,000; ❄) This friendly midrange hotel has comfortable, well-maintained bungalows and an above-average **restaurant** (set menu Ar25,000) set amid coconut palms. The atmospheric bungalows on the river are especially good value. Local tours organised.

Hippocamp GUESTHOUSE €€€
(☎032 64 418 99; madahippocampe@live.fr; room Ar90,000, bungalow incl breakfast Ar120,000, set menu Ar24,000; 🏊) This interesting new *chambre d'hôte* (B&B) occupies a beautiful home on the canal, with six rooms and three bungalows, the latter lacking bathroom privacy. The range of activities on offer are a big plus here, but the unfiltered natural swimming pool, replete with fish, may not be to everyone's liking. Rates include airport transfer.

Hôtel du Centre HOTEL €
(☎032 40 773 39, 033 28 177 30; d Ar12,000, meals Ar5000) A basic place with rooms in wooden sheds. Meals can be arranged in the evenings.

Masoala Resort BUNGALOW €€€
(☎033 15 051 52, 032 11 075 51; www.masoalaresort.com; d €22-68; 🏊) This hotel occupies a fine location, with a grand view of Nosy Mangabe, but the Versailles fountain, the watertower in the shape of a tea cup, the enormous decorative boat on the lawn, the garish amateur murals, and the large water hazard (aka a swimming pool) make it look more like a mini-golf course than a hotel. Driver, please.

Le Maroa BUNGALOW €
(☎Tamatave 032 81 658 77; d Ar12,000) Near the Parc National de Masoala office, Le Maroa has a good **restaurant** (mains Ar6000) with lots of varieties of *soupe chinoise* and decent bungalows.

Eating

The only fine dining is to be had at Relais du Masoala. Coco Beach provides some hearty meals that are good value. For budget eating, locals praise the Chinese food at **Florida Snack**, on the main road near the Bank of Africa, as well as the chicken and fish at **Baguette d'Or** (300m north of the market on the main road, then right 50m.)

Entertainment

There are three discos that comprise Maroantsetra nightlife: **Eden Club**, **Miami**, and **Vatsy**, all of which attract a young and amiable crowd that dances into the wee hours. Miami edges out the rest as the renowned location of the annual Miss Maroantsetra beauty contest, a September tradition. As you'll be going at night, a taxi is the only way to find these places.

Information

Bank of Africa has a branch here for changing cash and travellers cheques.

MNP office (032 41 944 46) Located near the market.

Orange (per min Ar70; 7.30am-noon & 2.30-6pm) Internet on the main street.

Getting There & Away

Air

Air Madagascar flights connect Maroantsetra a few times a week with Antananarivo (€184, 45 minutes), Tamatave (€128, 30 minutes), and Sambava (€88, 30 minutes). The Air Madagascar office is a few kilometres from town on the road to the airport. Flights to/from Maroantsetra are often full, especially between June and November – be sure to reconfirm your ticket. Weather may affect plane schedules, particularly during the rainiest months (July to September).

Boat

The **Melissa Express** (Maroantsetra 032 05 733 58, Mananara 032 46 001 71, Tamatave 032 44 743 03, Ile Sainte Marie 033 18 732 69) passenger boat offers weekly service between Maroantsetra and Mananara (Ar40,000), Soanierana-Ivongo (Ar 100,000) and Ile Sainte Marie (Ar120,000). This is the only service of its kind on this coast, and inexpensive, but is subject to interruptions, particularly from July to September.

There are also unscheduled but regular cargo boats sailing between Maroantsetra and Ile Sainte Marie (10 hours), Tamatave (two days), Antalaha (12 to 15 hours) and Mananara (nine hours). Enquire at the port in Maroantsetra, and then be prepared for inevitable delays.

> **DON'T FORGET THE PROPRIETOR**
>
> The Madagascar travel scene is fascinating because hotels are rarely owned by large and soulless corporations. Due to the country's political and economic instability, there are no motel chains dotting the RN7, while in the cities the big international chains are noticeably absent. Instead, hotels in this stretch of the globe are run by the most interesting expats you will ever meet, from the wizened Frenchmen running end-of-the-Earth bungalows (see p167) to the impressive family-run resorts, such as Relais de La Reine in Isalo (French, p76), Princesse Bora in Ile Sainte Marie (Swiss, p180), La Pirogue in Mahambo (French-American, p173), and Relais du Masoala in Maroantsetra (French-American, p186).
>
> Each proprietor stamps his or her own personality upon a place, turning it, for better or worse, into a work of hospitality art. And oh, the stories they can tell! So when you do meet the proprietors, be sure to lift the lid on their treasuries of tales. A trip to Madagascar is not complete until you do.

The boats that take passengers are sometimes extremely overloaded, and some do capsize, so if the boat looks too full, don't get on. Good boats to look out for to Mananara are *La Baleine* and *Ambotosoa*. To Ile Sainte Marie or Tamatave, look out for *Savannah*, *Red Rose* or *Rosita*.

Taxi-Brousse

Maroantsetra lies 112km north of Mananara at the end of the infamous RN5 (see p175). Taxis-brousses depart for Mananara around 6am Tuesday, Thursday, and Saturday (Ar30,000) and carry on to Tamatave (Ar80,000). There are no roads anywhere else.

Private 4WD

Taxi-brousse company **Kofifen** (033 11 640 95) also rents private 4WDs. They quote Ar685,000 including driver to Mananara, Ar1.425 million to Manompana, Ar1.45 million to Soanierana-Ivongo, and Ar1.48 million to Tamatave, but in our experience hard bargaining can cut these prices nearly in half.

Getting Around

The airport is about 7km southwest of town. The taxi fare is Ar15,000.

Réserve de Nosy Mangabe

The island of Nosy Mangabe, easily visible 5km offshore from Maroantsetra, is a must-visit for anyone with a smidgin of romance in their blood. This is a thickly forested and mountainous tropical island, with huge soaring canarium trees arising from flying buttress roots, a rusty shipwreck piercing one side, waterfalls, a spyglass hill, a yellow sickle beach, elusive animals, foreign inscriptions, and the omnipresent sound of the jungle. Whew! If that doesn't bring out the Robinson Crusoe in you, check your pulse. It rains a lot, though, so be prepared.

You have the option of taking a day trip here, or staying overnight. MNP runs a very well-equipped beachside **campground** (camping per tent Ar5000) with picnic tables, a kitchen and toilets, and some rental camping equipment. There were also five basic bungalows under construction at the time of research. It's an idyllic spot, with a waterfall for a shower, and beckoning trail heads. A popular option takes you to the summit of the island, affording great views. Another leads to **Plage des Hollandais**, a beach with rocks bearing the scratched names of some 17th-century Dutch sailors. From July to September, you can see whales offshore.

The forest here is full of reptiles and amphibians, including the leaf-tailed gecko, one of nature's most accomplished camouflage artists; several species of chameleons; many frogs; and several harmless species of snake, including the Madagascar tree boa. It is also home to various lemurs, including the elusive aye-aye, which was introduced here in 1967 to protect the species from extinction. A sighting is by no means guaranteed.

Information

Entry permits can be obtained at the MNP office in Maroantsetra, or on the island itself. A permit costs Ar20,000 for three days, and does not include the nearby Parc National de Masoala.

Guides are compulsory. An experienced guide (with wildlife knowledge) is Ar35,000 per group per day. A simple trail guide is Ar15,000 per day. Night walks (recommended) cost Ar10,000 for groups of up to four, plus Ar2000 for the guide's evening meal. Some guides will cook in the evenings for an extra fee.

Getting There & Away

Boat transfers can be arranged through the MNP office. Rates per person for a return day trip are Ar100,000/60,000/40,000/35,000 for one/two/three/four people. The trip takes 30 to 45 minutes, but is weather-dependent, so it is best not to wait until your last day.

Parc National de Masoala

The magical Masoala (mash-wala) Peninsula is the site of a 210,000-hectare national park containing one of the best rainforests in the country. It also encompasses three protected marine areas: Tampolo Marine Park on the peninsula's southwestern coast, Cap Masoala Marine Park at the tip of the peninsula and Tanjona Marine Park on the southeastern coast. Most of the park is spread across the central part of the peninsula, extending southwest to Tampolo Marine Park. There are several small discrete parcels *(parcs détachés)* elsewhere on the peninsula as well. At the peninsula's southernmost tip is the beautiful Cap Masoala, which can be reached on foot or by bicycle from Cap Est.

The peninsula is famous for its vegetation, which includes primary forest, rainforest and coastal forest as well as a variety of palm and orchid species. Ten lemur species are found here, along with several tenrec and mongoose species, 14 bat species, 60 reptile species and about 85 bird species. The marine national parks protect mangrove ecosystems, coral reefs, dolphins, dugong and turtles.

There are excellent opportunities here for sea kayaking, snorkelling and swimming. The entire peninsula is exceptionally wet, however, particularly during June and July, when river levels are highest. The months between October and December are somewhat drier and best for trekking.

Park Fees & Guides

The main park headquarters is located at the MNP office in Maroantsetra. The guides here are well organised and many speak English. Treks can also be arranged at the MNP office in Antalaha or in Ambodirafia, near Cap Est, although the staff and guides there don't speak English.

Permits cost Ar20,000 for three days. Guides are mandatory in both terrestrial and marine parks. Experienced guides (with wildlife knowledge) are Ar35,000 per day. Trail guides are Ar15,000 per day, porters Ar10,000 to Ar15,000 per day. There is an additional fee of Ar30,000 if the boat has to wait overnight.

Activities

This is a hiker's paradise. If you are staying in the ecolodges on the west coast, there are many short trails that you can take. There are also three main long-distance trails for serious trekkers. The **Maroantsetra to Antalaha direct trip** (three to five days, Ar150,000) passes through rice paddies and gentler terrain. It is the easiest but also the dullest. For forest lovers, the **Maroantsetra to Cap Est route** (five to eight days, Ar240,000) is more interesting, but also more challenging, with river crossings. Most nights are spent in villages, where it is customary to pay a few thousand ariary per person to the village chief. Carry a tent, however, as some villages are too small to offer accommodation. Finally, one can walk the entire rim of the peninsula, from **Maroantsetra to Cap Masoala to Cap Est**. This long journey can be cut to two weeks or so by taking a boat from Maroantsetra to Cap Masoala (Ar390,000).

There is a flat fee of Ar35,000 return for a guide for all three main treks. Food, including for the guides and porters, is not included in these rates and is paid by the client.

All long-distance treks are fairly demanding and involve muddy stretches. At certain times of the year you may be wading up to chest height over slippery rocks. Inquire at the MNP office about trail conditions.

Sleeping & Eating

There are designated **camping grounds** (camping Ar3000) all the way around the peninsula, including at Marofototra, Ambodilaitry, Ifaho and Cap Est. Grounds have wells and shelters for tents, but you'll need to bring in all other equipment. Bottled water and basic supplies are usually available in bigger villages such as Mahalevona, Ampokafo and Antanandavahely, but you will need to be self-sufficient with most food and water (bring a purifier).

The three lodges occupy the same stretch of coast, near Tampolo on the southwestern side of the peninsula. Access is generally by boat. We recommend purifying your water.

TOP CHOICE **Masoala Forest Lodge** ECOLODGE €€€
(☎22 261 14, 032 05 415 86; www.masoalaforestlodge.com) Staying here is akin to going on a high-end safari, including the luxury tents (with hot water). Located on a 10-hectare forest reserve, the grounds are like a camp. The owner, who has run lodges elsewhere in Africa, focuses intently on his client's time, with a full range of activities (eg hikes, snorkelling, swimming and kayaking). The minimum program is €245 per person per day with a three-night stay, all inclusive (transfer, park permits, meals and activities). Kayak expeditions to Cap Masoala (100km, 10 days, €1800 per person) are a speciality from October to December. Check out the classy website.

Ecolodge Chez Arrol ECOLODGE €€
(☎032 40 889 02, 033 12 902 77; http://arollodge.free.fr; camping per person Ar3000) The most basic option, with simple thatched-hut bungalows and cold water. The cheapest package, including two days here and one day on Nosy Mangabe, all inclusive (taxi and boat transfer, guide fees, entrance permit and full board) is €400 per person for two people. Seven days here and two in Nosy Mangabe costs €881 per person, all inclusive. The lodge also offers camping and tree climbing in the canopy to see red-ruffed lemurs. Part of the proceeds go to support the local community.

Tampolodge ECOLODGE €€€
(☎034 31 747 97, 032 42 713 37; www.tampolodge.com) This lodge has the best location, on a fantastic arc of beach split by the alluring S-bend of a jungle river. Accommodation is in basic bungalows with cold water, but with nice large bathrooms. Pirogue trips can be arranged upriver (Ar10,000); go at sunrise. A double bungalow with bathroom is €60 per person with full board, and expensive transfers from Maroantsetra (€132 to €150 *per person*) make a short stay overpriced.

PARC NATIONAL DE MASOALA

Best time to visit August (for whales) to January

Key highlight Seeing humpback whales and red-ruffed lemurs in the same day

Wildlife Gold dust gecko, fork-marked lemurs, helmeted vanga shrike, serpent eagle, dugong

Habitats Low, middle and highland rainforest, mangrove, littoral forest, reefs and rivers

Gateway towns Maroantsetra, Antalaha

Transport options Boat or walk in

Things you should know Bring a raincoat. The sea can be rough in the afternoon.

Understand Madagascar

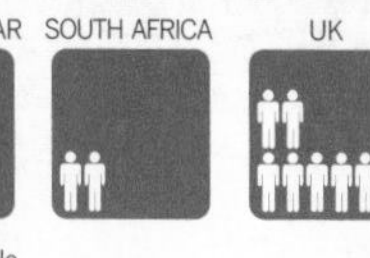

Madagascar Today

The Dark Years

Madagascar has been in the throes of a political crisis since Andry Rajoelina came to power following violent uprisings in March 2009; his predecessor, Marc Ravalomanana, handed power to the army and fled to South Africa.

The international community decided that Rajoelina's accession to power was unconstitutional and refused to recognise his High Transitional Authority (HAT) as a legitimate government.

A power-sharing deal brokered by France, South Africa and the African Union between HAT and the opposition was reached in August 2009, only to be dismissed by HAT a couple of months later. The sanctions were swift and drastic: all international aid funding, which represented about 50% of the government's public funding, was withheld.

In August 2010, Marc Ravalomanana was condemned, in absentia, to forced labour for life for the deaths of 30 protesters during the uprisings of February 2009 (the presidential guards had fired on the crowd without warning).

HAT's self-imposed deadline of running elections within 24 months came and went, but the Southern African Development Community (SADC) kept working behind the scenes on a compromise. In March 2011, after months of negotiations, SADC presented a draft roadmap for an exit to the crisis.

» Population: 19.6 million

» 77% live below the national poverty line

» Life expectancy: 60

» Literacy: 71%

» Average number of children per woman: 4.7

Light at the End of the Tunnel?

It took a few iterations but the roadmap was finally signed by all political parties on 17 September 2011, with the exception of former president and political exile Didier Ratsiraka. One of the insistences of SADC was the 'unconditional return' of all political exiles, a point that Rajoelina highlighted by adding that exiles would not be immune from judicial pursuits.

Dos & Don'ts

» Respect local *fady* (taboos), which are cultural and social dictates that relate to food, behaviour and certain times of the week or year. Guides will explain.

» Don't point; bend your finger or indicate with your palm.

» Bring rice or a bottle of rum if you're invited to a Malagasy home.

» Don't attend cultural celebrations such as exhumation or circumcision ceremonies unless you have been invited.

Top Books

A History of Madagascar (2001) by Mervyn Brown

The Eighth Continent: Life, Death and Discovery in the Lost World of Madagascar (2000) by Peter Tyson

The Aye-Aye and I (1992) by Gerald Durrell

belief systems
(% of population)

Indigenous Christian Muslim

if Madagascar were 100 people

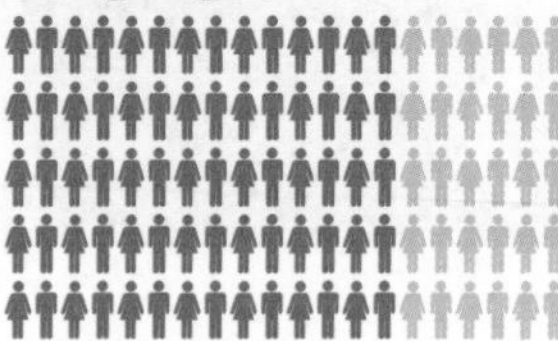

70 would live in a rural area
30 would live in an urban area

Despite Ratsiraka's refusal to sign the roadmap, the progress was held as a milestone. In December 2011, the EU announced it would conditionally support the transition process in Madagascar and work towards restarting its development cooperation.

Tourists also started to come back in 2011; after deserting the country since the events of 2009, visitor numbers were back to mid-noughties levels – welcome morale and economic boosts.

At the time of writing, HAT was planning to run elections in 2012. A number of contentious issues remained, none trickier than the return of Rajoelina's nemesis, disgraced former president Marc Ravalomanana.

Prospects

Madagascar has suffered immensely from the political crisis: it affected its international standing and cut off vital donor funding for public investments, notably infrastructure. Foreign investment has also been affected, with investors unsure about whether a contract signed with one administration would be honoured by the next.

There is much activity in the extractive industry, where iron ore, oil and gas exploration concessions have showed promising results. The Malagasy are anxious to see the proceeds of their mineral wealth trickle through, but there is concern too about the social and environmental impacts of such projects.

More than anything else, though, the Malagasy want to move on. In a country where half the population is under the age of 18, the desire for change is palpable. As one Malagasy put it, 'we have all the ingredients to make a great dish but we've never found a good cook'. So bring on the elections.

The political crisis increased poverty levels by more than 9% between 2005 and 2010. In 2009, Madagascar's GDP actually decreased by nearly 4%, and only grew by 0.3% in 2010 and 0.7% in 2011. Projections predict a more dynamic 2% in 2012.

Top DVDs

Madagascar (2005) With a stellar cast of voice-overs, this cartoon raised Madagascar's profile.

Madagascar (2011) A three-part series by the BBC, narrated by Sir David Attenborough, showcasing the island's wildlife.

Top News Sources

Jeune Afrique (www.jeuneafrique.com/pays/madagascar/madagascar.asp)

All Africa (http://allafrica.com/madagascar/)

La Tribune de Madagascar (www.madagascartribune.com)

Top Websites

Wild Madagascar (www.wildmadagascar.org) Background information and conservation news.

David Attenborough's Madagascar (www.bbc.co.uk/nature/collections/p00db3n8) Lots of inspirational videos and images.

History

In the grand scheme of history, Madagascar is a baby. Although the country has existed in its current form for nearly 100 million years, humans only set foot on the island about 2000 years ago.

Madagascar's first settlers came from Southeast Asia and were soon joined by migrants from neighbouring Africa and the Arabian Peninsula. This melting pot of Indian Ocean populations evolved in distinct kingdoms, which were only brought together as a unified people in the 18th century, and after much resistance.

This newfound unity proved too weak to sustain the repeated onslaught of European imperialists, however. The French eventually claimed Madagascar as their own in 1896, a title they retained until 1960. The independence movement had started during the 1930s, and after a brief interruption during WWII, regained momentum in the 1950s.

It took another decade or so to shake off colonialism's long shadow, and in 1975 President Didier Ratsiraka took Madagascar on a radically different path to socialism. The experiment came to an unhappy end in 1993, following elections brought about by two years of violent protests.

Since then, Madagascar has bumped from one violently ousted leader to the next. In 1996, Albert Zafy was impeached for abuse of power and Ratsiraka made a brief comeback; he was eventually forced into exile in France after contesting the victory of Marc Ravalomanana in the 2001–02 presidential elections. In 2009, it was Ravalomanana's turn to be given the boot, after popular uprisings brought Andry Rajoelina to power.

Malagasies now, understandably, hope for peaceful, fair and free elections to choose their next president.

Best History Books

» *A History of Madagascar*, by Mervyn Brown

» *Madagascar: A Short History*, by Solofo Randrianja and Stephen Ellis

Arrivals from Asia & Europe

Considering that human beings evolved on the African continent just across the Mozambique Channel, their arrival in Madagascar was comparatively

TIMELINE

5th century BC

Although hard evidence has yet to be found, some scholars believe that humans may have arrived in Madagascar as early as the 5th century BC.

5th century AD

Madagascar is settled by Indo-Malayans who migrate by sea from the distant shores of Indonesia and Malaysia. They bring with them agricultural, linguistic and cultural traditions.

15th century

Arabic script brought by Muslim immigrants is adapted to Malagasy language. Sorabe ('Great Writings') is the preserve of a selected few and used only for high-profile documents.

SORABE

Sorabe ('Great Writings', from the Arabic word *sora*, 'to write', and the Malagasy *be*, meaning 'big') is an early written form of Malagasy using Arabic script. The earliest Sorabe manuscripts were written sometime after the 15th century under the influence of Muslim traders (academics disagree on whether they were from the Arabian Peninsula or what is now Indonesia) who wanted to reproduce pages of the Koran. Sorabe was later used to write histories and genealogies, astrologers' predictions and various works on traditional medicine. Knowledge of the script was primarily the preserve of specially trained scribes known as *katibo*. Most Sorabe manuscripts are in the possession of the Antaimoro and Antambohoaka tribes in southeast Madagascar, although the oldest surviving example is conserved in a library in Paris.

late (around AD 400) and by a rather circuitous route. Anthropological and ethnographical clues indicate that Indo-Malayan seafarers may have colonised the island after migrating in a single voyage, stopping en route at various points in the Indian Ocean. Their coastal craft possibly worked their way along the shores of India, Arabia and East Africa, trading as they went, before finally arriving in Madagascar. Linguistic clues also support this theory, as elements of Sanskrit have been identified in the Malagasy language.

These first settlers brought with them the food crops of their homelands, such as rice. This Asian influence was tempered over the years by contact with Arab and African traders, who plied the seas of the region with their cargoes of silks, spices and slaves. Gradually the Asian culture of the new settlers was subsumed into a series of geographically defined kingdoms, which in turn gave rise to many different Malagasy tribes.

Marco Polo was the first European to report the existence of a 'great red island', which he named Madagascar, after possibly having confused it with Mogadishu in Somalia. But Arab cartographers had long known the island as Gezirat Al-Komor, meaning 'island of the moon' (a name later transferred to the Comoros). It wasn't until 1500 that the first Europeans set foot on Madagascar, when a fleet of Portuguese vessels arrived. The Dutch and British tried to establish permanent bases at various points around the coast, only to be defeated by disease and less-than-friendly locals.

More successful were the efforts of buccaneers from Britain, France and elsewhere, who from the end of the 17th century onwards made Madagascar a base from which they attacked merchant ships sailing between India and Europe.

The word for zebu cattle in Malagasy is *hen'omby*, which is of Bantu origin. Linguists have established that all words used for domestic animals have African roots, confirming the fact that African migrants who settled on the island brought with them the prized animals.

1500

Portuguese sailors under the command of Diego Dias become the first Europeans to set foot on Madagascar; Dias names the island Ilha de São Lourenço.

1600

Malagasy kings do a brisk trade in slaves with African, European and Arab traders. It is estimated that up to 150,000 slaves were exported during the 17th century.

Late 18th century

Merina chief Ramboasalama assumes the throne at Ambohimanga and, with the help of European arms traders and military advisors, unifies the various Merina peoples into a powerful kingdom.

1817

Radama I enters into diplomatic relations with Great Britain, beginning a period of British influence that carries on well into the 19th century. Missionaries convert the Merina court to Christianity.

'No Frontier but the Sea'

As Malagasy trade with Europe grew during the 18th century, several rival kingdoms began to vie for dominance. The Menabe people under Andriamisara I founded a capital on the banks of the Sakalava River, from which the modern-day Sakalava tribe took its name. Meanwhile on the east coast, Ratsimilaho – the son of an English pirate and a Malagasy princess – succeeded in unifying rival tribes into a people that became known as the Betsimisaraka. In central Madagascar a certain Chief Ramboasalama took the snappy name Andrianampoinimerinandriantsimitoviaminandriampanjaka (Andrianampoinimerina for short), meaning 'Hope of Imerina', and unified the Merina into a powerful kingdom that soon came to dominate much of Madagascar.

Criminal suspects under Queen Ranavalona I were forced to drink a strong poison called *tanguin*. If they vomited profusely enough, they were declared innocent. Most died.

In 1810 Andrianampoinimerina was succeeded by his equally ambitious son Radama I, who organised a highly trained army that conquered Boina (the main Sakalava kingdom in northwestern Madagascar), the Betsimisaraka peoples to the east, the Betsileo to the south and the kingdom of Antakarana in the far north, whose warrior princes preferred suicide or exile to surrender. Unable to take the Sakalava kingdom of Menabe by force, Radama prudently married Princess Rasalimo, daughter of the Menabe king, thereby fulfilling a vow made by his father that the Merina kingdom would have 'no frontier but the sea'.

His empire-building complete, Radama I set about courting European powers, especially Great Britain. The London Missionary Society (LMS) soon arrived with a contingent of Welsh missionaries who set about converting the Merina court and educating children in schools.

In 1828 Radama died at the tender age of 36. His successor was his widow Ranavalona I, who promptly set about reversing Radama's policies. Ties with European powers were almost severed, and those who refused to abandon Christianity (a European import) were hurled over the cliffs outside the Rova in Antananarivo (Tana). During her 33 years in power, Ranavalona elevated torture and execution to new plateaus of inventiveness. She was said to be sexually insatiable and had a stream of lovers.

When Rainilaiarivony assassinated Radama II, he strangled him with a silken cord to avoid the *fady* (taboo) over the shedding of royal blood.

French Conquest & Colonialism

Ranavalona died in 1861, understandably unlamented by what remained of her subjects. Her son Radama II succeeded her. He was a reformer, and he rescinded most of his mother's policies and welcomed back the Europeans.

In May 1862, however, Radama II was assassinated. Rainilaiarivony, the king's assassin, took the post of prime minister and married Radama's widow, who took the title Rasoherina I. He quickly issued an edict

1828

Ranavalona I becomes queen, commencing a 33-year reign. She declares Christianity illegal and denounces European influence, with the exception of industrialist Jean Laborde.

1835

The Bible is published in Malagasy, following the London Missionary Society's transliteration of the language in Roman alphabet. Until then, Malagasy had been written in the Arabic script Sorabe.

1840s

French engineer Jean Laborde kick-starts Madagascar's industrial revolution by building an industrial complex in Mantasoa complete with brickworks, blast furnaces, arms and munitions factory and textile mills.

1861

Ranavalona dies and Radama II becomes king, abolishing forced labour and reinstating freedom of religion. Missionary activity begins to expand, and Christianity becomes the predominant religion of Madagascar.

stating that the queen could act only with the consent of her ministers – effectively leaving the real power to him, her husband.

Rasoherina survived until 1868 and was succeeded by Ranavalona II, who died in 1883 and was succeeded by Ranavalona III. Prime Minister Rainilaiarivony had married both queens and became the principal power behind the throne, building a magnificent residence in Antananarivo.

By the late 19th century, British interest in Madagascar had begun to wane, and French influence had increased. That influence turned into outright aggression in 1883, when French warships occupied major ports and forced the Malagasy government to sign a treaty declaring the island a French protectorate. Further demands ensued, and in 1894 the French accused the Merina government of tyranny and demanded the capitulation of Queen Ranavalona III. When she rejected their demands, a French army marched on Antananarivo, taking the capital in September 1895.

On 6 August 1896 Madagascar was officially declared a French colony. A year later Queen Ranavalona III was sent into exile in Algeria, and the Merina monarchy was abolished.

Merina Sights in Antananarivo

» Ambohimanga

» Rova

» Musée Andafivaratra

» Ilafy

» Antsahadinta

JEAN LABORDE

One of the few Europeans Queen Ranavalona tolerated was a French engineer, Jean Laborde (he was in fact her lover). Laborde was shipwrecked on the east coast of Madagascar in 1831, at a time when Ranavalona was busy sending Europeans packing. Laborde's engineering skills didn't go unnoticed, however, and Ranavalona, ever the cunning ruler, sensed an opportunity: she granted Laborde large tracts of land and access to unlimited forced labour if he could provide her with weapons, that would in turn expedite the job of getting rid of foreigners.

Laborde set to work and within a few years he had not only built an arms and munitions factory in Mantasoa (about 60km east of Antananarivo), but a complete industrial complex, too, with blast furnaces to produce cast iron, puddling mills to produce wrought iron, a steel plant, glassworks, brickworks, a cement plant and textile mills. He also built a summer palace for Ranavalona in Ambohimanga and contributed to a host of engineering projects, from roads to bridges.

As Ranavalona became more and more tyrannical, Laborde decided to take part in a plot to overthrow her in 1857. The coup failed and Laborde was banned from the island. The 1200 or so labourers that had slaved on the Mantasoa industrial complex took the opportunity to rebel and torched the place – the few buildings left standing can still be viewed in Mantasoa.

Laborde was invited back in 1861 by Radama II, Ranavalona's son, and was made France's first consul to the Merina court by Napoleon III. Laborde died in 1878 in Madagascar and is buried in Mantasoa, on a hill overlooking what was once the engine of Madagascar's industrial revolution.

1862

Radama II is assassinated by Rainilaiarivony, who becomes prime minister and marries Radama's widow, Rasoherina I. He will also marry the next two queens, Ranavalona II and Ranavalona III.

» Rainilaiarivony's palace

1896

Madagascar becomes a French colony; Governor-General Joseph Gallieni declares French the official language and sets about destroying the power of the Merina and removing all British influence.

1930s

A Malagasy independence movement begins to gather momentum, fuelled by resentment of the French colonials by a growing, educated middle class and led by nationalist leader Jean Ralaimongo.

Malagasy Nationalism & Independence

In the early 20th century Madagascar's new rulers abolished slavery, although it was replaced with an almost equally exploitative system of taxes. Land was expropriated by foreign settlers, and a coffee-based import and export economy developed. With economic growth and an expanding education system, a new Malagasy elite began to emerge, and resentment of the colonial presence grew in all levels of society. Several nationalist movements evolved among the Merina and Betsileo tribes, and strikes and demonstrations became more frequent.

Nationalist leader Jean Ralaimongo began the Malagasy independence movement in the 1930s, but his campaign was cut short by the outbreak of WWII. During the first half of WWII the French in Madagascar came under the authority of the pro-Nazi Vichy government. But the Allies, fearing the Japanese could use Madagascar as a base to attack shipping, launched a seaborne attack and captured the town of Diego Suarez. Antananarivo and other major towns also fell to the British after months of fighting but were handed back to the Free French (those who fought on the side of the Allies in WWII) of General de Gaulle in 1943.

Nationalist leader Jean Ralaimongo became a slave at the age of seven; he was freed in 1898, when the colonial government abolished slavery. After serving with the French during WWI, he stayed in France and met the young Ho Chi Minh, from whom he got many of his communist ideologies.

Postwar Madagascar experienced a nationalist backlash, with resentment towards the French culminating in a rebellion in March 1947. The rebellion was eventually subdued after an estimated 90,000 Malagasy were killed. During the 1950s nationalist political parties were formed, the most notable being the Parti Social Démocrate (PSD) of Philibert Tsiranana, and reforms paved the way to independence.

On 14 October 1958 the Malagasy Republic was proclaimed, becoming an autonomous state within the French Community. After a period of provisional government, a constitution was adopted in 1959 and full independence was achieved on 26 June 1960, with Tsiranana the country's first president.

Following the euphoria, however, discontent with the country's ongoing ties with France and its poor economic performance grew. Following uprisings in 1971 and 1972, Tsiranana was forced to resign and hand over power to his army commander, General Gabriel Ramanantsoa.

The Third Republic

In February 1975, after several coup attempts, General Ramanantsoa stepped down and was replaced by Colonel Richard Ratsimandrava, who was assassinated within a week of taking office. The rebel army officers who had announced the military takeover were quickly routed by officers loyal to Ramanantsoa, and a new government headed by Admiral Didier Ratsiraka, a former foreign minister, came to power.

WWII

Madagascar is under the authority of the pro-Nazi Vichy French government. Fearing the Japanese could use the island as a base, the Allies attack and capture several towns.

1947

A rebellion led by Joseph Raseta and Joseph Ravoahangy is brutally suppressed by the French; thousands of Malagasy are killed and the rebellion's leaders are sent into exile.

26 June 1960

Madagascar gains full independence from France in a peaceful transition; Philibert Tsiranana is elected president, though in effect the French still run the country and maintain military bases.

1975

General Gabriel Ramanantsoa steps down after coup attempts; his followers appoint Admiral Didier Ratsiraka as leader. Ratsiraka adopts Soviet-style ideology and cuts ties with France, leading to economic decline.

Ratsiraka attempted radical political and social reforms in the late 1970s, severing all ties with France and courting favour with former Soviet-bloc nations.

In March 1989, Ratsiraka was returned for a third seven-year term in an election that some regarded as questionable. It sparked riots, and 1991 was marked by widespread demonstrations demanding the president's resignation. The country ground to a halt as a result of general strikes and riots, and protests left dozens dead.

In late October 1991, an agreement was signed with opposition politicians in preparation for popular elections and the birth of the so-called 'Third Republic'. However, Ratsiraka still refused to step down. In July 1992 there was an attempted civilian coup, but the rebels failed to gain popular support and were forced to surrender.

Elections were finally held in 1993 and resulted in victory for opposition candidate Professor Albert Zafy, ending Ratsiraka's first 17 years in power. After trying to sack his prime minister, Zafy was unexpectedly impeached by his parliament in July 1996 for abuse of authority. New presidential elections were called in November 1996 and to the surprise of everyone, including international monitors, Ratsiraka (who had been in exile in France for the previous 19 months) won.

Reform & a New Optimism

Self-made millionaire Marc Ravalomanana began his path to success by pedalling around his home town on a bicycle selling pots of homemade yoghurt. By the time he became mayor of Antananarivo in 1999, his company, Tiko, was the biggest producer of dairy products in Madagascar.

Ravalomanana announced his candidacy for the presidency of Madagascar under the banner of his TIM party (which stands in Malagasy for 'I Love Madagascar') in December 2001 and went head to head with Didier Ratsiraka. Upon hearing the results, both men insisted they had won; a bitter six-month struggle for power ensued. As Ravalomanana swore himself in as president, Ratsiraka declared a state of emergency and imposed martial law.

The military eventually swung towards Ravalomanana, tipping the balance of power, and in April 2002 the Malagasy High Constitutional Court declared Ravalomanana the outright winner. By August Ravalomanana's administration had received endorsement from the UN, then won a convincing majority in elections for the National Assembly. Ratsiraka refused to accept that the game was over but left for exile in France anyway.

Ravalomanana quickly set about his reform agenda, introducing a new currency (the ariary). Foreign investors were cheered by a major hike in economic growth, and wooed by laws that provided tax breaks and allowed foreigners to own land.

At the World's Park Conference in Durban in 2003, then president Marc Ravalomanana announced his intention to triple Madagascar's protected areas, a commitment that remains on the agenda.

Late 1970s

Ratsiraka pushes his nationalist agenda; French is no longer taught in primary schools and he decrees that towns must be known by their Malagasy names.

1991

Economic decline ignites widespread strikes and protests; the 'Third Republic' calls for elections but Ratsiraka refuses to step down. Opposition leader Albert Zafy is eventually elected president in 1993.

1996

Among widespread accusations of criminal activities, President Zafy is impeached for abuse of power and general elections are called. Ratsiraka is returned to power and becomes president again in 1997.

2001

Former yoghurt peddler Marc Ravalomanana swears himself in as president. Ratsiraka declares martial law, and violent protests ensue; Ravalomanana is declared the winner after a six-month showdown.

Ravalomanana comfortably won a second term in office in 2006; on the back of his electoral success, he organised a referendum to change the constitution, many of the amendments conferring on him more power (notably the option of standing for two more terms). The referendum scraped by, but the opposition was outraged by what they saw as an increasingly autocratic government.

The Coup

Despite growing discontent, in July 2008 Ravalomanana signed a 99-year lease with Korean company Daewoo Logistics for 13,000 sq km of land for maize cultivation, half of all arable land on the island. The deal caused consternation (and was later rescinded) in a country where land customarily belongs to ancestors.

For many, the Daewoo deal was the straw that broke the camel's back. Andry Rajoelina, then mayor of Antananarivo and a former DJ, rallied opponents under his new TGV party. Following the closure of his TV channel TV Viva in December 2008, violent protests ensued. On 7 February 2009, the army opened fire on protesters gathered in front of the presidential palace, killing 40 and injuring more than 200. With international pressure mounting, Ravalomanana finally handed his resignation to the army on 17 March 2009 and fled to South Africa. Within a few hours the army had swiftly passed all powers to Rajoelina, who was sworn in as president of the High Transitional Authority (Haute Autorité de Transition; HAT).

The events were widely condemned by the international community as a coup, and the result was that the EU, the US and the UN refused to recognise Rajoelina as Madagascar's legitimate leader and turned off the international aid taps.

The HAT had promised to hold elections within 24 months, but as this book went to press, a firm date had yet to be announced.

TIKO

Once one of the largest companies in the country, Tiko, Marc Ravalomanana's yoghurt empire, was ransacked, pillaged and forced to suspend operations following the uprisings of 2009. It was rumoured in 2011 that Ravalomanana's son was keen to restart it.

2006

Marc Ravalomanana is swept to office for a second term as president. Encouraging economic growth leads the World Bank to wipe US$20 billion from Madagascar's national debt.

GAMMA-RAPHO VIA GETTY IMAGES ©

» Marc Ravalomanana

July 2008

Ravalomanana signs a deal with Korean company Daewoo Logistics to lease 13,000 sq km of arable land for 99 years, a move widely perceived as treason.

March 2009

Antananarivo mayor Andry Rajoelina overthrows Ravalomanana in an army-backed coup. The UN and the EU refuse to recognise the new government; international donors withhold all aid.

Malagasy Life

Behaviour & Etiquette

On arrival in Madagascar your first impression is likely to be of a polite but rather reserved people. This apparent timidity is a reflection of *fihavanana*, which means 'conciliation' or 'brotherhood': it stresses avoidance of confrontation and achievement of compromise in all walks of life. It is unseemly to discuss some subjects, such as personal problems, even with close friends. Likewise, searching or indiscreet questions are avoided at all costs.

Politeness in general is very important to the Malagasy, and impatience or pushy behaviour is regarded as shocking. Passengers queuing for a flight, for instance, will place their tickets in a neat row on the check-in desk or put their luggage in an orderly line before patiently awaiting their turn.

The welcoming of strangers and the traditions of hospitality are held sacred throughout Madagascar. It is considered a household duty to offer food and water to a guest, no matter how poor the inhabitants are themselves. In return, travellers should always honour this hospitality by accepting what has been offered to them.

Most Malagasy surnames start with the honorary prefix 'Ra', the equivalent of 'Mr'. Similarly, many kings' names started with 'Andriana', a term that roughly translates as 'noble'.

Population & Language

Malagasy people are divided into 18 tribes, whose boundaries are roughly based on old kingdoms. Tribal divisions are still evident between ancient enemies such as the Merina and the Antakàrana. Also important is the distinction between Merina highlanders – who have more prominent Asian origins and are associated with the country's aristocracy – and so-called *côtiers* (literally, 'those from the coast'), whose African influences are more pronounced and who are often looked down on by the Merina. In Antananarivo, well-off *côtières* (women from the coast) often straighten their hair to avoid discrimination against their coastal origins.

The main ethnic groups are Merina, who make up 27% of the population, Betsimisaraka (15%), Betsileo (12%), Tsimihety (7%), Sakalava (6%), Antaisaka (5%) and Antandroy (5%). There are also small groups of Indian, Chinese, Comorian and French living on the island.

FADY

Fady is the name given to local taboos designed to respect the ancestors. *Fady* can take innumerable forms and vary widely from village to village. It may be *fady* to whistle on a particular stretch of beach, to walk past a sacred tree, to eat pork or to swim in a certain river.

Although foreigners will be excused for breaking *fady*, travellers should make every effort to respect these taboos. The best thing to do is to ask locals for information, and to be particularly careful on sacred sites and in the vicinity of tombs or burial sites.

Malagasy Ethnic Groups

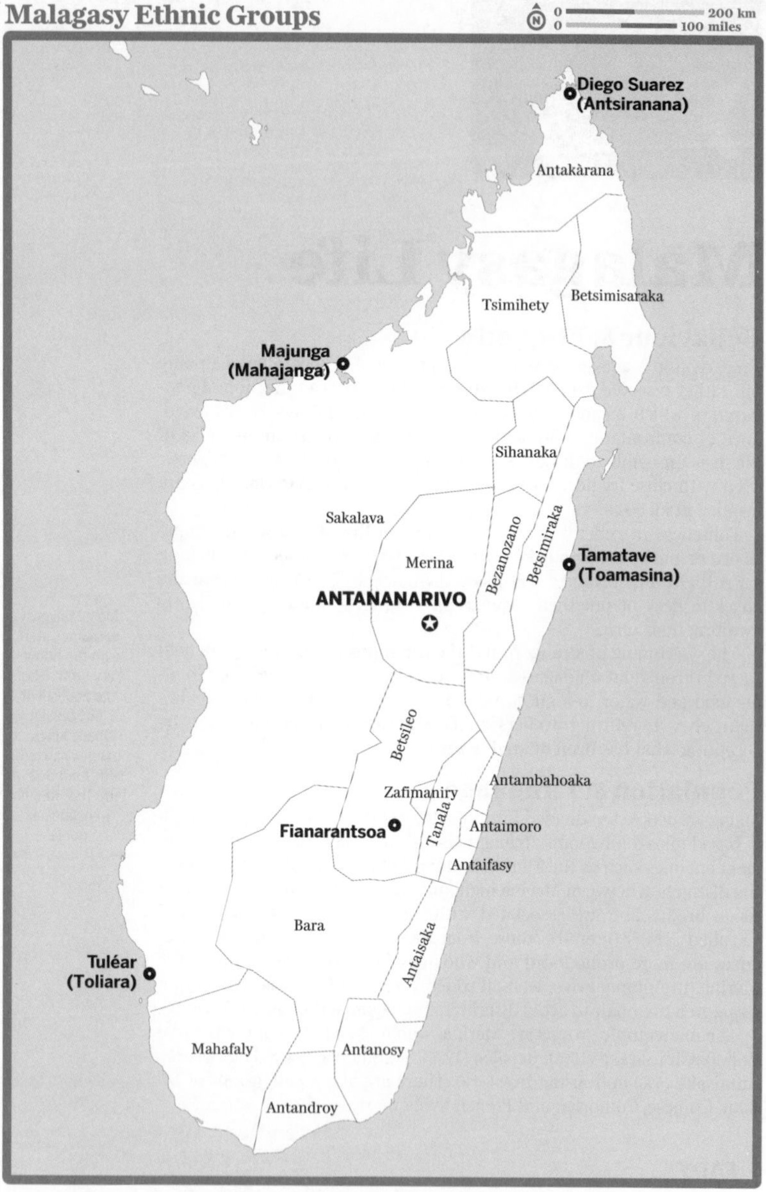

0 200 km
0 100 miles

Diego Suarez (Antsiranana)
Antakàrana
Tsimihety
Betsimisaraka
Majunga (Mahajanga)
Sihanaka
Sakalava
Merina
Bezanozano
Betsimiraka
Tamatave (Toamasina)
ANTANANARIVO
Betsileo
Antambahoaka
Zafimaniry
Tanala
Antaimoro
Fianarantsoa
Antaifasy
Bara
Antaisaka
Tuléar (Toliara)
Mahafaly
Antanosy
Antandroy

This ethnic patchwork is matched by a hotchpotch of dialects. The official Malagasy language of newspapers and schools is based on the Malagasy of the Merina people, but each region has its own dialect. Vocabulary and accents vary to the extent that people from different provinces struggle to understand one another.

Religion & Beliefs

About half of Madagascar's population adheres to traditional beliefs, while the efforts of proselytising Europeans during the 19th century have resulted in the other half worshipping at Catholic and Protestant churches. A small proportion is Muslim. In recent years, evangelical churches have become popular, too, with charismatic preachers, inspirational singing and dancing, and unusual venues (from stadiums to town halls).

Even Christian Malagasies retain great respect for traditional beliefs, which are rooted in reverence for one's ancestors and their spirits. Among most tribes, this is manifested in a complex system of *fady* (taboos) and burial rites, the best known of which is the ceremonial exhumation and reburial known as *famadihana* (literally, 'the turning of the bones').

Malagasies invoke spirits for protection, fertility or good health at sacred sites, be it a baobab tree, a forest waterfall or a royal tomb; you'll recognise these sites from the offerings (zebu horns, *lamba* scarves, small denominations, blood, honey, sweets etc). Praying and offering ceremonies are popular Sunday family outings and are often accompanied by a picnic.

Concepts of time and date also have a great influence. Malagasies strongly believe in *vintana* (destiny), which determines the most auspicious date for activities (building a house, planting a new crop etc) or events such as circumcisions, weddings or funerals. Each day of the week has its connotations: Wednesdays and Fridays are good for funerals; Saturday, which is associated with nobility, is considered good for celebrations. To make sure that they choose the most favourable date for an occasion, Malagasies will consult a *mpanandro* (astrologer) for guidance on *vintana*.

Every ceremony is invariably accompanied by the slaughter of a zebu, more than one if the family is wealthy or influential in the community. The blood and the horns are valuable offerings, and the meat is shared by those attending.

The complex set of beliefs of the Malagasy has been constructed through the assimilation of diverse influences. The funeral rites of many tribes, for example, have Austronesian roots, while the status of cattle is thought to have African roots; belief in *vintana*, on the other hand, is thought to originate from Islamic cosmology.

A common ritual after the death of a family member is for the entire family to go down to a local river and wash all their clothes, an event you'll often see from the roadside, with clothes drying along the river banks.

RITUALS

FAMADIHANA

On the crest of a hill, a grove of pine trees whispers gently. In the shade, trestle tables are spread with sticky sweetmeats and bowls of steaming rice. A band plays a rollicking, upbeat tune as the stone door of a family tomb is opened. Old ladies wait at the entrance, faces dignified under their straw hats. Middle-aged men indulge in lethal homemade rum, dancing jerkily to the rhythms of the band.

One by one the corpses are brought out of the tomb, wrapped in straw mats and danced above the heads of a joyful throng. The bodies are rewrapped in pristine white burial *lambas* (scarves), sprayed with perfume and meticulously labelled by name with felt-tip pens. Everyone wants to touch the ancestors and talk to them. A period of quiet follows, with family members holding the bodies on their laps in silent communication, weeping but happy at the same time. The air is charged with emotion. Then the bodies are danced one more time around the tomb, a few traditional verses are read out and the stone is sealed with mud for another seven years.

Famadihana ceremonies take place between July and September in the *hauts plateaux* (highlands) region from Antananarivo south to Ambositra. These days it's generally OK to attend one, as long as your visit is arranged through a hotel or local tour company. On no account should you visit without an invitation and never take photos unless specific permission has been granted.

Family Life & Home

The family is the central tenet of Malagasy life, and includes not only distant cousins but also departed ancestors. Even urban, modern Malagasies, who reject the belief that ancestors have magic powers, regard those who are no longer alive as full members of the family. *Famadihanas* are an opportunity to communicate with ancestors. Families spend a great deal of time and money on family reunions, and taxis-brousses (bush taxis) are often full of individuals visiting relatives.

If you see a young Malagasy man wearing a comb in his hair, he's advertising his search for a wife.

Malagasy homes are arranged according to astrological principles: the northeast corner is the noble and auspicious part of the house; doors always face west. Many Malagasies think that life on earth is temporary, whereas life after death is permanent, so families will favour lavish tombs and keep a modest house.

Marriage is a pretty relaxed institution and divorce is common. Children are seen as the primary purpose of marriage, and essential to happiness and security. The idea that some people might choose not to have children is greeted with disbelief.

Women

Women are a dynamic force in Malagasy society. They are very active in the workplace and are represented at every echelon of society: from street vendor to politician, school teacher to entrepreneur. Women are also regarded as the head of the domestic sphere, even if they also go out to work.

Women tend to marry and have children young: 16 or younger is typical in rural areas, 20 is about average in urban areas, where women are more likely to go through secondary and superior education. A woman will generally move to her husband's village. Polygamy exists but is not commonplace.

Sexually, Malagasy society is fairly liberated; women can dress however they want, and they can be quite forward with sexual advances to men, including foreigners. Prostitution is rampant in a number of areas, and travellers should be aware that sex tourism is heavily punished, particularly if minors are involved.

Economy

Most Malagasies bemoan the fact that their country, despite having so much going for it, has failed to develop economically. The political instability and economic mismanagement are to blame. Madagascar therefore remains one of the world's poorest countries. It ranked 151 out of 182 countries in the 2011 Human Development Index of the UN Development Programme (UNDP); its GDP in 2010 was US$8.7 billion (130 on the World Bank's ranking), lower than that of Afghanistan, Yemen or the Congo.

Household Facts

- Households with access to sanitation: 40%
- Households that have drinking water: 45%
- Children who go to primary school: 73%
- Students who carry on to university: 1%

Madagascar's economy is mainly subsistence agriculture, with rice, cassava, bananas and yam as the main food crops. The principal cash crops are coffee, vanilla, sugar cane, lychee, cloves and cocoa, with coffee and vanilla earning a substantial percentage of foreign exchange. Most foreign trade is with France, the EU and the USA.

There is a small amount of manufacturing, largely restricted to agricultural products, but the textiles industry was dealt a severe blow when Madagascar lost its eligibility for the African Growth and Opportunity Act (AGOA) – a legislation that allowed sub-Saharan countries preferential access to the US market – in the wake of the political meltdown of 2009. Some 40,000 people lost their jobs as a result.

Public investment has also suffered greatly in the last few years: foreign aid represented nearly 50% of the state's budget, but international donors have withheld all funds since the 2009 coup.

VANILLA

The vanilla plant was introduced to Madagascar from Mexico by French plantation owners over the course of the 19th century. They named it *vanille* (*lavanila* in Malagasy), from the Spanish *vainilla* or 'little pod'. It is a type of climbing orchid, *Vanila planifolia*, which attaches itself to trees. Each flower must be hand-pollinated, which makes vanilla production extremely labour-intensive. The vanilla seeds grow inside long pods hanging from the plant, which are collected and cured in factories.

Madagascar produces about 65% to 80% of the world's vanilla. The plant grows most abundantly in the northeastern parts of the country, particularly the SAVA region (comprising Sambava, Andapa, Vohémar and Antalaha), where the hot and wet climate of the coast is ideally suited for its cultivation.

Cyclone Hudah destroyed more than 20% of Madagascar's vanilla crop in 2000, causing a shortage of supply and a huge escalation in price. Combined with the political instability of the 2002 elections and more bad weather in 2003, prices of vanilla spiked at US$500 per kilogram in 2004. Since this historic high, however, vanilla prices have remained relatively flat, at around US$30 to US$40 a kilo.

Sport

Malagasies love watching international football (soccer; the English Premier League, in particular) and rugby (the French and European leagues, notably). For all this enthusiasm, however, the national football and rugby teams have yet to make a splash on the international stage.

Where Malagasies punch above their weight is in the rather niche sport of *pétanque*, a form of boule (played with metal balls on dirt ground). A French import, it's become a case of the student outdoing (or certainly equalling) the master: Madagascar won the Pétanque World Championship in 1999, it was vice-world champion in 2010 and Africa champion in 2011 (it will represent Africa at the world championship in France in 2012). Madagascar has also won numerous international opens, so don't be surprised to see the game played up and down the country, on the beach, in village squares or wherever there is a flat enough bit of ground.

Arts

Literature

The earliest Malagasy literature dates from historical records produced in the mid-19th century. Modern poetry and literature began to flourish in the 1930s and 1940s. The best-known figure was the poet Jean-Joseph Rabearivelo, who committed suicide in 1947 at the age of 36 – reputedly after the colonial administration decided to send a group of basket-weavers to France to represent the colony instead of him.

Two excellent collections of Malagasy writing are *Voices from Madagascar: An Anthology of Contemporary Francophone Literature*, edited by Jacques Bourgeacq and Liliane Ramarosoa, which contains Malagasy writing in French and English, and *Hainteny: The Traditional Poetry of Madagascar*, by Leonard Fox, with translations of beautiful Merina poems charting love, revenge and sexuality.

Modern-day literary figures include Michèle Rakotoson, Johary Ravaloson, David Jaomanoro and Jean-Luc Raharimanana. Nearly all of their works are published in French or Malagasy.

Oral Traditions

Hira gasy are popular music, dancing and storytelling spectacles held in the central highlands of Madagascar. Brightly clad troupes of 25 performers compete for prizes for the best costumes or the most exciting spectacle. An important part of *hira gasy* is *kabary,* in which a performer delivers an oratory using allegory, double entendre, metaphor and simile. *Hira gasy* has long been used to deliver important information or raise awareness of certain topics (health, politics, environmental issues, respecting family values etc). Unfortunately, unless you are fluent in Malagasy, you're unlikely to agree with the proverb that says: 'While listening to a *kabary* well spoken, one fails to notice the fleas that bite one'. All the same, it is a cultural event well worth seeing.

More accessible are the songs and dances after the *kabary*. Dancers are dressed in bright gowns called *malabary*, and women also wear the traditional *lamba* (scarf). The competition winner is decided by audience members, who throw small denominations at their favourite troupe.

Music

Most traditional Malagasy music revolves around favourite dance rhythms: the *salegy* of the Sakalava tribe, with both Indonesian and Kenyan influences; *watsa watsa* from Mozambique and the Congo; the *tsapika*, originating in the south; and the *sigaoma*, similar to South African music.

Over the Lip of the World: Among the Storytellers of Madagascar, by Colleen J McElroy, is a journey through Malagasy oral traditions and myths.

The most widely played traditional wind instrument is the *kiloloka*, a whistlelike length of bamboo capable of only one note. Melodies are played by a group of musicians, in a manner similar to a bell ensemble. The tubular instrument you'll see on sale at tourist shops and craft markets is a *valiha*, which has 28 strings of varying lengths stretched around a tubular wooden sound box; it resembles a bassoon but is played more like a harp. It has fallen out of favour in Madagascar but is still played in Malaysia and Indonesia, which may suggest that it was brought to Madagascar by the earliest settlers of the island.

Apart from at special events such as the Donia festival in Nosy Be, traditional Malagasy music can be hard to find and it is often restricted

MADAGASCAR'S GOSSAMER

In 1710, Frenchman François Xavier Bon de Saint Hilaire published a paper considering the use of gossamer (spider silk) instead of that of the silkworm. Silk was – and still is – a hugely valuable material, and finding an alternative source of production was the holy grail of the weaving industry. Bon's experiments were promising – he made gloves and stockings for King Louis XIV – but he struggled to unravel the spider's cocoon into a single continuous strand because of a binding glue.

It wasn't until 1761 that Spanish Jesuit Raimondo de Termeyer worked out a way of extracting the thread directly from the spider's spinnerets. A number of experiments continued until the early 20th century, but spider silk never really took off on a large scale.

Madagascar's golden orb spider – which you'll see everywhere in the highlands if you look up at branches and cables – has long been known for the quality of its silk: as well as being a divine saffron colour, it is about five times stronger than steel by weight.

In 2004, British textile expert Simon Peers and US entrepreneur Nicholas Godley decided to give gossamer another go. A million golden orb spiders, a few bites, and miles of gossamer later, Peers and Godley were able to display an 11ft-long, hand-woven golden-hued shawl at the American Museum of Natural History in New York in 2009. The design of the brocaded shawl was inspired by 19th-century Merina weaving traditions.

The shawl captivated the public's imagination with its ethereal beauty, and it was displayed at the Art Institute of Chicago the following year. In 2012 it was exhibited at London's Victoria & Albert Museum, along with another cape specially made for the exhibition.

to rural areas. Malagasy pop music is usually a cheesy blend of guitar rock, rough-and-ready rap and hip hop, and soulful ballads, a genre best represented by national treasure Poopy (yes, that's her real name). For more traditional sounds, Jerry Marcos, a master of *salegy*, is guaranteed to have you shaking your stuff like there is no tomorrow.

A number of musicians have artfully mixed pop and traditional influences, including the wonderful singer-songwriter Nogabe Randriaharimalala (www.nogabe.com), Njava (www.myspace.com/njava) and Tarika.

Apart from the Donia and Zegny'Zo festivals, the best place to see live performances is at the bigger venues in Antananarivo – look in the newspapers on Friday for event details (p39).

Arts Performances

- *Hira gasy*, Antananarivo
- Zegny'Zo festival, Diego Suarez
- Donia festival, Nosy Be
- Le Glacier, Antananarivo
- Institut Français, Antananarivo

Architecture

Each region of Madagascar has its own architectural style and building materials. The Merina and Betsileo of the *hauts plateaux* (highlands) live in distinctive red-brick houses that are warm on cold nights. The typical Merina home is a tall, narrow affair with small windows and brick pillars in the front that support open verandahs. The Betsileo areas dispense with the pillars and trim their houses with elaborately carved wood. Coastal homes are generally constructed of lighter local materials, including *ravinala* (literally, 'forest leaves'; also known as travellers' palm) and raffia palm.

The interesting film *Quand les Étoiles Rencontrent la Mer* (When the Stars Meet the Sea), directed by the Malagasy Raymond Rajaonarivelo, is the story of a young boy born during a solar eclipse.

Textile Arts

Textiles have always played a huge part in Malagasy society, with some types of cloth even being imbued, it is believed, with supernatural powers. The Merina used cocoons collected from the wild silkworm to make highly valued textiles called *lamba mena* (red silk). The silks were woven in many colours and pattern combinations, and in the past had strong links with royal prestige, expressed by the colour red. Worn by the aristocracy in life and death, *lamba mena* were also used in burial and reburial ceremonies.

Lamba are still used in funeral rites and you'll see red-and-white cloths tied to sacred trees across the country, tokens of gratitude to ancestors for fulfilled prayers.

Malagasy Cuisine

Food is taken seriously in Madagascar, where French, Chinese and Indian influences have blended with local eating traditions into an exciting and often mouth-watering cuisine. Regional variations are many, with a variety of fruit, vegetables and seafood dictating local tastes and recipes.

Malagasy Classics

Eating rice three times a day is so ingrained in Malagasy culture that people sometimes claim they can't sleep if they haven't eaten rice that day. In fact, the verb 'to eat' in Malagasy, *mihinam-bary*, literally means 'to eat rice'.

Rice is eaten on its own for breakfast, in porridge form; for lunch and dinner it is generally accompanied by a helping of meat, such as *hen'omby* (boiled zebu), *hen'ankisoa* (pork), *hen'akoho* (chicken or duck) or *hen'andrano* (fish). Common preparations include *ravitoto* (stew – usually beef or pork – with manioc greens and coconut), *sauce coco* (a delicious coconut curry, usually with chicken, fish or seafood) and the nondescript *sauce* (generally a tomato-based affair; served with anything from chicken to fish).

The growth of a rice plant is described in Malagasy using the same words as those for a woman becoming pregnant and giving birth.

To keep things interesting, the Malagasies have developed an arsenal of aromatic condiments, such as *sakay* (a red-hot pepper paste with ginger and garlic), *pimente verde* (a fiery green chilli) and *achards* (hot pickled fruit, such as tomato, lemon, carrot or mango, used as relish – you'll see bottles of the stuff sold by the roadside).

Rice Alternatives

The most common alternative to rice is a steaming bowl of *mi sao* (fried noodles with vegetables or meat) or a satisfying *soupe chinoise* (clear noodle soup with fish, chicken or vegetables) – dishes that show the Asian origins of the Malagasy. Poorer rural communities supplement their rice diet with starchy roots such as manioc or corn.

WHERE TO EAT

What you eat in Madagascar will largely depend on *where* you eat. *Hotelys* or *gargotes* are small, informal restaurants found in every city and town; they are cheap and serve no-frills, typical Malagasy fare such as *romazava* (beef and vegetable stew), *poulet sauce* or grilled fish, with a mountain of rice for bulk. The quality ranges from rough to delicious. The tastier Malagasy food is often served in private homes, and what better excuse to make friends with the locals!

Restaurants, which range from modest to top-end establishments, serve various types of cuisines, including fancier versions of Malagasy standards. Quality is invariably good, sometimes outstanding. Many restaurants offer a *menu du jour* (three-course set menu), or a *plat du jour* (daily special), which are generally good value. Prices for these are usually around Ar15,000 to Ar25,000. For à la carte menus, the average price of a main course is Ar10,000 to Ar15,000.

NATIONAL FAVOURITES

Romazava A beef stew in a ginger-flavoured broth; it contains *brêdes mafana*, a green leaf reminiscent of Indian *saag* in taste that will make your tongue and lips tingle thanks to its anaesthetic properties!

Ravitoto Another well-loved Malagasy dish, it is a mix of fried beef or pork with shredded cassava leaves and coconut milk; truly delicious.

Pizza Just like Europeans and Americans, Malagasies have succumbed to pizzas! They are a popular treat among middle-class families and you'll find an inordinate amount of pizza joints (often with takeaway) in every large town and city.

Seafood

Given that Madagascar is an island, it's hardly surprising that seafood features prominently on the menu. Prices are so low that all but those on the tightest budgets can gorge themselves at whim on fish, freshwater crayfish, prawns, lobster and even tiny oysters (from Morondava). Adhering to the motto that less is more, seafood is often cooked simply, grilled or fried, or in *sauce coco*.

The African Cookbook, by Bea Sandler, has some good recipes from Madagascar.

Vegetarians & Vegans

The Malagasy don't find vegetarianism difficult to understand, and they are often more than happy to cater for special diets if you give them enough notice. If you eat eggs, you will have no problem as any restaurant can whip up an omelette. If you don't, getting enough protein could be a problem, as beans and lentils are not widely available.

Snacks & Munchies

One of the first things you'll notice on arriving in Madagascar is the dizzying variety of snacks available at street stalls. Savoury snacks include meat samosas (called *sambos*), small doughnuts called *mofo menakely*, and *masikita* (skewers threaded with grilled beef).

The log-like cake you'll see sold on roadsides is *koba*, a concoction of ground peanuts or pistachios, rice flour and sugar, wrapped tightly in banana leaves, baked and sold in slices. *Hotelys* also make delicious sweet doughnuts, which they serve with a cup of black coffee.

Ma Cuisine Malgache (Karibo Safako), by Angéline Espagne-Ravo, contains the best collection of Malagasy recipes in French.

In towns and cities, you'll also find plenty of patisseries selling cakes, croissants, pastries and meringues. Baguettes can be bought from every street corner, although the quality is often poor.

Gourmet Cuisine

Madagascar has developed a unique strand of haute cuisine that blends Malagasy and French influences and makes the best of local ingredients. Among our favourites are zebu steak with green pepper sauce and *frites* (fries), roast chicken with vanilla mashed potatoes, and grouper in pink peppercorn sauce with sautéed potatoes. For starters, there is *foie gras* (duck-liver pâté), of course; desserts are equally exciting, with chocolate cakes and vanilla custard, crêpes and local fruit jams, exotic sorbets and ice cream.

Gourmet cuisine is served up and down the country in better restaurants and is an absolute highlight of any trip to the red island.

If you're invited to a Malagasy celebration, bring a present (a small amount of money or a bottle of rum). Hold your wrist with the opposite hand when passing food or drinks.

Hot Drinks & Soft Drinks

Most Malagasies like to accompany a rice meal with a drink of rice water. This brown, smoky concoction, known as *ranovola* or *ranon'apango*, is made from boiling water in the pot containing the burnt rice residue –

THE MIGHTY ZEBU

Zebu cattle not only provide status and transport, they are also well known for their excellent meat. Zebu beef is prepared in much the same way as European cattle beef: in stews, kebabs (known locally as *masikita*, often tiny in size) and as succulent steak.

Zebus are synonymous with status and wealth (a zebu costs €500 to €800, a huge amount of money for a Malagasy family); zebu meat is therefore the festive food par excellence. Zebus will be slaughtered for weddings, *famadihanas* (exhumation and reburial ceremonies), circumcisions and other important festivals or events.

The hump, which is brown fat, is a delicacy (it used to be the preserve of the nobility); it is seldom served in restaurants, but it is a must at Malagasy celebrations, where it is served grilled or in kebabs.

definitely an acquired taste. That said, it is the safest water to drink in *hotelys* since it has been boiled.

When you order a beer, you'll generally be asked 'PM ou GM?' Moderately thirsty travellers will opt for PM or Petit Modèle (Small Model, 33cl); parched visitors shall quench their thirst with a GM or Grand Modèle (Big Model, 66cl).

Despite the fact that coffee is grown in Madagascar, only the most upmarket establishments offer espresso or good filter coffee. Elsewhere, you'll have to content yourself with weak black coffee and learn to love condensed milk. Tea is better; TAF-brand teabags are excellent, and the vanilla-flavoured black tea is highly recommended.

Soft drinks (Coke, Pepsi, Fanta) are sold at every bar under the Malagasy sun; Madagascar also produces its own sodas, including the synthetic-tasting Bonbon Anglais ('English sweet'), a lemonade.

Far and away the best sweet drinks, however, are the *jus naturels* (freshly squeezed fruit juices). Local wonders include *corossol* (soursop), *grenadelle* (passionfruit), papaya, mango and whatever is in season. In coastal areas, street vendors sell green coconuts, which they will split open so that you can drink the vitamin-packed juice.

Boozie Delights

The most popular Malagasy beer is Three Horses Beer (universally known as THB). Up a notch in the alcoholic stakes is the island's rum. Most bars and restaurants offer *rhum arrangé* – rum in which a variety of fruits and spices have been left to soak. Common flavours include lemon, ginger, cinnamon, lychee and vanilla, and these alcoholic concoctions generally line the back of the bar in an array of demijohns worthy of an apothecary. *Rhum arrangé* is drunk neat as an aperitif or an after-dinner liqueur.

Although illegal, moonshine (generally known as *toaka gasy*) is widely available; its alcohol content will blow your socks off so go easy on the shots. In eastern Madagascar, the local tipple of choice is *betsa-betsa* (fermented sugar-cane juice), while in the north, *trembo* (palm wine) is popular.

Although Malagasy wines still have some way to go to rival regional counterparts, the Vin Blanc Doux from Clos Malaza is generally held to be the best local vintage and works a treat with the local *foie gras*.

Madagascar's small wine industry is centred on Fianarantsoa. You'll probably want to try a glass out of curiosity, but it's definitely not the island's forte. Imported French and South African wine is served in better restaurants throughout the country.

Celebrations & Customs

A Malagasy proverb says 'the food which is prepared has no master'. In other words, celebrating in Madagascar means eating big. Weddings, funerals, circumcisions and reburials are preceded by days of preparations. Extended family, friends and often passers-by, too, are invited to share the food, usually a combination of meat dishes (note that turkey is considered a meat for special occasions), vegetables and, of course, a mountain of rice. At Malagasy parties, copious quantities of home-brewed rum are consumed, and helpless drunkenness is entirely expected.

Environment

Madagascar is the world's fourth-largest island, after Greenland, Papua New Guinea and Borneo. Its incredibly diverse landscapes and unique wildlife are a product of history: cast adrift from Africa about 165 million years ago, Madagascar took with it a cargo of animals and plants that have been evolving in isolation ever since.

The Land

In the Beginning

What is now the island of Madagascar was once sandwiched between Africa and India as part of the supercontinent Gondwana, a vast ancient land mass that also included Antarctica, South America and Australasia.

Gondwana began to break apart about 180 million years ago, but Madagascar remained joined to Africa at the 'hip' – in the region of modern East Africa – for another 20 million years. About 88 million years ago the eastern half of Madagascar broke off, moving northward to eventually become India, by which time modern Madagascar had drifted to its present position. Since then, Madagascar has remained at its present size and shape, geographically isolated.

The Natural History of Madagascar, by Steven Goodman and Jonathan Benstead, provides the most comprehensive overview of the island's precious natural heritage.

The Eighth Continent

Madagascar measures 1600km on its longest axis, aligned roughly northeast to southwest, and 570km from east to west at its widest point. Almost the entire island is in the tropics, albeit well south of the equator, and only the southern tip protrudes below the Tropic of Capricorn. The 5000km-long coastline features many long, sweeping sandy beaches, with coral reefs and atolls offshore in some areas, and is dotted with some 250 islands, of which Nosy Be and Ile Sainte Marie are the largest. It is such epic numbers that have earned Madagascar the nickname 'the eighth continent'.

A chain of mountains runs down the eastern seaboard, forming a steep escarpment and trapping moisture that helps create the island's

LOST GIANTS

When humans first arrived, Madagascar supported many animals much bigger than contemporary species: hippopotamuses, aardvarks, gorilla-size lemurs and giant flightless birds, similar to modern African birds such as the ostrich, roamed the island. With the arrival of humans, many of the larger animals, which no doubt provided a ready supply of protein, were wiped out. Over the last thousand years, scientists estimate that 16 species of lemur, plus tortoises, the hippopotamuses, giant aardvarks, the world's largest bird (the 3m-high elephant bird *Aepyornis*) and two species of eagle, have become extinct.

See p92 for more on the tragic story of the elephant bird.

rainforests, which are rich in biodiversity. There is no modern volcanic activity on the island, although volcanoes previously erupted in the central highlands.

The island's highest point is 2876m Maromokotro, an extinct volcanic peak in the Tsaratanana massif, followed by the 2658m Pic Imarivolanitra (formerly known as Pic Boby) in Parc National d'Andringitra.

The Eighth Continent: Life, Death and the Discovery in the Lost World of Madagascar, by Peter Tyson, is a scientific travelogue that guides readers through the island's unique natural history and biodiversity.

Mineral Beauty

Going east from the western coastline, limestone is replaced by sandstone, which rises into majestic formations in places such as Parc National de l'Isalo.

Northern and western Madagascar host impressive limestone karst formations – jagged, eroded rocks that contain caves, potholes, underground rivers and forested canyons rich in wildlife, such as crocodiles, lemurs, birds and bats. Karst is known locally as *tsingy*, and is protected within one of Madagascar's three World Heritage Sites, Parc National des Tsingy de Bemaraha, as well as in the Parc National de l'Ankarana.

Wildlife

Madagascar's 80-million-year isolation has allowed its wildlife to take a remarkable evolutionary turn. Unperturbed by outside influences and human beings (who 'only' arrived 2000 years ago), the fauna and flora followed their own interpretation of the evolution manual; the result is that 70% of animals and 90% of plants found in Madagascar are endemic.

As well as being completely unique, their sheer variety is staggering: Madagascar hosts 5% of all animal and plant species known to man. Habitat degradation threatens much of this incredible natural wealth, and habitat conservation is now a worldwide priority. For more information, see the Parks & Reserves chapter (p241).

Fauna

Lemurs

Madagascar's best-known mammals are the lemurs, of which there are about 50 species. As well as being entertaining to watch (they are primates after all, and therefore distant cousins of ours), it's hard to overrate how unique they are: Madagascar's lemurs are found nowhere else on earth, which also explains why primatologists class Madagascar in a category of its own, the other three being Africa, Southeast Asia and the Americas.

Lemurs are divided into five families: the beautifully marked sifakas and indris (of which only one species is extant), all known for their leaping abilities; a family of small, nocturnal mouse lemurs that includes the world's smallest primates; the 'true' lemurs, such as the ring-tailed and ruffed lemurs; the sportive lemurs; and, most remarkable of all, the bizarre, nocturnal aye-aye, which extracts grubs from under bark with its long, bony middle finger.

Where to See Lemurs

- Indri: Parc National d'Andasibe-Mantadia
- Silky sifaka: Parc National de Marojejy
- Red-ruffed lemur: Parc National de Masoala
- Aye-aye: Aye-aye Island
- Ring-tailed lemur: Anja
- Coquerel's sifaka: Parc National d'Ankarafantsika

Other Mammals

Madagascar has many species of small mammal, such as bats, rodents and tenrecs. Tenrecs are related to shrews and fill a similar niche as tiny hunters of the leaf litter. Among their diverse forms are shrew tenrecs, the hedgehog-like spiny tenrecs and even an otter-like aquatic species.

There are six species of carnivore – all are mongooses and civets – including the ring-tailed mongoose, the fanaloka and the puma-like, lemur-eating fossa.

Madagascar's waters harbour rich marine life – dolphins, dugongs and humpback whales. Whales come to Madagascar to give birth and mate during winter months. See p180 for more on the whales' migration.

GOING, GOING...BACK AGAIN!

The last century saw several Malagasy bird species pushed perilously close to the brink of extinction. Waterbirds have fared particularly badly: the Alaotra Grebe was last seen in the 1980s and was declared extinct in 2010.

All three of the country's endemic duck species are rare. One, the Madagascar Pochard, had last been observed in 1994 when a female was rescued by a conservation worker from a fisherman's net on Lac Alaotra. The rescuer kept the bird alive in a bath in the hope that a mate would be found, but it succumbed and the Madagascar Pochard was presumed extinct. But in 2006 the unthinkable happened: nine adult Madagascar Pochards were discovered with young on a remote lake in the Alaotra basin in northern Madagascar. In a desperate effort to save the species from extinction, the Durrell Wildlife Conservation Trust and the Wildfowl and Wetlands Trust (WWT) recovered eggs about to hatch and set up an emergency captive breeding programme, with the long-term aim of reintroducing the rare duck to its habitat. Only 20 Pochards are now left in the wild.

Birds

Madagascar's birdlife has the highest proportion of endemic birds of any country on earth: of the 209 breeding species, 51% are endemic. A large percentage of birds are forest-dwelling and therefore under pressure from land clearing.

Among Madagascar's unique bird families are the mesites – skulking, babblerlike birds thought to be related to rails; the spectacular ground-rollers, including a roadrunner-like species unique to the spiny forests; the tiny, iridescent asities, similar to sunbirds and filling a similar niche; and the vangas, which have taken several strange twists as they evolved to fill various forest niches. There are a number of predators – including the highly endangered Madagascar serpent eagle and fish eagle – and nocturnal species as well.

Most species are resident (ie nonmigratory), although a few are seasonal migrants to East Africa. Waterbirds are rather poorly represented in Madagascar because there are comparatively few large bodies of water; some of the best concentrations are on the west coast in the Mahavy-Kinkony Wetland Complex. The richest habitat by far for birds (and all other terrestrial life forms) is the rainforest of the eastern seaboard, although many of these species are rare and poorly known.

The BBC's seminal three-part series *Madagascar*, narrated by Sir David Attenborough, makes for an inspirational introduction to the great island. It features the island's iconic fauna and flora, as well as its more obscure specimens, in fascinating details and stunning images.

Reptiles & Amphibians

There are 346 reptile species on Madagascar, including most of the world's chameleons, ranging from the largest – Parson's chameleon, which grows to around 60cm – to the smallest, the dwarf chameleons of the genus Brookesia, which fits on your thumbnail! You might also spot the king of camouflage, the leaf-tailed gecko, and the amazingly colourful Labord's chameleon. Equally attractive are some of Madagascar's 200 species of frog, including the bright-red tomato frog and iridescent Malagasy poison frogs.

Amazingly, the verdant forests support not a single snake species harmful to people; among the many beautiful snakes are the Madagascar boa and leaf-nosed snake. In contrast, the Nile crocodile is just as dangerous here as it is in Africa and it kills people every year.

Five of the world's seven species of marine turtle can be found in Madagascar (all endangered); the country is also home to several species of tortoise, many of which are highly endangered (see p108 for information on conservation efforts to save the ploughshare tortoise).

Since 1999, an incredible 615 species have been discovered in Madagascar, including 41 mammals, 61 reptiles, 42 invertebrates, 17 fish, 69 amphibians and 385 plants.

ICONIC TREES

The photogenic Allée des Baobabs in western Madagascar has done much for the popularity of this giant tree. Madagascar is home to seven of the world's eight baobab species, of which six are native and endemic (the seventh species is that found on mainland Africa; the eighth in Australia).

The trees stand out for their size (up to 30m high), huge trunks (one of the largest in the country is in Majunga, with a circumference of 21m), old age (many are thought to be several centuries old) and signature scraggly branches, in full view over the winter months, when baobabs have lost their foliage. The trees store water in their trunks and are therefore well adapted to dry environments.

Another of Madagascar's iconic plants – it is, technically, not a tree – is the *ravinala*, or travellers' palm, named so after the large quantities of watery sap it can store at the base of its leaves and which could be drunk. *Ravinala*, which is native to the island, has many uses in Madagascar: the leaves are dried and used for building roofs in traditional houses. Bundles of dried leaves are sold by the roadside everywhere in northern and eastern Madagascar. Done well, a *ravinala* roof can last 10 years. The tough stems are often used to make beautiful ceiling or wall panels. The wood from the trunk is also used for various building purposes.

Perhaps as a nod to its durability, Air Madagascar chose the *ranivala* tree as its emblem.

Invertebrates

As you might expect from somewhere that has such thriving wildlife, the bugs in Madagascar are out in force. It is thought there are some 100,000 species of insects on the island; amongst the most charming specimens are hissing cockroaches, scorpions, giraffe-necked weevils, tarantulas, giant millipedes, stick insects and the incredible flatid bug, which looks more like a giant bit of paper confetti than an insect.

Best Whale-Watching

- Baie d'Antongil
- Ile Sainte Marie
- Fort Dauphin
- Ifaty
- Nosy Be

Fish

Freshwater fish are one of the most endangered groups of animal on Madagascar, owing to silting of rivers through erosion. A survey by the International Union for the Conservation of Nature (IUCN) of 98 endemic species of freshwater fish found that 54% of the fish in Madagascar were either critically endangered, endangered or vulnerable.

Marine life is incredibly diverse, but similarly vulnerable to erosion run-off, notably the country's beautiful coral. Madagascar harbours the world's fourth-largest coral reef, but overfishing, pollution, climate change and sediments from soil erosion have greatly impacted its health.

Madagascar's waters teem with sharks, which, depending on your point of view, is either great (conservationists, fishermen, some divers) or scary (swimmers, surfers, the other divers). Risks of attacks are particularly high on the east coast, less so in areas where fringing corals protect the shores.

Flora

Madagascar's plants are no less interesting than its animals and its flora is incredibly diverse. About 6000 species are known to science, including the bizarre octopus trees, several species of baobab and a pretty flower that is used to treat leukaemia.

Common tenrec mothers can give birth to 25 infants at one time, the most of any mammal in the world.

The island's vegetation can be divided into three parallel north–south zones, each supporting unique communities of plants and animals: the hot, arid west consists of dry spiny desert or deciduous forest; the central plateau (*hauts plateaux*) has now been mostly deforested; and the wettest part of the country, the eastern seaboard, supports extensive tracts of rainforest. Mangrove forests grow in sites along the coast, particularly near large estuaries. All of these habitats have suffered extensive disturbance.

Arid Landscapes

The spiny desert is truly extraordinary: dense tangles of cactus-like octopus trees festooned with needle-sharp spines are interspersed with baobabs whose bulbous trunks store water, allowing them to survive the dry season. The baobabs' large, bright flowers are filled with copious amounts of nectar, often sipped by fork-marked lemurs. About 60 species of aloe occur in Madagascar, and many dot the spiny desert landscape.

Dry deciduous forests are a feature of the western half of the country, although they do not look quite as bare as their northern hemisphere counterparts in the depths of winter. The thinner winter foliage does make it prime bird- and lemur-watching time however.

The rosy periwinkle – a flower endemic to Madagascar – has been a source of alkaloids that are 99% effective in the treatment of some forms of leukaemia.

The Highlands

The vast areas of blond grassland of the *hauts plateaux* are actually the result of extensive felling by humans. The boundary of the sole remaining patch of natural forest, at Parc National Zombitse-Vohibasia, stands in forlorn contrast to the degraded countryside surrounding it.

Growing among the crags and crevices of Parc National de l'Isalo are nine species of *Pachypodia*, including a tall species with large fragrant yellow-white blossoms, and the diminutive elephant-foot species that nestle in cliff crevices on the sandstone massif.

Rainforest

Madagascar's eastern rainforests once covered the entire eastern seaboard and still support the island's highest biodiversity, most of which is found nowhere else on earth. Giant forest trees are festooned with vines, orchids and bird's-nest ferns (home to tree frogs and geckos).

There are 1000 species of orchid in Madagascar, more than in all of Africa, and more than 60 species of pitcher plants are found in swampy parts of rainforests. Insects are attracted to the nectar of these carnivorous plants, but are trapped by downward-pointing spines along the inside of the 'pitcher' and are eventually dissolved and absorbed by the plant.

BAOBABS

The Malagasy have nicknamed baobabs 'roots of the sky', after their scraggly branches. Legend has it that God made the baobab the most beautiful tree on earth. The devil was so jealous that he decided to plant baobabs upside down so that he could view them from hell!

Environmental Issues

Madagascar faces tremendous environmental challenges, none greater than deforestation. Just like every other country, Madagascar is also going to have to contend with the effects of climate change on its unique biodiversity.

Deforestation

Around 95% of Malagasy households rely on firewood and charcoal for their domestic energy needs. This reliance has put immense pressure on Madagascar's forests, as have the need for agricultural and grazing land (slash-and-burn, or *tavy* in Malagasy, is widespread): scientists estimate that 90% of the island's original forest cover is now gone.

WHAT YOU CAN DO

» Offset your air miles to Madagascar: some of your credits may come from the country's budding carbon-offsetting projects.

» Do not buy items made from precious wood: their trade is illegal.

» Never buy lemurs, tortoises or other protected species, no matter how sorry they look: instead, report them to the police or the nearest MNP office.

» If you buy gemstones, make sure you buy them from an established dealer and get an export permit.

ILLEGAL ROSEWOOD LOGGING

In April 2000, Cyclone Hudah tore through the Masoala Peninsula in northeast Madagascar. The storm left a trail of devastation in its wake: satellite images revealed that some 3% of the forest was severely damaged. Although rosewood exploitation had been banned, then president Marc Ravalomanana exceptionally allowed fallen trees to be sold as timber. Little did he know that this would open the floodgates of illegal logging.

The practice has since continued unabated. The traffic in precious wood is driven by consumer demand for luxury furniture and musical instruments from China, the US and the EU: a rosewood bed sells for US$1 million in China.

In 2009, an investigation by Madagascar National Parks, the environmental NGO Global Witness and the US Environmental Investigation Agency uncovered the scale of the pillaging, which had reached catastrophic proportions following the presidential coup of February 2009. The report revealed that 100 to 200 trees were being taken down every day, a bounty worth US$80,000 to US$460,000; it also found that the police and officials at every level of the forestry sector had colluded with traffickers.

The Malagasy authorities reacted by forbidding all precious wood exports in April 2010. Its implementation remains patchy, but the news in September 2011 that rosewood and ebony had been added to the Convention on International Trade in Endangered Species (CITES) was another boost for the forests of the northeast. Global Witness and the EIA have also called on individual countries to crack down on illegal imports.

The impact of deforestation on such a large scale is multiple, from habitat loss to soil erosion. The latter is particularly dramatic: during the rainy season, Madagascar's laterite soils 'bleed' in the country's streams and rivers. The red earth saturates coastal waters, threatening fragile marine ecosystems, including precious coral reefs.

Natural Resource Exploitation

Madagascar has immense natural wealth: oil, gas, minerals (nickel and iron in particular), gemstones and precious woods. But with such richness comes great pressure to make the best of this natural endowment.

There are a number of large-scale mining projects in the works, which, if administered well, could bring prosperity to a population that has long suffered. Poorly executed, they could wreck havoc in the country's fragile environment.

Amongst the most controversial projects are plans to develop tar sand deposits in the west of the country. Tar sands have the worst environmental footprint of all oil projects: they are energy-intensive to extract and require huge amounts of water, a particularly sticky point in the arid west.

Madagascar's seas also suffer from overfishing. Human population growth and lack of food and employment alternatives in the south have pushed marine ecosystems to the brink. A number of NGOs are currently working with coastal communities to improve their livelihood's sustainability. Similar work is being done with communities practicing slash-and-burn agriculture in forest areas.

Forest Guises

- Spiny forest, Arboretum d'Antsokay, Tuléar (Toliara)
- Rainforest, Parc National de Masoala
- Dry deciduous forest, Parc National d'Ankarafantsika

Wildlife

When Madagascar broke away from Africa some 160 million years ago, its cargo of primitive animals evolved in some novel directions, free from the pressures felt on other land masses, such as human hunters. The result is one of the most important biodiversity hot spots in the world, and thanks to a great network of reserves and excellent local naturalist guides, Madagascar is also one of the world's great ecotourism destinations. Lemurs are the main attraction for most nature lovers, but the island also offers superb birdwatching and there is a host of smaller animals that could keep you occupied for several trips.

Suraka silk moth, Parc National de l'Isalo (p74)

Colourful Typical Lemurs

Lemurs are an extraordinarily diverse group of prosimians (primate ancestors) found only in Madagascar. 'Typical' lemurs are long-tailed, monkey-like animals with catlike faces, prominent ears and prehensile hands with separate fingers and toes.

Ring-Tailed Lemur

1 These sociable lemurs forage on the ground in groups of 13 to 15, searching for fruit, flowers, leaves and other vegetation in spiny and dry deciduous forest. Habituated troops live at Réserve d'Anja (p67). *Length 95–110cm; weight 2.3–3.5kg.*

Black & White Ruffed Lemur

2 This species' social behaviour is complex: males and females may occupy separate territories, or live in mixed social groups. They are easily seen at the Andasibe area parks (p159). *Length 110–120cm; weight 3.1–3.6kg.*

Red Ruffed Lemur

3 Like other ruffed lemurs, this species primarily eats fruit, is highly vocal and sometimes hangs by its hind feet while feeding. It is found only in lowland primary rainforest on the Masoala Peninsula (p188). *Length 100–120cm; weight 3.3–3.6kg.*

Mongoose Lemur

4 Recognisable by their piercing orange eyes and strongly marked bibs, mongoose lemurs live in pairs with their offspring. They tend to be more secretive than other 'typical' lemurs, but can be readily seen at Parc National d'Ankarafantsika (p107). *Length 75–83cm; weight 1.1–1.6kg.*

1

4

2

KARL LEHMANN/LONELY PLANET IMAGES ©

3

KARL LEHMANN/LONELY PLANET IMAGES ©

Plain Typical Lemurs

Many lemurs are plainly marked with mousy brown or grey colours that make them inconspicuous in the shaded forests where they live. Lemurs don't need strong social markings because they rely on scent to mark territories and signal their readiness to breed.

Crowned Lemur

1 Male and female (pictured) crowned lemurs have different colourations. They live in dry deciduous forest and rainforest in northern Madagascar. Habituated troops can be seen at Parc National de l'Ankarana (p148). *Length 75–85cm; weight 1.1–1.3kg.*

Common Brown Lemur

2 Living in groups of three to 12, these lemurs are active during the day but may be partly nocturnal in the dry season. Common at the Andasibe area parks (p159). *Length 100cm; weight 2–3kg.*

Black Lemur

3 Males are dark brown or black, while females vary from golden brown to rich chestnut with flamboyant white ear and cheek tufts. They're easily seen in Réserve Naturelle Intégrale de Lokobe (p130). *Length 90–110cm; weight 2–2.9kg.*

Red-Bellied Lemur

4 You can tell male red-bellied lemurs from females by the white 'teardrops' of bare skin under their eyes. See them at Parc National de Ranomafana (p57), especially from May to June. *Length 78–93cm; weight 1.6–2.4kg.*

Eastern Lesser Bamboo Lemur

5 The most common of the bamboo lemurs is widespread in eastern rainforests at Parc National de Ranomafana (p57) and the Andasibe area parks (p159). *Length 56–70cm; weight 0.7–1kg.*

1

4

2

KARL LEHMANN/LONELY PLANET IMAGES ©

3

ARIADNE VAN ZANDBERGEN/LONELY PLANET IMAGES ©

1

THOR VAZ DE LEON/LONELY PLANET IMAGES ©

4

ARIADNE VAN ZANDBERGEN/LONELY PLANET IMAGES ©

KARL LEHMANN/LONELY PLANET IMAGES ©

PETE OXFORD/NPL/MINDEN PICTURES ©

Sifakas & Indri

Also known as simponas, sifakas are prodigious leapers that move rapidly by propelling themselves from tree to tree with their elongated back legs. Many are attractively marked and easily seen at national parks where troops have been habituated. Indris and sifakas are members of the same family.

Verreaux's Sifaka

1 This beautiful lemur is famous for balletic bounds across clearings, leaping sideways on its strong back legs. The species is restricted to dry deciduous forest in the south and is easily seen at Parc National de l'Isalo (p74). *Length 90–110cm; weight 3–3.5kg.*

Coquerel's Sifaka

2 These attractive sifakas commonly travel in groups. They're restricted to dry deciduous forest in Madagascar's northwest, such as Parc National d'Ankarafantsika (p107). *Length 93–110cm; weight 3.7–4.3kg.*

Decken's Sifaka

3 Protected by a strong local *fady* (taboo), these little-known sifakas sometimes live in towns in western Madagascar. They're common in Parc National des Tsingy de Bemaraha (p110). *Length 92–110cm; weight 3–4.5kg.*

Diademed Sifaka

4 Arguably the most beautiful of all lemurs, this species is almost the same size as the indri. It's widely distributed on the eastern seaboard but is best seen at the Andasibe area parks (p159). *Length 94–105cm; weight 6–8.5kg.*

Indri

5 Known locally as *babakoto*, the indri is the largest lemur and has the strongest voice, which can travel 3km through the forest. Indris can leap up to 10m between tree trunks, and they travel in family groups of two to six while foraging, mostly for leaves. See them at the Andasibe area parks (p159). *Length 69–77cm; weight 6–9.5kg.*

Common Nocturnal Lemurs

Approximately half of all lemur species are nocturnal. The nocturnal species are the smallest lemurs, and include mouse lemurs (the smallest of all primates), dwarf lemurs and sportive lemurs. The aye-aye is classified in its own family and even among lemurs stands out as unique.

1

Gray Mouse Lemur

1 Like most mouse lemurs, this species can be very common in suitable habitats, which include deciduous dry forest, spiny forest and secondary forest. It is typically active in the lower tree layers, although it moves very quickly and often retires from torchlight soon after being spotted. Mouse lemurs eat insects, fruit, flowers and other small animals, and are preyed upon by forest owls. *Length 25–28cm; weight 58–67g.*

Aye-Aye

2 With its shaggy, grizzled coat, bright orange eyes, leathery bat-like ears and long, dextrous fingers, the aye-aye is a strange-looking animal and the subject of much superstition. The middle digit of each forehand is elongated, and is used to probe crevices for insect larvae and other morsels. Aye-ayes are difficult to see but widely distributed in rainforests and dry deciduous forests. See them on Aye-Aye Island (p184). *Length 74–90cm; weight 2.5–2.6kg.*

Weasel Sportive Lemur

3 Found in rainforests of east-central Madagascar, these lemurs have dense woolly fur and spend the night munching on leaves, often staying for hours in the same tree. Males are solitary and highly territorial, while females remain with their offspring. *Length 30–35cm; weight 0.5–1kg.*

3

A & J VISAGE/ALAMY ©

2

KARL LEHMANN/LONELY PLANET IMAGES ©

1

3

NHPA/PHOTOSHOT ©

Rare Nocturnal Lemurs

Nocturnal lemurs are hard to find and may require the assistance of expert guides to spot. Some are thought to be highly endangered, while so little is known about others that their numbers and distribution have not been accurately determined.

Milne-Edwards' Sportive Lemur

1 Long, powerful back legs enable the eight species of sportive lemur to leap from tree to tree, balanced by their long tails. They sleep during the day in holes in trees and emerge after dark to feed. This species lives in dry deciduous forest in the west and northwest and can generally be seen at Parc National d'Ankarafantsika (p107). *Length 54–58cm; weight 1kg.*

2
PREMAPHOTOS/ALAMY ©

Western Avahi

2 The two species of avahi have dense fur that gives them a woolly appearance, hence their alternative name of 'woolly lemurs'. Their diet consists of a large variety of leaves and buds, and families huddle together during the day in dense foliage in the forest canopy. Avahis are restricted to dry deciduous forest in west and northwest Madagascar. They're commonly seen at night at Parc National d'Ankarafantsika (p107). *Length 59–68cm; weight 0.9–1.3kg.*

Pygmy Mouse Lemur

3 Owing to its size and nocturnal habits, this very small lemur went undetected for more than 100 years until it was rediscovered in 1993. It has been found in dry forests at Parc National des Tsingy de Bemaraha (p110), but almost nothing is known of its history, whether it's threatened or if new populations will be found. *Length 12–13cm; weight 43–55g.*

Carnivorous Mammals

Although lemurs are the undoubted highlight, Madagascar has many other types of native land mammal, including eight predators, dozens of bats and rodents, and tenrecs (primitive, shrew-like animals that have evolved into at least two-dozen forms, including spiny and aquatic species). A few of the island's unique carnivores are highlighted here.

Fossa

1 The legendary fossa is a solitary and elusive predator of lemurs and other animals. It is extremely agile and catlike, even descending trees head first. It is reputed to follow troops of lemurs for days, climbing trees to pick them off as they sleep at night. Fossas were the villains in the animated film *Madagascar*. *Length 140–170cm; weight 5–10kg.*

Fanaloka

2 Also known as the Malagasy or striped civet, the nocturnal, fox-like fanaloka is found in eastern and northern rainforests. It hunts mostly on the ground but can climb well, eating rodents, birds and other animals. During the day it sleeps in tree hollows and under logs. It is regularly seen on night walks at Parc National de Ranomafana (p57). *Length 61–70cm; weight 1.5–2kg.*

Ring-Tailed Mongoose

3 This attractive mongoose is widespread and active by day, and is therefore probably the easiest carnivore to spot. Family parties communicate with high-pitched whistles as they forage for small animals, including reptiles, birds and eggs, insects, rodents and even small lemurs. Generally seen at Parc National de Ranomafana (p57) and Parc National de l'Ankarana (p148). *Length 60–70cm; weight 0.7–1kg.*

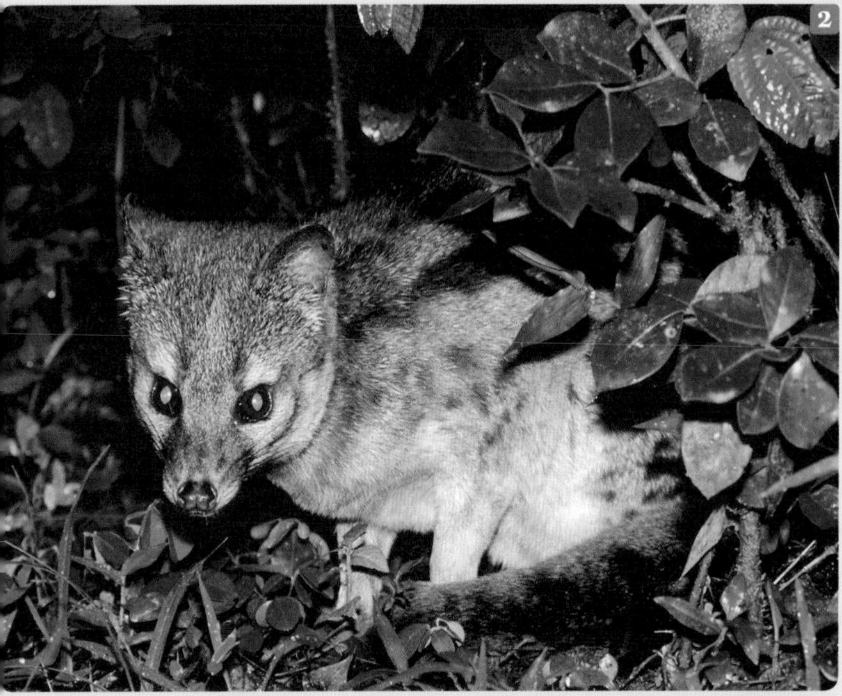

KARL LEHMANN/LONELY PLANET IMAGES ©

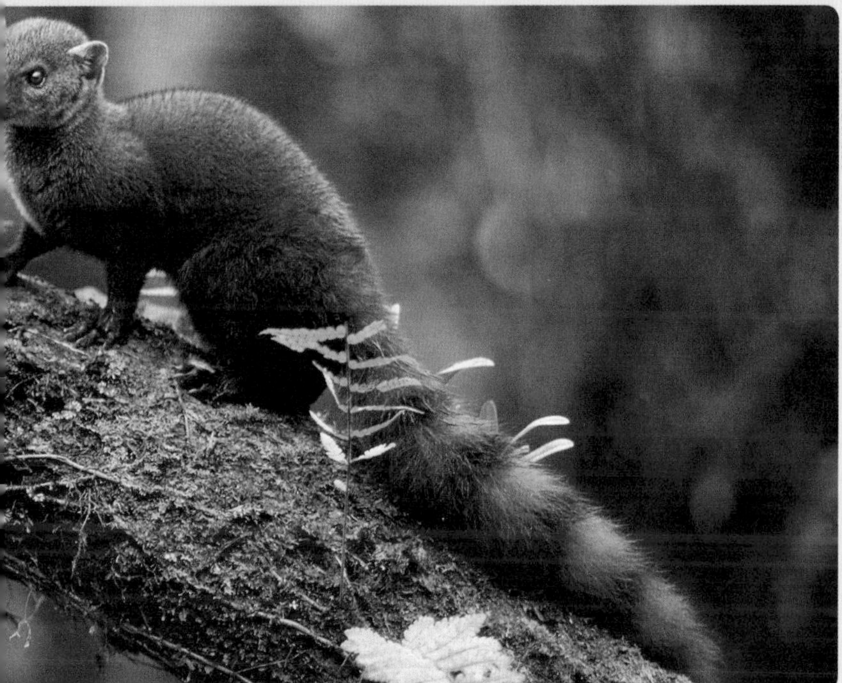

FRANS LANTING/CORBIS ©

1

3

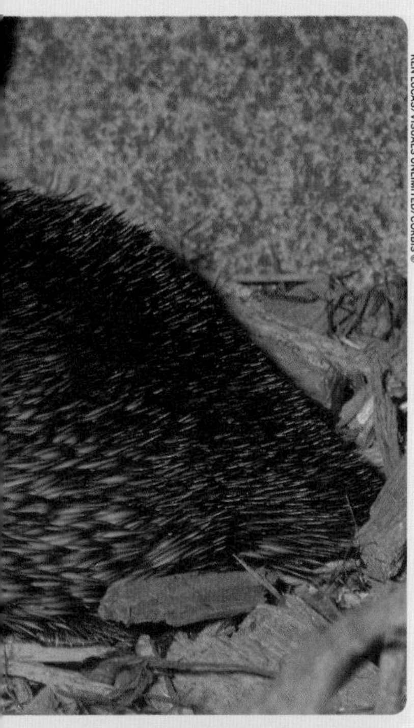
KEN LUCAS/VISUALS UNLIMITED/CORBIS ©

Omnivorous Mammals

Many of Madagascar's mammals are omnivorous, which means they eat a little bit of everything they come across, including insects, berries, fruit and seeds. Some specialise in fruit; others vary their diets according to which foods are available at different times of the year.

Hedgehog Tenrec

1 Nocturnal hedgehog tenrecs forage by sniffing out insects and their larvae and fallen fruit among leaf litter. During the day they shelter in tunnels under logs or tree roots. They are found in many habitats, including forests near Antananarivo, and are usually seen on nocturnal walks in Parc National Montagne d'Ambre (p147). *Length 16–22cm; weight 180–270g.*

Madagascar Flying Fox

2 Flying foxes roost upside down in big, noisy colonies, like most bats, but use trees rather than caves as roosting sites. Colonies can number up to a thousand individuals and great flocks take to the wing at dusk, fanning out across the countryside to feed on fruit. A colony of this species is a permanent fixture at Réserve Privée de Berenty (p92). *Length 23–27cm; wingspan 1–1.2m; weight 500–750g.*

2

DEA/DANI-JESKE/GETTY IMAGES ©

Giant Jumping Rat

3 Madagascar's largest rodent is strictly nocturnal. Pairs live in burrows with their offspring, foraging for seeds and fallen fruit after dark. They generally move on all fours but also hop on their hind legs. They were formerly more widespread but now live in a relatively small area of dry deciduous forest in western Madagascar and are regularly encountered at Réserve Forestière de Kirindy (p116). *Length 54–58cm; weight 1.1–1.3kg.*

Birds of Open Country

Madagascar's birds are unusual: many evolved in isolation and 80% of the country's species are found nowhere else in the world. Sadly, many of these are now rare or endangered and others have become extinct within the last 100 years or so.

1

Madagascar Bee-Eater

1 Best seen in full sunlight, loose flocks of these graceful birds forage for flying insects over open country. They nest in hollows in river banks and road cuttings. *Length 23–31cm.*

Madagascar Kingfisher

2 A flash of orange usually gives this bird away when it dives into water for small fish and tadpoles. Otherwise, it sits still for long periods and could be overlooked. It is common everywhere near fresh water. *Length 15cm.*

Madagascar Kestrel

3 Madagascar has comparatively few birds of prey but this is a common species. It is often seen hovering over grasslands near highways before swooping down to catch small animals. *Length 25–30cm.*

Madagascar Hoopoe

4 In flight this extraordinary bird shows off its stripes and looks like a huge butterfly. Its crest can be fanned but normally lies flat. It is common across the island, especially in dry deciduous forest. *Length 32cm.*

Sickle-Billed Vanga

5 This crow-sized bird lives in noisy flocks that move through forests making nasal *waa waa waa* calls, and probes for food under bark and crevices with a long, downcurved bill. It's common at Parc National d'Ankarafantsika (p107). *Length 32cm.*

4

2

FRANS LANTING/CORBIS ©

3

PREMAPHOTOS/ALAMY ©

Rainforest Birds

Madagascar's rainforests support the island's highest bird diversity; birdwatching in this environment can be both challenging and extremely rewarding. Long, quiet spells can be suddenly broken by a frenetic 'wave' of feeding birds composed of a dozen or more different species that will have you flipping through your field guide trying to identify them before they disappear into the foliage.

1

Madagascar Paradise-Flycatcher

1 Females of this large, active rainforest flycatcher are rufous with a black head, while males sport 12cm tail streamers and may be rufous, white or black, or a combination of all three. They're common at Parc National de Ranomafana (p57). *Length 18–30cm.*

Helmet Vanga

2 The helmet vanga looks like no other bird – its extraordinary, bright-blue bill is incongruously large, almost toucan-like, and thought to act as a resonator when it calls in the forest. Restricted to intact rainforests of the Masoala Peninsula (p188). *Length 29cm.*

Blue Vanga

3 The stunning vanga is unmistakable and common in a variety of forest types across the island. Vangas can be conspicuous birds that travel in pairs or small groups, often in the company of other forest birds. *Length 16cm.*

Nelicourvi Weaver

4 Most weavers are found in grasslands, but this rainforest species often associates with flocks of greenbuls while foraging in the forest. Both sexes have yellow heads but females lack the striking black mask of males. *Length 15cm.*

4

2

NICK GARBUTT/NATURE PICTURE LIBRARY ©

3

PETE OXFORD/NATURE PICTURE LIBRARY ©

1

ARIADNE VAN ZANDBERGEN/LONELY PLANET IMAGES ©

4

MARTIN HARVEY/CORBIS ©

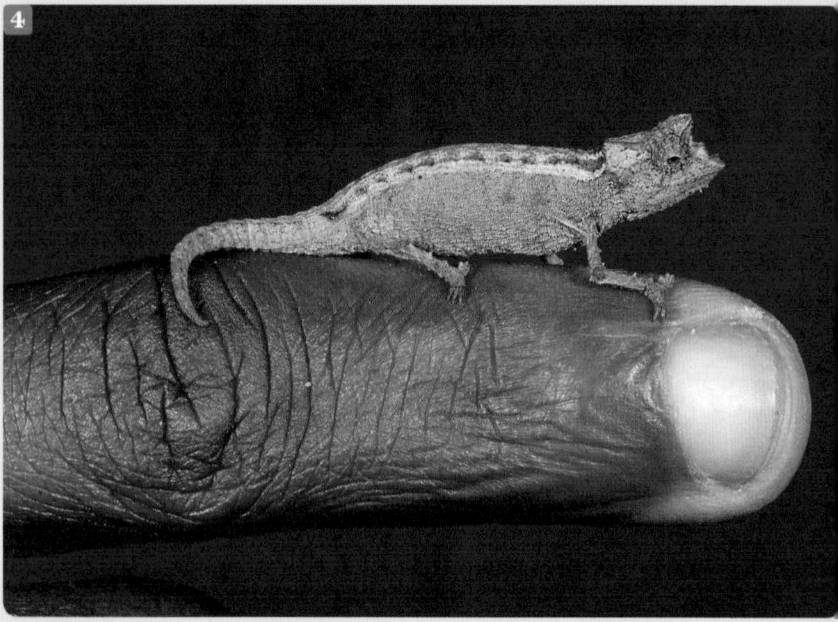

INGO ARNDT/NATURE PICTURE LIBRARY ©

Reptiles & Amphibians

Reptiles are usually overlooked, but chameleons are among Madagascar's most famous animals – for good reason. They have a fantastic ability to change their colours, and have eyes that swivel independently of each other on raised cones, and sticky tongues that shoot out to catch prey.

Nile Crocodile

1 Crocodiles are found in freshwater habitats, including the Pangalanes Lakes (p162), and in the cave system of Parc National de l'Ankarana (p148). *Length up to 5m.*

Parson's Chameleon

2 The world's largest chameleon prefers rainforests and lives in the forest canopy. Males have a massive casque (helmet-like structure) and two blunt 'horns'. *Length up to 40cm, in rare cases up to 69cm (males); females are smaller.*

Radiated Tortoise

3 Confined to dry forests in southern Madagascar, this striking tortoise is endangered due to hunting. It is the subject of an intensive conservation program and is being bred in captivity at Arboretum d'Antsokay (p80). *Length 40cm; weight 15kg.*

Pygmy Leaf Chameleon

4 This chameleon is one of the world's smallest vertebrates. It can be found on Nosy Be (p121), where it hunts among leaf litter and on low branches. *Length 28mm (males), up to 33mm (females).*

Tomato Frog

5 This bizarre frog is restricted to northwestern Madagascar and endangered because of the pet trade. Females are larger and brighter than males, and both sexes exude sticky mucus when threatened by a predator. *Length 6cm (males), up to 10.5cm (females).*

OLIVIER CIRENDINI/LONELY PLANET IMAGES ©

Fish & Coral-Reef Animals

Coral reefs and marine environments are among Madagascar's most overlooked and relatively unstudied treasures. The island's southwest coast alone has the fifth-largest coral-reef system in the world. While reefs in the southwest have suffered massive damage from coral bleaching, scientists were stunned to discover on a recent survey that the reefs of the northeast coast are remarkably healthy and have the highest coral diversity in the western Indian Ocean.

Hawksbill Sea Turtle

1 These attractive coral-reef sea turtles were once abundant in the waters around Madagascar but are now globally endangered because their shells are made into colourful trinkets. *Length 1m.*

Humpback Whale

2 Whale-watching has recently become a popular activity at the Baie d'Antongil (p183) and Ile Sainte Marie (p175) when several hundred humpbacks arrive from Antarctica in June and linger with their calves until September. *Length 12–16m.*

Clown Triggerfish

3 This exceptionally colourful reef fish has a stout orange-lipped mouth adapted for crushing sea urchins and clams. When threatened they wedge themselves among rocks with their rigid fins. *Length 25–50cm.*

Bicolour Parrotfish

4 The parrotfish is a blast of fluorescent orange, blue and purple. The fish plays a major role in reef ecosystems by ingesting coral and breaking it down into sand with the special teeth in its throat. *Length 50–80cm.*

1

3

INAKI RELANZON/NATURE PICTURE LIBRARY ©

2

JENNY & TONY ENDERBY/LONELY PLANET IMAGES ©

Insects & Other Invertebrates

Madagascar's forests support thousands of fascinating and unusual invertebrates. Most are insignificant and easily missed, but you will also encounter clouds of brilliant butterflies, huge moths and bizarre beetles unlike anything you've ever seen.

Comet Moth

1 These stunning yellow moths with long dangling tails are bigger than your hand. Their habitat is threatened but fortunately the legendary moths are being successfully bred in captivity. *Wingspan up to 22.5cm; tail length 20cm.*

Flatid Leaf Bug

2 Looking at first glance like clusters of tiny fuchsia flowers, colonies of adult leaf bugs have evolved in this way as protection against predators. Their young, known as nymphs, look like pieces of lace or lichen attached to branches. *Length 5mm.*

Giraffe-Necked Weevil

3 This bizarre little beetle with an outrageously long neck is found only on the small tree *Dichaetanthera cordifolia*. They are quite common in Parc National de Ranomafana (p57) and the Andasibe area parks (p159). 'Necks' on males are much longer than on females. *Length 2.5cm.*

Madagascar Hissing Cockroach

4 Strangely, this flightless cockroach has become a popular pet outside its native Madagascar. In the wild it lives in rotting logs, where females give birth to live young. Females are gregarious but males are solitary. When disturbed, both sexes can emit a hissing sound by forcing air through their spiracles (breathing pores) as a defence mechanism, although rival males also hiss to assert dominance. *Length 12.5cm.*

Parks & Reserves

A Brief History

Although protected areas in Madagascar have existed since the 1950s, the environmental movement began in earnest in 1985 with an international conference of scientists, funding organisations and Malagasy government officials. Biologists had long known that the country was an oasis of amazing creatures and plants, but the clear felling and burning of forests all over the island were threatening these treasures. Concerned international donors and the Malagasy government joined together to plan a major conservation programme.

By 1989 Madagascar had a national Environmental Action Plan, which offered a blueprint for biodiversity action for the next 15 years. The first step was to create a national park system, called the Association Nationale pour la Gestion des Aires Protégées (Angap; National Association for the Management of Protected Areas), and then set Angap to work on creating new parks and training staff. The last phase of the program, with started in earnest in the naughts, aimed to develop sustainable tourism in the country's protected areas.

Although not perfect, great strides have been achieved in the country's protected areas since 1985: Angap changed its name to **Madagascar National Parks** (MNP; www.pacs-madagascar.com) in 2009, and there are now 19 national parks, 23 special reserves and five strict natural reserves, with more in the pipeline.

Lords and Lemurs, by Alison Jolly, is a history of the Réserve Privée de Berenty that skilfully weaves together the stories of the spiny desert Tandroy people, three generations of French plantation owners, lemurs and lemur-watchers.

An Uncertain Future

At the World's Park Conference in Durban in 2003, then president Marc Ravalomanana announced a bold plan to triple the extent of Madagascar's protected areas. Sadly, since the political turmoil of 2009, conservation efforts have faced major setbacks with the illegal logging of rosewood and

UNESCO HERITAGE SITE IN DANGER

In 2007, Unesco declared the eastern-seaboard Rainforests of the Atsinanana a World Heritage Site. The site includes six rainforest national parks: Parc National de Marojejy, Parc National de Masoala, Parc National de Zahamena, Parc National de Ranomafana, Parc National d'Andringitra and Parc National d'Andohahela. Unesco acknowledged the importance of these forests in maintaining Madagascar's high levels of biodiversity.

But in July 2010, the World Heritage committee decided to move the Rainforests of the Atsinanana to its List of World Heritage in Danger because of illegal logging and hunting of endangered species on site. The committee noted that 'despite a decree outlawing the exploitation and export of rosewood and ebony, Madagascar continues to provide export permits for illegally logged timber'.

Unesco urged Madagascar to respect the legislation, but as of 2012, there was no sign that the rainforests of Atsinanana would be moved off the red list any time soon.

ebony from the national parks of Masoala and Marojejy, and the withdrawal of funding from international donors.

A small silver lining came in June 2011 in the form of an emergency US$52 million funding from the World Bank to support the national parks network. Like most international donors, the World Bank stopped all funding to the country following the 2009 coup. But in a communiqué, it noted that the new funding did not 'signal the World Bank's reengagement with Madagascar, but [rather] its recognition that the environmental and social costs of inaction are too high'.

The funding will cover the management costs of MNP and will help pursue Madagascar's commitment to extend its protected surface area. The next national park to be gazetted should be the Makira Forest, an

MADAGASCAR'S NATIONAL PARKS & RESERVES

PARK	FEATURES	ACTIVITIES
Parc National Andasibe-Mantadia	Pristine forest, excellent local guides, well-marked trails	Hiking, lemur-watching, birdwatching
Parc National d'Andohahela	Three types of forest: humid, transition and spindly	Hiking, camping, birdwatching
Parc National d'Andringitra	Rugged granite peaks, fantastic trails and scenery	Trekking, climbing
Parc National d'Ankarafantsika	Diverse landscapes, from dry forest to canyon and lakes	Hiking, birdwatching, lemur-watching, boat trips
Parc National de l'Ankarana	*Tsingy* (limestone pinnacles), caves, dry forest	Hiking, caving, birdwatching, night walks
Parc National de l'Isalo	Sandstone mountains, gorges with natural swimming pools	Hiking, swimming
Parc National de Kirindy-Mitea	Sand dunes, dry forest, brackish-water lakes, mangroves	Hiking, birdwatching, pirogue trips
Parc National de Marojejy	Remote mountain peaks, lush rainforest, canyons	Trekking in the Marojejy Massif, lemur-watching
Parc National de Masoala	Primary rainforest, mangroves and protected marine areas	Trekking, sea kayaking
Parc National Montagne d'Ambre	Humid forest, old French botanical gardens, waterfalls	Hiking, birdwatching, lemur-watching
Parc National de Ranomafana	Rainforest, mountain streams	Hiking, night walks, lemur-watching
Parc National des Tsingy de Bemaraha	Spectacular limestone pinnacles, Unesco World Heritage Site	Climbing, hiking, pirogue trips
Réserve d'Anja	The 'three sisters', three mountain-size boulders; forest; scenery	Hiking, climbing, lemur-watching
Réserve Forestière de Kirindy	Dense, dry deciduous forest	Hiking, night walks, lemur-watching
Réserve Naturelle Intégrale de Lokobe	Primary forest on an isolated peninsula	Hiking, lemur-watching, pirogue trips
Réserve de Nosy Mangabe	Rainforest-covered island	Hiking, camping, night walks
Réserve Spéciale de Cap Sainte Marie	Stark, windswept cape, Madagascar's southernmost point	Hiking, camping, searching for elephant bird eggshells

area adjacent to Masoala Peninsula and the Baie d'Antongil, which, together, form an important biodiversity hot spot nicknamed the MaMa-Bay Land/Seascape.

Sustainable Conservation

Enlightened conservationists know that for conservation programmes to succeed in poor developing nations, local people must be involved.

From the beginning, the needs of the people living in and around the parks were incorporated into park management plans, and 50% of park admission fees are returned to local communities. This money is used to build wells, buy vegetable seeds, help with tree nurseries, rebuild schools and build small dams to facilitate paddy, rather than hillside, rice cultivation.

WILDLIFE	BEST TIME TO VISIT	PAGE
Indri, birds, Parson's chameleon, orchids	Sep-Nov	p159
Spiny iguana, birds, including harrier hawk	Apr-Dec	p93
Ring-tailed lemur, orchids	Oct-Nov	p68
Birds, Coquerel's sifaka, brown lemur, mongoose lemur	Year-round	p107
Bats, birds (several species of flycatchers), Sanford's lemur	Apr-Nov	p148
Verreaux's sifaka, ring-tailed lemur, pachypodium	May-Jun, Sep-Oct	p74
Birds, including flamingos	Year-round	p119
Silky sifaka, reptiles, amphibians, millipedes	Aug-Nov	p152
Red-ruffed lemurs, humpback whales, dugongs, turtles, orchids	Aug-Dec	p188
Brookesia chameleon, amphibians, crowned lemur, Sanford's lemur	Year-round	p147
Red-bellied lemur, diademed sifaka, red-fronted lemur, golden bamboo lemur	Sep-Dec	p57
Decken's sifaka, brown lemur	Apr-Oct	p110
Ring-tailed lemur	Year-round	p67
Fossa, giant jumping rat, flat-tailed lemur, mouse lemur	Apr-Oct	p116
Black lemur, boa constrictor, birds, including owls	Year-round	p130
Aye-ayes, whales, reptiles and amphibians	Jul-Sep	p188
Radiated tortoise, spider tortoise, whales offshore	May-Oct	p92

Tourism has also fostered employment opportunities in villages around major national parks, with rangers, guides, porters and those working in guesthouses and restaurants all benefiting.

About US$15 million of the US$52 million donated by the World Bank in June 2011 were specifically earmarked for community development, with the goal of building long-term sustainability in the livelihood of the parks' communities. Activities will include income-generating projects, training in ecosystem mapping, training for park rangers etc.

Scientific Research & Parks

The biodiversity that Madagascar's parks and reserves protect is of great interest to scientists, and many of the country's protected areas host research programs in primates, biodiversity, endemicity, the effects of climate change, deforestation and much more.

In 1986, scientists 'rediscovered' the greater bamboo lemur (previously thought extinct) in what is now Ranomafana national park. They also discovered a new species, the golden bamboo lemur. So extraordinary were these findings that they led to the creation of the park.

The Institute for the Conservation of Tropical Environments set up the ValBio research centre next to Parc National de Ranomafana; the Wildlife Conservation Society is highly involved in the management and protection of Parc National de Masoala and the Baie d'Antongil area; the Durrell Wildlife Conservation Trust has had a captive tortoise breeding centre at Parc National d'Ankarafantsika for nearly 25 years; the German Primate Centre has been researching Réserve Forestière de Kirindy's lemurs since 1993; WWF is working with the government on the designation of new protected areas; and Conservation International is working on wildlife corridors between protected areas.

These are just a handful of projects taking place in the country's parks but they highlight how important protected areas are to the scientific community, a fact that is, sadly, not always well explained to visitors.

Admission Fees

National park admission prices for adult foreign nationals depend on the park's category. Andasibe-Mantadia, Ankarafantsika, Ankarana, Isalo, Montagne d'Ambre, Ranomafana and Tsingy de Bemaraha parks are Category A; all other national parks are Category B. Malagasy nationals pay Ar1000 per day. Children pay Ar200 per day.

Admission to other protected areas varies between Ar3000 and Ar20,000 per day for an adult. Children generally pay a nominal fee.

Gerald Durrell's hilarious book *The Aye-Aye and I* is an account of the Durrell Wildlife Conservation Trust's expedition to capture aye-ayes, gentle lemurs, giant jumping rats and other endangered species in a bid to set up captive breeding programs.

Guides

Guides are compulsory in all MNP protected areas (national parks, special reserves and strict nature reserves). You don't need to book a guide in advance: just turn up at the MNP Office on the day (or the day before if you'd like to discuss itineraries) and you will be assigned a guide who matches your request (guides work in rotation). Guides are generally well-trained and hugely knowledgeable in local fauna and flora. All MNP guides speak French, and an increasing number now speak English. Fees vary depending on the skills of the guide, the park and the length of walks, but in any case, they are generally clearly displayed at the local MNP office. Charges of Ar30,000 for half a day's walk is about

NATIONAL PARK ADMISSION FEES

	1 DAY (AR)	2 DAYS (AR)	3 DAYS (AR)	4 DAYS (AR)
CATEGORY A	25,000	37,000	40,000	50,000
CATEGORY B	10,000	15,000	20,000	25,000

average. In other protected areas, guides are not always necessary; fees are generally in line with those of MNP.

Camping in Protected Areas

Almost all national parks have designated camping areas; the locations are invariably atmospheric, but facilities vary from pretty good to really basic.

Don't be put off if you haven't come equipped for camping: most parks rent tents and you can hire porters and cooks. All you really need is a warm sleeping bag.

If you would like to camp in a park, you should go to the MNP office by at least the afternoon before, or call them if you're going to arrive later, to organise a guide, porter, supplies etc.

Réserve d'Anja is the country's most successful community-managed private reserve. Started in 1999, it is run and managed by Anja Miray, whose members are local residents.

Survival Guide

Directory A–Z

Accommodation

Listings in this book quote full board when the accommodation rate includes three meals a day, and half-board when it includes breakfast and dinner.

Accommodation in Madagascar is cheap compared to Europe or North America, but not as cheap as you might perhaps expect.

Madagascar's winter months (July to September) are the busiest; it's a good idea to book ahead at this time of year, particularly in popular destinations such as Nosy Be, Ile Sainte Marie or Parc National des Tsingy de Bemaraha.

Few hotels have official low-/high-season prices, although many offer discounts at quiet periods, notably during the rainy season.

Hotels in this book have been classified as budget, midrange or top end.

ACCOMMODATION PRICE RANGES

Budget	€	<Ar35,000	Simple room, often with shared facilities, normally with fan and mosquito net (where needed).
Midrange	€€	Ar35,000-70,000	A notch above budget in terms of decor; rooms are generally ensuite (but hot water does not always work). Air-con may be available.
Top end	€€€	>Ar70,000	All mod cons, good hotel facilities (pool, wi-fi etc). Prices quoted in euros in most upmarket establishments.

The top-end category is the most heterogeneous, with some luxury resorts costing as much as €500 (Ar1.4 million) per night for a double room with full board.

Prices for top-end hotels are often quoted in euros, but you will generally have to pay in ariary, at the day's exchange rate.

The *vignette* (tourist tax) of Ar500 to Ar4000 per night is included in prices quoted in this book.

Camping & Gîtes d'Etape

Camping is possible, mostly in national parks.

Facilities vary, from showers, toilets and well-equipped cooking areas, to nothing more than a cleared area of bush and a long-drop toilet.

Tents are often available for hire, although you'll need your own sleeping bag.

Some national parks also have basic hostels known as *gîtes d'étape*.

Homestays

In rural areas you can sometimes arrange homestays by politely asking around a village for a place to sleep. Pay a fair fee – about Ar20,000 per couple is appropriate.

If you can, bring some rice (the main staple) too – you can generally buy it by the measure (about 300g) in markets and village shops.

Hotels & Bungalows

Hotels in Madagascar come in many guises, from simple *pensions* to luxury resorts. Bungalows are stand-alone structures; they are often wooden and popular in seaside locations and scenic areas. Bungalows can be anything from very basic to plush and elegant.

Hot water is rare in budget accommodation, hit and miss in midrange places but reliable in top-end places.

Air-con is only really necessary in summer months (December to March) in the highlands; elsewhere, it'll very much depend on how much breeze the hotel gets at night.

Hot water and a decent blanket or two are luxuries worth paying for if you're staying in the highlands, especially in winter since hotels don't have central heating, and cheaper places are notorious for draughts.

All but the most basic hotels provide mosquito nets in coastal areas; they are not commonplace in Antananarivo (Tana) or the highlands, where mosquitoes are less of a problem.

Activities

Madagascar is an excellent destination for sporting activities. Climbing, diving, trekking and canoeing/kayaking are all in plentiful supply.

The key is to pick a reliable operator, particularly with high-risk activities such as diving, kite-surfing and rock climbing. Check the operator's affiliations, the instructors' qualifications and inspect your gear.

Divers, note that there is no hyperbaric chamber in Madagascar, so should you have a mishap underwater, you will have to go to Réunion to be depressurised.

Business Hours

Reviews in this book don't list opening hours unless they differ from the standard hours given here.

Businesses (Antananarivo) 8am to 4pm Monday to Friday

Businesses (rest of the country) 7.30am to 11.30am and 2pm to 4.30pm Monday to Friday

Restaurants 11.30am to 2.30pm (lunch) and 6.30pm to 9.30pm (dinner)

Bars 5pm to 11pm

Shops 9am to noon and 2.30pm to 6pm Monday to Friday, 9am to noon Saturday

Children

There are few dedicated children's facilities in Madagascar; that said, Malagasies love children and will always do their best to accommodate families.

Many hotels provide *chambres familiales* or double rooms with an extra single bed geared for use by parents and children.

Disposable nappies are available in Antananarivo and other large cities, but are hard to find elsewhere.

Some national parks and zoos have exhibitions geared towards helping children understand issues of biodiversity and conservation.

For more information, check out Lonely Planet's *Travel with Children*.

Customs Regulations

Travellers are allowed to leave the country with the following:

- 2kg of vanilla (dried)
- 1kg of hallmarked jewellery with receipts
- 1kg peppercorns
- 1kg coffee

Precious stones and woods must come with an export certificate; if the retailer doesn't provide it to you, enquire at the customs desk at the airport.

For a full list of regulations, check Douanes Malgaches (Malagasy Customs; www.douanes.gov.mg).

Electricity

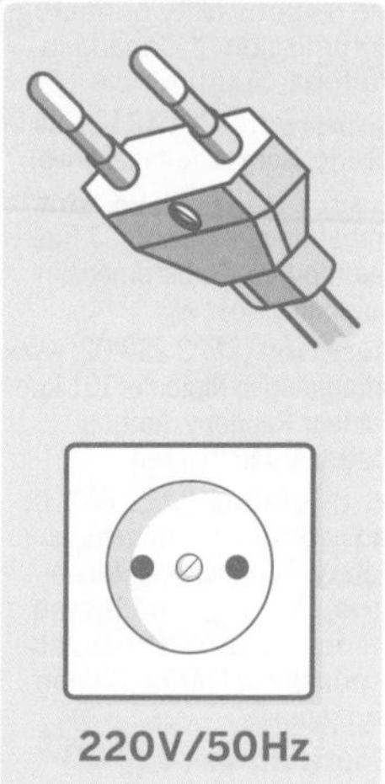

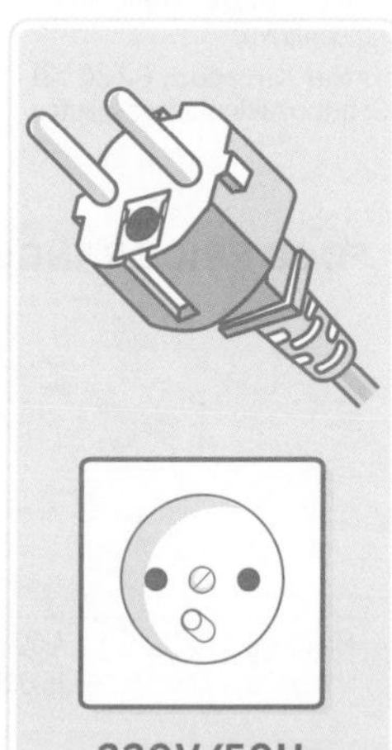

Embassies & Consulates

Australia (☎+230 202 0160; www.mauritius.embassy.gov.au;

BOOK YOUR STAY ONLINE

For more accommodation reviews by Lonely Planet authors, check out http://hotels.lonelyplanet.com/madagascar/. You'll find independent reviews, as well as recommendations on the best places to stay. Best of all, you can book online.

Mauritius) The Australian High Commission in Mauritius has consular responsibility for Madagascar.

Canada (☎22 397 37; consulat.canada@moov.mg; Immeuble Fitaratra, Ankorondrano, Antananarivo) Consulate, under the responsibility of the High Commission of Canada in Pretoria, South Africa.

Comoros (☎24 542 12; Rue Dr Villette, Isoraka, Antananarivo)

France (☎22 398 98; www.ambafrance-mada.org; 3 Rue Jean Jaurès, Ambatomena, Antananarivo)

Germany (☎22 238 02; www.antananarivo.diplo.de; 101 Rue Pasteur Rabeony, Ambodiroatra, Antananarivo)

Netherlands (☎22 682 31; rad.ned@dts.mg; Immeuble Galaxy, Andraharo, Antananarivo) Consulate under the responsibility of the Dutch Embassy in Dar Es Salaam, Tanzania.

South Africa (☎22 433 50; antananarivo.consular@foreign.gov.za; Rue Ravoninahitriniarivo, Ankorondrano, Antananarivo)

United Kingdom (☎24 521 80; http://ukinmadagascar.fco.gov.uk) The embassy closed in 2005 although consular services remain.

United States (☎23 480 00; www.antananarivo.usembassy.gov; Point Liberty, Andranoro, Antehiroka) Located about 15km north of Antananarivo, on the road to Ivato airport.

Food

Eating in Madagascar is a treat: food is generally good, and excellent value.

Restaurants reviewed in this book have been classified as budget, midrange and top end according to the price of a main course.

The majority of restaurants in Madagascar fall in the midrange category and standards are often excellent.

Meal times are as follows:

» Breakfast 6am to 9am

» Lunch 11.30am to 2.30pm

» Dinner 6.30pm to 9.30pm

For more information on the kind of food you're likely to come across in Madagascar, see p208.

FOOD PRICE RANGES

Budget	€	<Ar10,000	Food stalls, *hotelys* or *gargottes* (informal Malagasy eateries). Rice dishes are the staple, and there is also a huge variety of fritters.
Midrange	€€	Ar10,000-15,000	Restaurants, some of which are very fancy. A small increase in price but a big jump in quality; zebu steaks, grilled seafood and vegies, which are often delicious.
Top end	€€€	>Ar15,000	Expect haute cuisine, elaborate presentation, decadent wine or rum selections and elegant surroundings.

Gay & Lesbian Travellers

Homosexuality is legal in Madagascar but not openly practised. The age of consent is 21.

Overt displays of affection – whether the couple is of the same or opposite sex – are considered to be culturally inappropriate.

Insurance

A travel-insurance policy to cover theft, loss and medical problems is essential. Some policies specifically exclude dangerous activities, which can include scuba-diving, motorcycling or even trekking.

Check that the policy covers an emergency flight home. This is an important consideration for Madagascar, given the cost of air tickets to most destinations.

For more advice about health-insurance policies, see p262.

Worldwide travel insurance is available at www.lonelyplanet.com/travel_services. You can buy, extend and claim online anytime – even if you're already on the road.

Internet Access

» Internet cafes can be found in all major towns and cities.

» An increasing number of hotels, including budget and midrange places, have complimentary wi-fi.

» Connection speeds vary from pretty good to woefully slow.

» Prices range from Ar30 to Ar100 per minute.

Legal Matters

Malagasy authorities take sex tourism very seriously – offenders risk five to 10 years in jail and forced labour; sentences are particularly severe when minors are affected.

The use and possession of marijuana and other recreational drugs is illegal in Madagascar, including the stimulant *khat* (even though the latter is widely and openly consumed in the north; see p152).

If you are arrested, ask to see a representative of your country.

Maps

Regional maps and street maps of provincial capitals are produced by Foiben Taosarintanin'i Madagasikara (FTM). FTM maps can be fairly dated but are generally accurate, although they can be hard to find (normally in bookshops for around Ar20,000).

Edicom and Carambole both publish detailed maps of Antananarivo, which are widely available at bookshops and cost about Ar15,000.

Topographical maps are hard to find in Madagascar, so buy one before you leave.

Money

Madagascar changed its currency from the Malagasy franc (FMG) to the ariary (Ar) in 2005. But despite having had a few years to get used to the new currency, many Malagasies still count in FMG (one ariary is worth five FMG), so it is essential you clarify which currency a price is being quoted in, particularly in rural areas.

Inflation is rampant in Madagascar, and the denominations are struggling to keep up. The biggest bank note currently available is Ar10,000, but with a main course at a restaurant costing Ar10,000 to Ar15,000, many agree it won't be long until larger denominations are printed.

For travellers, it means that changing just €300 will produce a wad some 85 notes thick...

Only the most upmarket resorts will accept payments in foreign currency.

ATMs

» You'll find ATMs in all major towns and cities.

» Withdrawals from ATMs are capped at Ar300,000.

» All ATMs accept Visa.

» Crédit Agricole (BNI-CA) ATMs also accept MasterCard.

Credit Cards

Visa credit cards are accepted at some upmarket hotels and shops, Air Madagascar, and at some larger travel agencies.

Although MasterCard can now be used at Crédit Agricole (BNI-CA) ATMs, you will not be able to make payments with it.

Some places levy a commission of about 5% to 8% for credit-card payments.

Visa and MasterCard can be used at most banks to obtain cash advances of up to Ar10 million; commission rates go as high as 5%, depending on the bank.

Moneychangers

The main banks:

» Bank of Africa (BOA)

» Bankin'ny Indostria-Crédit Agricole (BNI-CA)

» Banky Fampandrosoana'ny Varotra-Société Générale (BFV-SG)

» Banque Malgache de l'Océan Indien (BMOI)

All banks will readily exchange euros; US dollars are generally accepted, too.

British pounds, Swiss francs, Japanese yen and South African rand will be harder to exchange outside major cities.

Most banks will refuse €100 or US$100 notes (for fear of counterfeit), so bring small denominations only.

Upmarket hotels often have currency-exchange facilities but check how competitive their rates are.

ADDRESSES IN MADAGASCAR

Addresses in Madagascar are complex affairs – locals don't tend to go by street numbers and there's no standard system. In this book we've included addresses for places on prominent streets, but if the street is not well known we've simply given the area of town where you'll find the place, or a description of how to locate it. If in doubt, ask around locally.

The bureau de change at Ivato airport will change Malagasy currency back into euros or dollars, but requires a minimum of €50.

Travellers Cheques

All banks in Antananarivo exchange travellers cheques.

Outside of the capital, the BFV-SG is your best bet, although some branches of BOA and BNI-CA also offer the service.

As with cash, prefer euros and stick to small denominations (banks need the approval of their headquarters to exchange denominations of €100 or more).

Post

There are post offices located in every town and city. The postal service is slow but generally OK for postcards and letters. Parcels, however, seem to be regularly stolen and Malagasies never send valuables through the post.

The cost for a postcard is Ar1620 to Europe and Ar1720 to North America or Australia, and for a letter it's Ar2700 to Europe and Ar3000 to North America or Australia.

MADAGASCAR'S CULTURAL CALENDAR

Alahamady Be (March) The low-key Malagasy New Year.

Santabary (April/May) The first rice harvest.

Fisemana (June) A ritual purification ceremony of the Antakarana people.

Sambatra (June to December) Circumcision festivals held by most tribes between June and September, and in November and December in the southwest.

Famadihana (July to September) The 'turning of the bones'.

Public Holidays

Accommodation and flights can be harder to find during French school holidays, when residents from neighbouring French territories Mayotte and Réunion travel in the region. To find out when these holidays are, visit www.ac-reunion.fr/outils/infos-pratiques/calendrier-scolaire.html.

Government offices and private companies close on the following public holidays; banks are generally also closed the afternoon before a public holiday.

New Year's Day 1 January

Insurrection Day 29 March; celebrates the rebellion against the French in 1947

Easter Monday March/April

Labour Day 1 May

Anniversary Day 8 May

Organisation of African Unity Day 25 May

Ascension Thursday May/June; occurs 40 days after Easter

Pentecost Monday May/June; occurs 51 days after Easter

National Day 26 June; Independence Day

Assumption 15 August

All Saints' Day 1 November

Christmas Day 25 December

Safe Travel

Crime Insecurity has increased in Antananarivo since the political crisis started; always travel by taxi at night and watch out for pickpockets, especially around Ave de l'Indépendance.

Natural disasters Cyclone season runs from December to March; the east coast is the most affected but cyc-lones can also hit the west coast. Heed local warnings and seek advice at the time for transport and activities.

Robbery There has been a spate of robberies on vehicles and taxis-brousses travelling at night along the RN2, RN6 and RN34. Police have responded by increasing their presence on the road, but you should avoid travelling at night, particularly in private vehicles.

Telephone

The country code for Madagascar is +261. Phone numbers have 10 digits.

Landline numbers start with 020; this prefix must be added to all landline numbers quoted in this book. For example, to dial a landline number in Antananarivo, dial ☎020 22 999 99. From abroad, dial ☎+261 20 22 999 99.

Mobile numbers start with 032, 033 or 034.

To call out of Madagascar, dial +00 before the country code.

If you don't have a mobile (cell) phone, there are cardphones in major cities (on the street and at post offices). *Télécartes* (phone cards) are sold at post offices and in some shops.

Rates for international calls from payphones are around Ar2700 per minute to France and the Comoros, and about Ar4100 per minute to the rest of Europe and North America.

You can send a fax from some post offices, upmarket hotels and internet cafes.

Mobile Phones

Mobile (cell) phone coverage is pretty good across Madagascar, but a number of remote areas only have coverage from one network instead of the three available.

SIM cards are very cheap (Ar500 to Ar2000) and can be bought pretty much anywhere in the country.

You can buy credit at literally every street corner in big cities and every grocery shop across the country in the form of electronic credit or scratch cards (Ar1000 to Ar100,000).

A national/international SMS costs around Ar120/340.

National calls cost around Ar350 to Ar400 per minute.

International calls from mobile phones cost Ar870 to Ar4000 per minute.

Main Mobile Networks

The main mobile networks are **Telma** (www.telma.mg; prefix 034), which is government-owned; **Airtel** (http://africa.airtel.com/madagascar; prefix 033); and **Orange** (www.orange.mg; prefix 032).

Tourist Information

Madagascar's **tourist offices** (www.madagascar-tourisme.com) range from useless to incredibly helpful. They will generally be able to provide listings of hotels and restaurants in the area, and in the best cases help you organise excursions or find a guide.

Travellers with Disabilities

Madagascar has no facilities for travellers with disabilities. This, combined with a weak infrastructure in many areas of the country, may make travel here difficult.

Wheelchair users will struggle with the lack of surfaced paths; visually-impaired travellers should be especially careful of open drains and irregular pavements.

Public transport is very crowded and unable to accommodate a wheelchair unless it is folded up; private vehicle rental with a driver is commonplace, however, and would offer a good alternative. Make sure you talk through any special requirements with the agency at the time of booking.

In Antananarivo and most of the provincial capitals there are hotels with either elevators or accommodation on the ground floor. While most bungalow accommodation – a common type of lodging in Madagascar – is generally on the ground floor, there are often steps up to the entrance, and inner doorways can be too narrow for a wheelchair.

Few bathrooms are large enough to manoeuvre a wheelchair in, and almost none have any sort of handles or holds.

PRACTICALITIES

» Madagascar is three hours ahead of GMT; there is no daylight saving.

» The main French-language newspapers are *Midi Madagasikara*, *Madagascar Tribune* and *L'Express de Madagascar*.

» Madagascar TV stations include the state-run TVM (TV Malagasy) as well as the private channels MATV, RTA and MBS TV.

» Madagascar uses the metric system.

Organisations that provide information on world travel for the mobility impaired include the following:

Mobility International USA (☎+1 541 343 1284; www.miusa.org; USA)

National Information Communication Awareness Network (Nican; ☎+612 6241 1220; www.nican.com.au; Australia)

Royal Association for Disability & Rehabilitation (☎+44 20 7250 3222; www.radar.org.uk; UK)

Society for the Advancement of Travel for the Handicapped (SATH; ☎+1 212 447 7284; www.sath.org; USA)

Visas

All visitors must have a visa to enter Madagascar. Travellers will need to provide a return plane ticket, have a passport valid for at least six months after the intended date of return, and one free page in their passport for the visa stamps.

Visas of up to 90 days can be purchased at the airport upon arrival.

» 30-day visas are free

» 60-day visas cost €45

» 90-day visas cost €70

Longer or different types of visas must be arranged before travel – note that applications can be long.

Always check with your nearest representation on the latest conditions and fees.

GOVERNMENT TRAVEL ADVICE

The following government websites offer up-to-date travel advisories and information on current events.

Australian Department of Foreign Affairs (www.smartraveller.gov.au)

British Foreign & Commonwealth Office (www.fco.gov.uk)

Canadian Department of Foreign Affairs & International Trade (www.voyage.gc.ca)

French Ministry of Foreign Affairs (www.diplomatie.gouv.fr)

US State Department (www.travel.state.gov)

Volunteering

More people are showing interest in volunteering for community-enhancement and scientific-research projects in Madagascar. There are many ways to give something back in Madagascar, from 'traditional volunteering' in schools or orphanages to the more recent 'working holidays', where you pay to work on a project.

The following organisations all offer different types of experiences; check their websites to see what fits your budget and skills.

Akany Avoko (☎24 150 27, 032 04 331 21; www.akanyavoko.com) An Antananarivo-based children's home that cares for around 120 orphans, street kids and youngsters with little or no family support. Akany Avoko has been around for

RESPONSIBLE DIVING & SNORKELLING

Consider the following tips when diving, and help preserve the ecology and beauty of reefs.

» Never use anchors on the reef, and take care not to ground boats on coral.

» Don't touch living marine organisms or drag equipment across the reef. Polyps can be damaged by even the gentlest contact. If you must hold onto the reef, only touch exposed rock or dead coral.

» Be conscious of your fins. Even without contact, the surge from fin strokes near the reef can damage delicate organisms.

» Take great care in underwater caves. Spend as little time within them as possible as your air bubbles may be caught within the roof and thereby leave organisms high and dry.

» Resist the temptation to collect or buy corals or shells or to loot marine archaeological sites (mainly shipwrecks).

» Ensure that you take home all your rubbish and any litter you may find as well. Plastics in particular are a serious threat to marine life.

» Do not feed fish, even if operators offer it.

» Never ride on the backs of turtles.

40 years, and is sustained by charitable donations and income-generating projects. It welcomes volunteers, whether they have half a day or six months to spare. Inexpensive accommodation can be provided.

Blue Ventures (☎+44 20 7697 8598; www.blueventures.org) Based in London, with a field site located in Andavadoaka, this organisation coordinates teams of volunteer divers to work with local NGOs and biologists. Volunteering stints range from three to 12 weeks (£1500 to £3700) and include PADI scuba-diving certification.

Dodwell Trust (www.dodwell-trust.org) This British charity runs a variety of projects accepting volunteers for one- to 12-month stays. The emphasis is on teaching English in primary schools; there are also opportunities to help local radio programs, teach basic IT skills and work on local conservation issues. Programs cost between £700 and £3700.

Earthwatch Institute (☎+44 1865 318 838; www.earthwatch.org) This Oxford-based company runs 13-day scientific research trips (£1800) to track and monitor fossas at Parc National d'Ankarafantsika in western Madagascar.

Women Travellers

Most women do not feel threatened or insecure in any way when travelling in Madagascar. The most you can expect is some mild curiosity about your situation, especially if you are single and/or don't have children (Malagasy women marry and have children young).

A limited selection of tampons is available in Antana-narivo and some of the larger towns, but it's best to bring your own supply.

Transport

GETTING THERE & AWAY

Entering Madagascar

If you are coming from a yellow-fever infected country, you will be asked for a yellow fever vaccination certificate.

Air

Airports & Airlines

International flights come into **Ivato airport** (www.adema.mg), 20km north of Antananarivo (Tana). The airports in Majunga (Mahajanga), Diego Suarez (Antsiranana) and Tamatave (Toamasina) also handle flights from Réunion, Mauritius and the Comoros. The following airlines fly to/from Madagascar:

Air Austral (www.air-austral.com) Flies between Madagascar, Réunion and Mayotte.

Air France (www.airfrance.com) Four flights a week between Paris and Tana.

Air Italy (www.airitaly.it) Weekly flights between Milan and Nosy Be.

Air Madagascar (www.airmadagascar.com) The national carrier; has direct flights from France, South Africa, Kenya, Thailand and Guangzhou in China and neighbouring Indian Ocean islands. Its planes were blacklisted from European airspace in early 2011, it therefore leases an aircraft from Air Italy to operate Europe-bound flights.

Air Mauritius (www.airmauritius.com) Flies between Mauritius and Tana almost daily.

Corsair (www.corsair.fr) Up to three flights a week between Paris and Antananarivo.

Kenyan Airways (www.kenya-airways.com) Has four flights a week between Nairobi and Tana.

South African Airways (www.flysaa.com) Daily flights between Johannesburg and Tana.

Tickets

Because there isn't much competition to fly to Madagascar, airfares can be expensive.

Expect to pay €800 to €1500 for a return ticket from Europe (where there are more options), at least €1700 from North America and at least €2000 from Australia.

Sea

Ship

The mixed cargo and passenger ships *MS Mauritius Trochetia* and *MS Mauritius Pride* sail between Tamatave on the east coast and the islands of Réunion and Mauritius once every two weeks or so. One-way fares to Réunion are €264/232 for a 1st-/2nd-class cabin (based on two people sharing), and €303/282 to Mauritius. Book through **Tropical Service** (☎53 336 79;

CLIMATE CHANGE & TRAVEL

Every form of transport that relies on carbon-based fuel generates CO_2, the main cause of human-induced climate change. Modern travel is dependent on aeroplanes, which might use less fuel per kilometre per person than most cars but travel much greater distances. The altitude at which aircraft emit gases (including CO_2) and particles also contributes to their climate change impact. Many websites offer 'carbon calculators' that allow people to estimate the carbon emissions generated by their journey and, for those who wish to do so, to offset the impact of the greenhouse gases emitted with contributions to portfolios of climate-friendly initiatives throughout the world. Lonely Planet offsets the carbon footprint of all staff and author travel.

AIR PENNY SAVER

Domestic flights are about 30% cheaper when bought in Madagascar compared to when purchased abroad. If your itinerary is flexible, this is a great way to save money. But bear in mind that flights on popular routes are booked far in advance and that it is difficult to get tickets at short notice.

Air Madagascar also offers a 50% discount on domestic flights to travellers who flew the airline to Madagascar. (The discount doesn't apply to taxes, so the final saving is about 30% of the final fare; still, not to be sniffed at.)

Prices quoted in this book do not take either discount into account.

www.croisiere-madagascar.com; 23 Blvd Joffre, Tamatave).

Private Yacht

Yachts regularly sail to Madagascar to/from from South Africa, Mozambique, Mayotte, Réunion and Mauritius, and travellers may be able to join the crossing as crew members. Your best options to find a boat are online forums, word of mouth and asking around at ports (Nosy Be in particular).

Tours

Adventure Associates (www.adventureassociates.com; Australia) Runs tours to Madagascar, combined with Réunion.

Baobab Travel (www.baobab.nl; Netherlands) Offers a south and east circuit.

Comptoir de Madagascar (www.comptoirdemadagascar.com; France) General interest tours.

Cortez Travel & Expeditions (www.air-mad.com; US) Well-established operator with an agency in the US and one in Madagascar.

Madagaskar Travel (www.madagaskar-travel.de; Germany) General and specialist fauna and flora itineraries.

Priori (www.priori.ch; Madagascar) Cultural and wildlife tours; run by a Swiss national, long-time Madagascar resident.

Rainbow Tours (www.rainbowtours.co.uk; UK) Specialist and general-interest guided trips to Madagascar; highly recommended by travellers.

Reef & Rainforest Tours (www.reefandrainforest.co.uk; UK) Focuses on wildlife holidays.

Terre Malgache (www.terre-malgache.com; France) A wide range of tours to Madagascar.

Trauminsel Reisen (www.trauminselreisen.de; Germany) Itineraries all over Madagascar.

Wildlife Worldwide (www.wildlifeworldwide.com; UK) Wildlife-viewing tours.

Zingg (www.zinggsafaris.com; Switzerland) Individual and group circuits.

GETTING AROUND

Air

Flying within Madagascar can be a huge time-saver considering the distances and state of the roads. Unfortunately most domestic routes are between Tana and the provinces, with few direct routes between provinces.

Airlines in Madagascar

Air Madagascar (www.airmadagascar.com) is the only airline to provide domestic flights. Cancellations and delays occur but the airline is generally reliable.

Tickets are expensive (one-way €125 to €187) but generally exchangeable. You can pay for tickets by credit card or in ariary, euros or US dollars at the head office in Antananarivo and Air Madagascar offices in larger towns. Smaller offices may only accept ariary or euros, however.

Certain routes such as Morondava–Tuléar (Toliara) during the high season (May to September) and all flights to/from Sambava during the vanilla season (June to October) are often fully booked months in advance.

Bicycle

» A mountain bike is normally essential if cycling in Madagascar.

» Inner tubes and other basic parts are sometimes available in larger towns.

» The terrain varies from very sandy to muddy or rough and rocky.

» It's usually no problem to transport your bicycle on taxis-brousses or on the train.

» You'll find mountain bikes for hire (Ar5000 to Ar20,000 per day) in most large towns and tourist hot spots such as Ile Ste Marie (Nosy Boraha) or Nosy Be.

Boat

Cargo Boat

In parts of Madagascar, notably the northeast coast and Canal des Pangalanes, cargo boats (sometimes called *boutres*) are the primary means of transport. Cargo boats have no schedules and leave with the tides. Some cargo boats have passenger cabins, but most have deck space only.

Capsizing occurs regularly, so don't get in if the seas are rough or if the boat is overcrowded. Some precautions to keep in mind:

Major Domestic Air Routes

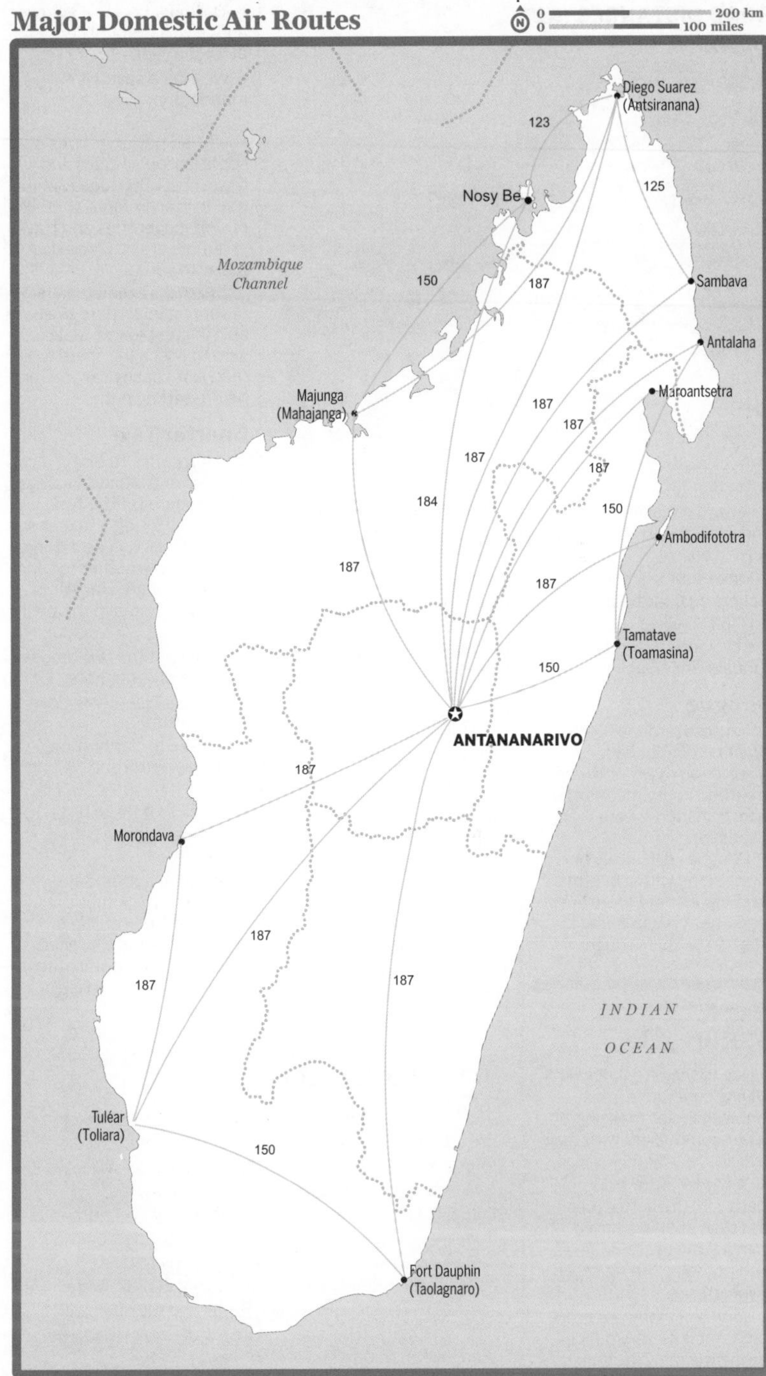

ROAD DISTANCES (KM)

	Antananarivo	Antsirabe	Diego Suarez	Fianarantsoa	Fort Dauphin	Tamatave	Tuléar (Toliara)	Majunga	Morondava	Nosy Be
Antsirabe	162									
Diego Suarez	1093	1254								
Fianarantsoa	405	243	1497							
Fort Dauphin	1103	941	2195	699						
Tamatave	324	485	1255	729	1428					
Tuléar (Toliara)	923	761	2015	519	595	1246				
Majunga	552	713	805	956	1654	873	1474			
Morondava	646	485	1197	460	1158	969	978	1197		
Nosy Be	880	1054	235	1280	1980	1042	1797	574	1505	
Soanierana-Ivongo	488	649	1420	893	1591	167	1411	1037	1134	1204

» Always check the forecast and ask local advice before setting off.

» Make sure there are life jackets on board.

» Don't travel at sea during the cyclone season, between January and March.

Pirogue

Engineless pirogues or *lakanas* (dugout canoes), whether on rivers or the sea, are the primary means of local transport where roads disappear.

Pirogues can easily be hired, along with a boatman, but bear in mind there are no amenities on board and the ride can be quite rough.

Car & Motorcycle

» Due to the often difficult driving conditions, most rental agencies make hiring a driver compulsory with their vehicles.

» Of Madagascar's approximately 50,000km of roads, less than 20% are paved, and many of those are riddled with potholes the size of an elephant.

» Routes in many areas are impassable or very difficult during the rainy season.

» The designation *route nationale* (RN) is sadly no guarantee of quality.

» Driving in Madagascar is on the right-hand side.

» Police checkpoints are frequent (mind the traffic spikes on the ground) – always slow down and make sure you have your passport and the vehicle's documents handy.

» If you see a zebu on the road, slow right down as it can panic; also, there may be another 20 in the bushes that haven't yet crossed.

Car Hire

If you insist on driving yourself, note the following rules:

» You must have an International Driving License.

» You must be age 23 or over and have had your license for at least a year.

» Wearing a seatbelt is mandatory.

You'll find petrol stations of some kind in all cities and towns. Fuel shortages are frequent, even in Tana, so stock up. For longer trips and travel in remote areas, take extra fuel with you.

Spare parts and repairs of varying quality are available in most towns. Make sure to check the spare tyre (and jack) of any car you rent before setting out.

Charter Taxi

An alternative to hiring a car and driver (difficult in areas where there is little tourism), chartering a taxi or a taxi-brousse can be a good alternative, whether for one or several days. Here are some tips to make the best of it:

» Enquire at the taxi-brousse stand or ask your hotel what the going rate for your journey is.

» Be sure to clarify such things as petrol and waiting time.

» Check that the vehicle is in decent shape before departing.

» For longer, multiday journeys, check that the driver has the vehicle's documents and a special charter permit (indicated by a diagonal green stripe).

ROAD SOLIDARITY

Public transportation is few and far between in remote areas – and sometimes nonexistent during the six months of the rainy season. If you've hired a 4WD to drive through remote areas, you'll see many locals hitching for a lift to the next town or village; your driver may be keen to help out his fellow countrymen, but he will always ask you whether you're happy to take on extra passengers. Note, too, that villagers reuse water bottles to store chutneys and juices and will often ask you whether you have any spare (to the cry of 'Eau Vive! Eau Vive!'), so don't throw them away.

» Prepare a contract that you and the driver will sign stipulating insurance issues, the agreed-upon fee (including whether or not petrol is included) and your itinerary.

Motorcycle

» Motorcycles can be hired by the half day or full day at various places in Madagascar, including Tuléar, Nosy Be and Ile Ste Marie.

» Chinese motorbikes are increasingly replacing the well-known Japanese brands.

» Wearing a helmet is compulsory; they should be provided in the rental.

Hitching

Hitching is never entirely safe in any country in the world, and we don't recommend it. Travellers who do decide to hitch should understand that they are taking a small but potentially serious risk. People who do choose to hitch will be safer if they travel in pairs and let someone know where they are planning to go.

Traffic between towns and cities is thin, and most passing vehicles are likely to be taxis-brousses or trucks, which are often full. If you do find a ride, you will likely have to pay about the equivalent of the taxi-brousse fare.

Along well-travelled routes or around popular tourist destinations, you can sometimes find lifts with privately rented 4WDs.

Local Transport

Charette

In rural parts of Madagascar, the *charette*, a wooden cart drawn by a pair of zebu cattle, is the most common form of transport. Fares are entirely negotiable.

Pousse-Pousse

The colourful *pousse-pousse* (rickshaw) is a popular way to get around in some cities. Fares vary between Ar500 and Ar2000 for a ride, depending on distance. When it's raining and at night, prices increase.

Taxi-Brousse

The good news is that taxis-brousses are cheap and go everywhere. The bad news is that they are slow, uncomfortable, erratic and sometimes unsafe.

Despite the general appearance of anarchy, the taxi-brousse system is actually relatively well-organised. Drivers and vehicles belong to transport companies called Coopératives (co-operatives). Coopératives generally have a booth or an agent at the taxi-brousse station (called *gare routière* or *parcage*), where you can book your ticket.

Although the going can be slow, taxis-brousses stop regularly for toilet stops, leg stretching and meals (at *hotelys* along the road).

SEATS & LUGGAGE

» Most taxis-brousses, notably the Japanese minibuses used for long journeys, stick to the number of seats in the vehicle. This is less true of *bâchés* and *camions-brousses*.

» The two front seats beside the driver are usually the most spacious and most sought after. They are, however, the most dangerous in case of an accident since there are no seatbelts.

» Seats at the back of minibuses will be very uncomfortable for anyone taller than 1.65m and downright impossible for anyone taller than 1.85m.

» You can buy more than one seat.

» Specific seats can be booked, but you'll have to

TAXI-BROUSSE GLOSSARY

The term taxi-brousse (literally 'bush taxi') is used generically in Madagascar to refer to any vehicle providing public transport. When you buy your taxi-brousse ticket, therefore, you could be about to climb into anything from a pickup truck to a rumbling juggernaut with entire suites of furniture tied to its roof.

The most common guise of the taxi-brousse is the 14-seater Japanese minibus (Toyota and Mazda especially). On long and popular routes (eg Tana–Morondava or Tana–Tuléar), you'll also find Mercedes 18-seater minibuses, which are the most spacious and comfortable of the lot (comparable to a low-cost European airline).

For shorter journeys (eg Diego Suarez to Joffreville) and in rural areas, ancient Peugeot 504s or 505s are the go. They are smaller and therefore fill quicker and also tend to fill more than their theoretical number of seats (three at the front and four or five at the back).

A *bâché* is a small, converted pick-up, which usually has some sort of covering over the back and benches down each side. *Bâchés* are used on shorter, rural routes and are hideously uncomfortable.

The *camion-brousse* is a huge 4WD army-style truck, fitted with a bench or seats down each side, although the majority of passengers wind up sitting on the floor, on top of whatever supplies the truck is carrying. They are used for particularly long or rough journeys.

book at least the day before at the taxi-brousse station.

» Luggage goes on the roof under a tarpaulin and is tightly roped in.

» Taxis-brousses leave when full, which can take an hour or a day. If you'd like to speed up the process, buy the remaining seats.

» The choice of a taxi-brousse will often come down to joining the next vehicle to leave, which will be packed to the roof, or holding out for a decent seat in a later taxi-brousse.

COSTS

» Fares for all trips are set by the government and are based on distance, duration and route conditions. Ask to see the list of official fares.

» *Never* buy your ticket from a tout – always get it from the cooperative booth at the taxi-brousse station or from the driver if in doubt. In any case, get a receipt.

CAR & DRIVER Q&A

In Madagascar the road transportation system is such that most rental cars come with a mandatory driver, making the choice of both a critical decision in your travel planning. Here are the key issues to consider.

Why do I need a car?

If you take a taxi-brousse (bush taxi), it takes a great deal of time. You will go to the station and wait for it to fill up with passengers. This can take an hour or a day, and you may need to do this more than once if you need a connection. Having your own car allows you to stop wherever you want.

Do I need a 4WD?

It depends on your route. If you're sticking to the RN7 between Tana and Tuléar, you don't need a 4WD. But most roads in Madagascar are dirt or sand, and frequently require 4WD.

Why do I need a driver?

The roads can be very rough, so you have to know how to drive on them. Even if you do, navigation is tricky: tracks change, depending on traffic and rainfall. There are a lot of police checkpoints: you have to know how to deal with them. If you get in an accident or something goes wrong with the car, you may be far from anywhere. You will have to contact someone and describe where you are. There may be no mobile phone (cellphone) signal. You have to know how to find spare parts. The driver is responsible for all this.

So how do I find a good driver?

You either go through a tour agency or hotel or hire one directly. Either way, it is essential you shop around. Talk to the driver ahead of time. Make sure you speak a common language and that the driver has experience in your region. If you're not hiring through a reputable agency, take a look at the car, particularly if you are going on a long journey. See how well he takes care of it. If you are out of the country, ask him to send you pictures.

How much does a car and driver cost?

The car and driver are one package. Fuel is generally extra, although not always. Prices for a car are typically Ar80,000 to Ar100,000 per day. Prices for a 4WD are Ar150,000 to Ar240,000 per day. Some drivers will charge by the road surface, dirt or paved, regardless of the car. Prices also decrease with long-term rentals of 10 days or so. This is negotiable, but a 10-day 4WD rental typically ranges from Ar130,000 to Ar200,000 per day. Also, the renter is responsible for paying to return the vehicle to where it began, which involves both a daily rental fee plus fuel. Finally, make sure you clarify whether or not extras, such as toll roads and ferry crossings, are included as they can add up quickly.

What about food & lodging for the driver?

The renter is not responsible. Usually your hotel will provide food and board free of charge for the driver (they have special driver rooms for this purpose).

How can I pay?

If you go through an agency, you may be able to pay by card or bank transfer. Otherwise you'll have to pay cash: 50% up front, the remaining half at the end of the trip.

TRAIN JOURNEYS

JOURNEY	DAYS	DEPARTURE TIME	ARRIVAL TIME	FARE (AR)
Moramanga–Tamatave	Mon	7am	5pm	20,000
Tamatave–Moramanga	Tue	8.20am	7pm	20,000
Moramanga–Ambila	Thu	3pm	10pm	20,000
Ambila–Moramanga	Fri	8am	5.30pm	20,000
Moramanga–Ambatondrozaka	Wed & Sat	9.30am	4.30pm	12,000
Ambatondrozaka–Moramanga	Thu & Sun	8.30am	2.30pm	12,000
Fianarantsoa–Manakara	Tue, Thu & Sat	7am	2-7pm	20,000
Manakara–Fianarantsoa	Wed, Fri & Sun	7am	2-7pm	20,000

» Prices are the same for locals and foreigners. However, fares can vary between vehicle types.

» Children under five travel free (but must sit on a parent's lap).

SAFETY

Japanese minibus taxis-brousses are generally in pretty good condition (which can't be said of the ancient Peugeots or *bâchés* plying rural areas), but the one thing to watch out for are smooth tyres. General safety advice is not to travel after dark, but on longer routes, it simply can't be helped. On some routes where highway robbery is on the increase, taxis-brousses are required to travel in convoys at night.

Tours

Madagascar's many tour operators and freelance guides can organise anything from a three-week discovery trip with car and driver to more specialist tours such as mountain-bike excursions, walking tours, wildlife-viewing trips, and cultural and historic tours. All have English-speaking guides and/or drivers.

Following is a nonexhaustive list of reliable companies that can arrange excursions throughout Madagascar.

Boogie Pilgrim (☎22 530 70; www.boogiepilgrim-madagascar.com) Adventurous ecotours and camps in several places in Madagascar, including Parc National d'Andringitra and Canal des Pangalanes. English and German speaking.

Cortez Travel & Expeditions (☎22 219 74; www.air-mad.com) US-Malagasy agency offering a wide range of itineraries for individuals and groups.

Espace Mada (☎22 262 97; www.madagascar-circuits.com) Vehicles, guides and 4WD excursions; specialist for Tsiribihina River and Parc National des Tsingy de Bemaraha trips.

Madamax (☎22 351 01; www.madamax.com) Specialist in adventure-packed holidays; rock-climbing and river trips are their forte.

Mad Caméléon (☎22 630 86; www.madcameleon.com) Tours focusing on western and southern Madagascar, including the Tsiribihina River descent, Parc National des Tsingy de Bemaraha, and pirogue trips down the Manambolo River.

Malagasy Tours (☎22 356 07; www.malagasy-tours.com) A reliable, upmarket operator offering tours in all areas of the country, with trekking and trips along the Tsiribihina River and the Canal des Pangalanes.

Ortour (☎032 07 704 64; www.ortour.com) All kinds of tours, including excellent trekking or birdwatching tours and budget/luxury options on the standards.

Tany Mena Tours (☎22 326 27; www.tanymenatours.com) This agency specialises in sustainable tourism; as well as taking in the country's main sights, all circuits have an emphasis on cultural experiences, with village visits and specialised Malagasy guides.

Za Tours (☎22 424 22; www.zatours-madagascar.com) Well-regarded English-speaking tour company.

Train

The Malagasy rail system, known as the Réseau National des Chemins de Fer Malgaches (RNCFM), is made up of over 1000km of tracks but is used mostly by freight transport.

The only regular passenger train routes are highlighted in the train journeys table. There is momentum to increase passenger rail travel, so check whether new lines have been opened, notably to/from Tana.

Madarail (www.madarail.mg; Gare Soarano, Antananarivo) Operates lines from Moramanga, as well as the tourist-oriented Micheline between Tana and Andasibe (Périnet) or Antsirabe (which only runs at weekends).

FCE (Fianarantsoa-Côte Est) Operates trains between Fianarantsoa and Manakara.

Health

As long as you stay up to date with your vaccinations and take some basic preventive measures, you'd have to be pretty unlucky to succumb to most of the health hazards covered in this chapter.

BEFORE YOU GO

Get a check-up with your dentist and your doctor six to eight weeks before coming to Madagascar to ensure you are up to date with immunisations, to discuss malaria prophylaxis and to make sure tooth decay won't turn into an abscess while you're away.

Insurance

Find out in advance whether your insurance plan will make payments directly to providers or will reimburse you later for overseas health expenditures (most medical facilities and doctors in Madagascar expect payment upfront).

It's vital to ensure that your travel insurance will cover the emergency transport required to get you to a good hospital – in South Africa or Réunion, or all the way home – by air and with a medical attendant if necessary. Not all insurance plans cover this, so check the contract carefully.

Medical Checklist

It's a good idea to carry a medical and first-aid kit with you. Following is a list of items you should consider packing. Contact-lens wearers should also make sure they have spares and plenty of lens solution.

- Acetaminophen (paracetamol) or aspirin
- Adhesive or paper tape
- Antibacterial ointment for cuts and abrasions
- Antibiotics (if travelling off the beaten track)
- Antidiarrhoeal drugs (eg loperamide)
- Antihistamines (for hay fever and allergic reactions)
- Anti-inflammatory drugs (eg ibuprofen)
- Antimalaria pills
- Bandages, gauze and gauze rolls
- Insect repellent for the skin
- Insect spray for clothing, tents and bed nets
- Iodine tablets (for water purification)
- Oral rehydration salts
- Scissors, tweezers and safety pins
- Steroid cream or hydrocortisone cream (for rashes)
- Sunblock (very difficult to find in Madagascar)
- Syringes and sterile needles (if travelling off the beaten track)
- Thermometer

Websites

It's a good idea to consult your government's travel health website before departure, if one is available. The following websites can help:

Australia (www.smartraveller.gov.au)

Canada (www.phac-aspc.gc.ca)

Lonely Planet (www.lonelyplanet.com)

MD Travel Health (www.mdtravelhealth.com)

United Kingdom (www.fitfortravel.nhs.uk)

United States (www.cdc.gov/travel)

World Health Organization (www.who.int)

IN MADAGASCAR

Availability & Cost of Health Care

Getting Treated

Pharmacies For minor problems such as cuts, bites, upset stomachs or colds, pharmacies should be your first port of call in Madagascar. Pharmacists are, on the whole, well trained, the pharmacies are clean and well stocked, and there is an efficient on-call rotation in most towns and cities (generally displayed in the window). Most drugs and bandages cost the same or a little less than in developed countries (generic drugs are used more widely).

Medical centres & hospitals For more serious conditions, you will need to go to a medical centre or a hospital. Public hospitals are, on the whole, poorly equipped and underfunded, but they are sometimes the only option available (note that patients often have to buy medicine, sterile dressings, intravenous fluids etc from the local pharmacy). There are good medical centres in touristy areas such as Nosy Be and good private facilities in Antananarivo. For anything serious, however, you will need to be evacuated to Réunion (a French territory) or South Africa.

Dentists There are dentists across Madagascar, and their standard of care varies from excellent to bad.

Standards

Health care standards vary a lot from one practitioner to another and from one hospital to the next: standards are on the whole pretty good in Antananarivo, but are patchy outside the capital. If you find yourself in need of medical assistance, contact your embassy or consulate for a list of recommended practitioners or establishments in your area. Your insurance company may also have advice.

REQUIRED & RECOMMENDED VACCINATIONS

The **World Health Organization** (WHO; www.who.int) recommends the following vaccinations as routine (many are administered as part of standard childhood immunisation programs in developed countries, but adults may need a booster):

» diphtheria, tetanus and pertussis (DTP)

» Haemophilus influenzae type b (HIB) – this is the leading cause of bacterial meningitis

» hepatitis B

» measles, mumps and rubella (MMR)

» pneumococcal disease

» polio

» rotavirus

» tuberculosis

» varicella

Vaccinations for the following are also recommended for Madagascar:

» hepatitis A

» typhoid

Rabies is endemic in Madagascar, but vaccination is only recommended for visitors who will be spending extensive periods of time in remote areas.

Many vaccines don't ensure immunity until two weeks after they are given, so visit a doctor four to eight weeks before departure.

Ask your doctor for an International Certificate of Vaccination or Prophylaxis (otherwise known as ICVP or 'the yellow card'), listing all the vaccinations you've received.

Infectious Diseases

Despite the intimidating list of infectious diseases in Madagascar, most are extremely rare among travellers. However, if you do experience unusual symptoms for more than three days, seek medical advice.

Cholera

Spread through Contaminated drinking water.

Symptoms & effects Profuse watery diarrhoea, which causes debilitation if fluids are not replaced quickly.

Prevention Cholera is usually only a problem during natural or artificial disasters, eg cyclones, war, floods or earthquakes. An oral cholera vaccine is available, but it is not particularly effective. Boil drinking water or drink bottled water.

Dengue Fever

Spread through Mosquito bites.

Symptoms & effects Feverish illness with headache and muscle pains similar to those experienced with a bad, prolonged attack of influenza.

Prevention Avoid mosquito bites by covering up and wearing repellent during outbreaks. Seek medical advice if flulike symptoms persist.

Diphtheria

Spread through Close respiratory contact with an infected person.

Symptoms & effects A temperature and a severe sore throat. Sometimes a membrane forms across the throat, and a tracheotomy may be needed to prevent suffocation.

Prevention Vaccination (DTP) is recommended and lasts 10 years.

Hepatitis A

Spread through Contaminated food (particularly shellfish) and water.

Symptoms & effects Jaundice and prolonged lethargy. First symptoms include dark urine and a yellow colour to the whites of the eyes. Sometimes a fever and abdominal pain might be present.

Prevention Vaccination is available and recommended.

Hepatitis B

Spread through Infected blood, contaminated needles and sexual intercourse.

Symptoms & effects Jaundice and occasionally liver failure.

Prevention Vaccination is available and recommended.

HIV

Spread through Infected blood, contaminated needles and sexual intercourse.

Symptoms & effects Attacks the body's immune system.

Prevention HIV prevalence in Madagascar is very low (0.2%, similar to Europe), so risk to travellers is minimal, but the same precautions apply here as at home: never have unprotected sex and make sure all hospital equipment is sterile.

Malaria

Spread through Bite of the female *Anopheles* mosquito.

Symptoms & effects The early stages of malaria include headaches, fever, generalised aches and pains, and malaise, which could be mistaken for flu. Other symptoms can include abdominal pain, diarrhoea and a cough. If not treated, the disease can progress to jaundice, reduced consciousness and coma, followed by death.

Prevention Malaria is present throughout Madagascar, although the risks of contracting the disease are higher on the coast (particularly in the east) than in the highlands. It is recommended that all travellers take prophylaxis: there is a variety of drugs available nowadays, ranging in price, regime and secondary effects. Atovaquone/proguanil (Malarone), doxycycline and mefloquine (Lariam) seem to be the most commonly prescribed – discuss your options with a medical professional. It is essential you seek medical help if you suffer from a persistent high fever during your stay or in the six weeks afterwards, as hospital treatment is essential.

Plague

Spread through Bite from infected fleas carried by rodents, handling infected animals (rodents, rabbits and cats in particular) or inhaling droplets from coughs of infected individuals.

Symptoms & effects Pneumonic plague is the most common type of plague in Madagascar. Sufferers will experience shortness of breath, blood-stained sputum and, in the worst cases, septicaemia (blood poisoning) and respiratory failure.

Prevention Plague occurs in small but regular outbreaks in remote areas of Madagascar. There is no vaccine. Travellers are very unlikely to be affected, but as a precaution, never handle animals and use insect sprays to avoid flea bites.

TAP WATER

Madagascar's water is not safe to drink from the taps anywhere in the country – including the most expensive hotels. Bottled water (Ar1800 to Ar4000) is available throughout the country. If you can get clear water from a tap or well, water-purifying tablets are a good option.

If you're planning to get off the beaten track, consider investing in a portable water filter/steriliser such as SteriPen (about US$100) or LifeStraw (about US$20).

Avoid ice in drinks without first asking if it's been made from filtered water.

Poliomyelitis

Spread through Contaminated food and water.

Symptoms & effects Polio can be carried asymptomatically (ie showing no symptoms) and can cause a transient fever. In rare cases it causes weakness or paralysis of one or more muscles.

Prevention The vaccine is given in childhood and should be boosted every 10 years.

Rabies

Spread through Bite or lick on broken skin by an infected animal.

Symptoms & effects Rabies causes acute encephalitis (inflammation of the brain). It is always fatal once the clinical symptoms start, which might be up to several months after an infected bite.

Prevention A preventive vaccine of three injections exists, which gives a person bitten by an infected animal more time to seek medical help. If you have not been vaccinated you will need a course of five injections within 24 hours of being bitten.

Schistosomiasis (Bilharzia)

Spread through Flukes (minute worms) that are carried by a species of freshwater snail; the snails shed the flukes in slow-moving or still water. The parasites penetrate human skin during paddling or swimming and migrate to the bladder/bowel.

Symptoms & effects Transient fever and rash, and blood in stools or urine. In chronic cases, schistosomiasis can cause bladder cancer or damage to the intestines.

Prevention Avoid paddling or swimming in suspect freshwater lakes or slow-running rivers. A blood test can detect antibodies if you suspect you have been exposed, and treatment back home is then possible in specialist travel or infectious-disease clinics.

TRAVELLER'S DIARRHOEA

Although it's not inevitable that you will get diarrhoea while travelling in Madagascar, it's certainly very likely. Diarrhoea is the most common travel-related illness: figures suggest that at least half of all travellers to Africa will get diarrhoea at some stage. Sometimes dietary changes, such as increased spices or oils, are the cause. To avoid diarrhoea, only eat fresh fruits and vegetables if cooked or peeled, and be wary of dairy products that might contain unpasteurised milk. Although freshly cooked food can often be a safe option, plates or serving utensils might be dirty, so you should be highly selective when eating food from street vendors (make sure that cooked food is piping hot all the way through).

If you develop diarrhoea, drink plenty of fluids, preferably an oral rehydration solution containing lots of salt and sugar. A few loose stools don't require treatment, but if you start having more than four or five loose stools a day, you should start taking an antidiarrhoeal agent (such as loperamide) or an antibiotic (usually a quinoline drug, such as ciprofloxacin or norfloxacin). If diarrhoea is bloody, persists for more than 72 hours or is accompanied by fever, shaking chills or severe abdominal pain, you should seek medical attention.

Tuberculosis (TB)

Spread through Close respiratory contact and, occasionally, infected milk or milk products.

Symptoms & effects TB can be asymptomatic, only being picked up on a routine chest X-ray. Alternatively, it can cause a cough, weight loss or fever, sometimes months or even years after exposure.

Prevention The BCG vaccination is recommended for those mixing closely with locals, although it gives only moderate protection.

Typhoid

Spread through Food or water contaminated by infected human faeces.

Symptoms & effects Usually a fever or a pink rash on the abdomen. Sometimes septicaemia can occur.

Prevention A vaccine is available and gives protection for three years.

Environmental Hazards

Heat Exhaustion

Causes Heavy sweating and excessive fluid loss with inadequate replacement of fluids and salt.

Symptoms & effects Headache, dizziness and tiredness.

Prevention & treatment Aim to drink sufficient water to produce pale, diluted urine. To replace salt loss, drink oral rehydration fluids or plenty of savoury and sweet liquids (soup, fruit juice etc).

Heatstroke

Causes Occurs when the body's heat-regulating mechanism breaks down because of extreme heat, high humidity, dehydration and physical exertion.

Symptoms & effects An excessive rise in body temperature, irrational and hyperactive behaviour and, in the most serious cases, loss of consciousness.

Prevention & treatment Acclimatisation to different climate conditions is the best way to prevent heatstroke. Cool the person down with water and keep them in a cool, dark place. Treatment is similar to that for heat exhaustion, but emergency fluids (intravenous) may be needed for extreme cases.

Insect Bites & Stings

Causes Mosquitoes, fleas, scorpions, bedbugs, spiders.

Symptoms & effects Aside from the fact that some bugs can transmit diseases, insect bites or stings can cause irritation, infections and pain. Scorpion stings can be very nasty (fever is common), and sometimes fatal in people with heart conditions, so seek medical help if you're stung.

Prevention & treatment Avoiding getting bitten or stung is obviously the best way to go: wear trousers and long sleeves in the evenings as well as insect repellent. In Ankarana, where scorpions are rife, don't sit on large rocks or logs, and if you camp, check your shoes in the morning and take great care when folding your tent. Antihistamine or steroid creams can help relieve itching from the most benign bites. Painkillers are also efficient to deal with painful bites. If you have a severe allergy (anaphylaxis) to bee or wasp stings, carry an adrenalin injection or similar with you as you won't find any outside of major cities.

Traditional Medicine

Although Western medicine is available in larger cities and towns, *fanafody* (traditional medicine or herbal healing) plays an important role in Madagascar, particularly in rural areas where there are few alternatives. *Ombiasy* (healers) hold considerable social status.

Language

WANT MORE?

For in-depth language information and handy phrases, check out Lonely Planet's *French Phrasebook* and *Africa Phrasebook*. You'll find them at **shop.lonelyplanet.com**, or you can buy Lonely Planet's iPhone phrasebooks at the Apple App Store.

Madagascar has two official languages: Malagasy and French. Malagasy is the everyday spoken language while French is often used for business and administrative purposes, and in the more upmarket sectors of the tourism industry. Unless you travel on an organised tour, stick to big hotels in major towns or speak Malagasy, some basic French will help you get by comfortably in the cities. In rural areas, where knowledge of French is less widespread, you may need to learn a bit of Malagasy too.

FRENCH

The sounds used in French can almost all be found in English. There are a couple of exceptions: nasal vowels (represented in our pronunciation guides by o or u followed by an almost inaudible nasal consonant sound m, n or ng), the 'funny' *u* (ew in our guides) and the deep-in-the-throat *r*. Bearing this in mind and reading our pronunciation guides as if they were English, you'll be understood just fine.

Note that French has two words for 'you' – use the polite form *vous* unless you're talking to close friends or children, in which case you'd use the informal *tu*. Of course, you can also use *tu* when a person invites you to do so.

All nouns in French are either masculine or feminine, and so are the adjectives and articles *le/la* (the) and *un/une* (a) that go with the nouns. We've included masculine and feminine forms where necessary, separated by a slash and indicated with 'm/f'.

Basics

Hello.	*Bonjour.*	bon·zhoor
Goodbye.	*Au revoir.*	o·rer·vwa
Excuse me.	*Excusez-moi.*	ek·skew·zay·mwa
Sorry.	*Pardon.*	par·don
Yes.	*Oui.*	wee
No.	*Non.*	non
Please.	*S'il vous plaît.*	seel voo play
Thank you.	*Merci.*	mair·see

How are you?
Comment allez-vous? ko·mon ta·lay·voo

Fine, and you?
Bien, merci. Et vous? byun mair·see ay voo

You're welcome.
De rien. der ree·en

My name is ...
Je m'appelle ... zher ma·pel ...

What's your name?
Comment vous appelez-vous? ko·mon voo·za·play voo

Do you speak English?
Parlez-vous anglais? par·lay·voo ong·glay

I don't understand.
Je ne comprends pas. zher ner kom·pron pa

Accommodation

Do you have any rooms available?
Est-ce que vous avez des chambres libres? es·ker voo za·vay day shom·brer lee·brer

How much is it per night/person?

Quel est le prix par nuit/personne?	kel ay ler pree par nwee/per·son

Is breakfast included?

Est-ce que le petit déjeuner est inclus?	es·ker ler per·tee day·zher·nay ayt en·klew

campsite	*un camping*	un kom·peeng
dorm	*un dortoir*	un dor·twar
guesthouse	*une pension*	ewn pon·syon
hotel	*un hôtel*	un o·tel
youth hostel	*une auberge de jeunesse*	ewn o·berzh der zher·nes

a ... room	*une chambre ...*	ewn shom·brer ...
single	*à un lit*	a un lee
double	*avec un grand lit*	a·vek un gron lee

with (a)...	*avec ...*	a·vek ...
air-con	*climatiseur*	klee·ma·tee·zer
bathroom	*une salle de bains*	ewn sal der bun
window	*fenêtre*	fer·nay·trer

Directions

Where's ...?

Où est ...?	oo ay ...

What's the address?

Quelle est l'adresse?	kel ay la·dres

Could you write it down, please?

Pourriez-vous l'écrire, s'il vous plaît?	poo·ryay·voo lay·kreer seel voo play

Can you show me (on the map)?

Pouvez-vous m'indiquer (sur la carte)?	poo·vay·voo mun·dee·kay (sewr la kart)

at the corner	*au coin*	o kwun
at the traffic lights	*aux feux*	o fer
behind	*derrière*	dair·ryair
in front of	*devant*	der·von
far (from)	*loin (de)*	lwun (der)
left	*gauche*	gosh
near (to)	*près (de)*	pray (der)
next to ...	*à côté de ...*	a ko·tay der...
opposite ...	*en face de ...*	on fas der ...
right	*droite*	drwat
straight ahead	*tout droit*	too drwa

KEY PATTERNS

To get by in French, mix and match these simple patterns with words of your choice:

Where's (the entry)?

Où est (l'entrée)?	oo ay (lon·tray)

Where can I (buy a ticket)?

Où est-ce que je peux (acheter un billet)?	oo es·ker zher per (ash·tay un bee·yay)

When's (the next train)?

Quand est (le prochain train)?	kon ay (ler pro·shun trun)

How much is (a room)?

C'est combien pour (une chambre)?	say kom·buyn poor (ewn shom·brer)

Do you have (a map)?

Avez-vous (une carte)?	a·vay voo (ewn kart)

Is there (a toilet)?

Y a-t-il (des toilettes)?	ee a teel (day twa·let)

I'd like (to book a room).

Je voudrais (réserver une chambre).	zher voo·dray (ray·ser·vay ewn shom·brer)

Can I (enter)?

Puis-je (entrer)?	pweezh (on·tray)

Could you please (help)?

Pouvez-vous (m'aider), s'il vous plaît?	poo·vay voo (may·day) seel voo play

Do I have to (book a seat)?

Faut-il (réserver une place)?	fo·teel (ray·ser·vay ewn plas)

Eating & Drinking

What would you recommend?

Qu'est-ce que vous conseillez?	kes·ker voo kon·say·yay

What's in that dish?

Quels sont les ingrédients?	kel son lay zun·gray·dyon

I'm a vegetarian.

Je suis végétarien/ végétarienne.	zher swee vay·zhay·ta·ryun/ vay·zhay·ta·ryen (m/f)

I don't eat ...

Je ne mange pas ...	zher ner monzh pa ...

Cheers!

Santé!	son·tay

That was delicious.

C'était délicieux!	say·tay day·lee·syer

Please bring the bill.

Apportez-moi l'addition, s'il vous plaît.	a·por·tay·mwa la·dee·syon seel voo play

I'd like to reserve a table for ...	*Je voudrais réserver une table pour ...*	zher voo·dray ray·zair·vay ewn ta·bler poor ...
(eight) o'clock	*(vingt) heures*	(vungt) er
(two) people	*(deux) personnes*	(der) pair·son

Key Words

appetiser	*entrée*	on·tray
bottle	*bouteille*	boo·tay
breakfast	*petit déjeuner*	per·tee day·zher·nay
children's menu	*menu pour enfants*	mer·new poor on·fon
cold	*froid*	frwa
delicatessen	*traiteur*	tray·ter
dinner	*dîner*	dee·nay
dish	*plat*	pla
food	*nourriture*	noo·ree·tewr
fork	*fourchette*	foor·shet
glass	*verre*	vair
grocery store	*épicerie*	ay·pee·sree
highchair	*chaise haute*	dewn shay zot
hot	*chaud*	sho
knife	*couteau*	koo·to
local speciality	*spécialité locale*	spay·sya·lee·tay lo·kal
lunch	*déjeuner*	day·zher·nay
main course	*plat principal*	pla prun·see·pal
market	*marché*	mar·shay
menu (in English)	*carte (en anglais)*	kart (on ong·glay)
plate	*assiette*	a·syet
spoon	*cuillère*	kwee·yair
wine list	*carte des vins*	kart day vun
with	*avec*	a·vek
without	*sans*	son

Meat & Fish

beef	*bœuf*	berf
chicken	*poulet*	poo·lay
cod	*morue*	mo·rew
herring	*hareng*	a·rung
lamb	*agneau*	a·nyo
mackerel	*maquereau*	ma·kro
mussel	*moule*	mool
oyster	*huître*	wee·trer
pork	*porc*	por
salmon	*saumon*	so·mon
seafood	*fruit de mer*	frwee der mair
shellfish	*crustacé*	krew·sta·say
squid	*calmar*	kal·mar
trout	*truite*	trweet
turkey	*dinde*	dund
veal	*veau*	vo

Fruit & Vegetables

apple	*pomme*	pom
apricot	*abricot*	ab·ree·ko
asparagus	*asperge*	a·spairzh
beans	*haricots*	a·ree·ko
beetroot	*betterave*	be·trav
cabbage	*chou*	shoo
cherry	*cerise*	ser·reez
corn	*maïs*	ma·ees
cucumber	*concombre*	kong·kom·brer
grape	*raisin*	ray·zun
lemon	*citron*	see·tron
lettuce	*laitue*	lay·tew
mushroom	*champignon*	shom·pee·nyon
peach	*pêche*	pesh
peas	*petit pois*	per·tee pwa
(red/green) pepper	*poivron (rouge/vert)*	pwa·vron (roozh/vair)
pineapple	*ananas*	a·na·nas
plum	*prune*	prewn
potato	*pomme de terre*	pom der tair
pumpkin	*citrouille*	see·troo·yer
spinach	*épinards*	eh·pee·nar
strawberry	*fraise*	frez
tomato	*tomate*	to·mat
vegetable	*légume*	lay·gewm

Other

bread	*pain*	pun
butter	*beurre*	ber

Signs

Entrée	Entrance
Femmes	Women
Fermé	Closed
Hommes	Men
Interdit	Prohibited
Ouvert	Open
Renseignements	Information
Sortie	Exit
Toilettes/WC	Toilets

cheese	*fromage*	fro·mazh
egg	*œuf*	erf
honey	*miel*	myel
jam	*confiture*	kon·fee·tewr
oil	*huile*	weel
pasta	*pâtes*	pat
pepper	*poivre*	pwa·vrer
rice	*riz*	ree
salt	*sel*	sel
sugar	*sucre*	sew·krer
vinegar	*vinaigre*	vee·nay·grer

Drinks

beer	*bière*	bee·yair
coffee	*café*	ka·fay
(orange) juice	*jus (d'orange)*	zhew (do·ronzh)
milk	*lait*	lay
red wine	*vin rouge*	vun roozh
tea	*thé*	tay
(mineral) water	*eau (minérale)*	o (mee·nay·ral)
white wine	*vin blanc*	vun blong

Emergencies

Help!
Au secours! o skoor

I'm lost.
Je suis perdu/perdue. zhe swee·pair·dew (m/f)

Leave me alone!
Fichez-moi la paix! fee·shay·mwa la pay

There's been an accident.
Il y a eu un accident. eel ya ew un ak·see·don

Call a doctor.
Appelez un médecin. a·play un mayd·sun

Call the police.
Appelez la police. a·play la po·lees

I'm ill.
Je suis malade. zher swee ma·lad

It hurts here.
J'ai une douleur ici. zhay ewn doo·ler ee·see

I'm allergic to ...
Je suis allergique ... zher swee za·lair·zheek ...

Question Words

How?	*Comment?*	ko·mon
What?	*Quoi?*	kwa
When?	*Quand?*	kon
Where?	*Où?*	oo
Who?	*Qui?*	kee
Why?	*Pourquoi?*	poor·kwa

Shopping & Services

I'd like to buy ...
Je voudrais acheter ... zher voo·dray ash·tay ...

Can I look at it?
Est-ce que je peux le voir? es·ker zher per ler vwar

I'm just looking.
Je regarde. zher rer·gard

I don't like it.
Cela ne me plaît pas. ser·la ner mer play pa

How much is it?
C'est combien? say kom·byun

It's too expensive.
C'est trop cher. say tro shair

Can you lower the price?
Vous pouvez baisser le prix? voo poo·vay bay·say ler pree

There's a mistake in the bill.
Il y a une erreur dans la note. eel ya ewn ay·rer don la not

ATM	*guichet automatique de banque*	gee·shay o·to·ma·teek der bonk
credit card	*carte de crédit*	kart der kray·dee
internet cafe	*cybercafé*	see·bair·ka·fay
post office	*bureau de poste*	bew·ro der post
tourist office	*office de tourisme*	o·fees der too·rees·mer

Time & Dates

What time is it?
Quelle heure est-il? kel er ay til

It's (eight) o'clock.
Il est (huit) heures. il ay (weet) er

It's half past (10).
Il est (dix) heures et demie. il ay (deez) er ay day·mee

morning	*matin*	ma·tun
afternoon	*après-midi*	a·pray·mee·dee
evening	*soir*	swar
yesterday	*hier*	yair
today	*aujourd'hui*	o·zhoor·dwee
tomorrow	*demain*	der·mun

Monday	*lundi*	lun·dee
Tuesday	*mardi*	mar·dee
Wednesday	*mercredi*	mair·krer·dee
Thursday	*jeudi*	zher·dee
Friday	*vendredi*	von·drer·dee
Saturday	*samedi*	sam·dee
Sunday	*dimanche*	dee·monsh

Transport

boat	*bateau*	ba·to
bus	*bus*	bews
plane	*avion*	a·vyon
train	*train*	trun

I want to go to ...	
Je voudrais aller à ...	zher voo·dray a·lay a ...
Does it stop at (Amboise)?	
Est-ce qu'il s'arrête à (Amboise)?	es·kil sa·ret a (om·bwaz)
At what time does it leave/arrive?	
À quelle heure est-ce qu'il part/arrive?	a kel er es kil par/a·reev
Can you tell me when we get to ...?	
Pouvez-vous me dire quand nous arrivons à ...?	poo·vay·voo mer deer kon noo za·ree·von a ...
I want to get off here.	
Je veux descendre ici.	zher ver day·son·drer ee·see

first	*premier*	prer·myay
last	*dernier*	dair·nyay
next	*prochain*	pro·shun

a ... ticket	*un billet ...*	un bee·yay ...
1st-class	*de première classe*	der prem·yair klas
2nd-class	*de deuxième classe*	der der·zyem las
one-way	*simple*	sum·pler
return	*aller et retour*	a·lay ay rer·toor

aisle seat	*côté couloir*	ko·tay kool·war
delayed	*en retard*	on rer·tar
cancelled	*annulé*	a·new·lay
platform	*quai*	kay
ticket office	*le guichet*	ler gee·shay
timetable	*l'horaire*	lo·rair
train station	*la gare*	la gar
window seat	*côté fenêtre*	ko·tay fe·ne·trer

I'd like to hire a ...	*Je voudrais louer ...*	zher voo·dray loo·way ...
4WD	*un quatre-quatre*	un kat·kat
car	*une voiture*	ewn vwa·tewr
bicycle	*un vélo*	un vay·lo
motorcycle	*une moto*	ewn mo·to

Numbers

1	*un*	un
2	*deux*	der
3	*trois*	trwa
4	*quatre*	ka·trer
5	*cinq*	sungk
6	*six*	sees
7	*sept*	set
8	*huit*	weet
9	*neuf*	nerf
10	*dix*	dees
20	*vingt*	vung
30	*trente*	tront
40	*quarante*	ka·ront
50	*cinquante*	sung·kont
60	*soixante*	swa·sont
70	*soixante-dix*	swa·son·dees
80	*quatre-vingts*	ka·trer·vung
90	*quatre-vingt-dix*	ka·trer·vung·dees
100	*cent*	son
1000	*mille*	meel

child seat	*siège-enfant*	syezh·on·fon
diesel	*diesel*	dyay·zel
helmet	*casque*	kask
mechanic	*mécanicien*	may·ka·nee·syun
petrol/gas	*essence*	ay·sons
service station	*station-service*	sta·syon·ser·vees

Is this the road to ...?	
C'est la route pour ...?	say la root poor ...
(How long) Can I park here?	
(Combien de temps) Est-ce que je peux stationner ici?	(kom·byun der tom) es·ker zher per sta·syo·nay ee·see
The car/motorbike has broken down (at ...).	
La voiture/moto est tombée en panne (à ...).	la vwa·tewr/mo·to ay tom·bay on pan (a ...)
I had an accident.	
J'ai eu un accident.	zhay ew un ak·see·don
I have a flat tyre.	
Mon pneu est à plat.	mom pner ay ta pla
I've run out of petrol.	
Je suis en panne d'essence.	zher swee zon pan day·sons
I've lost my car keys.	
J'ai perdu les clés de ma voiture.	zhay per·dew lay klay der ma vwa·tewr

MALAGASY

Malagasy has around 18 million speakers. It belongs to the Malayo-Polynesian branch of the Austronesian language family and is unrelated to other African languages – its closest relative is a language from southern Borneo. Over the centuries Malagasy has incorporated influences from Bantu (particularly in some of the west coast dialects) and Arabic. It has also been influenced by English and French – first in the 19th century by British and French missionaries, and later as a result of colonisation by the French in the first half of the 20th century. Malagasy was first written using a form of Arabic script. Its modern Latin-based alphabet was developed in the early 19th century.

The pronunciation of Malagasy words is not always obvious from their written form. Unstressed syllables can be dropped and words pronounced in different ways depending on where they fall in a sentence. If you read our pronunciation guides as if they were English, you'll be understood. Note that dz is pronounced as the 'ds' in 'adds'. The stressed syllables are indicated with italics.

Basics

Hello.	*Manao ahoana.*	maa·*now* *aa*·hon
Goodbye.	*Veloma.*	ve·*lum*
Good night.	*Tafandria mandry.*	taa·faan·*dri* *maan*·dri
Yes.	*Eny.*	e·ni
No.	*Tsia.*	*tsi*·aa
Please.	*Azafady.*	aa·zaa·*faad*
Thank you.	*Misaotra.*	mi·*sotr*
Sorry.	*Miala tsiny.*	mi·*aa*·laa tsin

Mr	*Ingahy*	in·*gaa*
Mrs	*Ramatoa*	raa·maa·*tu*
Miss	*Ramatoakely*	raa·maa·*tu*·kel

How are you?
Manao ahoana ianao? maa·*now* aa·ho·*ni*·aa·now

Fine, and you?
Tsara, ary ianao? tsaar aa·ri·*aa*·now

What's your name?
Iza no anaranao? *i*·zaa nu aa·*naa*·raa·now

My name is ...
... no anarako. ... nu aa·*naa*·raa·ku

Do you speak English?
Miteny angilisy ve ianao? mi·*ten* aan·gi·*lis* ve *i*·aa·now

I don't understand.
Tsy azoko. tsi *aa*·zuk

Accommodation

Where's a ...? *Aiza no misy ...?* *ai*·zaa nu mis ...

campsite	*toerana filasiana*	tu·e·raan fi·laa·*si*·naa
guesthouse	*tranom-bahiny*	traa·num·*baa*·hin
hotel	*hôtely*	*o*·tel
youth hostel	*fandraisana Tanora*	faan·*drai*·saa·naa *taa*·nur

Do you have a ... room? *Misy ... ve ato aminao efitra iray ...?* mis ... ve aat·waa·*mi*·now e·fi·traa i·*rai* ...

single	*ho an' olon-tokana*	waan u·lun·to·*kaa*·naa
double	*misy fandriana lehibe*	mis faan·*dri*·naa le·hi·*be*
twin	*misy fandriana kely*	mis faan·*dri*·naa kel

How much is it per night/person?
Ohatrinona isan' alina/olona? o·trin *i*·saan *aa*·lin/*u*·lun

Can I camp here?
Mahazo milasy eto ve aho? maa·*haa*·zu mi·*laas* e·tu ve *ow*

Place Names

Although most people continue to use French place names in Madagascar, since the time of independence places have been known officially by their Malagasy names. The following list may help alleviate confusion.

Malagasy	*French*
Ambohitra	Joffreville
Anantsogno	St Augustin
Andasibe	Périnet
Andoany	Hell-Ville
Antananarivo	Tananarive
Antsiranana	Diego Suarez
Fenoarivo	Fénérive
Iharana	Vohémar
Mahajanga	Majunga
Mahavelona	Foulpointe
Nosy Boraha	Île Sainte Marie
Taolagnaro	Fort Dauphin
Toamasina	Tamatave
Toliara	Tuléar

DIALECTS

Despite the linguistic unity of Malagasy, regional differences do exist, and in some coastal areas, you'll hear little standard Malagasy. The three broad language groups are those of the highlands; the north and east; and the south and west. However, even within these areas there are local variations. The following list indicates a few of the lexical and phonetic differences between standard Malagasy and some of the regional dialects.

English	Highlands	North & East	South & West
Greetings.	*Manao ahoana.*	*Mbola tsara anarô.*	*Akore aby nareo.*
(in response)	*Tsara.*	*Mbola tsara.*	*Tsara./Soa.*
What's new?	*Inona no vaovao?*	*Ino vaovaonao?*	*Talilio?*
Nothing much.	*Tsy misy.*	*Ehe, tsisy fô manginginy.*	*Mbe soa.*
Where?	*Aiza?*	*Aia?*	*Aia?*
Who?	*Iza?*	*La?*	*La?*
spouse	*vady*	*vady*	*valy*
ancestor	*razana*	*raza*	*raza*

Directions

Where's the ...?		
Aiza ...?	ai·zaa ...	
What's the address?		
Inona ny adiresy?	i·nu·naa ni aa·di·*res*	
Can you write it down, please?		
Mba afaka soratanao ve izany azafady?	mbaa *aa*·faak su·raa·*taa*·now ve *i*·zaan aa·zaa·*faad*	
Can you show me (on the map)?		
Afaka asehonao ahy (eoamin'ny sarintany) ve?	aa·faak aa·se·u·*now* waa (e·uaa·min·*ni* saa·rin·*taan*) ve	
How far is it?		
Hafiriana avy eto?	haa·fi·*ri*·naa *aa*·vi et	
How do I get there?		
Ahoana no lalako mankany?	ow·o·naa nu *laa*·laa·ku *maa*·kaan	
Turn left/right.		
Mivilia ankavia/ ankavanana.	mi·vi·*li* aan·kaa·*vi*/ aan·kaa·*vaa*·naan	

It's ...	*... ilay izy.*	... *i*·lai iz
behind ...	*Ao ambadiky ny ...*	ow aam·*baa*·di·ki ni ...
in front of ...	*Manoloana ny ...*	maa·nu·*lo*·naa ni ...
near	*Akaiky ny*	aa·*kai*·ki ni
next to ...	*Manaraka ny ...*	maa·naa·*raa*·kaa ni ...
on the corner	*Eo an-jorony*	e·waan·*dzu*·run
opposite ...	*Mifanatrika ...*	mi·*faa*·naa·trik ...
straight ahead	*Mandeha mahitsy*	maan·*de* maa·*hits*
there	*Eo*	e·u

Eating & Drinking

Can you recommend a ...?	*Afaka manoro ahy... tsara ve ianao?*	*aa*·faa·kaa maa·*nur* waa ... tsaar ve *i*·aa·now
bar	*bara*	*baa*·raa
dish	*sakafo*	saa·*kaaf*
place to eat	*toerana hisakafoanana*	tu·e·raan i·saa·kaa·fu·*aa*·naan

I'd like ..., please.	*Mba mila ny ..., azafady.*	mbaa *mi*·laa ni ... aa·zaa·*faad*
the bill	*fakitiora*	faak·ti·*ur*
the menu	*lisitra sakafo*	*lis*·traa *saa*·kaaf
a table for (two)	*latabatra ho an' (olon-droa)*	laa·*taa*·baa·traa waan (u·lun·*dru*)
that dish	*iny sakafo iny*	in saa·*kaa*·fu in

cup of coffee/tea ...	*kafe/dite iray kaopy ...*	kaa·*fe*/di·*te* i·*rai* kop ...
with milk	*misy ronono*	mis *ru*·nun
without sugar	*tsy misy siramamy*	tsi mis si·*raa*·maam

Could you prepare a meal without ...?	*Mba afaka manao sakafo tsy misy ... ve ianareo?*	mbaa *aa*·faak *maa*·now *saa*·kaaf tsi mis ... ve i·aa·*naa*·re·u
eggs	*atody*	aa·*tud*
meat stock	*hena*	*he*·naa

Do you have vegetarian food?	
Manana sakafo tsy misy hena ve ianareo?	*maa*·naa·naa *saa*·kaaf tsi mis *he*·naa ve i·aa·naa·re·u

beer	*labiera*	laa·*bi*·er
bottle	*tavoahangy*	taa·vu·*haan*·gi
breakfast	*sakafo maraina*	*saa*·kaaf maa·*rai*·naa
coffee	*kafe*	kaa·*fe*
cold	*mangatsiaka*	maan·gaa·*tsik*
dairy products	*ronono*	ru·*nun*
dinner	*sakafo hariva*	saa·*kaa*·fu aa·*ri*·vaa
drink	*zava-pisotro*	zaa·vaa·*pi*·su·tru
eggs	*atody*	aa·*tud*
fish	*trondro*	*trun*·dru
food	*sakafo*	saa·*kaaf*
fork	*forisety*	fu·ri·se·ti
fruit	*voankazo*	vu·aan·*kaaz*
glass	*vera*	*ve*·raa
hot	*mahamay*	*maa*·mai
hungry	*noana*	*no*·naa
knife	*antsy*	*aant*·si
lunch	*sakafo atoandro*	saa·*kaaf* waa·tu·*aan*·dru
meat	*hena*	*he*·naa
milk	*ronono*	*ru*·nun
nuts	*voanjo*	vu·*aan*·dzu
plate	*lovia*	lu·*vi*
restaurant	*hôtely fisakafoana*	o·*te*·li fi·saa·kaa·*fu*·aa·naa
seafood	*hazan-drano*	haa·zaan·*draa*·nu
spoon	*sotro*	*su*·tru
sugar	*siramamy*	si·*raa*·maam
tea	*dite*	di·*te*
thirsty	*mangetaheta*	maan·ge·taa·*he*·taa
vegetarian	*tsy misy hena*	tsi mis *he*·naa
waiter	*mpandroso sakafo*	paan·*dru*·su *saa*·kaaf
(boiled) water	*rano (mangotraka)*	*raa*·nu (maan·*gu*·traak)
wine	*divay*	di·*vai*
without ...	*tsy misy ...*	tsi mis ...

Question Words

When?	*Oviana?*	o·*vi*·naa
Where?	*Aiza?*	*ai*·zaa
Who?	*Iza?*	*i*·zaa
Why?	*Nahoana?*	naa·*hon*

Emergencies

Help!
Vonjeo! — vun·*dze*·u

I'm lost.
Very aho. — *ve*·ri ow

Where are the toilets?
Aiza ny trano fivoahana? — *ai*·zaa ni *traa*·nu fi·vu·*aa*·haan

Call the doctor/police.
Antsoy ny dokotera/ polisy. — aant·*su*·i ni duk·*ter*/ po·*lis*

It hurts here.
Marary eto. — maa·*raa*·ri e

I'm allergic to (penicillin).
Tys mahazaka (penisilina) aho. — tsi maa·haa·*zaa*·kaa (pe·*ni*·si·lin) ow

Shopping & Services

I'm looking for ...
Mitady ... aho. — mi·*taa*·di ... ow

How much is it?
Ohatrinona? — o·*trin*

Can you write down the price?
Mba afaka soratanao ve ny vidiny? — mbaa *aa*·faa·kaa su·raa·*taa*·now ve ni *vi*·din

What's your lowest price?
Ohatrinona ny vidiny farany? — o·*trin*·naa ni *vi*·din *faa*·raan

There's a mistake in the bill.
Miso diso ny fakitiora. — mis *di*·su ni faak·*tu*·raa

I'd like a receipt, please.
Mba mila resiò aho, azafady. — mbaa *mi*·laa re·si·*u* ow aa·zaa·*faad*

It's faulty.
Tsy marina io. — tsi maa·ri·*ni*·u

Can I have my ... repaired?
Afaka amboarina ve ny ... -ko? — aa·faa·kaamb·*waa*·rin ve ni ... ·ku

When will it be ready?
Rahoviana no vita? — row·*vi*·naa nu *vi*·taa

I'd like to change money.
Mba te hanakalo vola aho azafady. — mbaa te haa·naa·*kaa*·lu *vu*·laa ow aa·zaa·*faad*

market	*tsena*	tsen
mobile phone	*paoritabila*	por·*taa*·bi·laa
internet cafe	*sibera*	*si*·ber
pharmacy	*farimasia*	faa·ri·*maa*·si
post office	*paositra*	*po*·si·traa
tourist office	*biraon' ny vahiny*	bi·row·ni *vaa*·hin

Time & Dates

What time is it?
Amin'ny firy izao? aa·min·*ni*·fi *ri*·zow

It's (two) o'clock.
Amin'ny (roa) izao. aa·min·*ni* (ru) *i*·zow

Half past (one).
(Iray) sy sasany. (rai) si *saa*·saan

Quarter past (one).
(Iray) sy fahefany. (rai) si faa·*he*·faan

Quarter to (eight).
(Valo) latsaka fahefany. (vaal) *laat*·saa·kaa faa·*he*·faan

At what time ...?
Amin'ny firy ...? aa·min·*ni* fir ...

At ...
Amin'ny ... aa·min·*ni* ...

yesterday	*omaly*	*u*·maal
today	*androany*	aan·*dru*·aan
tomorrow	*rahampitso*	raa·haam·*pits*

Monday	*Alatsinainy*	aa·laat·*si*·nain
Tuesday	*Talata*	*taa*·laat
Wednesday	*Alarobia*	aa·laa·*ru*·bi
Thursday	*Alakamisy*	aa·laa·*kaa*·mis
Friday	*Zomà*	zu·*maa*
Saturday	*Asabotsy*	aa·saa·*buts*
Sunday	*Alahady*	aa·laa·*haad*

Numbers

1	*isa/iray*	*i*·saa/*i*·rai
2	*roa*	ru
3	*telo*	tel
4	*efatra*	e·faatr
5	*dimy*	dim
6	*enina*	e·nin
7	*fito*	fit
8	*valo*	vaal
9	*sivy*	siv
10	*folo*	ful
20	*roapolo*	ru·aa·*pul*
30	*telopolo*	te·lu·*pul*
40	*efapolo*	e·faa·*pul*
50	*dimampolo*	di·maam·*pul*
60	*enimpolo*	e·ni·*pul*
70	*fitopolo*	fi·tu·*pul*
80	*valopolo*	vaa·lu·*pul*
90	*sivifolo*	si·vi·*ful*
100	*zato*	zaat
1000	*arivo*	*aa*·riv

Transport

A ... ticket (to Toliary), please.	*Tapakila ... (mankany Toliary) iray, azafady.*	taa·paa·*kil* ... (*maa*·kaan tu·*li*·aar) *i*·rai aa·zaa·*faad*
one-way	*mandroso*	*maan*·drus
return	*miverina*	mi·*ve*·rin

Is this the ... to (Toamasina)?	*Ity ve ny ... mankany (Toamasina)?*	i·*ti* ve ni ... maa·*kaan* (to·*maa*·sin)
boat	*sambo*	saamb
bus	*aotobisy*	o·to·bis
plane	*roaplanina*	*ro*·plaan
train	*lamasinina*	laa·*maa*·sin

bus stop	*fijanonana*	fid·zaa·*nu*·naan
economy class	*kilasy faharoa*	ki·*laa*·si faa·haa·*ru*
first class	*kilasy voalohany*	ki·*laa*·si vu·aa·*lu*·haan
train station	*gara*	*gaa*·raa

How long does the trip take?
Hafiriana ny dia? haa·fi·*ri*·naa ni di

Is it a direct route?
Tsy mijanojanona ve? tsi mi·dzaa·nu·*dzaa*·nu·naa ve

How long will it be delayed?
Hafiriana ny fahatarany? haa·fi·*ri*·naa ni faa·haa·*taa*·raan

How much is it to ...?
Ohatrinona ny ...? o·*trin*·naa ni ...

Please take me to (this address).
Mba ento any amin' (ityadiresy ity) aho azafady. mbaa *en*·tu *aa*·ni *aa*·min (tiaa·di·*res* ti) ow aa·zaa·*faad*

I'd like to hire a car/4WD.
Mba te hanarama fiara/4x4 aho azafady. mbaa te haa·naa·*raa*·maa *fi*·aar/kaat·*kaat*·raa ow aa·zaa·*faad*

Is this the road to (Antsirabe)?
Ity ve ny lalana mankany (Antsirabe)? i·*ti* ve ni *laa*·laan maa·*kaan* (aan·tsi·raa·*be*)

bicycle	*bisikileta*	bis·ki·*le*·taa
highway	*lalambe*	laa·*laam*·be
motorcycle	*môtô*	mo·*to*
oil (engine)	*menaka*	*me*·naa·kaa
park (car)	*fijanonana*	fid·zaa·*nu*·naan
petrol	*lasantsy*	laa·*saant*·si
tyre	*kodiarana*	*ku*·di·aa·raan

GLOSSARY

andriana – noble

Antaimoro – east coast tribe from the region around Manakara; also the name given to a type of handmade paper

Antakarana – tribe from northern Madagascar

ariary – Madagascar's unit of currency

aye-aye – rare nocturnal lemur

bâché – small, converted pick-up truck

baie – bay

Basse-Ville – lower town

be – 'big' in Malagasy; denotes larger parts of a town

Betsileo – Madagascar's third-largest tribe after the *Merina* and the *Betsimisaraka*

Betsimisaraka – Madagascar's second-largest tribe

boutre – single-masted dhow used for cargo

camion-brousse – large truck used for passengers

cassava – root vegetable also known as manioc

Creole cuisine – a blend of African, Asian and European influences

fady – taboo, forbidden

famadihana – exhumation and reburial; literally 'the turning of the bones'

fossa – local name for the striped civet

gare routière – bus station

gargote – cheap restaurant

gasy – Malagasy (pronounced 'gash')

gîte – rustic shelter

Haute-Ville – upper town

hauts plateaux – highlands; the term is often used to refer to Madagascar's central plateau region

hira gasy – music, dancing and storytelling spectacles

hotely – small roadside place that serves basic meals

Imerina – region ruled by the *Merina*

indri – largest of Madagascar's lemur species

kely – 'small' in Malagasy; often used to denote a township or satellite town

lac – lake

lalana – street

lamba – white cotton or silk scarf

maki – Malagasy term for a lemur

Merina – Madagascar's largest tribe, centred in Antananarivo

MNP – Madagascar National Parks

mora mora – 'slowly, slowly' or 'wait a minute'; often used to mean the Malagasy pace of life

nosy – island

Nouvelle-Ville – new town

parc national – national park

parcage – *taxi-brousse* station

pic – peak

pirogue – dugout canoe

pousse-pousse – rickshaw

ravinala – literally 'forest leaves'; also known as travellers' palm, the most distinctive of Madagascar's palm trees

réserve spéciale – special reserve (often similar to a national park)

RN – route nationale; national road (often still no more than a track)

rova – palace

Sakalava – western tribe

sambatra – mass circumcision ceremony

SAVA – region comprising Sambava, Andapa, Vohémar (Iharana) and Antalaha

sifaka – a type of lemur, known in French as a 'propithèque'

taxi-be – literally 'big taxi'; also known as a 'familiale'

taxi-brousse – bush taxi; generic term for any kind of public passenger truck, car or minibus

tenrec – small mammal resembling a hedgehog or shrew

THB – Three Horses Beer; Madagascar's most popular beer

tilapia – freshwater perch (fish)

tsingy – limestone pinnacle formations; also known as karst

vazaha – foreigner or white person

Vezo – nomadic fishing subtribe of the *Sakalava*, found in the southwest

via ferrata – mountain route equipped with fixed cables, stemples, ladders and bridges

ylang-ylang – bush with sweet-smelling white flowers used to make perfume

Zafimaniry – a subgroup of the *Betsileo* people who live in the area east of Ambositra, and are renowned for their woodcarving skills

zebu – a type of domesticated ox found throughout Madagascar; it has a prominent hump on its back and loose skin under its throat

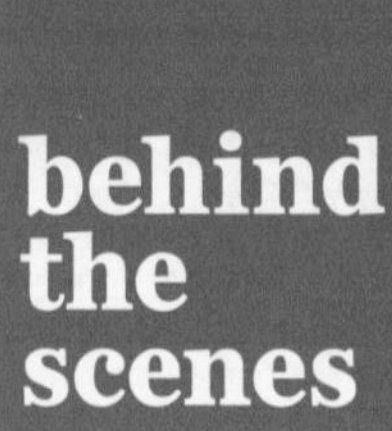

SEND US YOUR FEEDBACK

We love to hear from travellers – your comments keep us on our toes and help make our books better. Our well-travelled team reads every word on what you loved or loathed about this book. Although we cannot reply individually to postal submissions, we always guarantee that your feedback goes straight to the appropriate authors, in time for the next edition. Each person who sends us information is thanked in the next edition – the most useful submissions are rewarded with a selection of digital PDF chapters.

Visit **lonelyplanet.com/contact** to submit your updates and suggestions or to ask for help. Our award-winning website also features inspirational travel stories, news and discussions.

Note: We may edit, reproduce and incorporate your comments in Lonely Planet products such as guidebooks, websites and digital products, so let us know if you don't want your comments reproduced or your name acknowledged. For a copy of our privacy policy visit lonelyplanet.com/privacy.

OUR READERS

Many thanks to the travellers who used the last edition and wrote to us with helpful hints, useful advice and interesting anecdotes:

Daniella Antberg, Victoria Bei, Rachel Blackamore, Victoria Booth, Isabelle Bovey, Julian Brill, Sonja Brocatus, Michael Conneally, Carol Craven, Lilian De Boer, Carin Deanwales, Thomas Dobler, Heinz Effertz, John Gardiner, Freek Glas, Claire Goldschmidt, Gavin Hickey, Daniel Hutley, Stephen Johansen, Katie Kemp, Jessica Killaspy, Michael Leach, Tessa Liebman, Alain Madaplouf, Saskia Martens, Callista Meeusen, Vera Molberg, Volker Mueller, Tanja Nijhoff, Michelle Nissen, Richard Osmond, Pia Ottacher, Rochelle Pincini, Lennart Pyritz, Jonathan Rae, Peter Riebeek, Ada Rimon, Judith Rosendahl, Ray Schrire, Costantino Sertorio, Inger-sigrun Slagstad Vik, John Soar, Riswana Soundardjee, Petr Spas, Richard Swatman, Jacqui Symonds, Tina Thorburn, Marieke Van Der Spek, Erika Van Heeringen, Olivier Walgraffe, Jonas Wernli, Michael Westendorp, Polly Whyte, Janine Widler, Anton Wittwer, Manuele Zunelli

AUTHOR THANKS

Emilie Filou

Thanks to Heritiana Rakotondrazaka for insight and good times; Christopher Holmes, director of WCS in Madagascar, for background info on the environment; Gérald Razafinjato, director of Sandandrano, for his time and inspiration; Philippe Fontayne and Mado at Millot Plantations for all the tips and introductions; Sido and Benj for their Mada review; my local-knowledge interviewees for their time; and, finally, thank you to my husband, Adolfo, for his patience, moral support and comedy calls: next time, together!

Paul Stiles

Special thanks goes to the many Peace Corps volunteers who helped make this a better book, including Megan Van Aelstyn (Antsirabe), Natalie Mundy (Ambositra), Alison Thieme (Ranomafana), Emily Burgess (Manakara), Liz Toomey (Andringitra), Jessica Carag (Fort Dauphin), Hilary Brueck (Andapa), Matt Amato (Antalaha) and Sara Tolliver (Andasibe). Particular thanks goes to Mike Westendorp, who organised all of the above, and helped research all aspects of the book during two weeks of constant travel. You've all made Madagascar a better place.

ACKNOWLEDGMENTS

Climate map data adapted from Peel MC, Finlayson BL & McMahon TA (2007) 'Updated World Map of the Köppen-Geiger Climate Classification', *Hydrology and Earth System Sciences*, 11, 163344.

Cover photograph: Chameleon, Nosy Be. Jean-Bernard Carillet/Lonely Planet Images.

Many of the images in this guide are available for licensing from Lonely Planet Images: www.lonelyplanetimages.com.

THIS BOOK

This 7th edition of Lonely Planet's *Madagascar* was researched and written by Emilie Filou and Paul Stiles; the Wildlife section was updated and expanded by David Lukas. The previous edition was written by David Andrew, Aaron Anderson, Becca Blond and Tom Parkinson. This guidebook was commissioned in Lonely Planet's Melbourne office, and produced by the following:

Commissioning Editors David Carroll, Will Gourlay, Sam Trafford

Coordinating Editors Carolyn Boicos, Monique Perrin

Coordinating Cartographer Andras Bogdanovits

Coordinating Layout Designer Virginia Moreno

Managing Editors Brigitte Ellemor, Angela Tinson

Senior Editors Victoria Harrison, Susan Paterson

Managing Cartographers Shahara Ahmed, Adrian Persoglia, Mandy Sierp

Managing Layout Designer Jane Hart

Assisting Editors Alice Barker, Carly Hall, Andi Jones, Amy Karafin

Cover Research Naomi Parker

Internal Image Research Rebecca Skinner

Language Content Branislava Vladisavljevic

Thanks to Anita Banh, Lucy Birchley, Ryan Evans, Jennifer Johnston, Yvonne Kirk, Annelies Mertens, Trent Paton, Martine Power, Kirsten Rawlings, Gerard Walker

index

000 Map pages
000 Photo pages

000 Map pages
000 Photo pages

O

P

000 Map pages
000 Photo pages

Q

R

S

T

V

W

Z

000 Map pages
000 Photo pages

how to use this book

These symbols will help you find the listings you want:

- Sights
- Beaches
- Activities
- Courses
- Tours
- Festivals & Events
- Sleeping
- Eating
- Drinking
- Entertainment
- Shopping
- Information/Transport

These symbols give you the vital information for each listing:

- Telephone Numbers
- Opening Hours
- Parking
- Nonsmoking
- Air-Conditioning
- Internet Access
- Wi-Fi Access
- Swimming Pool
- Vegetarian Selection
- English-Language Menu
- Family-Friendly
- Pet-Friendly
- Bus
- Ferry
- Metro
- Subway
- Tram
- Train

Reviews are organised by author preference.

Look out for these icons:

- TOP CHOICE — Our author's recommendation
- FREE — No payment required
- A green or sustainable option

Our authors have nominated these places as demonstrating a strong commitment to sustainability – for example by supporting local communities and producers, operating in an environmentally friendly way, or supporting conservation projects.

Map Legend

Sights
- Beach
- Buddhist
- Castle
- Christian
- Hindu
- Islamic
- Jewish
- Monument
- Museum/Gallery
- Ruin
- Winery/Vineyard
- Zoo
- Other Sight

Activities, Courses & Tours
- Diving/Snorkelling
- Canoeing/Kayaking
- Skiing
- Surfing
- Swimming/Pool
- Walking
- Windsurfing
- Other Activity/Course/Tour

Sleeping
- Sleeping
- Camping

Eating
- Eating

Drinking
- Drinking
- Cafe

Entertainment
- Entertainment

Shopping
- Shopping

Information
- Bank
- Embassy/Consulate
- Hospital/Medical
- Internet
- Police
- Post Office
- Telephone
- Toilet
- Tourist Information
- Other Information

Transport
- Airport
- Border Crossing
- Bus
- Cable Car/Funicular
- Cycling
- Ferry
- Metro
- Monorail
- Parking
- Petrol Station
- Taxi
- Train/Railway
- Tram
- Other Transport

Routes
- Tollway
- Freeway
- Primary
- Secondary
- Tertiary
- Lane
- Unsealed Road
- Plaza/Mall
- Steps
- Tunnel
- Pedestrian Overpass
- Walking Tour
- Walking Tour Detour
- Path

Geographic
- Hut/Shelter
- Lighthouse
- Lookout
- Mountain/Volcano
- Oasis
- Park
- Pass
- Picnic Area
- Waterfall

Population
- Capital (National)
- Capital (State/Province)
- City/Large Town
- Town/Village

Boundaries
- International
- State/Province
- Disputed
- Regional/Suburb
- Marine Park
- Cliff
- Wall

Hydrography
- River, Creek
- Intermittent River
- Swamp/Mangrove
- Reef
- Canal
- Water
- Dry/Salt/Intermittent Lake
- Glacier

Areas
- Beach/Desert
- Cemetery (Christian)
- Cemetery (Other)
- Park/Forest
- Sportsground
- Sight (Building)
- Top Sight (Building)

OUR STORY

A beat-up old car, a few dollars in the pocket and a sense of adventure. In 1972 that's all Tony and Maureen Wheeler needed for the trip of a lifetime – across Europe and Asia overland to Australia. It took several months, and at the end – broke but inspired – they sat at their kitchen table writing and stapling together their first travel guide, *Across Asia on the Cheap*. Within a week they'd sold 1500 copies. Lonely Planet was born.

Today, Lonely Planet has offices in Melbourne, London and Oakland, with more than 600 staff and writers. We share Tony's belief that 'a great guidebook should do three things: inform, educate and amuse'.

OUR WRITERS

Emilie Filou

Coordinating Author, Plan Your Trip, Antananarivo, Western Madagascar, Northern Madagascar (except SAVA Region), Madagascar Today, History, Malagasy Life, Arts, Malagasy Cuisine, Environment, Parks & Reserves, Directory A–Z, Transport, Health Emilie first travelled to Africa at age eight to visit her grandparents, who had taken up a late-career opportunity in Mali. Many more trips and a geography degree later, Emilie now works as a freelance journalist focusing on development issues in Africa. Her most memorable moments in Madagascar include singing and dancing around the campfire on the banks of the Tsiribihina River, sitting on somebody's lap in a full-to-bursting taxi-brousse and striking up a conversation with the 'host', driving from Belo to Morondava (with no breaks) and revelling in the supremely beautiful landscapes around Nosy Be.

Read more about Emilie at:
lonelyplanet.com/members/emiliefilou

Paul Stiles

Central Madagascar, Southern Madagascar, Eastern Madagascar, SAVA Region (Northern Madagascar) When he was 21, Paul bought an old motorcycle in London and took off on the adventure of a lifetime, ending up in Tunisia. That did it for him. Since then he's explored 60 countries, including four wonderful years in the Canary Islands, and currently inhabits the rocky coast of Scotland. With a passion for exotic travel, ecotourism and islands, he's roamed from Morocco to Hawaii for Lonely Planet. For this book he made a marathon 4WD journey along the Great Reef, trekked into Marojejy and climbed Pic Boby, where he left his compass in the box at the summit.

Read more about Paul at:
lonelyplanet.com/members/paulwstiles

Contributing Author

David Lukas David Lukas wrote the Wildlife section. David is a freelance naturalist who lives next to Yosemite National Park in California. He writes extensively about the world's wildlife, and has contributed wildlife chapters for eight African Lonely Planet guides, ranging from *Ethiopia & Eritrea* to *South Africa, Lesotho & Swaziland*. He also wrote *A Year of Watching Wildlife*, which covers the top places in the world to view wildlife.

Published by Lonely Planet Publications Pty Ltd
ABN 36 005 607 983
7th edition – March 2012
ISBN 978 1 74179 175 4

10 9 8 7 6 5 4 3
Printed in China